1968

MEXICO

RADICAL AMÉRICAS
A series edited by Bruno Bosteels
and George Ciccariello-Maher

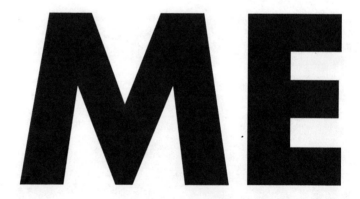

Duke University Press Durham and London 2018

SUSANA DRAPER

1968

MEXICO

Constellations of Freedom and Democracy

Printed in the United States of America on acid-free paper ∞
Designed by Courtney Leigh Baker
Typeset in Garamond Premier Pro and Futura by
Westchester Publishing Services

Library of Congress Cataloging-in-Publication Data
Names: Draper, Susana, [date] author.
Title: 1968 Mexico : constellations of freedom
and democracy / Susana Draper.
Description: Durham : Duke University Press, 2018. |
Series: Radical Américas | Includes
bibliographical references and index.
Identifiers: LCCN 2018001471 (print)
LCCN 2018007843 (ebook)
ISBN 9781478002499 (ebook)
ISBN 9781478001010 (hardcover : alk. paper)
ISBN 9781478001430 (pbk. : alk. paper)
Subjects: LCSH: Mexico—History—1946–1970. |
Nineteen sixty-eight, A.D.
Classification: LCC F1235 (ebook) |
LCC F1235 .D73 2018 (print) | DDC 972.08—dc23
LC record available at https://lccn.loc.gov/2018001471

Cover art, top: Protestors, 1968. Photo by Óscar Menéndez.
Courtesy of the photographer. Bottom, from left: M8 "Greyhound"
tanks at a demonstration at the Zócalo, Mexico City, August 28,
1968; Student demonstration, Mexico City, August 27, 1968. Photos
by Marcel·lí Perelló.

"What was **'68** for you?"

MARTÍN DOZAL
"For me it was a party, at the beginning . . .
  this awakening: an awakening that woke us up
  and that did not wake us up."

GUADALUPE FERRER
"'68 for me was the opening of thought."

ESMERALDA REYNOSO
"'68 absolutely revolutionized my life."

GLADYS LÓPEZ HERNÁNDEZ
"'68 was like an awakening, not only for me,
  but the young people of this time here in Mexico:
  to see other horizons, other paths, other ways
  of thinking, of living, of knowing, like an awakening to
  a real reality, pardon the redundancy, not what
  they put on television, in the family."

—Interviews with Susana Draper
and Vicente Rubio-Pueyo, *México 68:
Modelo para armar; Archivo de memorias
desde los márgenes*

MERCEDES PERELLÓ
"We had strong disagreements about how to make
  revolution. In '68 for the first time we stopped fighting
  and we all joined together in the same struggle."

—Interview with Heidrun Hozfeind,
*México 68: Entrevistas con activistas
del movimiento estudiantil*

Contents

Preface **ix**   Acknowledgments **xv**

Introduction. THE MOVEMENT OF 1968 **1**

1. THE PHILOSOPHICAL AND
LITERARY CONFIGURATION OF '68
José Revueltas on Cognitive Democracy
and Self-Management **35**

2. THE EFFECTS OF '68 ON CINEMA
The Image as a Place of Political Intervention **91**

3. WHERE ARE THE WOMEN OF '68?
Fernanda Navarro and the Materialism
of Uncomfortable Encounters **127**

4. REMEMBRANCES FROM THE WOMEN'S
PRISON AND THE POPULAR PREPARATORY
Of Freedom and Imprisonment by Roberta "La Tita"
Avendaño and *Ovarimony* by Gladys López Hernández **157**

Conclusion. '68 AFTER AYOTZINAPA **191**

Notes **199**   Bibliography **229**   Index **245**

There are interruptions: moments in which one of the machines that makes time function stops—it can be the machine of work, or of School. There are likewise moments when the masses in the street oppose their agenda to that of governmental apparatuses. These "moments" are not only ephemeral instances that interrupt the temporal flow, which is later normalized. They are also effective mutations of the landscape of the visible, the seeable, and the sayable, transformations of the world of the possible. —JACQUES RANCIÈRE, "Desarrollar la temporalidad de los momentos de igualdad"

The moment of '68 is a figure saturated by projections and evaluations: *point of origin, watershed of history, democratizing instance, historical failure.* However, the more we look and read, the more its contours, its dates, its coherence are blurred. In writing *Amulet,* this great poetic gesture about '68 Mexico, Chilean writer Roberto Bolaño plays with this confusion. His protagonist, Auxilio Lacouture, inspired by Alcira Soust, a Uruguayan poet who lived in Mexico without papers, is obsessed with how, in attempting to remember them, dates intertwine in a curious process of becoming: "The year 1968 became the year 1964 and the year 1960 became the year 1956. But it also became the years 1970 and 1973 and the years 1975 and 1976."[1] Locked in the women's bathroom at the School of Philosophy and Letters during the military occupation of the Universidad Nacional Autónoma de México (UNAM, National Autonomous University of Mexico), Alcira-Auxilio feels "as if time were coming apart" and '68 becomes a lookout point of history.[2] One of the keys to *Amulet,* published thirty years after the student popular movement, resides in the emphasis on the disproportion that is involved in all acts of imagining the past. This implies a compelling critical gesture: not thinking about the past, en masse, as great failure or defeat that uses the present as a measure for projecting another future; but on the contrary, the text destabilizes all notions of progressive linearity in time, making us think about the singularity connected to the ways of making history perceptible, the leap implied by the passage from experience to its narrativization. This strikes me as important because the Mexican '68 (or "the '68s" everywhere) are encircled by a certain moralizing way of assessing it (did it fail, did it triumph, did it lead to a "transition," was it fruitful?), which disregards the singular character of the event as mobilizing an entire political context, more than as a process that should lead to concrete results. As Jacques Rancière suggests in the epigraph that opens this chapter, there are moments in history in which certain interruptions take place and open up a transformation of language and a visibility of the political that is difficult to translate into an evaluative form. This also relates to a reconfiguration of the political that is key to 1968 around the world.

This book seeks to investigate some of the ways in which the emancipation and reconfiguration of the political took place, during and after '68. This involves bringing the question of emancipation to the realm of memory—a possible *emancipation* of memories of '68—and also to the reconfiguration of a series of movements that express the unique polyphony of the moment. It is a matter of avoiding a sense of property and ownership over meanings, expressed through certain *camouflaged or visible monopolies over words* about '68, thereby opening up and multiplying the archives, voices, and images that helped identify crucial problems of the time, such as self-management, the democratization of knowledge, a mass exodus into the streets, the circulation of words in numerous assemblies, the opening up of diverse processes of liberation from heteropatriarchal schemes of life, the permanent provocation of singular encounters, and so on. Thus 1968 emerges here as *the name and locus* of a series of revolts that seek a different language in which to discuss and perform modes of emancipation and liberation. It is a moment profoundly marked by changes to the way we understand the meaning and function of the word *revolution*, which we could see as in transition from noun (*revolution* as state takeover) to verb (*revolutionize*). One of the many crucial edges of '68 was the fact that the word *revolution* was grounded in everyday practices that affected a range of public, private, and common spaces. This was expressed through various *problematic units* particular to the time, which served to define the specific characteristics of each movement in different parts of the world. When I speak of problematic units, I am referring to several key forms of expression that composed new political horizons out of a desire to ascertain the meaning of self-management, practices of equality, participation in everyday acts, horizontality, creative forms of organization, and the displacement of the roles and functions performed by sectors of authority and of knowledge.

In thinking about this book, the notion of the constellation comes to mind as a way of naming what emerges here as '68: to follow the trace that links different flickering points in a multiplicity of concepts, images, bodies, and memories that emerge as modes of continuing it in thought, in image, and in a distant present. The idea of approaching 1968 as a constellation (and less as a monumental and fixed instant of history) reconfigures 1968 as the name and place of an event that is constantly reconstructed, debated, and re-created. Hence, I do not think of this book as a way of accounting for the moment, in the sense of what a historian or a sociologist does, often reconstructing events from the demand for the truth required by the discipline. Incorporating those readings, but attempting to take them elsewhere, my desire has been to suspend a certain criterion of positivist veracity expressed in the proposal to "account for" what was right or wrong in a moment. In attending to the possibility of constructing a '68 constellation composed of a series of materials that open up different disciplines, I investigate the ways '68 is expressed, continued, and thought about on various planes: philosophical, essayistic, testimonial, visual. Thus, more than an analysis of an archive that '68 creates as an object, I look into how the *'68 effect* is configured and how it affects certain practices of writing, visualization, and subjectivization: that is, how '68 is repeated as a gesture that not only destabilizes politics and bodies but also institutes different forms of critical language, thought, cinematography, and pedagogy. Thus, I was interested in bringing to the structure of the book something that in '68 was a key for reflecting on self-management and the democratization of knowledge: interdisciplinarity, or dialogue among different languages and practices as a way of taking on a university that reiterated the technocratic mandate of hyperspecialization, which partitioned knowledge to the point that it lost sight of its connection to social problems.

On a personal note, it should be said that a book develops in many periods, to the rhythm of countless conversations, readings, experiences, and encounters. The writing of the book was interrupted by the emergence of Occupy Wall Street (OWS) in 2011, a moment in which '68 became present in many forms in the imaginary and poetics capable of naming the innovative nature of these movements. Participating in the movement suspended my writing for a long time, since, in addition to lacking time in the first months of an intense moment of projects and assemblies, I began to feel a strong distance from what I was writing. The proximity between many issues that we were putting forward connected to the idea of a democracy of knowledge, to the encounters among different people and the potential for dialogue—an entire series of points that were crucial in my project about '68. Suddenly, I felt full of questions, and the idea of writing in an individual way became something distant. At the same time, the sense of opening that the movements brought amid a fossilized, politically neoliberal scene at the center of capital made me want to dig deeper into some of the leading ideas of this project: Revueltas's cognitive democracy and the role of the encounters that provide one of the most singular characteristics of these movements. Conversations among those who do not usually converge are some of the sparks in such moments.

As I reconnected with the project, all these learning experiences made me think of the kind of book I wanted to write. In order to analyze the idea of a democracy of knowledge and bring other voices to the stage, following some traces, like the "workshop on words" ("taller de palabras") at Lecumberri Prison that Revueltas names in "Imprisoned Words," or to look at the different memories of women who participated in different ways, I had to look for what was not in the usual writings and archives.[3] In conversation with me about this, Vicente Rubio-Pueyo came up with the idea of video-recording the interviews, and we embarked on a parallel project of creating what we see as an open archive of memories, thus continuing the research into the Mexican '68 in another way: assembling an archive of voices and memories of '68 that were not always the same, opening the space of the word toward other zones, taking the form of the assembly to the practice of memory. With the help of Ángel Luis Lara and Luis Hernández Navarro, we embarked on a series of conversations, editing them as video interviews with the help of Lur Elaizola and Yolanda Pividal. This took the shape of a virtual archive (https://www.mexico68conversaciones.com/) that we called *Mexico '68: Model for Assembly; Archive of Memories from the Margins*, borrowing from Julio Cortázar's experimental novel published in 1968, and also following the title used by Héctor Aguilar Camín.[4] As we embarked on the process of listening to different people, new ideas and suggestions planted the seeds that would help me continue the process of writing this book. In part, I could not have continued without this other side of the process, the *conversation* and the act of poring over the words of those who had made fundamental contributions but who had not written their "book about '68," as others had done. The work of gathering voices coincided with the unexpected emergence of #YoSoy132, which brought up '68 as an inspiring reference, making similar demands for opening the language of information, for a change in the script, and denouncing the political monopoly of the Partido Revolucionario Institucional (PRI, Institutional Revolutionary Party) and the Partido de Acción Nacional (PAN, National Action Party). Comrades from 132 traveled to New York as part of this collective feeling that the new movements opened, making dialogue and different assessments possible.

My return to a more systematic process of writing this book in 2013 (two years after the beginning of OWS and once the movement had lost the intensity of its first two years) during the course of a Princeton graduate seminar about '68 was a way of demanding that I think about various times and problems simultaneously, but now with the pleasant feeling of patience that the distance of time provides. This allowed me to see in a more nuanced way the relevance of these historical instances that, like '68, are able to gather many peoples, groups, and sectors, as well as the need to insist on the form of elaborating their memories from polyphony and the desire for connectivity. We live in an age in which the necrological apparatuses of the state, the *narcos*, the war machines, insist on continuing to punctuate the circuits for demanding justice, democracy, and equality with an accumulation of corpses. Nevertheless, sometimes it seems that we pass from one demand to the next, from one necrologic to another, *losing sight of the need for struggles to construct a common language, a historicity that enables exiting the unusual presentism with which neoliberalism punctuates life.* In this sense, bringing to the present the memory of moments that were so profound in their demand for another form of politics, another way of participating from within the everyday and from within the social fabric, from dialogue and cooperation, continues to be relevant. To attempt to cross the horizon of fixed identities with which a certain politics maintains controllable order implies reflecting on the encounter between different people as an essential element of the political. Here *equality* is not the demand of a small group but rather *a demand for the reconfiguration of the stage that makes the political possible.* On this stage, words and images exist as elements with which we narrate the possibility of change, the historicity of the present in constant dialogue with the past, the relationships of learning that we establish, almost without thinking, between pasts and presents, times and places, which all of a sudden connect and generate critical constellations.

Acknowledgments

A book is the result of a long process of conversations. I would like to thank friends and colleagues who invited me to share fragments of this project at different stages, to participate in conferences and share work in progress: Jens Andermann, Elixabete Ansa, Gavin Arnall, Manuela Badilla, Bruno Bosteels, Oscar Cabezas, Ivonne del Valle, Eugenio Di Stephano, Claudia Feld, Gabriel Giorgi, Erin E. Goodman, Erin Graff Zivin, Merilee S. Grindle, Katherine Hite, Pablo La Parra, Jacques Lezra, Vania Markarian, Lidia Mateo, Graciela Montaldo, Alberto Moreiras, Cristina Moreiras, Jaime Ortega, Jennifer Rodríguez, Marcelo Rodríguez, Raúl Rodríguez Freire, Rafael Rojas, Ana Sabau, Emilio Sauri, Marcelo Starcembaum, José Luis Villacañas, Esther Whitfield, Gareth Williams; and the graduate students in Comparative Literature and in Spanish and Portuguese at Princeton, New York University, Cornell, and the University of Illinois–Chicago. Special gratitude goes to the graduate students who participated in the "1968 and the present" graduate seminar at Princeton in 2013, where the main lines of this project were discussed; to the editors of the series Radical Américas, Bruno and Geo, for encouraging me to participate; and to Courtney Berger, for her invaluable comments and guidance through the publishing process.

Most of the book relies on the conversations that built onto the project of *Mexico '68: Model for Assembly*. Immense gratitude to the generosity of Angel Luis Lara and Luis Hernández Navarro, for thinking aloud about people who would become key to the project. The thinking process would not have been possible without the generosity and openness of those who shared their memories and reflections on 1968: Jesús Martín del Campo, Martín Dozal, Guadalupe Ferrer, Alberto Híjar, Gladys López Hernández, Óscar Menéndez, Fernanda Navarro, Esmeralda Reynoso, Ramón Vela, and Juan Villoro. Their words and memories opened many itineraries and made me come up with the imaginary lines that mapped different constellations.

The research was carried out with the support of my colleagues in Comparative Literature and Spanish and Portuguese, and with grants from Princeton Latin American Studies, the David A. Gardner Grant, and the University Committee on Research on the Humanities and Social Sciences. Its English version was possible thanks to the patient work of editing and translation at different stages by Andrew Ascherl, Patricia Draper, Audrey Hall, Ruth Halvey, and Margarita Rosario.

Thanks to all the *compañerxs* from many spaces in New York City (Making Worlds, 16beaver, Free University, Socio-Praxis at Sunset Park, Critical Resistance) that since and after Occupy made Revueltas's ideas on cognitive democracy, which inspired this project, be experienced in many forms; gratitude to Ayreen Anastas, David Andersson, Pablo Benson, Ina Bransome, Sara Burke, Maria Byck, Isabel Cadenas-Cañón, George Caffentzis, Jim Constanzo, Silvia Federici, René Gabri, Sofia Galisá, Malav Kanuga, Jesal Kapadia, Janet Koenig, Kara Lynch, Brian Mac Carthy, Janet Mangia, Luis Moreno-Caballud, Marina Sitrin, Conor Tomás Reed, Maleni Romero-Córdoba, Chris Rude, Begonia Santa Cecilia, Antonio Serna, Kristin Soerianata, Babak Tofighi, Brian Welton, Marlene Ramos, and Marcos Wasem, among many others.

This book is for Vicente—who made it possible through a sustained encouragement and reminder that it was worth doing it, through conversations, ideas, and the intensity of sharing and building different "commons" dreams—and for our little explorer and *libertador de rutinas*, *el peque* Simón.

Early versions of parts of chapters 2 and 4 were published in *Efectos de imagen: ¿Qué fue y qué es el cine militante?* (Santiago: LOM Ediciones, 2014), edited by Elixabete Ansa Goicoechea and Óscar Ariel Cabezas, and in *Reflections on Memory and Democracy*, edited by Merilee S. Grindle and Erin E. Goodman (Cambridge, MA: David Rockefeller Center for Latin American Studies, Harvard University, 2016).

THE MOVEMENT OF 1968

Acts of Memory and Struggles of Signification

We often talk about '68, and the many '68s around the world, as if the date itself were the site in which a singular plural memory took place. In contrast to earlier periods of mass uprising (such as 1848), 1968 is usually considered one of the first moments in which more spontaneous and simultaneous uprisings took place across the globe, including northern and southern regions of the so-called Third World.[1] Yet the movements of '68 are often mired in the realm of the unclassifiable for having demanded a process of emancipation and democratization that did not conform to traditional representative politics (a party or a specific petition). To play off the idea proposed by Daniel Bensaïd and Henri Weber in *May 1968: a General Repetition*, 1968 has gradually become a kind of open "rehearsal" of history: a rehearsal whose premiere is missing and yet lingers on as a promise of future performances.[2] The idea is taken up again in the classic study by Giovanni Arrighi, Terence Hopkins, and Immanuel Wallerstein on antisystemic movements, suggesting that '68 resurfaces as a historical citation, inspiration, or reference each time a new social movement breaks out—particularly those that are characterized by their brevity and the breadth of their demand for political transformation.[3]

Thus 1968 has continually reappeared in the streets, tweets, and memes circulated across the globe from 2011 onward (i.e., simultaneously in Greece, Spain, the United States, Mexico, Chile), concurrent with the crafting of new social responses to political and economic crises (15-M, Occupy Wall Street, #YoSoy132, the Chilean student movement). Taken as either something to leave in the past—as shown by an iconic piece of graffiti in Klafthmonos Square, Greece, at the beginning of the mobilization of 2008: "Fuck May 68, Fight Now"—or as an inspiration for overcoming local obstacles and evaluating the relationships between movements worldwide (the "global" revolution), *1968* keeps recurring in the imaginaries of different presents. Throughout the decades, it has returned or reemerged—as a cascade of singular emancipatory moments around the world, or as a sort of *scream* that reverberates over and over again—to use the image that John Holloway proposes in order to approach movements that attempt to *change the world without taking power*.[4] In the introduction to a recent journal issue dedicated to examining the relationship between 1968 and its futures, Kostis Kornetis uses the terms *surplus of utopia* and *inheritance of utopia* as connecting threads that bind reincarnations of '68 together more broadly and across time.[5] Recent works on the global 1968s, such as *The Long 1968* and *Protests in the Streets*, make reference to the global mobilizations that started in 2011, pointing to a common impulse to change the system without relying on the authority of a specific ideology or a party.[6] At the same time, references to '68 made by 2011 movements mention this axial year either to put words to something that is difficult to qualify as positive or negative (the idea of a movement without specific demands) or to defer to the authority of those who participated in '68 and their "judgment" of the new movement. In a paradoxical gesture, '68 works as a signal that helps to name the ambiguity and open character of the new movements; that is, it becomes a reference for something difficult to define from within the parameters of traditional politics.

We can ask ourselves: How does 1968 manifest itself in each of these returns? How has it been evoked in so many disparate circumstances? If we strip away the stigma imposed by the dominant European and American imaginary, what meaning lies beneath? For several decades, these questions have begun to take shape, questioning the leading imaginaries of '68 so often shaped by stigmas from the Global North. As we approach the fiftieth anniversary of '68, we face a series of inquiries: Is there anything left to say? What kind of memories can intervene to destabilize the dominant imaginary at such a crucial moment, which is widely considered the inception of a global consciousness? Nearly five decades after '68, we may find it curious that the proliferation of monuments that freeze the dynamic of the time contrasts with the need to go on constructing detailed studies that purport to *open up* the mainstream media narrative to other voices and views. Although the majority of anniversaries function as opportunities for monumentalization, they can also become *spaces for questioning* and *reconsidering timelines*, thus raising the possibility of depicting historical watersheds in new ways. As Katherine Hite contends, commemorations operate not only as exercises in recognition (generally led by the state with a conciliatory bent) but also as moments that revive the potential to transform "past meanings" in order to mobilize the present.[7] Clearly, many of the chords that 2011 strikes with 1968 have to do with the emergence of a series of views and forms of experimenting with the political that seemed to have been mutilated by the neoliberal era. By this I refer to the development of a capacity for self-organization, mutual aid, horizontal assemblies, the occupation of public spaces, and the development of sui generis organizational strategies. Also, 2011, like '68, occurred at a time when mobilizations could acquire a new global scope, thanks to new information and communication technologies—in this case, social networks.[8] This marks the reemergence of something from the distant past that seemed to have been crushed by the overwhelming force of repressive acts in response to the collective organization of the sixties. This "something" seemed to have more to do with a horizon of change—the opening of the present to an array of possible transformations—than to specific, tangible content at each juncture. In this particular recurrence of '68, the connection between past and present was forged by an emancipatory desire for the collective transformation of the everyday, suspending more dominant versions of the memory of the past, which are usually darkened by the repression that followed. Generally, within discursive as well as media spheres, the idea of a "politics of memory" is often related to traumatic moments of repression, forging a metonymic bond between memory and atrocity that we have somehow naturalized; however, this connection buries the memory of movements in which a desire for collective and everyday forms of emancipation awakened. Consequently, from the expansion of studies on memories of the Holocaust, to official or camouflaged dictatorial regimes in Latin America and southern Europe, to the proliferation of wars and antiterrorist campaigns, a general *imbalance* seems to exist between the memory of horror and that of collective processes of emancipation.

In the introduction to her classic *May '68 and Its Afterlives*, Kristin Ross alludes to this phenomenon when she says that the near-instantaneous association between memory and atrocity has "in turn . . . de-familiarized us from any understanding, or even perception, of a 'mass event' that does not appear to us in the register of 'catastrophe' or 'mass extermination.' 'Masses,' in other words, have come to mean masses of dead bodies, not masses of people working together to take charge of their collective lives."[9] Undoubtedly, this observation prompts us to consider how we might configure a memory that elicits forms of pleasure, collective empowerment, and disappointment instead of trauma. Trying to move slightly beyond the ongoing history punctuated by state and capital with their multiple forms of repression, it is important to note that the general preponderance of interest in studying memories of horror and death remains problematic when those memories are stripped from an analysis of the struggles for collective emancipation embodied by the repressed movements.

Clearly, the as-yet-"unofficial" nature of much of the violence employed in the sixties, seventies, and eighties explains this, but it is also important to expand the practical and semantic boundaries of the word *memory* so as to encompass processes that are not merely punctuated by the necrological apparatuses of a repressive state. In the case of Latin America, "museums of memory" usually concentrate more on accounting for violence and state repression in those decades than on uncovering the processes of reconfiguring freedom that were also characteristic of the historical moments that had been harshly annihilated. A crucial issue at stake here is how, by overemphasizing the role of repression and death, one loses sight of the means by which the state perpetuates its prolonged massacre of movements and dreams of freedom. As we will see, this is a particularly crucial problem when we approach Mexico 1968 because, as Bruno Bosteels states, the merciless state massacre at Tlatelolco "put its stamp retroactively on any interpretation of the events leading up to the brutal repression." This made melancholy and shame the main forces guiding the signifying processes of one of the most important political events. He argues that a different history of the events could be written "not from the perspective of the state but from the *subjective principle of equality* that universally resists the excessive power of the state."[10] Thus, a challenge for nearly "fifty years" of '68s—in all their manifestations (the long 1960s, the long 1968s)—consists of figuring out how to disentangle memory from massacre and terror without committing a naïve act of pure positivity or an epic affirmation of militancy that refuses to interrogate its own internal problems and contradictions. This task entails weaving dominant narratives of memory together with the sui generis mobilizations of those years, thus opening up memory to forms of communication and transformation that expand its capacity, particularly when that memory is linked to a historical moment marked by the radical interrogation of classic representational politics. Along these lines, I am reminded of Alain Badiou's reflections, when he says that we are contemporaries of '68, at least regarding its problematization of emancipation: "We can say that we are still struggling with the difficult questions raised by May '68. We are the contemporaries of '68 from the point of view of politics, the definition of politics, and the organized future of politics. I therefore use the word 'contemporary' in the strongest possible sense.... Of course, the world has changed, and of course, categories have changed.... But *we have the same problem*, and are the contemporaries of the problem revealed by May '68: the classical figure of the politics of emancipation proved ineffective."[11] We may well ask what this question regarding emancipation would mean if we were to transpose it into the realm of *memories* of '68, especially when it requires suspending the automatism with which official memories of '68 have been reproduced. In short, *what would an emancipation of memories of '68 look like*? Surely this possibility would introduce a new field of sayability, forging new meanings from the figure of emancipation in question. Thus, rather than entering into a discussion of the oversaturation of memorialist cultures in recent decades, I would like to briefly address the question of what it would mean to go beyond the "depoliticization" of '68, which Bosteels, Luisa Passerini, and Ross associate with those memorial processes, in the interest of opening other horizons for political memories.

Ross examines how forms of depoliticization, understood as the erasure of the innovative political dimension of '68, accomplished two processes that can be projected onto the experience of other countries, three of which are directly applicable to Mexico: reducing the event to a family conflict ("kids" versus adults) that is both generational ('68 as the concern of a particular generation) and transitional ('68 as a transition "toward"). To this Passerini adds the strategy of oscillating between mythicization and denigration, whereby a number of memorialist works end up producing a "void full of words of exaltation or denigration."[12] Depoliticization connotes a powerful moralizing operation, postulating the question of how we might foster alternative approaches to memories and processes of transformation that extend beyond good and evil. Thus, the question of whether it is possible to avoid those registers bears important implications for our intellectual work, where we operate as collectors of memories, activating or paralyzing their potentiality through reflection. It also affects our critical capacity to indicate how the very idea of memory has often been weighed down by the same habits of accumulation encouraged by the glorified consumption of recent decades.[13]

Although this book focuses on 1968 Mexico, it is important to note that over the past few decades, a shift began to take place in academic studies of the so-called global sixties in reaction to the fact that common mappings of the movement systematically exclude the countries of the Global South. This has opened up a number of new lines of questioning about the 1960s and '68; take for example a recent volume, *The Third World in the Global 1960s*, edited by Samantha Christiansen and Zachary Scarlett, which attempts to map the global sixties by including only so-called Third World countries, while omitting connections to similar experiences in the United States and Europe. Although it is clear that the goal of the editors was to redraw the map of the decade from a totally different perspective, there is also a danger in omitting the 1968s in the north, as this runs the risk of reproducing the same division the authors are trying to overcome. For across many 1968s, significant events involved the possibility of acknowledging and visualizing the many "souths" within the north, and vice versa, particularly because hard north-south divisions were a problematic structure that the 1968s made visible.[14] Another work, *New World Coming: The Sixties and the Shaping of Global Consciousness*, offers an alternate view of the decade; bridging north and south, it proposes to examine how a global consciousness was built, adopting the struggles for liberation and decolonization in Third World countries as its focus.[15] In the same tone but from a different perspective—centered on northern and southern Europe—the journal edited by Kornetis looks at the periodization of and communication among various 1968 and "long 1960s" movements: "This period . . . was characterized by a series of 'cultural transfers' that provided the missing link between protest movements; anti-authoritarian clashes and liberation struggles were facilitated by the globalizing tendencies that were brought about by new technologies, in particular television, that led to new forms of communication."[16] By identifying a series of points, Kornetis configures what he calls a mechanism of "cultural transfer" to explain the connectivity between '68 in various mediums (rock music, the news, libraries, certain authors, etc.).

In addition to the different lines of study that the global sixties have opened, I would like to call attention to the rich line of analysis of the '68s that focuses on studies of local mobilizations that defied national imaginaries. Perhaps it is the pioneering work of Ross that furnishes us with a series of fundamental questions that we need in order to uniquely deconstruct and analyze the version of '68 that was promoted most around the world (as in the case of France's May 1968). By discharging the ideological burden of monumentalization and studying the long exercise in depoliticization and dehistoricization that followed, Ross provides a new way of approaching the event. She dismantles the assumed "national" categories and acknowledges the internal colonialism so crucial to that moment. Along these lines, comparing the 1968s has been a task largely undertaken by sociologists and historians, with studies of individual nations united in volumes, anthologies, and so on. However, it is important to remember that 1968 was a key moment for the expression of a deep crisis within national grammars. Most of the liberation movements involved a radical critique of national tropes, as well as a national and international labor of deconstruction that laid the groundwork for new methodological queries. According to George Katsiaficas, "the worldwide episodes of revolt in 1968 have generally been analyzed from within their own national context; but it is in reference to the global constellation of forces and to each other that these movements can be understood in theory as they occurred in practice."[17] This is crucial, and it also makes us wonder about what perspective we can take in order to come up with these simultaneous relations and processes. That is, how can a broad international analysis hope to achieve a deep and critical analysis of the political transformations at stake in so many disparate protests? While I agree with Katsiasficas's point, I would caution that international views often become *panoramic* overviews of a moment, wherein little attention is paid to the *nuances* and *complexities* of the specific form that each 1968 took within its own national-international dialectic. For instance, the expansive international scope of Katsiasficas's book leaves little room for analyzing the singular forms that movements took *beyond a mere description of protest-repression*. References to the "international" scene usually relegate minor instances of 1968 to the simple trope of "protest-*repression*," disregarding the struggle and political reinvention implicated in them.[18] These take us back to the question of the primacy that repressive categories have when mass events are studied.

I would like to introduce the idea of the singular-plural as a form of decentering the narrative of a national unity that is radically split by such movements, simply by asking basic questions about the internal colonialism and racism of the era. I suggest that the singular-plural provides a way to write a history of the poetic political gesture that is 1968 from within the very crisis of national imagination that it brought about. How do we relate the singular-plural (non-unified, nonhomogeneous) to a fragmentary totality (the world, in the process of being changed)? In other words, how do we reconcile singularity with a process of historicizing complex unities? Given the singular-plural element of the event, we could make an argument for sustaining two simultaneous maps that honor the double temporality of '68. The first would present *a new way of inhabiting the present*—an irreverent impulse that opposes established cultural and political authorities and suffuses the present with the possibility of change. The second endeavors to reveal *an alternate history*, or the voicing of historical realities that had been smothered by dominant national narratives.[19] The latter refers to a long history of internal colonialism that emerged in the sixties and became a crucial channel through which to reconfigure temporal and political circumstances. In the case of Mexico, many accounts describe '68 not only as a watershed moment but also as an *awakening* to a previously unknown Mexico, to a reality that had been stifled or marginalized up until that point. In the great northern metropolises, this same awakening—the role Algeria played in France's May revolt, as Ross masterfully demonstrates; the parallel role of the African American liberation movement in the United States, and so on— is often omitted from the mass-media stereotypes of the '68s.[20] Accordingly, the plurality of expressions of this unprecedented dislodging of the universal narrative of nations takes us down two branching paths: national and international, each influenced by similar tropes—that is, the desire to democratize political structures, the participation of people who had never gotten involved in politics before, and the re-signification of freedom beyond the dichotomy hitherto imposed on the emancipatory narrative: the liberal imaginary versus dogmatic Marxism.

We can say that nearly fifty years after '68, much remains to be analyzed. The emergence of new perspectives on '68—such as Vania Markarian on the Uruguayan '68 and Ross on the French '68—signals a desire to build alternative memories, disentangling and deconstructing official attempts to undermine the movement's singular political force by controlling how it is remembered. They bring forth the disruptive capacity of '68 as a sui generis opportunity to proactively challenge sclerotic political institutions, triggering a dislocation of roles, social classes, and even accepted ways of intervening in politics. Markarian stresses the importance of identifying counterculture and singular forms of militancy that have been removed from the dominant memory of Uruguay '68, which is usually framed within a teleological process that leads to military dictatorship. Opening up the past to its own singularity means looking at still indistinct, everyday forms of organization that remain muffled beneath the crushing landslide of history. Ross approaches the same problematic from a different angle by studying the way mainstream memory domesticated France's '68, concealing the power and uniqueness of such a radical upheaval of fixed social positions and roles. Trapped in the familiar frame of a generation, a category of youth (a passing, fitful rebellion), the month of May, and a single neighborhood in Paris (*le quartier latin*), this revolution—an entire national political process that transcended sectors and classes—has been restricted to a small university yard and the primacy of a single voice: masculine authority and leadership. As we will see, many voices have begun to contribute to the discursive effort to rewrite Mexico '68, pointing out similar problems. It is almost as though, when the time came to think and remember the '68s, some dominant patron took over and privileged certain subjects—students, men, leaders—over others. So besides problematizing the northern paradigm (Paris, United States, Prague), there is still much to review and contemplate. For example, how does changing the perspective on and composition of memories of '68 alter our conception of the moment? Each instance of re-creation entails tracing a path from the event to the discourses that have reconfigured it in the present.

As for various discourses on Mexico '68, one can perceive a certain contemporary impulse to question dominant voices by opening the past to other interpretations. Consequently, a text such as Gladys López Hernández's, published in 2013, which I will analyze in the final chapter, compels us to acknowledge how the official memory of '68 has not only reiterated masculine leadership but also upholds a clear schema of social class by elevating certain memories and discarding others. Usually, the symbol of the National Strike Council (Consejo Nacional de Huelga, CNH) works as a space for authorizing dominant memories of '68; but this tends to omit all the structures that made that organization possible: assemblies, committees of struggle (*comités de lucha*) at each school, brigades that wove the movement into the social fabric. Omitted too are certain crucial agents of the democratization of knowledge, such as the Popular Preparatory (Preparatoria Popular) schools or efforts to establish cooperative forms of knowledge(s) between students and the people of Topilejo.[21] Seen in this light, it is intriguing that such hierarchical structures of memory have been imposed on such a profoundly democratizing moment. Half a century after the event, we can begin to delve into other areas, seeking more horizontal, less "proper" forms or memory that add ethical depth to current narratives. In so doing, we perceive how the democratization of memory can itself become a new iteration of the poetic gesture of that moment. Thus, the memory of the life and afterlife of '68 around the world becomes a field of struggle for conflicting modes of signifying the past from the present that demands new, more democratic perspectives on a democratizing event. Creating space for new memories offers us recourse to interrupt and influence the present with a more expansive, singular past.

The Struggle for Signification:
Memories and Accounts of '68 in Mexico

In the dominant map of the 1968s, Mexico occupies a peculiar interstitial space of north and south because it hosted the Olympic games that year, generating considerable visibility just days after the Tlatelolco massacre. Thus, on the international stage, the Mexican '68 is typically characterized by two events: Tlatelolco and the Olympic games. The paradoxical and perverse juxtaposition of the massacre to the games (diversion, repression) is generally supplemented by the act of political protest that took place during the awards ceremony, when African American athletes Tommie Smith and John Carlos made the "Black Power salute" in a gesture that spread around the world like wildfire but dampened their future careers considerably.[22] Due to the international nature of the Olympic Games and their immediate association with the terrible massacre in Tlatelolco—with which the state attempted to dissolve the noise of the mobilizations and attract the entire international tourist population—Mexico strikes a paradoxical, dissonant chord in the greater symphony of '68s. The international memories of the moment's capacity to question the roots of state authority and its developmentalist fantasy (of which the Olympic Games were one expression) still tend to be limited to the punctuation of state and international capital, leaving the distinct political relevance of the actual movement of '68 aside. Undeniably, the question at stake here involves more than a mere choice between "games/massacre" and "political movement"; instead, it relates to the possibility of thinking through these instances side by side, reincorporating certain memories of '68 that may not yet be included in the state's political spectacle.

In the interest of creating a wider field of reference, Mexico '68 assumes different forms in this book: the specific year in which the student popular movement was formed, as well as a field of reflections and reconstructions that endeavor to consider the event or continue its existence in various afterlives. In this sense, '68 also relates to the site of a series of struggles for signification that help to shed light on various marginalized perspectives and provoke deeper thoughts about its implications via written or reflexive processes that do not necessarily focus on a mere account of "what happened"—a positivist accumulation of dates and actions. In those struggles for signification, a collage of narrative images depicting the afterlife of the event takes shape—something that involves an insistence of building a memory of disruptive politics that forces us to confront the official, instrumentalist, and fossilized ways in which the event has been domesticated by national history and confined to a specific legibility. Ross argues that the dominant management of the memory of France '68 erased a key component of the time: the flight from harsh social determinations that designated people's places and roles within a determined order.[23] Paradoxically, the prevailing memory adheres to a criterion of normalization, by which the story of '68 is inscribed in a familiar frame: a generation of young people rebelled against authority and helped to modernize the country by transferring power from the authoritarian state to a liberal and financial bourgeoisie.[24] In the case of France, this official frame eliminates a whole host of elements necessary for understanding the centrality and breadth of the phenomenon—the Algerian conflict, for example, as well as working-class immigration and participation. In Mexico, 1968 has also been placed within a temporal and developmental frame in which the rupture effectuated by the event is reterritorialized in the language of a "transition to" democracy. Samuel Steinberg argues that, in contrast to the role that transition played in the Southern Cone, in the case of

Mexico, the category has been left unanalyzed in more critical and speculative ways outside the field of social sciences.[25] Esmeralda Reynoso questions the discourse that has marked '68 as part of a successful democratic "transition," postulating that, for her, what occurred during that time was a series of victories in terms of social rights that usually are more difficult to measure than a transition to democracy. This includes, for example, the form in which the lives of many women changed quite radically, along with the changing attitudes of youth and the forms of imagining existential paths, among other things.[26] This involves a transformation that does not fit within the normalizing strategy that usually situates a transition as moving forward within a temporal line, an advancement within the narrative of progress. Under the shadow left by the disappearance in 2014 of forty-three students at Iguala, Rafael Lemus argues that Ayotzinapa shows how the so-called transition to democracy that had marked one way of framing '68 in a narrative of success (from above) never took place.[27] At stake here is the sense of what is conceived as democratic and political, something that was at the heart of the movement, where the reconfiguration of democracy and politics related to a right *to transform the political* in ways that went beyond the logic of party representation and electoral alternation between the parties in power. Somehow, the radical transformation of the horizon of politics that crystallized in 1968 has been also naturalized under the repetition of separate levels: on the one hand, the notion that the "personal is political" (with its different equivalents), and on the other, the analysis of the political sphere, with the discourses of transition, end of the monopoly of the PRI, and so on. However, this separation omits the complications that the events of 1968 made possible in terms of reconceptualizing politics as a form of daily imagination at different micro- and macropolitical levels. As Bosteels states, "One of the lasting consequences of the events of 1968 . . . consists precisely in *displacing the borders of the political* so as to include the everydayness—the infra-ordinariness, so to speak—of those who are the subjects of struggles for justice."[28] I take this displacement of the borders of the political to the temporal imaginary in which the lives and afterlives of 1968 can be staged; this also involves problematizing the relations between temporality and politics that question the developmental narrative that usually permeates the imagination of change, both left and right.[29]

In terms of style, we might say that three tendencies have prevailed in studies of Mexico 1968: first, the testimonial form, wherein the dominant views of leaders or principal actors are reproduced; second, montages of repressive or traumatic moments that cast '68 in a more or less dramatic light; and lastly, studies that attempt to reconstruct '68 through the remembrance of activism and social movements. Generally speaking, these tendencies do not intersect or dialogue very much, and the resulting fragmented image makes it impossible to draw a more dialectical map of interrelations and possibilities. However, it does seem possible to trace the emancipatory paths of various experiences of '68, which collectively hint at an international landscape—one of the common creative responses to the rejection of politics as usual—keeping in mind their long-term trajectory, as well as the repressive forces that penetrated many areas. In other words, we can compose a dialectical view in which affirmation and negativity complement one another, thus avoiding the one-sidedness of affirmative mania (the pure positivity of the time) or the obituary form (obsession with repressive structures).

With the passing decades, the dominant generational, modernizing, and transitional frameworks that undermine the narratives of multiple '68s have been modified in several key ways. In her classic *State Repression and the Labors of Memory*, Elizabeth Jelin alerts us to the metamorphosing dynamic characteristic of the social processes of memory. "New historical processes, as well as changing social and political conjunctures and scenarios, inevitably produce alterations in the interpretive frameworks for understanding past experience and for constructing future expectations," she writes. "The complexity, then, refers to the multiplicity of temporalities at play, the multiplicity of meanings, and the ongoing transformation and change in actors and historical processes."[30] This dynamic is clearly evident in the case of Mexico, where the narrative of the memory of '68 has changed a great deal over the decades. Eugenia Allier Montaño's detailed study describes it as transferring primacy from the figures of the "fallen" to those of "social activists."[31] The construction of Memorial 68—inaugurated in 2007 in the Tlatelolco complex where the October 2 massacre took place—brings about a synthesis of this process. Erected on the very site of the atrocity, the monument features a series of activist testimonies that trace the general course of events from July to December 1968. Although a book like Elena Poniatowska's *Massacre in Mexico* accomplished this double function perhaps more polyphonically, the memorial still represents a spatial materialization that speaks to the new epoch dominated by what Allier Montaño calls the "eulogy of '68," whereby '68 is read as "a movement that propelled the democratization of Mexico forward." This reading doubles as a paradoxical example of instrumentalized memory, "convenient for the ends of diverse social and political actors; for PRI as a symbol of divergence from earlier PRI government, for PAN (especially Vincent Fox's government), and for the many parties of the left, as the effective democratization of Mexico demanded."[32]

To introduce another point of view, Esmeralda Reynoso, the current coordinator of Memorial 68, mentioned in an interview that it is necessary to rethink the space more dynamically and put it in dialogue with the present. She remarked that when young students from various schools visit the space, they usually leave with two impressions: the pain of the massacre and admiration for the valiant young people of the past. The past feels distant, and the chiefly epic tone of the narrative expressed through the videos shown—mostly featuring the memories of the male leaders of CNH—compounds that distance with admiration and respect.[33] Multiple analyses of the narrative structure of the memorial emphasize the problems that emerge from a memory that remains framed by a limited selection of voices, showing only one side of a polyphonic moment of protest and mobilization.[34] It becomes necessary to criticize certain monuments of '68 in order to invent new processes, new avenues to pursue, in which the weight of moralization gives way to a different way of reconstructing this vital moment. If we agree with Daniel Bensaïd's contention that "demoralizing" history equates to "politicizing it, opening it to strategic conceptualization,"[35] we are faced with the challenge of designing new itineraries and listening to other voices, as if our acts of interpretation could re-create the dynamic of a horizontal assembly that allows the memories of lesser-known contemporaries to speak.

Héctor Aguilar Camín begins *Thinking '68* with a series of statements and questions: "Remembering is not the same as thinking. . . . To what degree has the 'socialized' image of the Student Movement become a fixed photograph? Can this memorable event still move?"[36] We might say that this fixed photograph emerges from at least two dominant nuclei of memory that thinkers have begun to problematize over recent decades: first, the primacy of the Tlatelolco massacre as an almost metonymic reference to '68 Mexico; and second, the primacy of a few masculine voices of leadership in the creation of a history of '68, based on their experience in the student movement's National Strike Council. In the first case, the stain that the October 2 massacre left on '68 generates an interesting paradox in that the relevance of that moment, which opposed authoritarianism, remains punctuated by an act of despotism in which the state slaughtered an as-yet-undefined number of people.[37] As Esteban Ascencio observes, "There was violence—not just on October 2, but for the whole duration of the movement: military and police seizures of schools, provocations, threats, censure, the media's distortion of the facts, arrests, etc. The violence always existed. But to reduce the movement of '68 to what happened on October 2—to pack an entire process of struggle into a single day—is to minimize, on the one hand, the multiplicity of its expressions; and, on the other, to pay tribute to a very basic kind of necrophilia."[38] Surely there is no need to minimize the scope and horror of the massacre, nor the untimely role it played in sapping the vitality of a movement that had hitherto rendered the state police impotent. However, there is something problematic about the fact that the quasi-metonymic relationship sometimes drawn between the movement and the Tlatelolco massacre allows a repressive act by the state to undermine the entire exercise of democratic revolution. As Bosteels's critical intervention at the moment of the fortieth anniversary of 1968 puts it, the force and imagination of the movement was captured by the discourses of a "revolution of shame."[39] In the past decade, scholars have underlined the limitations of this closure, arguing in different ways how the memory of a political event—which did have its happy, festive moments—came to be reduced to a martyrological imaginary in which horror and death reign supreme. This culminates in what Gareth Williams calls the "Christian narrative of 1968 as inescapable martyrdom, sacrifice, and social trauma," one that prevents us from grasping the revolutionary nature of the event, stripping it of the freshness that enveloped it.[40] Steinberg's recent book, *Photopoetics at Tlatelolco*, also proposes the need for "critically traversing the *double* repression that conditions its reception," understanding by this the "military and paramilitary policing of the student movement" on and *before* October 2, 1968, and the "subsequent *assumption* of that massacre as the point of departure of any future organized around 1968."[41]

However, I would like to add that the memory of '68 has been somehow limited to the viewpoint of a few, mostly male leaders from the National Strike Council, thus constituting another component of the "fixed photograph" that has recently come under scrutiny, primarily because it imposes a hierarchical memory on an extremely polyphonic, egalitarian movement. With so few voices contributing, it is difficult to reconcile the dominant conceptualization of the event with the common recollection of a vigorous, massive uprising in which, in the words of Gastón Martínez, "everyone was a protagonist."[42] According to David Vega, then a student at the Polytechnic, "sometimes, when we talk about the student movement, we mention one or two leaders or discuss warring personalities. But really, we are missing something much more profound and less individual that must be acknowledged in all of its magnitude."[43] Along the same lines, Pablo Gómez Álvarez underscores the horizontality that characterized grassroots efforts: "I never saw a movement generate so much action from the very bottom, at the grassroots level. The creative decentralization of propaganda and political action was both impressive and truly admirable."[44]

In spite of the fact that the testimonies, essays, and disputes among the leaders will undoubtedly be incorporated into my analysis and have a fundamental value in reconstructing a certain trajectory of the movement, it is time to begin to trace other itineraries and include other voices. It is curious that a movement characterized by the polyphony and multiplicity of participants ends up appropriated by such a reduced and nonrepresentative number of those participants. Expanding this fundamental question to the political economy of memory, we can observe the increasing problematization of masculine dominance over the management of memories in the past decades. Deborah Cohen and Lessie Jo Frazier's analysis inspired a series of reflections on gender inequality in the constitution of dominant narratives about '68.[45] This involves something of a desacralization of the way the reigning hierarchical, masculine memory was constructed, particularly how it erases the mass political mobilization and participation of women from the movement. Upon reading the vast body of texts on this moment, Gloria Tirado Villegas noted that the majority of accounts were written by "participants, members of the National Strike Council, certainly social activists (a few of them prisoners), well-read journalists, academics. . . . Where were the women of '68? In so many texts, they barely receive mention."[46] Similarly, in a 2002 interview, Ana Ignacia Rodríguez, "La Nacha," said, "Discrimination against the women of '68 is—seriously!—a huge problem. Our participation was a decisive factor . . . but only our male comrades get to speak for the movement."[47] It is striking that those who struggle against the predominantly masculine memory of '68 are mostly women; with the exception of certain key retellings such as *'68* by Paco Ignacio Taibo II and *Escritos sobre el movimiento del 68* (*Writings on the Movement of '68*) by Eduardo Valle, the egalitarian participation of women languishes offstage.[48] By bringing up the question of gender in relation to the memory of '68, I do not aim to fall onto an essentialist or identitarian gesture that would assume women to be a simple, "transparent" subject whose voice would be sufficient to problematize masculine dominance in the narratives of the moment. Although I will go through this in more detail in chapter 4, I would like to state here that, by this question, I aim to point to the figure of the encounter, which is crucial to the book, with the hope of avoiding falling into some of the more typical operations of essentialism and identitarianism. That is, my hope is to avoid framing the analysis of the excluded as if they provided more "real" and "true" *versions* of the events by the mere fact of their exclusion. To do so assumes an essentialist approach to "otherness" that would overlook the complexity of the forms in which power relations are exercised through associations and positions. Luisa Passerini poses this problem in the introduction to *Memory and*

Utopia, where she addresses the epistemological issue at stake by following a feminist perspective that does not fall for the notion that any account could achieve fullness. Following Sally Alexander's idea, what is at stake is not to "recover" a full past but to write "a history which might begin from somewhere else."[49] Attuned to this approach, I hope to pay attention to the ways in which those who are not dominant voices in the official narratives elaborate their own ways of remembering and reconstructing the events. Within the complexity I mentioned above, these voices come from different positions, and I approach them from the following question: if a masculine schematic of leadership has dominated the memory of '68, what type of epistemological and imaginative operations emerge when memory is opened to other, less heroic, less masculine sites that address the encounters among different kinds of people?

Symbolic struggles over the memories that construct and reconstruct the event are important insofar as they express a distinct rejection of a monopoly over words. They seek to broaden access in order to illuminate points, problems, and situations that have not yet been articulated, especially given the multifaceted composition of the movement. In discussing how the moment has been remembered, Reynoso remarks that stylistic differences in the memory of '68 mirror those that distinguished the National Strike Council from the more polyphonic life of the brigades and the committees of struggle in their work on the streets and their conversations with common people with whom they actually engaged.[50] In the most minoritarian stratum of memory, narratives emphasize one largely neglected component that I consider fundamental: the moment of experiencing a sensation of *equality in participation*, which functions as a democratic structure that plays out in different forms of the day-to-day activities of the brigades, with their back-alley actions, paintings, mimeograph impressions, and kitchens. That memory of equality almost always surfaces in remembrances of everyday practices of the movement, as well as in memories of highly relevant moments such as the struggle and self-management of the Popular Preparatory, the experiences of activists in the village of Topilejo, and the mass participation of women, among other issues. In *'68*, Paco Ignacio Taibo II mentions equality as a key experience of '68 and describes the participation of women as a type of equality that did not ask permission, which was a crucial political gesture of the time. He declares that '68 predated the "new feminism": "It was better than feminism. It was *violently egalitarian*—and if it wasn't always, it always could be."[51] These words capture something that emerged in various conversations with women who participated in the movement: a rebellion of participating as if every man and every woman were equal, without asking permission, with respect and camaraderie.[52]

Undoubtedly many of the philosophical themes that we discuss today are part of the afterlife of the experience of 1968. The events, singularities, multiplicities, and margins of 1968 configured what has been regarded as the French post-1968 philosophical map, producing many debates and political positions that subsequently spread internationally. In this book, I approach 1968 as a moment of *encounter and equality* that opened up the stage for new configurations of freedom. Although encounter and equality are taken as the main guiding words with which I have chosen to characterize the moment in this book, there is not a homogeneous theory of them behind these pages; on the contrary, I am interested in seeing how encounter and equality work as guiding forces that constantly change and transform their territories according to the existential, conceptual, and political contexts in which they emerge at different points of time, including their reconfiguration in different acts of memory in the decades that followed the sixties. For instance, the encounter emerges in the work of José Revueltas through the formulation of the theoretical act, as a reflection on historicity and the connectivity among different fragments and layers of histories of emancipation that have been systematically repressed. It emerges in the visual realm as a form of performativity made possible by the image, thought of as a place of encounter able to connect people from different social places and realities in the process of making a film short or a communiqué. The encounter is crucially problematized, reconfigured, and transformed in different forms in the philosophical and testimonial works written by women, such as Roberta Avendaño, Fernanda Navarro, and Gladys López Hernández, as they attempt—each in her own way—to shed light on the epistemological and existential implications of the encounter, when this involves an encounter with what is nonanalogous or nonsymmetrical to my own self and situation. Here, questions of alterity and class difference emerge as an internal problematization of the areas that 1968 *made visible* and that also point to the limitations of the moment, its internal blindness toward forms of alterity that would stay outside the frames that had been opened by the moment (for instance, the fear of lesbianism in Avendaño's account of prison). The situation of imprisonment works as a place of *uncomfortable encounters* as well as a trope that allows us to see the walls imposed by middle-class patriarchal morality. It is also in the works written by women that the encounter emerges in a constant tension with equality.

In each chapter of the book, equality also emerges in different forms. It usually arises in many conversations and testimonies as a sense of equality felt in political participation. However, *equality* can be a confusing, misleading word, as it could be taken to mean a share in the political as usual, an access or entry into the existing political world, as when we think of the access of minorities to an area that had been denied to them. In contrast to this sense of the word, the equality that emerges in many accounts of 1968 refers to a sense of *participation as a form of sharing the horizon of a transformative potential of the political*, which is different from an equal share in politics as usual; it is the possibility of being equal *within the common goal of transforming the system*.[53] This clarification is necessary, considering that one of the dominant, terrible destinies of the feminism that was gestated in this period was that this irreverent struggle was subsequently reterritorialized by a sense of equality that came to mean merely access (the idea of equal pay, equal rights that leave the inequality of the patriarchal system untouched).[54] In a similar way, the reterritorialization of 1968 as the path for a political transition in Mexico has also been framed as the creation of new parties that now have power equal to that of the PRI. Of course, access is important; however, what is essential to remember is that such access was intimately connected to a *transformative force of the political order*. It was not just about having equal access to the political system, as it was this political system itself that was being radically criticized. Sharing equality in participation was part of a bigger process of questioning politics and opening up a different sense for experiencing it. And this process of questioning relates to the possibility of changing the way in which politics is socially framed and experienced: it involves the passage from the passive sense of participation related to representation (the electoral process, voting) to a reconfiguration of the sense of politics as something that is happening in the everyday—an active form of transforming the components that make social life possible.

When I speak of equality, there are at least two horizons in question. One horizon refers to the *irreverent participation* of those who had been systematically excluded from or felt that they were outside the political arena. This included women of different ages or people who, having never been involved before, felt they knew nothing of the old politics. It also refers to the connectivity among different struggles that become equal, as democracy reconfigures a form of active participation in the everyday politics at stake at work, at home, and at school. The other horizon is related to worlds that still remain outside the radical reconfiguration of the political, which is the world that emerges mostly in writings by women remembering their imprisonment, a universe where a deep form of inequality emerges as the destiny of many invisibilized sectors of the population. This is what we could see as the world that refers to or constitutes the common form of imprisonment in these memories, and that poses a challenge for the revolutionary desire and scope of young educated women sharing a space in prison. What I am interested in seeing here is how a post-'68 landscape that takes its memory from re-creating the experience of women's imprisonment makes the key idea-forces of the book take on other tones and tensions: *encounter and equality*, essential in descriptions of 1968, face a limit or limitation that is worked out in the texts, when the recently politicized women enter into contact with women from other social classes. It relates to the world of the socially rejected (common women prisoners) in both Avendaño and López Hernández, and also of those rejected by the university in López Hernández's remembrance of the Popular Preparatory. What does '68 look like from here? From both meanings of equality, '68 appears as an open promise, and at the same time, it is as if this way of looking opened other landscapes that had remained outside the memories of the moment. The itinerary that these texts create allows us to see how equality (in participation) leads to the vision of so many forms of inequality that somehow permeate invisible social divisions that become clearer in prison. Equality that was felt through participation in the movement became a limited, reduced experience when compared to the realities of the imprisoned women. This signals a problematization of equality and democracy where, as Judith Butler states, "the point of democratic politics is not simply to extend recognition equally to all of the people, but, rather, to grasp that only by changing the relation between the recognizable and unrecognizable can (a) equality be understood and pursued and (b) 'the people' become open to a further elaboration."[55] This is a limit, or the space of an unfulfilled promise that we can see emerging in some reconfigurations of 1968 made by women in the decades that followed.

Equality emerges in my own approach as a problematization of the voices and themes that have usually been the focus of accounts of Mexico 1968 while persistently silencing so many others. In other words, equality has gained little attention in the many *places of memory* that comprise the itineraries of '68.[56] One objective of this book is to shift perspectives on '68 away from the voices that have traditionally presided over its reconstruction. I do not mean to say that I will not include them, since I believe they have helped facilitate an extensive memory of the moment without which it would be difficult to even recognize it for what it was. That said, it is necessary to blaze new paths through figures and voices that have been pushed to the margins, with the aim of configuring another kind of constellation that would encompass points that these other memories or continuations of '68 make possible. As with a kaleidoscope, we will adopt different lenses that permit us to see different points and problems of the moment. It is a matter of supplementing dominant views with a more polyphonic style capable of reconstructing the edges of that moment and its historical, philosophical, and political relevance. Instead of going through the main archive of 1968, I decided to look at different interventions that did not share an identical ground or position. Even though the usual names that constitute the main political and cultural archive of 1968 will be present in the background (Raúl Álvarez Garín, Gilberto Guevara Niebla, Luis González de Alba, Marcelino Perelló, Elena Poniatowska, Carlos Monsiváis), I decided to include other names and positions that would express a more varied, less canonical, constellation of the moment. Therefore, when reading the thinkers I analyze here, including José Revueltas, Fernanda Navarro, Roberta Avendaño, Gladys López Hernández; when watching the films of the *superocheros* (Super-eighters) and cooperative filmmakers; and when listening to the voices of Guadalupe Ferrer, Esmeralda Reynoso, Alberto Híjar, and Martín Dozal, taken from interviews carried out with the purpose of opening up 1968, I realized that even though the conceptual figures of the encounter and of equality emerged in all of them as a singularity of the moment that pointed to a radically new sense of freedom in their lives, they never emerge as stable and equal concepts. This is because they relate to different fields of signification and problematization, such as freedom and temporality in Revueltas, encounter and alterity in Navarro, and encounter and class inequality in Avendaño and López Hernández. Thus, 1968 is characterized by a polyphony of voices that express different and no less contradictory philosophical and political positions. Because of this, in each section the art of the encounter emerges as a *zone of both experimentation and struggle* that varies according to the different situations, practices, temporalities, and subjects involved. So, they become *conceptual territories* that are constantly changing and transforming their mappings in a heterodox way, posing a multiplicity of meanings and conflicts. This is one of the main characteristics of what I analyze here as *cognitive democratization* as a practice where paradoxes and contradictions are allowed to take place without expecting the transparency and coherence of an ideal theme or theoretical positioning. The open character of '68 addresses the poetics of a liberation that is not limited to specific and timely demands of a group, a union, or a party. In this sense, one of the distinctive characteristics of '68 was its zeal for *social connectivity*, that is, the way in which the demand for a change in the system was able to bring together the desires and feelings among diverse people and groups, who had mostly never met to act in common until this moment. Playing with an expression by Vinícius de Moraes, we could say that '68 could be defined as *the art of the encounter*, and that a great potentiality to illuminate other social processes resides in this figure.[57] Because of the connective character of the social fabric, I refer to its ability to manifest itself from the educational centers as a struggle beyond its particular situation, consolidating a national movement that had the support and participation of many groups united by a demand for democracy, equality, and freedom. This implied a reconfiguration of the political and of the right to politics. For this reason, the figure of encounter has an essential role in this book, given that it refers to the connective nature of '68, unlike other movements that have emerged over the course of time. A phrase used by Mercedes Perelló sums up the tone of the moment: "in '68 for the first time we stopped fighting and we all joined together in the same struggle," referring to the way in which the movement brought together people who had diverse political positions as well as those who perhaps did not have any experience in political participation.[58]

The moment of 1968 can be approached as an instant of opening where many contradictory positions coexisted; this made it possible to experience the political outside the dogmatism of party rules or ideologies. It is an instant when the relaxation of the rigidity of the political allowed for the creation of a space where disparate concepts could be articulated in a common language. One of the crucial differences between movements and parties is that the former allow for a freedom of positions without having fixed principles and rules that would guide further actions from above. This relates to the primacy that processes have in movement politics as well as to the notion of change that is at stake. Instead of being guided by a goal (such as state takeover), movement politics are permeated by the practice of finding the political in the everyday—that is, in what is closest and therefore most difficult to articulate and modify. This can be seen in the attempt to develop a sense of equality in its practices (assemblies, horizontality), as well as a form of uncertainty that sometimes makes movements illegible, as there is no goal other than to transform the system in a piecemeal, more micropolitical way. One of the most innovative points of the '68 moment that I am interested in delving into here is the destabilization that '68 provokes on the horizons that organize the field of the sayable and imagination about freedom and liberation from the perspective of liberalism and dogmatic Marxism. I say destabilization because it is not about an absolute rejection but rather forms of tension, deconstruction, and impure mixes of elements that form the languages to express and live freedom. In the philosophical field, this generates interesting positions within the tradition of a heterodox Marxism and refines modalities of understanding the practice of liberation. Philosophical figures and trajectories like those of Grace Lee Boggs, Angela Davis, Fernanda Navarro, Henri Lefebvre, and José Revueltas are marked by this moment and refer us to critical gestures and revolutionary movements within the field of the conceptualization of the free, something that makes them think in a critical and creative way the instances of the capture of dialectical thought without fully renouncing, at least in that moment, the language of Marxism. It is the possibility of thinking together, in a single space, the figures of the complex composition that mark the passage between more traditional political *language* (as Marxism was in the seventies) and the babbling that expresses other alternative forms of collective freedom. Such alternate forms were based on the role that the everyday, the marginalized, and the singularity of desires divergent from the norm begin to have, renewing the understanding of the free and of processes of emancipation in a revolutionary mode. In this sense, the '68 moment radically modified an entire philosophical, artistic, and political climate.[59]

The Transversality of the Movement and the List of Demands (pliego petitorio): Political Overflow and the Eruption of Dissent

Setting aside polemics for or against the popular nature of '68, one indisputable historical singularity of the movement was its desire for *social connectivity*; that is, refusing to limit itself to a specific group with a specific demand and instead interweaving many threads in the social fabric, as it partially succeeded in doing.[60] The new capacity for participating and transforming the political took on a kind of *demand for social democratization* that, originating in the university, was able to spread across various sectors of the population in many different parts of the country. Although the capital became the very center of signification of the movement as well as a space in which the symbolic takeover of a political history gathered uncommon momentum (takeover of the streets, the Zócalo, the seizure of the UNAM), one distinctive element of the movement was its ability to take root in many educational centers and social sectors across the country. Therein lies the national and popular element that constitutes and defines the movement, without intimating a kind of homogenous collective for struggle. Furthermore, although the movement specifically and crucially originated from the higher education offered in the capital, its *political impetus* is not constrained to the academic sphere but calls for a transformation of all possible fields of the political across various dimensions. These range from everyday practices and their forms of subjectification to the demands for liberty and equality contained in the list of demands put forth by the National Strike Council. The global nature of the movement aligns with the type of general demand to dismantle the state's monopoly over the very meaning of freedom, so enmeshed in violence and authoritarianism: a false, imposed consensus. Therefore, its demand for *democratization* can be understood as a demand for equal right to participation and dissidence, which, to quote Sergio Zermeño, "does not simply mean to solicit an aperture of already established institutional channels. Rather, participation took the form of criticism and a rejection of existing forms of participation and expression, and there we find that which united all sectors."[61]

Delving into the movement's imaginary, César Gilabert points out that the movement lacked a concrete, long-term agenda in the most traditional sense of a "political plan" to use as a platform, for its political power derived from opening up a utopic imaginary.[62] Within that utopia, we find a defense of the universal right to the political, which enables a reconfiguration of the political by shifting the meaning of democracy outside traditional schemas that limit it to a form of "partyocracy" and of electoral processes.[63] Given the demand for dialogue and active participation in the political on various levels, the movement postulated a reinterpretation of the very meaning of freedom and equality as a way to transform the realm of political possibilities. Thus '68 opens "a new dimension of Mexican politics," for unlike the conflicts that preceded it (such as the railroad workers', teachers', doctors', or telegraphists' movements), the students neither "made claims by and for themselves" nor acted as spokespeople for a union organization or a specific party.[64] Part of the everyday creativity that unfolded over those intense months originated from a collective effort to leave the academic sphere and generate more encounters in the streets, smashing automated life with happenings, fliers, and spontaneous conversations. It is relevant to note that some of the demands on the petition refer to a history of struggles that had been systematically imprisoned and repressed, as well as to a way of forging a link between *democracy, equality, and freedom* that went beyond the concrete in order to postulate a change in the political order itself—as Adolfo Gilly states, the Mexican '68 consisted in a *social mobilization for democracy*.[65] It is the *transversal* nature of '68 that makes it stand out from the many other movements that preceded and followed it; that is, its capacity to *traverse the social field* with a demand for democracy, freedom, and equality in participation that rethinks the terms and conditions of the political, its possibility and existence.

As Raúl Álvarez Garín states, the number of struggles unfolding through and around the repressive acts perpetrated by the police from July 22 onward began to highlight the need for unification of dispersed struggles. In this context, the idea of creating a *single* list of demands responded to the desire to create a common plane for the unification of all the struggles that had been progressing in various colleges and institutes.[66] These student mobilizations, which began in protest of the harsh repression dealt to Vocational Schools 2 and 5 after a fight over a soccer game with students at Isaac Ochoterena Preparatory, are generally considered to be the starting point of the movement. This said, it should not be forgotten that all of this occurred within a greater context of struggles that had been going on in educational centers in various regions *throughout the decade*. Gilberto Guevara Niebla provides a detailed analysis of the various student struggles and acts of solidarity that marked that turbulent decade. He also comments on the distinctive nature that the '68 movement acquired in its "national" form, as well as its dissolution of the student identity, which fused with the whole of society to issue a democratic demand.[67]

The disproportionate burden of repression that the riot police (*granaderos*) inflicted on vocational students in the wake of July 22—on top of the generalized repression that occurred on July 26 with the march to commemorate the Cuban Revolution and the National Federation of Technical Students' march to protest police repression—gathered force that found an outlet on July 27 in a takeover of various educational centers (UNAM Preparatory Schools 1, 2, and 3) and an organization of assemblies. Two days later, the police and the army raided the campuses, unleashing the monstrous bazooka shot that destroyed the colonial gate of Preparatory School 1. The following day, classes were suspended and a crucial march took place, headed by the rector of UNAM, Javier Barrios Sierra. In the first days of August, the National Strike Council had already formed, uniting students with the Coalition of Secondary and Post-Graduate Professors for Democratic Liberties (Coalición de Profesores de Enseñanza Media y Superior Pro Libertades Democráticas), a group of teachers in support of the student proposition. At that point, assemblies were proposed so that each school could designate three representatives to the council. Thus, the National Strike Council relied on representation from each of the seventy schools on strike, eventually accumulating 210 members who mediated the decisions made by the committees of struggle and the assemblies at their respective institutions.

The agreement about the list of demands became a moment of *unifying struggles in a common force* extending across all sectors that adhered to it, and the six points were an expression of the request for a political reconfiguration that first had to dismantle the repressive mechanisms of the state: (1) freedom for political prisoners; (2) the removal of police chiefs Luis Cueto Ramírez, Raúl Mendiolea, and Armando Frías; (3) the dissolution of the granaderos; (4) the repeal of Article 145 and 145A of the Federal Penal Code that sanctioned "crimes of social dissolution"; (5) compensation for the families of the dead and those who fell victim to the constant aggression perpetrated since July; and (6) the demarcation of responsibility in respect to the repressive excesses of the police, the granaderos, and the army. These articulated the disparate struggles realized in various educational centers under a common language, one that called for freedom, equality, and democracy by demanding that the repressive fabric of the state, which annulled any disagreement, be unraveled. In this sense, the list of demands constituted both an opening and a common point of encounter that enabled the movement to spread across various social sectors to form a national struggle. Its strength lay in the fact that the six points, detached from student and academic life, comprised a democratic demand that asked for freedom and equality in the participation and construction of a political system by and for all.[68] Zermeño characterizes it as a "point of confluence" of many different sectors, unveiling a "comprehensible dimension for all layers of society through the request for a public dialogue with the government to resolve these demands."[69]

Once the list of demands was agreed upon, it was proposed that "all postgraduate institutions of the national academy and numerous provincial universities go on strike" until the government responded to the above points. As for the government's response, the only thing that came of this request for a dialogue was an even greater increase in repressive deployments, which made the demand for political rights even more necessary.[70] From then on, creative forms of political action emerged everywhere: assemblies, brigades, committees of struggle, festivals, and acts of solidarity on the part of various groups and sectors of workers, including electricians, railroad workers, doctors, primary and secondary schoolteachers, and journalists.[71] This generated informative rallies, assemblies, and conversations in the street, at the gates of government offices, and in factories. According to Gilabert, the clout that the National Strike Council has in the '68 imaginary perpetuates a "myth of the Central Committee," which often obscures other decision-making and participatory bodies that tended to feature greater engagement and horizontality. These assemblies, committees, and brigades "offered the floor to anyone who wanted it, regardless of their status or political affiliation."[72] That said, many people in the National Strike Council also took part in everyday activism, where the movement held together best. Being in charge of public relations in Preparatory School 1's committee of struggle, Reynoso recalls that people came from all over with stories, problems, and demonstrations of solidarity: "I had to talk to people who came to ask questions or wanted to know things, but only for a little while. The rest of the time what we did was go out to paint buses and hold flash rallies in plazas and markets. I remember we went to a very famous factory—the Clemente Jacques—to hold flash rallies as the workers were heading home, passing out fliers . . . and it was our daily work, aside from being at the school awhile." Reconstructing the day-to-day of the movement, she also remembers the marches as a practice that brought all schools and social sectors under the same banner: "We were all comrades. The magic word was *compañero, compañera*. Being a *compañero, compañera* was a safe conduct that meant everyone supported you and took care of you."[73]

These spaces and sites of encounter functioned as intersections among "democratic, libertarian, anarchist, and lucid aspirations; reasonable and frustrated hopes, transgression and excess. Suddenly, designated political spaces—delineated by State authoritarianism—were overtaken by powerfully disruptive elements, united ideologically around everyday life instead of politics."[74] There are two important things about this characterization that will prove fundamental to this book: the suspension of an orderly system of fixed, designated spaces; and the overflow this suspension achieved on various levels once people started organizing in unexpected places. The possibility of breaking with designated political spaces unleashes the force of a true demand for *democratization* as a way of intervening in a structure that maintains a political order as an entity separate from society by situating it in privileged spaces.[75] Thus, essential to the '68 moment is the art of overflowing social spaces and roles, making us reconsider the eruption of the political as a series of crossings and flights from static forms of identification of actors within an authoritarian order that attempts to put everyone in their place. At the root of the demand for democracy is a form of intervention in the very spaces that had annulled the possibility of political democracy in an authoritarian regime.

The list of demands put forth a specific request to dismantle a police force that fed the repressive, authoritarian character of Mexican politics. This put an entire political order in question as it involved a momentary suspension of the force of authority underlying the social contract, which is dictated by a sort of mandatory consent in which any act of discrepancy against the state is repressed or annihilated. Thus, the idea of '68 as a *watershed* of the twentieth century, which appears in the majority of testimonies and accounts, has to do with the colossal way in which it suspended—practically for the first time—the official version of the revolution through a collective practice of emancipating its imaginary. In *Democracy in the Streets*, Guevara Niebla affirms that '68 constituted "the first great modern urban political crisis to confront the regime of the Mexican Revolution. Its outbreak spectacularly revealed the absurd degree of despotism, rigidity, and concentration of power that Mexico's political system had achieved during the cycle of industrialization, building out from a democratizing imperative."[76] It is important to underscore that this moment of satiation and rupture with a certain postrevolutionary state destiny opened up a completely different mode of conceiving the political. It implies a struggle against the disproportionate role that authority and authoritarianism play in the political system, as a constitutive component, something that is expressed in many ways but particularly through the use of force and repressive deployment whenever disagreement arises between a group of common people and the cupola of political elite (presidentialism and the monopoly exercised by the PRI). Moreover, it signifies a challenge to the ways in which authoritarianism permeates the life of institutions that organize life within a political order and their dominant processes of subjectivation. This involves not only the organization of an entire institutional bureaucracy but also various ways of controlling and co-opting any organized body of dissent, whether in a union organization (something that the railroad workers', peasants', and doctors' movements made apparent in the fifties and early sixties) or on a more personal level—such as, for example, authority within a patriarchal family structure and the gender inequality it reproduces, or relations of power reproduced in educational centers (who gives orders, who enforces the orders).[77]

The breaking point that was reached in '68 amounts to a loud cry of "Enough!"—a manifold, festive demand for democratization in which common people lay claim to basic freedom and equality in the political process as a common right that is expressed through their everyday and institutional lives. Thus, the demand for democracy entailed a new configuration of the discernible political order at as-yet-unexplored levels, because emancipation did not entail a specific, prompt demand issued by a determined group (in the style of union petitions) but rather a demand for freedom and equality. These words, emptied of meaning until that point, came alive as expressions of democracy in everyday communal life, in people's desires and in their bodies, in language that is opened up and analyzed for new meanings, in questions of how to rethink institutions and propose alternatives. In a country where the word *revolution* had been monopolized by an authoritarian state, the question of a *democratic revolution* became a space open to the exploration of new ways of experiencing the political. Undoubtedly this generated an unprecedented wealth of ideas, which facilitated the construction of connecting bridges between those who belonged to determined groups or parties, and those who had never been the least interested in participating in politics. The work of organizing into committees of struggle, participatory assemblies, brigades, mimeographs, kitchens, graphic designs, and festivals transformed educational centers into realms of collective democratic experimentation that traversed a world of affects and their own capacity for collective action. As Carlos Monsiváis observes, "Acts of individual and collective feelings of solidarity and political imagination were the solid foundation and clear raison d'être of the Movement."[78] We can describe the path that '68 begins to tread as a form of creative and revolutionary rupture with the fiction of a transparent national "unity," which, as Guevara Niebla argues, attempted to provide a "basis for the political regime of the Mexican revolution," thus stripping bare the despotic character "of a political system in which the relationship between the governors and governed are mediated by the principle of authority."[79] By reiterating the demand for a "dialogue" with the government, the movement proposed to establish a conversation founded on the basis of a radical disagreement over ways of understanding the political.

In his analysis of sovereignty and exception in the twentieth century in Mexico, Gareth Williams explains how the point of departure from Mexican modernity took the form of "a police state understood as the direct governmentality of the sovereign qua sovereign."[80] This is notable because the suppression of the duality of state and society implies a persistent repression and *invisibilization* of disagreement as the expression of alternative ways of constructing the political. In 1968 the division became even greater with a movement that cut across various sectors of society with an explicit political and democratic demand that was systematically invisibilized through silence, indifference, and the permanent *crescendo* of the state's repressive response. If we carefully examine, as Jorge Volpi does, the "Fourth State of the Union Address by President Gustavo Díaz Ordaz" on September 1, 1968, it would seem to present a kind of official pronouncement of the single order enforced by the state. In it, the president accomplishes the negation and invisibilization of the very existence of the list of demands: "To date, we have not received a single concrete petition, either from educational administrators or organizations or from groups of teachers, students or others." Not only does he declare the nonexistence of the list of demands, but he also insists on the invisibilization of the realities to which it alludes. For example, he says, "I do not concede that political prisoners exist. Political prisoners are those who are detained *exclusively* because of their political ideas, without having committed any crime"—which means that political prisoners do not *exist* in the eyes of the government; instead, they are "vandals" or delinquents.[81] Here the president reestablishes "order" and invisibilizes dissent: "By the same concept, having exhausted the means that good judgment advises, I will always exercise when strictly necessary the authority contained in Article 89, Section VI of the Constitution, which says, 'The authorities and obligations of the president are to utilize the totality of the standing armed forces, or the army, navy, and air force, for the interior security and exterior defense of the Federation.' "[82]

It is evident that this State of the Union communicated an explicit denial of the student movement and the entire population that supported it. By counteracting the list of demands point by point, it is admitting its existence through a performative declaration of inexistence: defining what does and does not count in its political order. In the next chapter, I am interested in examining how that declared invisibilization of the movement erases the meaning of its words and demands, dismissing them as mere noise because they do not conform to the state's monopoly on logos. Thus, the clash between two heterogeneous logics—the monological authority of the president and the movement's demand for equality and democratic participation—is followed by the silencing and invisibility of dissidence. As Rancière explains, "The police is thus first an order of bodies that defines the allocation of ways of doing, ways of being, and ways of saying, and sees that those bodies are assigned by name to a particular place and task; it is an order of the visible and the sayable that sees that a particular activity is visible and another is not, that this speech is understood as discourse and another as noise."[83] Undoubtedly, the verbal declaration of war that the State of the Union made when it symbolically invisibilized the list of demands was soon to find a physical correlate in the savage October 2 massacre and the subsequent torture and detention of all those who had inhabited that space of equality, which the power of authority still refused to recognize. In short, disagreement is first negated by order of logos and then by order of *bodies*, thereby reaffirming the badly perforated fiction of political and social unity. Sovereignty is both affirmed and immunized when confronted with a heterogeneous logic that threatens its authority, breaking the partition of a political order that since July had been gathering momentum in the social sphere. In this sense, words, images, and bodies would operate as sites of struggle: mechanisms of affirmation and aperture of what is officially negated and declared nonexistent.

The petition for democracy in the face of a partyocratic and presidentialist structure emerges as a kind of polyphonic culmination of actions and words that "revindicate and empower political content by emphasizing their quotidianity" and thus ask to speak: "The movement is to request the word. . . . In that sense, it is, as [Herbert] Marcuse says, more marginalized than oppositional."[84] On "freedom of the press" day, José Revueltas would write from Lecumberri Prison: "They have sought to rob us of the freedom of these words, the freedom that people exercised by yelling them in the streets. *We are persecuted words*, isolated in cellblocks, filtered through cellblocks."[85] Words, images, and bodies are territories that all texts that seek to analyze, historicize, or continue the movement must acknowledge as central to a vital struggle for that right to logos. In his fourth State of the Union address, the president carried out the symbolic closure through word and image that the Tlatelolco massacre and mass imprisonment of the movement would soon inflict on bodies. Therefore,

the objective of the next two chapters is to traverse the points of a constellation of '68 that allows us to see the concrete ways in which the essential disagreement underlying the struggle for the right to the political was expressed
in words, images, and subjective accounts. By continuing to practice dissidence
through language, images, and bodies, the world negated by authoritarianism
continues to sustain itself by the force of a struggle based on reflection, creativity, and uncertainty. If this was indeed a moment of redefining what freedom
means in a society, as well as the construction of subjectivities that live within
and rebel against it, one might ask: How did this problematization of freedom
affect the entire language with which it was designated and configured? Put differently, how did this moment of dislocation we call '68 affect various practices of
memory, texts, and disciplines? How was the freedom claimed by '68 expressed
by virtue of remembering, rethinking, and imagining the event through other
temporalities? What comes out of '68 if it is remembered through accounts that
do not adhere to the closed circuits that have traditionally defined the event? The
following chapters seek to answer these questions.

Chapter 1 focuses on the work of self-taught, heterodox Marxist thinker
José Revueltas. Questioning how Revueltas configures '68, as well as how '68
configures Revueltas's own thought, I analyze how the movement impacted his
late work, since its everyday practices of democratic, horizontal organization
and self-management required a reconsideration of finite ideas about freedom.
First, I look at his philosophical writings on self-management (*autogestión*); on
the democratization of knowledge (which he called "cognitive democracy");
and on the theoretical act, which is posed as a form of answering the question
of how we can interpret a historical singularity such as 1968 without either
assigning it an unhistorical spontaneity—thus depoliticizing the originality of
its political demands—or falling prey to the kind of linear causality that so
often typifies our definition of progress. These three interrelated idea-forces expose how 1968 is configured in relation to a broader philosophical landscape of
the time, when materialism, freedom, and dialectics had been radically transformed. I continue by analyzing two of Revueltas's literary works: *The Apando*
and the posthumous novel-project *Time and Number*, as well as miscellaneous
writings on the collective experiences of the political prisoners at Lecumberri
Prison. Revueltas problematizes language, historicity, and temporality in relation to the freedom of the movements and the constant waves of repression
and death that the Mexican state uses to paralyze them.[86] I relate reflections on
dialectics and the possibility of thinking about a different, nondevelopmentalist, manifold temporality of social movements to the horizon of questions

posed by other Latin American critical Marxists of the time (such as José Aricó and René Zavaleta Mercado).

Chapter 2 analyzes the effects of 1968 on the visual regime, paying attention to how the movement continued into the early seventies in different marginal cinema collectives. The chapter elaborates the meanings of the autonomy of the image and the ways in which these experiences reconfigured aesthetics and politics. I analyze two specific groups in Mexico that proposed different forms of articulating cinema and liberation as a path toward a fourth cinema (*cuarto cine*), diverging from the then-dominant currents of militant cinema. One is the Cooperative of Marginal Cinema (Cooperativa de Cine Marginal), made up of students and amateur filmmakers who decided to superimpose the experience of the movement on the visual real, at the moment of depoliticization following the Tlatelolco massacre and mass imprisonment. The cooperative filmed different communiqués that linked various independent strikes throughout the country. Both the plot and the sound of the movies were created by the workers, thereby decentering the role of the artist and the work of art. The other group I study is one led by filmmaker Óscar Menéndez that clandestinely brought Super 8 cameras into Lecumberri Prison. The prisoners became artists recording their own situations, able to visually confirm political imprisonment at a moment when the president denied that political prisoners existed. I analyze the fascinating international itinerary of the resulting film, *History of a document*, which, with Jean-Paul Sartre's help, was edited in Paris by a group convened specifically for this purpose: the Groupe de Recherches Technologiques—Atelier d'expérimentation Super 8.[87] *History of a document* was going to be broadcast by the Office de Radiodiffusion-Télévision Française (ORTF) but was censored at the last minute. These experiments dislocate the social place of the image and operate as mechanisms that respond to a certain demobilization after '68, continuing the event beyond its temporality and connecting it with a larger history of social realities.

Chapter 3 focuses on how memories and critical re-creations of 1968 have been placed in a masculine, hierarchical paradigm that has erased the participation of women. Here, I approach the question of how a moment characterized by radical forms of democratization and equality in participation ended up *remembered and configured* from the angle of male leaders, but with the idea of moving beyond the constancy of women's participation in order to study different interventions made by women in different fields. After analyzing a series of interventions by women and the connections between 1968 and the emergence of second-wave feminism in Mexico, I examine the forgotten philosophical work of Fernanda Navarro,

Existence, Encounter, and Chance.[88] I argue that Navarro's book reconstructs the figure of the encounter—a crucial figure in my approach to 1968—and re-elaborates it from a perspective that prioritizes bodies and gender relations. Thus, through Navarro's work, I enter into the wake left by second-wave feminism in the decade that followed the movement in order to address her philosophical intervention around a materialism of the encounter.

Chapter 4 analyzes how the figure of the encounter emerged in the nineties with the publication of a memoir of '68 written by Roberta "La Tita" Avendaño, *On Freedom and Imprisonment.*[89] One of the few women on the National Strike Council, Avendaño accomplishes an unusual task: instead of providing her account and evaluation of the movement (as most of the National Strike Council's male leaders have done), she offers a reflection on 1968 that focuses solely on the personal experience of political imprisonment at the women's prison. The text re-creates the complexity of everyday life in prison through the relationships that Avendaño established with common prisoners. These were lower-class women who had remained outside 1968's dominant imaginary, mostly populated by the epic figures of the political prisoners. Reflecting on class difference and imprisonment raises questions about the "democratization" at stake in the movement. This had remained completely outside the more dominant voices and points to a contextualized form of addressing dialogue and inequality in an environment that arose from and exceeded the forms of otherness (white- and blue-collar workers, peasants) that were closest to the students at the height of their mobilizations. Finally, I move to the present and analyze a memoir written by a working-class woman who was seventeen years old in 1968: *Ovarimony: Me, a Guerrilla Fighter?* by Gladys López Hernández.[90] The text offers insight into class and gender difference in both the movement and the experience of imprisonment, but from another angle and social space. The text develops around a series of memories of experiments of '68 that were crucial for the lives of so many young people of the lower classes and that have remained marginalized in the dominant memory of the university. *Ovarimony* provides one of most detailed histories of the experience of the Popular Preparatory located at 66 Liverpool Street, the embryo of an experience of self-management and cognitive democratization that brought into practice what Revueltas theorized as a crucial component of the moment. Connected to the UNAM's School of Philosophy and Letters—mostly through the Marxist group called "Miguel Hernández"—the Popular Preparatory was a space in which students from the lower classes could continue their studies. From this experience, a question arises regarding who are the privileged subjects of education; that is, who qualifies for and who is excluded from the right to postsecondary education, which creates the different futures that will make up the productive life of the country, its professionals and its laborers. From this perspective, '68 emerges in *Ovarimony* as a liberating learning process with respect to the possibility of breaking with the predestination of class and gender, thus opening a whole set of micropolitical memories.

This itinerary is marked by a temporal line that I have chosen to respect, as it moves through different decades, choosing works and figures that take us out of the "familiar" environment of memories. At the same time, the constellation of memories that I propose to trace here does not follow the dominant figure around which narratives of '68 have been predominantly constructed: the university student who was a leader. Outside the figure of "La Tita" Avendaño, who was one of the few women in leadership who is remembered, the rest are figures who introduce ways of looking that illuminate modes of thinking about or continuing '68 from other angles, almost forcing us to think about how an event survives its time in disparate and numerous ways. Therefore, this work proposes a configuration that, attending to the dominant history and conceptualization of the moment, also introduces other points that flicker on the margins, pointing to the possibility of reading a different constellation. *Self-management, in word and in image, the encounter among different people, the demand for equality*—these issues open a territory of questions and reflections that became possible through '68. They have to do with textual, reflexive, and visual processes that construct a face of the event or participate in it from certain acts of interpretation that recall it from fragile points (such as class or gender inequality) or strong points (the encounter among different people, the sensation of liberation and of the reality of an equal participation in the political). Thus '68 emerges in a multifaceted way: it is about the specific year in which the student and popular movement forms, and which, in the course of a few months, revolutionizes the social, political, and subjective lives of many people. The events of '68 are also about a constellation that goes beyond these months of action and continues in different ways afterward, what we could better denominate as the "*'68 moment*," taking inspiration from the study by Michelle Zancarini-Fournel. Her book *The 68 Moment: A Contested History* sets out to displace the way of looking at the temporal fixation made in France of the month of May, in order to be able to attend to a larger figure, a "moment" that has been continuously interpreted and made into a space of struggle for political and historical signification, as well as a "field of experience" in which the past is constantly mobilized by a present and the horizon of a future.[91]

THE PHILOSOPHICAL AND
LITERARY CONFIGURATION OF '68
José Revueltas on Cognitive Democracy
and Self-Management

The revolutionary movement of '68 is ongoing;
it has not yet ended, nor will it ever end.
—JOSÉ REVUELTAS, *México 68*

What does it mean to approach the *moment of '68* through the gaze and ideas of
a heterodox, self-taught, and irreverent Marxist philosopher who, at the age of
fifty-four, left his position at the Cultural Olympiad at the start of the university
strike and relocated to the Universidad Nacional Autónoma de México, where
he thought and wrote about this crucial moment in Mexican history? Concurrently, one may also ask: What does it mean to enter José Revueltas's prolific body
of work at the crucial juncture that was '68, which many conceive as a turning
point of the twentieth century? How does this vital moment *affect* the very style
of his Marxist thought, particularly his views of dialectics and history? Without
a doubt, to approach '68 through the kaleidoscopic lens imposed by such a complex and singular thinker as Revueltas decenters the usual tendency to rely on
more familiar '68 voices. Rather than starting with an analysis of the movement's
most prominent figures—former students, leaders, and members of the National
Strike Council, who powerfully shaped the narrative about this moment—I have
selected a thinker who, in addition to being older at the time, had never
even studied at a university. He had abandoned formal education at the age of
fifteen to begin his long vocation as an autodidact.

In Revueltas's work, '68 appears in various incarnations throughout his
philosophical, literary, affective, and personal lives; his writings on the impact
of that moment range from a radical revision of the dialectic to more intimate

ruminations on the impact that this historical moment had on his own life. In some respects, it would seem that the philosopher set about translating the complexity and freshness of those crucial months into many different styles of thought, elevating '68 as a transversal language of sorts—composed of philosophical, literary, political, and autobiographical words—that underpins his later work. From the universal to the singular and vice versa, the heart of '68 lies in its everyday practices, which adhere to finite ideas about freedom: democratic and horizontal organization, self-management, and the importance of cognitive democracy. From his position on the margins of academia, Revueltas intuited how remarkably important '68 would be to Mexican history and surrendered himself wholly to his experience of it. From that moment until his death, he would surpass all other thinkers in his obsessive and systematic consideration of the event. As Jorge Volpi recounts, "As soon as the movement began, Revueltas showed solidarity with the students and devoted himself, body and soul, to supporting them. The School of Philosophy and Letters became his headquarters. There he wrote his articles and lectures, and even slept when he needed to recover his strength. From August to September, Revueltas penned countless essays, articles, manifestos, and letters intended to provide theoretical support to the student protest."[1] The result is a rare crucible of discursive genres through which he "performs" and thematizes '68.

Unlike Louis Althusser, who underwent the experience of '68 from a certain political distance, Revueltas wholly commits to participating in the experience and endeavors to position it both inside and against the grain of an entirely closed narrative within Marxism. As early as May, captivated by news of events in France, Revueltas wrote, "*It is forbidden to forbid* Revolution," an open letter dedicated to "French revolutionaries, independent Marxists, workers, students, and intellectuals from the days of May 1968." In it, he expresses admiration for the radical novelty of that singular revolution, which occurred "despite and in conflict with the fetishes of political parties and syndicates." He calls attention to the wide-ranging significance of the phenomenon in the international panorama of Vietnam and the start of the nuclear era.[2] A few months later, he published "Our 'May Revolution' in Mexico," where he emphasizes the importance of occupying the university and sustaining the strike by means of a parallel system of academic self-management wherein the university would become "the most critical, active element of society," based on the notion that "learning is disputing."[3] From that point on, Revueltas continually produced notes, pamphlets, and essays about the national and international importance of '68. The texts comprising this phase of his work add a certain philosophical and conceptual density to '68, one that insists on the necessity of thinking about this politically creative moment *historically*. Thus, the varied spectrum of his texts conceptualizes '68 within a broader philosophical history of freedom and the struggle to transform the languages of collective emancipation.

One of Revueltas's uncommon perspectives hints at the possibility of analyzing this social movement using a multitude of languages that restore richness to the manifold horizon of contemporary thought about politics and freedom. Hence the two questions intimated above—namely, how Revueltas configures '68 as well as how '68 configures Revueltas's own thought—uncover myriad concrete and singular ways to access this event. When Revueltas wondered from his Lecumberri Prison cell, "Is our life the revolution? What is the revolution for each of us?" he was posing a crucial philosophical question regarding his personal experience and the uncertainty it generated at the precise moment when history was being made.[4] How can a revolution transverse such a plurality of layers: ways of thinking, living day-to-day, connecting the present to a history affected by this event, relating to one another as a collective that sows the seeds of its own destiny, and testing out various ways to be free and express it? By inquiring about these events, studying their everyday manifestations, and reflecting on their present historicity within the frame of a greater past, we are able to grasp the style of '68 as a time when political and personal, historical and quotidian, wove together in one smooth, unbroken fabric.

Still, it is important to note the peculiar degree of affinity Revueltas felt with '68. This closeness seems to have been mediated by constant, reflexive action, lending a shade of critical distance and historical perspective to that which hit so close to home. Roberto Escudero describes his singular habit of *being present* in an illuminating way: "It was hardly unusual for participants in the '68 movement to arrive at the School of Philosophy and Letters and find José Revueltas writing, at all hours of the day or night, behind a desk that very often doubled as a pallet where he would sleep or rest for a few hours. Withdrawn from everyone and everything, he consolidated the impressions and theoretical observations that the reader now holds in her or his hands."[5] This rich passage demonstrates how the thinker was suffused by his experience, *immersing* himself in his work in an effort to live it, conceive it, and conceptualize it.[6] By the same token, that kind of nearly obsessive commitment yielded a constant, reflexive meditation that shaped his writing for months and years to come, as if while "withdrawn from everyone and everything," the writer was in fact participating actively and translating what he witnessed onto paper. Such theoretical dexterity helped him develop a style of narrating the events of '68 that simultaneously acknowledged its uniqueness and situated it within a greater historical context.

His inseparable companion and former cellmate Martín Dozal, to whom he dedicated "Ezequiel, or the Massacre of Innocents," remembers him in precisely the same way: "He was a man who got up at six in the morning to write, then read. He dashed off *In Search of Lost Time* as a quick break. He would say, 'Look here, look what this says,' eager to share every emotion he experienced."[7] That nearly constant commitment to writing was one notorious symptom of the generational distance between Revueltas and the students. Dozal explains that the terms Revueltas used to describe the dialectic and alienation proved extremely challenging for students new to philosophy: "Revueltas's knowledge was so vast that it was hard to put yourself on his level, which made you feel like he was the greatest man in the world. But that wasn't enough. What you really wanted was to insert yourself in his philosophical arguments, his dialectical arguments. He had been working with all these materials for forty years."[8] Although Revueltas was always remembered as a "comrade" (*compañero*), Alberto Híjar admits that Revueltas's profound meditations on self-management and alienation sounded extremely abstract to the youthful audience of Philosophy and Letters, embroiled as they were in the intense process of agitation and rebellion.[9] Along these lines, his daughter Andrea maintains that starting in '68, a myth of Revueltas began to develop, as he became a "symbol of opposition and struggle" that channeled the sentiments of an entire group. However, she also points out the distance between the myth and the philosopher who advanced a series of ideas that sounded "abstract and iconoclastic."[10] In *La estela de Tlatelolco*, Álvarez Garín remarks that

> Revueltas was very prominent in intellectual circles; although at that time, his effectiveness at the level of concrete political action was limited.... During the Movement, Revueltas's ideas carried relative weight among professors and influenced the creation of the Committee of Intellectuals. Many of his ideas—his critique of the Mexican Revolution and the actions of the Mexican Communist Party (PCM, Partido Comunista Mexicano), his thesis about the lack of historical precedence for the Party, his emphasis on the necessity and importance of critical thought, and his criteria for self-management, the structure and militant organizing on base, the committees of struggle (comités de lucha) and coordinating bodies—were already widespread.[11]

In some sense, my interest in analyzing '68 *in and through Revueltas* has to do with the fact that he was neither the typical subject-stereotype of '68 nor an outsider. Rather, he was a person who lived in a singular way—in his own skin, from the very first day—the daily life of the student movement, enduring his imprisonment at Lecumberri, released under protest on May 13, 1971, but retaining criminal charges until his death on April 14, 1976.[12] In theorizing the philosophical, literary, and political implications of '68, Revueltas's ideas acquire a wild and more creative tone because they come from multiple sources and cleave to the concerns of the time: university self-management and criticism of the dogmatic nature of political thought. When I say a "wild" tone of thought, I mean that his work remained untamed by the specificity of a discipline. Revueltas lives and writes his obsessions in various registers—philosophical, literary, essayist, and cinematographic—without becoming a great academic specialist in any of them. His ability to consider freedom and the dialectic from many different angles coheres with his understanding of self-management and cognitive democracy. For him, a democratic and critical education meant being able to break with the growing specialist technocracy and its burgeoning role in tertiary education. Unequivocally, this issue lay at the core of the student demonstrations opposing a "lack of a global university purpose" and a "rupture between national problems and the academic objectives of the university."[13] Self-management was intimately related to the possibility of rethinking the role of the university and scrutinizing its function within a greater social schema, especially when knowledge threatens to become a mere mechanism for churning out "middle management for the industrial sector of the economy."[14]

The most difficult part of writing about a dialectical thinker is figuring out how to narrate successively the simultaneous co-implication of concepts that comprise a line of inquiry. In Revueltas, these concepts are theorizations derived from his innovative ways of organizing his thoughts on '68 via a constellation of ideas: theoretical act, self-management, critical university, and cognitive democracy. Faced with the challenge of how to develop the key points of Revueltas's work on '68, I decided to organize these sections by means of vital, deeply interconnected words and concepts: a ring of keys that unlock various horizons. Moreover, employing key words as signposts to guide us though '68 emphasizes the fundamental role of the word in periods of discursive and political opening. As we will see, for Revueltas, words were sites of reflection, liberation, and opening. They offered the chance to interrogate and propagate the meanings that sometimes cling to them—particularly when there is a certain *monopoly* over meaning, over what can and cannot be said. Delving into their meanings involves the work of opening up language, dissenting with the state's monopoly over language—thus democratizing it. Therefore, the task of re-signification creates the possibility of spacing out words and stringing them together to generate new ways of experiencing the language in which political life takes place. Preparing his "Literary Workshop" in prison, Revueltas wrote: "*Vocable and word.* We will always read badly, but we can always read better. In each text, we can *discover,* with constant rereading, *hidden words and unexpected uses* of the tiny bonds that make up language, which deliver previously unobserved richness.... The sundry 'meanings' of *the* word, of *a* word."[15] The same can be said of the words that persist in his written work from 1968 until his death, such as *theoretical act* and *cognitive democracy*, *self-management* and *critical university*, *apando* (the punishment cell), *time*, and *freedom*.

Placing '68 in History: Theoretical Acts, Self-Management, and Cognitive Democracy

In the epigraph for a collection of Revueltas's texts on '68, posthumously compiled and published by his daughter Andrea under the title *México 1968*, he asserts the need to reflect on events, almost as part of the political process. "I believe that the experience of 1968 is highly positive and that it is going to lead to enormous benefits," he writes, "on the condition that we know how to theorize the phenomenon."[16] Indeed, it could be said that nearly all his written material since 1968 constitutes a sustained effort to carry out this theorization. Although Revueltas's preoccupation with understanding the dialectic in finite and uncertain terms long predated '68, the outbreak of the movement inspired him to deepen and enrich this vein of thought. As Bruno Bosteels extensively analyzes, the *essence* of Revueltas's finite dialectic amounts to an awareness of the constant gap between what happens in the world and the ways in which we can conceptualize it; that is, the uncertainty that emerges in the wake of an "unrepresentable" event whose singularity exceeds thought.[17] The visions of dialectics found in Revueltas's texts from Lecumberri Prison—edited posthumously as *Dialectic of Consciousness*—create a deep backstage for the texts of *México 68*, allowing us to see the effects that the political event had on his views on dialectics and historicity.

By positioning '68 as a theoretical act, Revueltas sought to interpret the historicity of '68 while explaining this singular event as part of a greater history—one that, far from erasing its singularity, would deepen its already profound implications. In other words, the question guiding his thought is: how can we historicize the *radical singularity* of '68 without chalking it up to "youthful spontaneity" or subsuming it under the unity of a traditional category, such as a party or an ideology? One way or another, we ask this question every time we witness the eruption of a social movement that defies the typical categories created to make politics legible. Either the event is interpreted as spontaneous—lacking demands, coherence, and consistency—or it is absorbed, cataloged, or programmed within a greater narrative. Sometimes, '68 itself is made into a label used to classify phenomena that are incomprehensible to traditional modes of political organization. In the case of Occupy Wall Street or #YoSoy132, it is evident that when faced with the novelty of a nonpartisan movement, which nonetheless includes the tensions and conflicts among different positions, some use '68 to explain the outbreak of these movements.

In defiance of most cursory interpretations—which dismissed '68 as an act of youthful spontaneity—Revueltas strives to expose and examine the event's historical relevance. Until '68, his dialectical thought focused mostly on the problematization of the impossibilities of a Communist Party in Mexico, as the monopoly exerted by the PRI had its parallel in the organization of a Stalinist PCM that left no form of conflict to take place. After the irruption of the movement of '68, Revueltas was obsessed with how to figure the historicity of such revolt in the present without resorting to the temporal frames of developmentalism and teleology. That is, he is determined to encompass its singular, revolutionary character *while simultaneously situating it within a longer history*, with the ultimate goal of shifting focus from its apparent immediacy to its very real historicity. As we will see, Revueltas will also name the theoretical act a *historical act*. "The student movement of 1968," Revueltas wrote,

> was not simply the whim of a spontaneous generation, nor "just another" disturbance initiated by studious youth. The huge mass demonstrations that followed the first skirmishes with the grenadiers marked the onset of a real social groundswell, a broader problematic that outgrew the paradigm of pure student unrest, which seemed little more than a surprising, muddled echo of the event. The radical slogans, the new methods, the unique style—which, up to that point, had never taken a form that the masses could adopt as their own—rendered the Movement *an original, unforeseen phenomenon.* Indeed, it was very much intended to disconcert those who had been waiting on revolutions for different causes, revolutions that would evolve differently—in short, revolutions that better fit the classic molds. What did the names Che Guevara, Ho Chi Minh, [Vladimir] Lenin, and [Leon] Trotsky mean to the ranks of protestors? What had occasioned those revolutionary mottoes, those sophisticated and innovative slogans, found on the walls of the university and the Polytechnic Institute? How did the National Strike Council come to command such profound respect and authority? By what means did the party position itself in relation to the committees of struggle? *What sparked the devotion, the adoration, the pride of belonging to a political brigade; and what was the secret of its extraordinary and tireless activity?*[18]

This long passage articulates the far-reaching question that the "theoretical act" attempts to answer, insofar as it avoids naming spontaneity as a psychological feature of '68, which was and continues to be the cliché that obscures its political innovation. It questions how historical figures and names articulate in this different and novel configuration of politics and affects. Moreover, these questions hint at the absolute originality of those mechanisms of action and political feeling, as well as the role that a handful of names, scraps of graffiti, slogans, and emotions played in this historical singularity. Thus '68 forces Revueltas to face a crucial contradiction that undermined his specific heterodox and innovative brand of Marxism from the 1950s: how can we interpret a historical singularity without either assigning it an unhistorical spontaneity—that is, depoliticizing the originality of its political demands—or falling prey to the kind of linear causality that so often typifies our definition of progress?[19] Along the lines of this questioning, the theoretical act emerges from his obsession with grasping a way of understanding '68 as a *historical rupture* that was also *connected to* a long and interrupted history of emancipatory projects. As Bosteels observes, despite the comparison that Henri Lefebvre drew between Revueltas and Theodor Adorno, the revolution in dialectics drew Revueltas nearer to Walter Benjamin's historical materialism. When presenting his multifaceted *Arcades Project*, Benjamin reiterates that the key issue was to find the style of "a historical materialism that has annihilated within itself the idea of progress."[20] Along these lines, Revueltas remarks that "theoretical action, historical action, can only be understood in its flow [*en su fluir*], bound to a succession of moments *that never offer a linear continuity and resist a unanimous definition.* There is a kind of geology of historical currents in which these actions are subsumed; they run a subterranean and tortuous trajectory, only to emerge years later in different forms, acted out by different characters."[21] A central concept underpinning these texts is that the theoretical act points to a type of historical materialism that unravels the developmentalist linearity of progress and takes as its organizing principle not an abstract idea but a *transformative force*. In the above quote, it is self-management; elsewhere, it will appear as cognitive democracy or equality of participation. But the crux of the matter is that calling the act or an action theoretical does not mean that the people who perpetrated or participated in it are theoretical; rather, it means that a moment becomes critical of its own present through a *collective participation in the making of history*. The singular temporality of self-management, the polyphony of voices, and equality in doing—all collude to interrupt linear time and chronology. A crucial passage clarifies this notion: "Although we cannot say in absolute terms that a fairly high level of theoretical understanding existed within the Movement of

'68, we *can* say with total certainty that *all* protesters participated in making history—all of them, free of hierarchical distinctions."[22] In other words, this moment becomes one of Mexico's first great democratic events, one that destabilizes the notion of democracy as partyocracy and enables common action.[23] This is paramount, because one prominent feature of the moment is the participation of everyone as equals: a moment in which democracy ceased to be a distant, theoretical ideal (theorization as observation) and became an exercise, an everyday act that cultivates a sense of history in the making.

The '68 moment modifies Revueltas's materialism, making him think more concretely about the role of discontinuity in history and facilitating a line of thought that replaces the laws of dialectics with a dialectic of encounter. I say "dialectic of encounter" instead of "materialism of encounter" to follow the distinction Peng Cheah draws when analyzing how the latter strips away the primacy of negativity. In Revueltas, negativity remains a fundamental force, as an encounter can be one of many pieces of history that had been *denied* and live on in a process that does not end with simple negation.[24] "Here we must perceive that the theoretical act is the encounter of these sorts of ideas and that, on making contact with a given reality, they have the ability to remove—disrupt—its deepest strata," Revueltas explains.[25] Taking a singular event, he begins rewriting an entire subterranean history—not merely of Marxism but of all instances in which democracy as horizontal and egalitarian participation has interrupted political machinations. Starting with '68, we can assemble an entire alternate calendar of historical revolutions, a montage of supposed failures that we now read as singular turning points in history.

> It was the youth movement of France, Japan, the United States, and Mexico. Young people lifted trampled, torn, and bloodied banners.... Young people claimed *socialist democracy* as their own and actively reinstituted it, restoring the most creative and vivacious content to a discipline that had previously been suppressed by the international bureaucracy of *all* parties. The ancient democracy of open questioning, the play of opposing tendencies, the right to disagree within the bosom of labor and revolutionary parties, whatever their political platform may be. *Such is the extraordinary theoretical content of 1968 in every region—Tokyo, Berlin, Paris, Mexico.*[26]

One of the ways in which '68 affected Revueltas's style of Marxist thought was to translate it into a constellation of concepts imbued with the power to rewrite a history of emancipatory moments composed of horizontal, democratic encounters. With this maneuver, Revueltas seems to align the open, horizontal, and pluralistic nature of the movement with a materialism governed by freedom. In his view, one distinguishing characteristic of the time was the emergence and coexistence of a multiplicity of tendencies, without the corresponding prioritization of a single-party dogma, sector, or labor effort.

Previously, dialectics had been a vast theater in which matrices of dissidence played out—dissidence against both the structure of dogmatism within the official philosophy of the Communist parties and the ways of conceiving and criticizing a developmentalist theology within the political imaginary of change. Like Althusser in the 1980s, Revueltas obsessed in the 1960s over his vision of an open materialism capable of representing the connectivity of revolutionary struggles that had formerly been subsumed by the legislation of a dogmatic dialectic incapable of accepting freedom and innovation. That is, his idea was to stage a new materialism that would accommodate the singularity of related historical events without delivering them in the form of an immutable law. Here Revueltas turns to a consideration of the thesis young Karl Marx wrote about the materialism of Democritus and Epicurus, which late Althusser would consider "aleatory" (instead of "dialectical") materialism, and which Revueltas would consider a theoretical act.[27]

Marx's thesis offers a way to rethink and carry out a substitution of the very concept of hierarchical organization by prioritizing *encounters instead of purges*—that is, creating worlds instead of destroying them. In "The Actual Meaning of the Russian October Revolution," a text that Revueltas wrote from Lecumberri Prison in 1970 for a commemorative colloquium on the fifty-third anniversary of the October Revolution, the writer employs the idea of cognitive democracy to string together various temporalities that had been repressed throughout the century. "Lenin's extraordinary project . . . appeared first in the Bolshevik Party as a cognitive democracy and later, under the Soviets, as democracy in society," he writes. "This grandiose experiment lasted for barely six years, from October 1917 until the death of Lenin in 1924."[28] From there, Revueltas discusses cognitive democracy as "freedom of criticism, minority right to opposition, the free play of tendencies, the clash of opinions," which parties and their hierarchical authoritarianism systematically denied. This component of '68 prompted him to rethink an entire materialist narrative of varied revolutionary moments and therefore to rethink the role of what is deemed a necessity or should be of history. In Revueltas's view, we must be able to conceive *"fate and chance as part and parcel of what's necessary* (Marx's philosophy of nature in Democritus and Epicurus, as presented in his doctoral thesis, underscores this). History is not final—it does not move from one stage to another on an ascendant trajectory."[29] Chance and contingency offer ways of expressing what is necessary, abolishing the idea of some legislative "necessity" of history while leaving a distinct impression of common historicity across struggles for cognitive democracy, which become moments of critical and creative opening of history that rebel against the established state of things.

In short, the openness and coexistence of discordance within the university during the months of the strike made it possible to visualize a constellation of many different histories and styles of freedom, something that also inspired him in order to find a style for historicizing the '68 event itself. Encounters between truncated past events are, without a doubt, illustrative of what the theoretical act describes as a *capacity for relationality*, connecting two universes. First, on the level of historical imagination, it allows us to perceive how a rupture such as '68 instantly evokes a series of historical events that had previously remained silent, trapped underneath dominant temporal narratives. Second, on a philosophical level, it connects us to a way of thinking about the status and survival of what had been negated at one time but now resurfaces in the social imaginary when a revolutionary rupture catapults it back to the present. In short, on both historical and epistemological levels, the theoretical act facilitates *a connection among multiple acts of deviation* that seemed to be defunct, sketching the new *world map* of politics that emerged in '68: a long history of insurgent episodes heretofore excluded from the dominant historical narrative.

With this interpretation, Revueltas attempts to transform dialectical materialism by generating a *dialectic of encounter* among moments that break with their present, releasing the potential for transformation found in deviations from the given (*clinamen*), as well as creative forces that amplify that which had been negated in order to create a more inclusive and open history. He points to the construction of an alternative historical calendar for the century by focusing on moments when the community seized the reins of its own destiny and heightened its capacity for change. This elevates a philosophical conception of negation that Stalinism had effectively erased. In "Class and Party: The New Contents of Reality in the Second Half of the Twentieth Century," written in Lecumberri Prison in 1969, Revueltas continues developing this line of thought, threading his previous notion of unpredictability through the "unexpected courses" that bend the arc of history. The ensuing interpretation strongly emphasizes that which is outdated or failed.

> The vulgar dialectical method pretends that the facts of the situation are what they are because they cannot be any other way—and even if the opposing party had won out, the result would have been exactly the same. This mode ignores the dialectic and is incapable of *comprehending or explaining*

why unexpected courses arise and where they lead, dialectically speaking. (For example: "Despite the fact that the Bukharinist-Stalinist movement drove the China Revolution to defeat in 1927, it triggered the Maoist 'cultural revolution' of 1967–28.") The *nonvulgar* mode presupposes the analysis of the *dialectic of deformations* and recognizes that "false courses" are themselves dialectic.[30]

This dialectic of unexpected courses (which the dominant history sees as deformations or historical failures) breathes life into what had been falsely deemed "irrelevant" to common Marxism, thus subverting the idea that a failed effort cannot proceed on its course. If, according to the vulgar view, a suppressed revolt registers merely as a zero or a nothing, how do we explain the fact that such rebellions often blaze a path for other, future encounters? Although Revueltas's reasoning may sound abstract, it conjures an idea that helps us read social movements—'68 above all—in a novel way, paying attention to the role played by negativity in their invisible afterlives. For instance, once brutally repressed, '68 was officially considered to be over; and yet it spawned and inspired a plethora of later movements. By emphasizing the dialectical life of the lines of history usually silenced by dogmatic dialectical thought as dead or failed ones, he is arguing for the historical sense of that which had been repressed or rejected, looking for a figure that allows for thinking about the singular connectivity between past(s) and present(s) struggles. This is an obsession with figuring forms of temporality that makes it possible to understand the life of emancipatory instants in complicated ways, moreover when, after the end of the strike, the movement started to be seen as dead or over. But, is there any absolute way to decide when a movement is over? The railroad worker movement was considered over; yet it stands as the cornerstone of the student movement of '68. Viewed from this angle, the idea that Revueltas formulates in wake of '68 becomes clearer: "The revolutionary movement of the generation of '68 is ongoing; it has not yet ended, nor will it ever end."[31] Thus, "The Revolution—*our* Revolution—isn't the work of a single day or year, but of a lifetime."[32]

By suggesting that unexpected courses in history serve as vehicles for potential revolutionary events, Revueltas conceptualizes the lives of movements, which often seem to last "a short while" in chronological time but that nevertheless live on in other guises. Making sense of moments in history that are commonly understood to be fleeting means acknowledging that we cannot simply measure them out with a clock—indeed, they contain an intensity that no clock can count. This same impression recurs in almost all accounts of those who participated in the student movement: while it lasted only a few months in the chronological sense, those months felt like years or decades on the level of lived and shared time. Although I will return to this later, I think it is important to mention how the idea of the theoretical act calls for new ways of narrating and reflecting on stories whose sense of time diverges radically from clock time. In other words, it points to the significance of events that last a mere handful of months or years and yet, despite their brevity, manage to destabilize the most entrenched structures or alter the very fabric of political life. The theoretical act illuminates those flashes, stringing together a collection of historical moments that have been dismissed as insignificant because they lack numerical primacy.

These negated paths reemerge when a new divergence from the present brings them to life and forms a dialectical image that disrupts our linear conception of time. For Benjamin, an image is rendered at moments of suspension, whose unfulfilled promise illuminates a new relationship between the open past and present. What for Benjamin is a "critical constellation" would be for Revueltas a "theoretical act" that forges a critical and reflexive theoretical connection between negated struggles. In the diverse landscapes where theoretical acts are set, we find that the effect-transmitter (the connector) among negated moments is the very idea of a socialist democracy, the specter of an unfulfilled promise that endlessly returns; and from which an aleatory dialectic is reconfigured. Thus a bond is forged between two ideas—democracy and the dialectic—that had previously been difficult to reconcile (if not entirely contradictory); moreover, this occurred at a moment when conceptions of Marxism and international communism were split between Eurocommunism, which Althusserians recognized as a camouflaged form of Stalinism, and the dictatorship of the proletariat, which defenders of the dialectic continued to demand.[33] It is as if Revueltas were trying to suggest cognitive democracy as a substitute for the dictatorship of the proletariat without sliding into Eurocommunism.

It is useful to mention here Adolfo Sánchez Vázquez, whose lucid characterization of Revueltas's Marxism recalled that its founding principle was to "foreground the emancipation not of a class, but of Man. It is no coincidence that the categories of alienation and disalienation should be central to him."[34] What makes the theoretical act of '68 so revolutionary is its ability to show just how alienated and vulgarized self-proclaimed Marxist revolutions had in fact become. By upholding state takeover as telos, the be-all and end-all, Marxism had fallen into a fetishist imaginary of change, culminating in the forceful enslavement and bureaucratization of the political rather than the proliferation of strategies for freeing up ways of producing and reproducing common existence. Sánchez Vázquez underscores that "after the student movement of

'68 in Mexico, revolutionary subjectivity took a previously unforeseen turn for José Revueltas, into university and popular self-management."[35] Thus '68 gave him a cipher for deepening his reflections on how to imagine freedom as a process, not an end goal. The importance of freedom at this critical aperture of the political brings out two fundamental aspects of Revueltas's own conception of freedom, according to Sánchez Vásquez: "The first aspect adds a libertarian note to his Marxism, since what he is doubtless trying to reach, beyond any concession or compromise, is freedom. The second aspect has to do with praxis: that is, conscious revolutionary activity as a central element of thought and action, in spite of the illusion of mechanical, spontaneous development."[36] This will emerge in Revueltas's texts on "self-management" as a concrete praxis by which a process of social disalienation—that is, everyday awareness of communal production—is expressed.

Thus the idea of democracy as an exercise and a process emerges, distancing itself from the format of the political party: neither parliamentarianism nor dictatorship, neither vanguard nor rearguard, cognitive democracy appears as the possibility of staging an encounter between disparate movements (united in their divergence), a path away from the dichotomous figures embodying the political in that moment.[37] Revueltas speaks of "arithmetic" versus "qualitative" democracy: the first relates to the common idea of a democracy of numbers, where the majority decides what form its illusory freedom will take; the second affirms democracy as a way to practice "consciousness as a collective exercise," wherein the term *collective* refers not to a number (a majority or a minority) but to a process led by the group's capacity for confrontation, debate, and discussion.[38] Revueltas assigns a very particular understanding of freedom to each version of democracy: in its liberal, arithmetic form, "democracy" means the property by which the freedom of one individual ends where that of another begins (civil society and the state). In its revolutionary, qualitative form, "democracy" means building a community that has no use even for the concept of the majority as a number; rather, it refers to a collective conscience that remains constantly in the process of open self-determination (knowing). In this sense, the freedom conferred by a qualitative and cognitive democracy signals a different conception of change, in which the results of a single vote do not decide who "triumphs" and assumes the position of a "majority" whose members probably do not have much in common. *Rather, freedom relates to a manifold communal consciousness composed of many different temporalities, which can never be absolutely present or permanent.* It is the potential to create a space that allows for the coexistence of a multiplicity through the texturing or manufacturing of reflexivity around it. It would therefore be the arraignment of the multiple in a constant state of change.

These reflections, written from Lecumberri Prison, assert the need to approach revolutionary change as a slow and arduous transformation, putting aside the mystique of radical and instantaneous change. Within a teleological chain, liberation would seem to move from the territory of "less" to "more": moving through history to arrive at a key moment at which things change, almost by magic. In revolutionary imaginary, a revolution would be *the pivotal moment* when a change, a break, or a rupture takes place—the magical instant that must catalyze a transvaluation of everything. Paradoxically, the mystical or theological fetishization inherent in the revolutionary imaginary becomes a way of erasing the process—that is, the work that made the impossible possible. Such an imaginary seems to reproduce the world structure it purports to reject: it erases the work of a process of transformation in favor of exalting and sanctifying the product, severing it both from its potential and from the greater social schema in which it occurs. Bosteels shows how the idea of conceiving an emancipatory act as a sort of miraculous lucky strike generates a paradox in which the sensation of freedom is equated to the desire to abandon oneself to a greater plan, as if freedom itself were to become an automatism.[39] Thus one effect that '68 had on the conceptualization of freedom through self-management was to desacralize freedom as a phenomenon "separate" from the world, a distant ideal. Through an open process that weaves a collectivity out of words, imagination, bodies, times, and ways of making a common society, freedom implies a process of radical transformation of our experience of the political.

The characterization of 1968 as a theoretical act functions as a *dispositif* that allows us to trace the relationship between Mexican history and international history, stringing together disparate and distant historical moments that share the common impulse to self-management and cognitive democracy. Understood as a polyphonic moment of encounter and coexistence of many ways of thinking about the political, '68 makes an entire alternative history legible through the immediacy of its open promise of freedom. It seeks to break monopolies on ways of performing and speaking the political, opening the present to other possibilities. Meanwhile, for Revueltas, in his conflictive dialogue with a trivialized dialectical materialism, '68 sets the stage for interrogating and expanding the horizons of Marxism. Put differently, it inspired an open and sustained reflection on ways of imagining freedom and the dialectic in a language distinct from that of necessity and teleology. Thus, the theoretical act paved the way for conceiving of an open, multiple temporality capable of reconfiguring a materialism that could leave behind the *dogmatic forms of historical, positivist legislation* that had transformed the revolutionary imaginary into a closed and deterministic universe.

At a national level, in Revueltas's work the demystification of Mexican history results from a *deepening* of a series of themes and questions that had previously permeated his criticism of the Communist Party formation, while trying to visualize a dialectic capable of operating outside the notion of progress and the teleology of dogmatic Marxism. For him, the actions of '68 dramatize a radical critique of the gaping absence of democracy in politics. Revueltas considered this problem a "barbaric democracy" in which the different body politics (from PRI to PCM) were ruled by the same dogmatic and nonreflexive matrix inherited from the Porfiriato.[40] In his *Essay on a Headless Proletariat* (1962), his most radical critique of the Mexican Communist Party, Revueltas made clear the importance of conceiving of a type of organization capable of retaining critical thought as its core tenet.[41] Until then, every movement that had struggled against forms of monopoly (what is called *charrismo* on the union level) had been harshly repressed. Nevertheless, '68 appeared to have awakened a new mode of understanding all such struggles by positioning itself as a national movement—no longer an organization brought together by a specific, university-related demand. It adopted the political role of demystifier in response to the real democratic demand to exercise the right of egalitarian participation in the making of history. In other words, the movement's historical singularity lay in its ability to "group" many problems beneath a general petition of the right to politics—beyond demanding one or two things—positioning itself beyond the world of specific demands.

Gilabert adds greater depth to this singular aspect by pointing out how it distinguished the student movement from earlier mobilizations. "Certainly, the period between 1940 and 1968 witnessed the gestation of many important social conflicts, some bearing consequences that we perceive to this day," he wrote. "But the Student Movement of 1968 was responsible for inaugurating a new dimension of Mexican politics. Whereas the conflicts that preceded it had been structured around economic demands, the students' demands did not claim things by and for themselves, which was inconceivable and therefore justified the suspicion of bad faith. Without the mobilized realizing it, the students' reproach of state authoritarianism became a political argument made by civil society, not by some union or partisan organization."[42] Its nonstate, nonpartisan aspect made this movement a kind of scream against forms of authoritarianism and monopoly that dominated the political scene and life, making in their petition several concrete demands that, if followed, would redefine the political. The demands expressed a kind of conceptualization of the right to the political as the right to exercise egalitarian participation. Guadalupe Ferrer sums it up by describing '68 as "the search for an aperture in terms of political participation."[43] At the same time, it is interesting to consider whether the university contributed to the possibility of such a unique type of demand, which in turn raised the tentative possibility of an alternative political system. By seeking to define the content of the theoretical act, Revueltas emphasizes the role of self-management, a crucial theme of the moment that pins the local movement to an international map of debates.

> *Self-management* was, *in fact and without a doubt, the very practice of the Movement, its existential way of being,* in concordance with its own concrete reality and its content of questioning the regime. The first, most lively and tangible, of its demonstrations was the presence of more diverse ideological currents that acted in free concurrence with each and every one of its ruling bodies, from bottom to top. This mobilized democracy as an operative form of freedom, replacing arithmetic, *quantitative* democracy with *qualitative* democracy: democracy as a ceaseless confrontation of knowledge within itself—that is to say, of the tendencies that compose it.[44]

One significant impact '68 had on Revueltas's philosophical work, as Sánchez Vázquez argues, was to awaken his interest and study of self-management. This precipitated a displacement of his previous interest in the party's role as a mode of political and epistemological organization; in '68, self-management became his distinctive nucleus for thinking about political and cognitive transformation.[45] As Revueltas wrote alongside the university strike, self-management presented a crucial knot he would need to untie in order to understand other themes of the moment. In various texts, this appears as "concept and methodology," an act of a collective consciousness whereby the university emerges as a much-needed site for addressing the notion of "knowledge as transformation."[46] Like the theoretical act, self-management condenses a way of imagining '68 through various decentering operations relating to the life of the university and an understanding of its knowledge, as well as problems of alienation and social transformation.

In "Outline for a Conference on Academic Self-Management," Revueltas analyzes the movement through the lens of self-management, focusing on the movement's functional mechanisms: the National Strike Council, the brigades, the committees of struggle, and the dissemination of fliers and printed manifestos. In these processes, he perceives an "ample, direct democracy that operates with full and unrestricted freedom" outside the "cult of personality," existing in a space created by the free play of opposing tendencies and diverse stances ("social Catholics, democrat-Christians, Maoist and pre-Soviet Communists, Trotsky-Leninists, anarchists, liberals").[47] Revueltas finds that this system of direct and free democracy is accompanied by a solidarity ruled by "the same communal interest," which is manifested by "points of live contact with social reality and with the people," which brigades made every day in an extraordinary manner.[48] In fact, this entire communal life, which developed in just a few months, conferred practical consistency on a reconceptualization of the political through the everyday life of the movement. According to Enrique González Rojo, the problematic of self-management is paramount to this moment of his work and unfurled around political brigades, committees of struggle, and the National Strike Council. For him, direct democracy from below constituted autonomous power before the state.[49] At the same time, Revueltas perceives that self-management offers a wholly new form of exercising cognitive democracy by transforming the meaning of knowledge into a common practice, communal to society. Surely a slender link exists between this way of conceptualizing knowledge and concerns of alienation in a society where knowledge is privatized and compartmentalized. If the discussion of academic self-management is indeed centered on the university, the *crux* of the problem resides in being able to imagine its *social projection*; that is, a journey toward the idea of *social* self-management. It is important to remember that the growing interest in self-management triggered by the mobilizations of the sixties in other thinkers close to Revueltas, such as Lefebvre, was intimately linked to the problematic of social alienation. By recognizing self-management as a way of dealing with this, they were opening a fresh and creative alternative to dogmatic imaginaries of change rooted in the notion of revolution as a "state takeover." Within self-management, the problem of concrete and quotidian social transformation—namely, specific modes of production and reproduction of individual and social existence—surges to the fore.

This generates several distinct layers of analysis: on the one hand, we have the concrete practices at the moment of the strike, where self-management sustained university life; on the other, we have the relationships between these practices and the theme of social alienation, which likewise affects how they are performed. As José Joaquín Blanco notes, Revueltas's project concentrated on "the students and teachers who stood in solidarity with the movement. . . . They would seize certain university resources and close bureaucratic offices with the goal of realizing the fullest extent of university autonomy, where the very same students and teachers run the institution. A new kind of education based on the critical relationship between teacher and student would coalesce; developing similar critical relationships to the university and to the rest of society would convert institutions of higher education into a self-critical sector of society."[50] At the same time, Revueltas stresses the ever-present danger of confusing self-management with a mere administrative structure that replaces one management with another. In "Consideration of Academic Self-Management," he warns against transforming it into a mere "administrative concept," since the autonomous university would inevitably be reduced to a mere independent organism of the state that continued reproducing its logic.[51] That is, if the critical and transformational component of self-management is overlooked, the result would simply be a change of government, not a transformation, thus reiterating that the fundamental problem for self-management provides a solution: social alienation.[52] For him, the distinction between self-management and a mere administration (self-governance) lies in the reconceptualization of the politics of the movement: its potential to engage *critically* with the society in which it exists. Elsewhere, he writes, "If the university consciousness (the consciousness of universality) of the student body gets along acritically with the society in which it lives (namely, a bourgeois or socialist society), it ceases to be an active consciousness . . . instead becoming a frozen mirror of society, a negation of any form of consciousness, an academic appendix attached to society."[53]

The idea of a "critical university" was seen as a reflexive and open universe whose axis consists of the renovation of what it means to *know*. "In self-management, knowing is transforming. It requires more than the simple adoption of a fixed concept of the world. Rather, that conception must also act as a revolutionary displacement of the outdated, the no longer valid, the obsolete that refuses to disappear. *Self-management* demands, therefore, a militant consciousness that never conforms to established values."[54] In this regard, Eduardo Valle suggests, the movement "makes itself political by overflowing matters pertinent to centers of education and setting its sights on society."[55] Instead of retreating into isolation, the university becomes an exercise in social thought that seeks to determine—perhaps for the first time on so large a scale—the role that the production and communication of knowledge might take on in the society in which they take place. In some ways, self-management appears in Revueltas's writing as way of putting into practice a "critical university" capable of rethinking "social relationships and the structure of society."[56] Originating in the university, the movement shifted middle-class strata around and connected them to the struggles of lower social classes, prompting the question of how to connect with and translate others' struggles and realities—the experiences of the Popular Preparatory at 66 Liverpool Street and in Topilejo are perhaps the most expressive examples of this process. This is something he stresses in all his texts on academic self-management, namely that it is, above all, "a becoming-aware" (*una toma de conciencia*), a "militant, active, destructive, and creative exercise of a collective consciousness in perpetual inquietude."[57]

Similar to the theoretical act, self-management crystalizes a problem that merges theoretical and practical concerns on the national and international level. On one side, it touches on processes that had been disputed within the UNAM since at least 1966, when a group of teachers and students from the School of Philosophy and Letters founded the "Miguel Hernández" group, symbolizing a rupture with the philosophical establishment. As Híjar points out, around the year the group was formed, a kind of invisible battle broke out over the philosophical canon. Although Marxism was conspicuously absent from the curriculum, texts and discussions on how to connect philosophy to society began to circulate.[58] This group adopted an intensely creative style of self-management during its fight to consolidate the first Popular Preparatory in 1968. In 1967, when a high number of lower-income students were rejected, students and families from working classes launched a fight to reclaim the universal right to education, supported by the "Miguel Hernández" group. The conflict exposed a class system where students from the lowest social classes were denied the possibility of choosing a future that involved tertiary education. In 1968 the new university rectorship of Javier Barrios Sierra conceded the building at 66 Liverpool Street to a social and educational experiment that had never before been attempted. When they were granted the building without any economic support whatsoever, the students began organizing not only the basic management of the study center but also the principles of education that would govern it, actualizing many of Revueltas's dream ideas in quite a short period of time. (I analyze the experience of the Popular Preparatory in chapter 4.) Another response from the university sphere came from the School of Architecture, which pointed out the absence of real ties between the curriculum and society. A group of students and professors managed to modify the curriculum in 1972 and began a practice of self-governance (*autogobierno*) that went unrecognized by UNAM until 1976. Some of the discussions around this experience explore the distinction Revueltas outlined between self-management and self-governance (administrative bureaucracy).[59]

On an international level, self-management refers to a concrete way of dealing with the lack of creativity that the Soviet Union had imposed on the imaginaries of transformation. It also illuminates a crucial theme within the critical Marxism of the moment, which was constructed through a series of debates about Yugoslavia (where self-management constituted a disruption of the bureaucratization of socialist countries), as well as through readings on alienation dismantled in creative ways through praxis. Debates crop up everywhere, synthesizing the radical changes to the political that '68 bought about, disputing the idea of "state take-over" as the ultimate goal of change and presenting a clear critique of the hard centrist fate of the Soviet Union.[60] That is, self-management answers the question of how a society can begin to reinvent itself through concrete changes in praxis, which, in dialectical terms, refers to ways of reconfiguring what is and transforming it into ever-open, never-completed systems of social production. Lefebvre was among a group of thinkers obsessed with self-management as a site where questions about social transformation through critical Marxism can be raised. For him, the most crucial junctures for recasting dialectics and alienation can develop out of an interrogation of concrete ways of producing and reproducing everyday life, which can function as *exercises in disalienation*.

At the same time, self-management went hand in hand with the need of a total redefinition of dialectics in history. In *Dialectical Materialism*, Lefebvre proposes to establish connections between instances that seem isolated, moving from the singular to a greater map that sustains the uncertainty of that which is incomplete or never defined.[61] Along these lines, Revueltas posits that self-management "challenges society *from within*, as the part of it that it is; and which, in that circumstance, assumes the self-critical consciousness of said society."[62] While reflecting on the reinvention of a materialist dialectic and university self-management, he suggests that we need to recognize autonomy as more than a mere administrative function, which would make self-management a mere modularization of the university in respect to the state, but not in respect to ways of understanding knowledge and its transmission. "Managing" without transforming will do little more than replicate capitalist logic and maintain the same predicament of prioritizing property relations over socialization. That is why self-management requires a complete reconfiguration of what it means to "know" and involves the creation of a mode of militant knowledge capable of behaving like an evolving and transformative action, *questioning the context that produces it*. The dialectical component renders this act a transformation in permanent progress; that is, knowledge that does not merely manifest itself as a "genre shop" of various theories that "lies beneath the banner of 'take it or leave it.'"[63] Rather, it offers another way of exercising knowledge and its communicability as an always ongoing process. "Self-management departs from the basis of *cognitive democracy* in which knowledge constitutes a debate, an objection, a review (a viewing again) of its processes: its constant re-creation," Revueltas writes.[64]

This translates into a series of changes in ways of communicating knowledge, introducing a new pedagogical dynamic in which teachers and students explore together and rediscover the same course that original thought had to run during the process of creating ideas. . . . Far beyond memorizing the formula in which the laws of gravity are expressed, they can rediscover and recognize the spiritual process that carried [Isaac] Newton to his conclusions. Instead of counting the changing meter of the *Marienbad Elegy*, they can comprehend, assimilate, and consubstantiate the process that drove Goethe to consummate the poetic act. This would occur in every discipline, from mathematics to philosophy; from architecture to chemistry; from economics to medicine. So it's about abolishing specializations.[65]

Such an abolition would be an act of resistance against the ever more technocratic model of education in which each subject becomes isolated from its fellows as well as from the social context in which it originally acquired its sense, consistency, and critical agency. Revueltas uses an array of storage metaphors (cataloging, separating, price tagging, accumulating) to satirize the way an "alienated" university handles knowledge. A "critical university," by contrast, "no longer wants to be an archive in which knowledge is stored, classified, and made available—like old veterans out of service—for the use that each successive generation will want to make of them. Now it understands that knowledge is revolutionary in and of itself and does not obey any sense other than that of 'transforming that which it knows.'"[66] In other words, what Revueltas calls a "critical university" would materialize a rejection of the primacy of instrumentalized knowledge, which was becoming increasingly evident at the time. As Theodore Roszak analyzes in detail in his classic book *The Making of a Counter Culture*, this event demonstrates how the global dimension of '68 was cast as a reconsideration of how institutional practices of knowing and creating art split into disciplines and refused to have anything to do with society.[67] In this sense, abolishing specializations would indicate "a comprehensive technical education subject to human values of knowledge—as opposed to the skill and efficiency, which are treated as the sole purpose and endpoint of technical learning and training."[68]

Just as in Lefebvre's work, self-management serves as a key word or node from which to problematize modes of social production and reproduction through a critique of the state, while also raising the question of the possibility of their liberation on so many different levels of human life.[69] This makes it necessary to revisit Marx's fundamental question, which '68 brought to the fore: how the theme of autonomy and freedom interacts with the alienation of the senses, of knowledge, of language, of the body—a central point that Revueltas develops throughout his literary work and more specifically in *The Apando*. To summarize, the questions and analyses surrounding self-management transect various layers of the moment of '68 on both local and international levels: the disconnect between university and society; and the basis of a discussion of critical Marxism that began by shifting thoughts about *the temporality of change*, opening a dialogue about the everyday that leaves the notion of state takeover aside in favor of thinking about a potential transformation of the here and now. In this regard, '68 is a philosophical event through which Revueltas invents and proposes various strategies for moving away from the idea of revolution as a historical telos and toward a more evolving conception of change, one composed of concrete practices, such as self-management and the democratization of knowledge. The dichotomy that emerges between alienation and disalienation creates space for self-management as a practical concept that underscores the eternally open nature of change.

As we saw earlier, the questions surrounding self-management that proved so crucial to '68 mostly pertain to ways of approaching and responding to the theme of alienation and the search for paths to freedom that would not rely on the magical telos of a state takeover. Pursuant to other political and philosophical texts on the subject, Revueltas writes series of literary works that dramatize these problems, as if seeking to plant theoretical action and self-management in literary ground. From 1968 until his death in 1976, he wrote one literary text after another. Not only did his texts stage reflections on freedom in relation to time and language, but Revueltas himself also used them to explain philosophical problems central to his work. In these texts, literary language becomes a stage to dramatize philosophical problems of freedom and temporality in ways that make the connection between politics and the everyday visible from the lived perspectives of the subjects. I will focus now on the complicated role that these ideas play in Revueltas's literary work, particularly the texts he wrote from '68 until his death. In order to do this, I depart from a peculiar note at the end of "Academic Self-Management and the Critical University," a lecture Revueltas gave in the Che Guevara Auditorium, where the word *apando* comes up as a way of explaining the freedom that self-management expresses. In that moment, Revueltas had just been released from prison and took up the fundamental question of '68 once more: "Critical university and academic self-management are interchangeable with two other concepts: free consciousness and cognitive democracy." He adds: "No gap exists between them. They nurture and sustain each other mutually. Freedom of consciousness has a single, unequivocal meaning. It does not allow coordinates. It refuses to be caged. It cannot live in the *apando* [the punishment cell]."[70] As is typical in Revueltas's work, these words become bridges that connect and broaden concepts and problems. Within a reflection on self-management looms a spatial and conceptual device that, intriguingly, exemplifies Revueltas's idea of freedom of consciousness. The struggle against compartmentalization of knowledge is framed as a step away from the experience of Lecumberri and Revueltas's fixation with the apando, seen as the prime example of the alienation of human knowledge. Before delving into an analysis of the first literary work that Revueltas writes in Lecumberri, *The Apando*, it is important first to examine the word *apando*, which I prefer to leave untranslated as a reminder of the complexity of meanings involved in it. So, what is an apando?

On the level of functional architecture, the apando is a dark cell designed to punish prisoners. Originally, punishment cells were conceived on the basis of a positivist model that organizes the panoptic plan of Lecumberri as a space to house the most "incorrigible" prisoners, that is, the ones who were not "reformable" in the Porfiriato imaginary. In the language of the prisoners themselves, apando also refers to a nail that they use to lock the cell door from the inside and thus separate themselves from the guards.[71] In 1975, sometime after his release, Revueltas analyzes the latter meaning of the word: "At first glance, apando is a punishment cell, but it carries many more connotations: you can lock yourself up voluntarily so the guards won't bother you, especially when you have a conjugal visit. If you lock yourself in there, nobody can enter the cell. There is even a long nail (called the apando) to jam in the keyhole of the cell door to lock it. The nail is also an apando. We refer to it with phrases like 'my apando' and 'what a great apando.'"[72] The word condenses the complexity of how imprisonment informs alienated forms of freedom: on the one hand, *apando* refers to being locked in a jail within jail (being *apandado* as a punishment within a punishment); on the other, *apandarse* means "to release oneself from imprisonment by locking oneself up at will." Last but not least: *The Apando* is the literary work that Revueltas created as an exploration of complex philosophical problems—freedom of consciousness, as we saw above, and also nonlinear forms of synthesis, as we will see later. In its latter meaning, *The Apando* dramatizes Revueltas's search for a genre in which to express the tensions in figuring a process of liberation that has no end. With *The Apando*, the sense of an alienated freedom that is thought of in terms of a geometry of imprisonment makes us, the readers, look at the search for freedom in an alienated society that massacres and represses each attempt of collective liberation. By choosing the word *apando*, Revueltas prompts us to explore its tensions and nuances in terms of space and subjectivity (being *apandado*, *apandarse*, writing/reading/thinking of freedom in *The Apando*). In a conversation between Poniatowska and

Revueltas, the former expresses that she feels the work "doesn't fit in any genre" and that "it has great political content without a single direct reference to politics."[73] The abstraction of literal politics might lead us to think that the story offers an experience in the form of release, in its crudest and most creative sense. The fact that it belongs neither to a genre nor to any direct or referential brand of politics goes hand in hand with a crucial aspect of '68: the destabilization of traditional ways of thinking and living politics. In addition, indifferentiation can also refer to what the prisoners of the movement experienced when they were denied the status of political prisoners and convicted on criminal charges simply for having participated in the movement.

The Literary Configuration of the Movement: '68 in The Apando

In his last chronicle of imprisonment, Revueltas examines in greater depth his ideas about the forms that freedom can take in an alienated society, designating prison as the highest expression of alienated architectural knowledge. From there, the underlying principles of his thoughts on the theoretical act and self-management spin off in another direction. Life in prison replaces the everyday life of the university, eliciting a series of observations about language and freedom. The Apando, one of his most well-known fictional works at that time, is set in the context of the growing state repression that confined the movement. The story captures Revueltas's feelings of perplexity and pain after the October 2 massacre at Tlatelolco and the mass imprisonment of many who survived. Before his capture but twenty-two days after the massacre, while still in hiding, he wrote:

> What does it all mean? What is this business of stringing words together in a world—in an airless vacuum, that is—where all the words seem broken down and won't dare speak about what happened, let alone what it means. *It's not the horror but this emptiness, this orphanhood, with so many dead around us.* In fact, I had started taking notes at the beginning of May, before the Movement started. I'll reconstruct each day, one after another, *in the always-new light*—every moment, every hour—*of this dizzying, dynamic, elusive life, where something that bore enormous and agonizing importance in its time should seem unreal, dreamed, implausibly lived now.*[74]

The vacuum left by the massacre prompts a profound inquiry into words and their ability to express, amid the sense of orphanhood that accompanied the shock of the slaughter committed by the state, a series of questions about the movement. The sensation of unreality that the massacre engendered in those who remained alive seemed to acquire, in Revueltas's imagination, a type of literary status in everyday life, where everyone suddenly feels like a character in a story told by others. It seems that in the realm of prison, he had stumbled upon a chance to elaborate and imagine what happened during the demobilization.

Revueltas first got the idea for *The Apando* upon entering Lecumberri in November '68, when he was sent to join the common prisoners in Cellblock I, separated from the rest of the political prisoners. Various diary entries document the insufferable conditions of those days, in which he says he forced himself to stay awake around the clock, expecting to be either beaten or killed. The writer sent a letter to the authorities informing them that he would start a hunger strike unless he was transferred to where the rest of the political prisoners were being held (this occurred several days later). While awaiting their reply, Revueltas wrote in his diary that he spent hours watching the prisoners confined to the apandos press their heads against the tiny cell window and scream for cigarettes all day. Certainly this image—which resembled a head in the guillotine—was seared into his brain, for it would appear at several points in his story of the same name. The first work Revueltas wrote in prison, *The Apando* seems to connect the sense of fear that permeated his earliest days in Cellblock I to the question that began to haunt him around that time: Is it possible to imagine freedom even in the most alienating of contexts? What does freedom look like from the apando? How does freedom look from the figurative apandos that permeate an alienated society? By these questions, I aim to point out the complexity of the narrative structure and reflection that the apando's polyvalence allows: a prison within the prison and a form of finding moments of freedom within imprisonment.

The narrative structure of *The Apando* is symptomatic and reiterates the question it poses through style: it is comprised in a single paragraph that runs from the beginning of the story to the end. Its narrative structure bears some similarity to Sartre's *No Exit*, which suffuses readers with a creeping sense of entrapment within the *architecture of text-society: a language and a history that have been locked in the apando*.[75] One might say that the extensive paragraph that makes up *The Apando* conveys the sense of a society that is trapped within a complex structure of repression and surveillance: a prison within a prison, where *The Apando* is to the prison what the prison is to a society imprisoned by a political structure that can admit no form of liberation without repressing it. Ignacio Trejo Fuentes observes that "the story and its characters present themselves as prisoners not merely of the actual, concrete prison, *but of the very text that contains them*."[76] Similarly, Jaime Ramírez Garrido recognizes this mode as the continuation of a theme that runs through almost all of Revueltas's work:

"From [*Walls of Water*] to *The Apando* and [*The Stuff of Dreams*]—that is, from beginning to end—Revueltas's texts seem to close in on themselves in an obsessive, inescapable way."[77] Literature offers the dialectical thinker a space where he can consider different forms of apparent stagnation and problematic density related to the uncertainty produced by massive imprisonment of the movement. In the spatial design of the apando, the questions become: What does it mean to be released from prison when society is itself another prison? What kind of freedom is there to be gained when the apando is also the prisoner's word-tool for escaping the guards, locking himself up in his cell by choice?

Here is the plot: three prisoners *apandados* in a punishment cell—Albino, Polonio, and El Carajo—want to bring drugs into the prison to help them bear punishment in another form: to help them withdraw from the dark and suffocating exposure that is the apando. Aware that the women who visit them (Meche and La Chata) are always patted down on entry, Albino and Polonio convince El Carajo (Shithead) that his mother should be the one to carry drugs in her vagina, since she wouldn't be checked as thoroughly as the others. The plan is for Meche and La Chata to start screaming in front of the apando, staging a "women's strike," while El Carajo's mother would pass them the drugs through the window. Once he had the drugs in hand, Albino would kill El Carajo. Everything goes according to plan: the three women make it in, and Albino sticks his head out the window (guillotine) of the apando and screams so they know where to find them. The three women head for the apando as planned, but El Carajo's mother refuses to hand over the drugs to a stranger. She cries out for her son instead: "'Where is he? Where is he?' she repeated, eyes still fixed on the head and hand poking out of the steel shutter, swaying awkwardly as if drunk."[78] Since she refuses to budge until she sees her son, Albino retreats from the window to make space for El Carajo, who sticks his head out to beg his mother for drugs. Suddenly, the scene changes and the noise is swallowed by a silence that Revueltas describes almost cinematographically. Thus begins the somewhat tragic ending: "Something happened in this movie before the soundtrack began. Who knows what the Commander said to the monkeys and the women, but an unusual and tense quiet fell.[79] Two monkeys leaned against the cell padlock and *released* the three inmates, while the whole group—the three women, their men, and the jailers, calm despite the wild looks cast by Polonio, Albino, and even El Carajo—were forced down the stairs."[80] The jailers took them to the guard-monkeys' "drawer" (*el cajón*), a space that was the opposite of the apando in terms of functional geometry of the prison: "Although the 'drawer' formed part of the Cellblock—separated from it only by the same gates that marked the boundaries of both—the presence of the jailers, locked inside, gave it the appearance of another prison, a prison that imprisoned them, a prison inside of a prison."[81] Once the prisoners, the commander, and the three jailers are all locked "in the same monkey cage," Albino, seething with fury, engages Polonio in a fight to the death as the visitors watch from the other side of the gates, inside the very same cellblock. In a flurry of blood and screams, two new elements are transposed in the story. First, more monkeys arrive with metal tubes and ultimately dismember Albino and Polonio: "The task was to push them, tube by tube, between the bars of the gates and the gates of the cage," resulting in "a diabolical succession of mutilations of space—triangles, trapezoids, parallels, oblique and perpendicular segments, lines and more lines, bars and more bars, to impede every movement of the gladiators [apandados] and leave them crucified on the monstrous cross of *this gargantuan defeat of freedom at the hands of geometry*."[82] Second, El Carajo, who had not moved a muscle, "cowers against the bars, fiercely intent on shrinking his body as much as he could," and collapses at the feet of the official to inform on his mother. "She's the one who brought the drugs in here, stuffed up her pussy," he confesses.[83] While this denunciation occurs, heard only by the officer, the narrative voice focuses on the inner thoughts of Polonio and Albino, who, "dangling from the tubes, more prey than any prisoner . . . wondered, at the same time, what it would mean for everyone to kill the crippled. What for?"[84] The story's ending almost mirrors the space described at the beginning: a drawer where the monkeys are imprisoned without knowing it, "with no memory of it," now "imprisoned, fucked," now moving into the drawer with the prisoners, unable to find sense in their actions, in the "shit" meaning expressed by that "what for?" ("what the fuck for?," we might add).[85] As in all of Revueltas, this can be read in at least two ways. On the one hand, nothing changes—the prisoners remain imprisoned. But on the other hand, something changes in El Carajo's detachment from his mother. Revueltas describes this as giving birth to himself, breaking off his dependency on his mother.

In *The Apando*, drugs are the only way El Carajo can experience freedom, which is expressed in a near-circular sequence: "because nothing whatsoever mattered to him anymore *except* the small, ephemeral pleasure, the serenity produced by the drug; and because he had to struggle interminably, minute by minute and second by second, to obtain that rest, which was the only thing in life that he loved, simply *evading the nameless torment* to which he was subjected; and because he literally had to sell his body's pain, sliver by sliver, *in exchange for an indefinite, shapeless stretch of freedom where he sank, happier with each successive punishment*."[86] This passage describes the sensation of freedom that El Carajo relives in each cycle of his life: moving from the apando to the infirmary, obtaining drugs, returning to the apando, cutting himself again, going to the infirmary, and so on. In this cycle, drugs represent an alienated freedom that sustains the life of the prison—that is, a mere evasion of the conditions within it. Nevertheless, we do not know how El Carajo's cycle will proceed from here. In other words, no magic, automatic solution appears when he cuts the umbilical cord. This entirely inconclusive conclusion—consistent with the indefinite nature of many of Revueltas's texts from this period—rings hollow, just as freedom does when severed from the fictional notion of a happy resolution in "unity." To some degree, Revueltas's texts from Lecumberri utilize narrative to express the same problem that traverses the radical revision of freedom inherent in '68: the desacralization or de-auratization of freedom— namely the idea, common to the revolutionary imaginary, that state takeover magically leads to freedom. This fetishized freedom erases the imaginary of social transformation that self-management underlined, namely, the importance of the process by which the idea of a happily-ever-after in which all problems are resolved is stripped of meaning.

In Revueltas's work, the revision of the dialectic revolves around the task of rewriting the notion of synthesis; in fact, when he mentions his multifaceted view of synthesis in a conversation, he uses *The Apando* as an example. "Vulgar Marxists believe that the dialectic is progressive, that it flows from less to more, from delayed to advanced," he writes. "This is false, *because synthesis can be totally negative, as in the case of* The Apando. *The dialectical synthesis that follows the interpenetration of contraries yields neither 'more' nor 'advancement.'* Rather, it presents us with a *shadowy thing* [*cosa sombría*], which totally negates the human being while remaining affirmative in its negation."[87] Intriguingly, instead of citing passages from his *Dialectic of Consciousness*, he selects a literary work to illustrate the complexity of a dialectics that does not work within the logic of progress. He does so to dramatize the complexity of the processes through which synthesis refers to a "shadowy thing" rather than a path to a higher echelon of freedom. Revueltas experiments with a fictional setting that would stage a break with the developmentalist notions of progress and the linearity of a forward or backward movement. In order to do this, he relies on figures that express the complexity of what is co-implicated in a process without defaulting to the magic of an easy resolution. Breaking with the teleological fantasy of change as magical resolution (a fantasy underlying most revolutionary imaginaries) allows us to examine the everyday unhindered by magical elements; that is, one that would not transcendentalize the everyday, instead treating it as *the matter and body of life time*. It sees the everyday as a system of repetition of that which makes up life, elapsed time and future time—the vital fluid in its intermediate stage when the direction these actions will take is not entirely known. This translates into the complicated and no less dark task of organizing Revueltas's literary works, given that the stories we read feature mostly truncated endings—that is, endings that fail to resolve the entire network of problems but instead adjust situations within a wholly fixed context.[88] The same could be said of the characters he creates. Speaking of the need to avoid falling headlong into a teleological epic that transforms fiction into moralizing, Revueltas explains, "it is inevitable for the author to project himself onto his characters, but he should steer clear of characters that could be described as teleological: those who have an ethical, moral, or political finality, as this introduces a preconceived thesis into the material."[89] The idea of nonteleological characters shares the same purpose as turning attention to the everyday—as a reflexive transformation of habits and actions that we repeat almost automatically: "Without everyday life, without analysis of such, it is impossible to reach a general conception on a given problematic."[90] From '68 on, almost all of his literary reimagining of the everyday occurred in prison, which resembles an observatory imaginary where he can revise his own obsession with freedom. Revueltas explains, "Freedom is configured most fully in prison, perhaps because it reduces an individual to his pure *imaginary dimension* and thus strips all of society bare within its authentic spectrum of sunlight. In prison, everything acquires *a greater significance*, the sense of private property, the water dish, food."[91] We can juxtapose this idea to the sensation of unreality that Revueltas felt toward the massacre and the state's ever-tightening grip on the movement. The spatial component of *The Apando* furnishes a complexity that allows us to broach the topic of an ever-relative freedom chained to a new problematization of liberation: small apandos within a greater (social) prison.

Revueltas's reflections on freedom found a privileged space in the prison, understood as a situation and as a complex imaginative space. Before launching into an analysis of the role this question plays in *The Apando*, we must distinguish the role that prisons play in Revueltas's philosophical and literary work from the argument put forth by Lessie Jo Frazier and Deborah Cohen, namely that prison served to sustain the epic narrative of the movement's male leaders.[92] They argue that many leaders' narratives center on their experience at Lecumberri Prison, making a history of the movement that tends to focus on the epic story of masculine resistance. In addition to erasing memories of grassroots participation, such narratives relegate women to the mere task of cooking for the prisoners (in *The Apando*, we could replace the task of cooking food for the smuggling of drugs onto the prison). One thing that sets Revueltas's story apart from the others is the fact that prison permeates his entire political life, from his first experience as an adolescent imprisoned on the Islas Marías, where he wrote *Walls of Water* to his last imprisonment in 1968, where he wrote *The Apando*, among other texts.[93] For him, prison lacked the exceptional status it held for most students, appearing in his work as a symbol of a problem that affects the social diagram as well as the forms that alienated knowledge takes. As he writes in *Dialectic of Consciousness*, prison expresses "the maximum degree of alienation of architectural consciousness. It does not matter that prison represents—in the view of the State, which is the highest expression of organized compulsion—the isolation of individuals who are considered 'antisocial.' Prison is and always has been a *political* prison embedded in an alienated polis that *always*—across all societies and time periods—threatens political, religious, or philosophical adversaries to existing power. Who will remember the names of helpless common prisoners?"[94]

Assuming that the struggle of the movement's political prisoners was grounded in the defense of the recognition of their status of political prisoners (something denied by the authorities), the question posed by Revueltas at the end of this quote exposes prison as a space that perpetrates the invisibility and naturalization of the criminalization of poverty. For a dialectical thinker, prison becomes more than a mere phase in the lives of some people: it is an entry point to understanding an alienated society. Lecumberri is figured as a kind of "funnel" that drains away forms of freedom systematically repressed by the state, a repository filled with that which is negated, that which is branded useless and deviant. One striking sign is that no prisoner in Revueltas's fiction is a political one: he writes about common prisoners in various prisons (Lecumberri in *The Apando* and "Hegel and I"; Islas Marías in *Time and Number*).[95] Even when he textualizes his stay in captivity in the wake of '68, Revueltas deliberately fictionalizes prison conditions so as not to name the student movement outright, though he is clearly obsessed with its outcome. The prison works as a *literary and conceptual dispositif* that made visible that which could not be seen from outside; that is, the imaginary element that, for the isolated prisoner, casts everything—private property, food, language, animality—in a harsh and extreme light. We may also perceive in this difference a subtle stance that enables us to see ever more clearly the distance between the way Revueltas proposed to conceptualize '68 and the way the students characterized it. Moreover, in many sections of his work, the author plays with the prison as an essential framework for understanding freedom. *An existentialist framework—within which Revueltas says that freedom is incomprehensible without prison, and that he who cannot be free in prison can never understand freedom—weighs heavily in this decision.* Prison emerges as a systemic problem that nonetheless holds a unique visual and discursive capacity.

The Apando: *Word, Space, and Fiction*

The Apando, we might say, is a small limit-novel because it carries lines of questioning to their very limit. The prison itself is but a symbol, because it is the city-prison, the society-prison.
—JOSÉ REVUELTAS, quoted in *Conversaciones con José Revueltas*, by Gustavo Sáinz

The Apando pushes the limit of thought on freedom by means of an imaginary that is closed in on all sides. If the prison is not just Lecumberri or Santa Marta, but society: how can freedom come about within this society-prison? Revueltas raises this concern as a question about social change: How can we keep entertaining the possibility of political transformation and freedom in a society that criminalizes political dissidence and employs, as a cyclical, permanent recourse, mass murder or imprisonment? Examining the various repressive cycles of the Mexican state, it is necessary to seek alternatives to the classic revolutionary imaginary on which the state bases its fiction, for Mexico is a country where "revolution" is little more than a state-organized matrix on which political time is constructed. If every attempt to release the structures monopolized by state and party (including the *charro* union)—that is, if every act of liberation—is followed by repression, death, and disappearance, what is the sense of seeking liberation? If you know the script, why act it out? As the last words of *The Apando* state, as an open declaration to readers: "What for now? [¿*Ya para qué?*]" What kind of plot can emerge if the script is always the same and the ending is death, reclaiming the dead, and so on? Physical death (massacre) and social death (prison) stain political life and demand reflection on new ways of thinking. For someone who comes to Tlatelolco after decades of observing the repressive circuit of the state, the question is far from banal; in fact, it has become an enigma. *Insisting on raising and reformulating it constitutes perhaps one of the most profound acts of this moment of his thought.* It is also a moment when he introduces more figures in order to imagine liberation within the shackles of the tragic events that punctuate the political. Something fascinating about Revueltas's work from this period is his struggle to center on experimentation with figures of thought that make it possible to think of *freedom* in a complex way. Inscribed in this frame, Revueltas starts to test forms of fiction that permit us to see both sides in a curious fashion: on the one hand, he writes philosophical essays on dialectics; on the other, he uses literary fiction to set the scene for his experiments on dialectics, which stem from a persistent obsession with figures that dramatize an apparent form of stagnation related to the cyclical nature of political life—attempts at liberation followed by repression. When viewed through this lens, his fiction stages what Ramírez Garrido interprets as an aporetic instance where "Revueltas's characters never find a trapdoor, an exit, an aperture."[96] For a creative dialectical thinker like Revueltas, these experiments can be seen as laboratories where he not only tests his own limits for thinking a problem that permeates his whole political life but also causes us to reflect on our own forms of understanding and living certain words, such as *freedom* and *liberation*, when they are stripped from the tranquility of unity—that is, when they are seen from the perspective of a struggle in a present whose future is always uncertain. For, if we follow the premise that one of the distinctive components of 1968 was the attempt to de-fetishize freedom, wouldn't the expectation of finding "*an exit*" still assume that there is a way to predict the resolution to all problems? What happens when the unity of the dream of state takeover is suspended and one attempts to approach freedom without the tranquility of that telos? Of course, the dialectics at stake here pose a complication of the figure of synthesis that Revueltas posed, instead, as a "shadowy thing" within a nonlinear process. Complicating this through the word itself (*apando* as the name of punishment for the "incorrigible" but also the name for the freedom to lock oneself up from the guards), one could see that *The Apando* stages a subtle critique of what a "way out" could be.

The literary space emerges in Revueltas's work as a way to decenter a single, unilateral point of view working as one of the few sites that enables us to see the complexities of a dialectical thought deprived of magic. In short, it adds complexity to our ways of thinking about liberation by collapsing viewpoints that would ordinarily have been kept separate, including the role of fiction itself. Here, instead of using the work in order to transmit an easy message of liberation (using it as a means to an end, or as a drug that would make us feel like El Carajo when he is high), he makes us reflect more deeply on our ways of imagining what form "liberation" could take in this complex situation. In other words, what would "a way out" mean within the structure of *The Apando*, where guards and prisoners are locked up in the same prison, and where the last words of the play ask, "What for now?"—ending here the long paragraph that started fifty-five pages before.

In other writings, Revueltas states that it would be impossible to transform the political imaginary with pamphlets alone, which tend to flatten out language in an effort to inform. For Revueltas, the prison becomes a moment of radical exploration of the role of language in creating a political imagination in conflict with the monopoly on meaning exercised by the PRI and party

Marxism, *as if the physical prison replicated the prison of language.* One question that strikes me as fundamental to this moment is: what is the role of literary space in confronting the discursive and temporal monopoly held by the state—that is, as a site where *the very condition of perceptibility and the staging of divergent outbreaks for change can take place?* The word becomes a site for building a common dissident imaginary, not only in the sense that it *goes against* the state monopoly on words and meanings but also in that it can empower people to *think and make* other political imaginaries in language. For Revueltas, a revolution cannot occur without a revolution in language—namely, in the act of naming and imagining.[97] Literature is usually excluded from revolutionary processes; yet its role is fundamental, as it provides an essential space in which to revise the myths that make up social life, and to rehearse or practice ways of transforming them. Revueltas takes advantage of the singular opportunity offered by the literary space to stage a crucial issue of politics, such that the most urgent philosophical dramas are played out obsessively in various literary essays. In particular, literature generates the possibility of staging an open multiplicity of temporalities that political texts tend to homogenize.

The Apando can be read as a highly complex, figurative reflection on which kind of freedom persists—or lingers, as El Carajo does, after the movement had been massacred and repressed. The "shadowy thing" configured in the story's final scene illustrates the conundrum of a synthesis with no "more" and no "less"—that is, no concept of a "result"—as occurs when gains are disjoined from losses, and only the worthless, like El Carajo, are spared. Here we find a cipher for a truncated and ambiguous freedom, one that is inscribed in function of his very name (*el carajo*, or "piece of shit"), which comes from an everyday Spanish expression that is used to refer to something that is meaningless to us: "I don't give a shit" or "it's not worth shit" (*Me importa un carajo, no vale un carajo*). It is a *nothing* that one finds *in language*. In a similar vein, Revueltas says, "to be alienated is *to not realize that one is free*, but it certainly does not mean that one is not free."[98] Here it is helpful to incorporate John Kraniauskas's interpretation of the end of *The Apando*, which centers on the motif of *allotropic negation* that Revueltas develops in his *Dialectic of Consciousness* (which I mentioned above to illustrate the difference between self-management and self-governance in Revueltas). It involves a negation that "changes form but conserves content—like sugar, which, whether powdered or crystal, remains sugar."[99] Kraniauskas says that Revueltas uses this motif to distance himself from Friedrich Engels's dialectical materialism, eliciting a question about the type of transformation at stake in the negation at the end of the story: "Revueltas invents the term to apply it to the States' Stalinist repressors.

Therefore, El Carajo's gesture can also be seen as allotropic as long as *it transforms, but still secures, state power.*[100] According to this reading, the apando—the text's crucial motif—emerges as a way of presenting this transformation that simultaneously secures state power, exemplifying the type of (relative) freedom that can occur within prison; and, moreover, *within the very society that built the prison as a "solution" to a problem.* It is as if absolute freedom would only be possible in a society capable of imagining a way of handling dissidence without resorting to prison, or confining someone to a cage. At the same time, we could push the interpretation in another direction, one that can look at what Revueltas thinks, with El Carajo as a conceptual character through which he reads the rupture in the act of giving birth. Here a complex image emerges if we put together two moments of the text: at the beginning, the image of El Carajo, sticking his head through the window of the apando imitating the act of giving birth: "Sticking the head in—or out—the head of this iron rectangle, this guillotine . . . required careful, thorough effort, as one might extract a fetus from its mother's insides; a tenacious and deliberate self-birth with forceps that rip out tufts of hair and scratch the skin."[101] The parallel drawn between the act of "self-birth with forceps" counteracts the final scene, an alternative moment of emancipation, when El Carajo manages to cut the umbilical cord between him and his mother. This produces a differentiation in the unitary structure that makes the cycle apando-cut-infirmary-drugs, as his mother will not be providing him drugs anymore. Everything is uncertain, and there is no hint of a "better" future at stake; however, there is a break in the flow of the cycle. The image-action of cutting works in different ways: cutting his skin so as to get to the infirmary to get more drugs and then cutting the umbilical cord, distancing himself from his mother, who is also the source that makes the cycle possible. In the former sense, cutting makes the cycle possible; in the latter, it involves the rupture of unity.

We could read the final motif of the story as an allegory that crystallizes the kind of emancipation that took place in '68 even as it remains imprisoned or confined within the state structure—the moment of rupture that made the historical act happen, the rupture with the state use of the word *revolution* to name national unity. In this sense, prison operates as a space for Mexican political history and fiction, revealing many interacting, problematic layers: prison within a prison, formal liberation instead of real liberation, the repetition of a cycle, and the search for an alternative language. In part, *The Apando* explores several iterations of the same question raised by self-management: how can we realize a transformation of the everyday, rather than a mere substitution of one authority for another? The metaphorical complex of the apando helps

Revueltas approach these questions from multiple angles as he works to actualize a political imagination centered on everyday ritual within an alienating context.[102]

In his final work, Revueltas attempts to permanently record and emphasize his defense of the notion of freedom tied to thought—fighting for a democracy of knowledge, of openness to criticism, of the right to dissent. In Revueltas's meditation on words, language is a final battleground, a final lull in a fight that may quickly turn to slaughter. Attention must be paid to the role that words can play in prison, as materials or tools in a struggle within a specific context and situation, as *language seems to offer a particular materiality, a site in which freedom can take shape and affect the body.* A key is to be found in Revueltas's reflections on language in relation to the political prisoners' hunger strike: *imprisoned words that need rethinking.* In a metafictional sense, it seems as if Revueltas were testing zones of passage or new paths *in and through* language. What words might make those new paths possible? He uses the word-symbol-place *apando* in various contexts, as if it were his philosophical, literary, and political obsession. Words are figured as both "thought and action," and Revueltas remarks that the '68 militants are held prisoner by words, and by their defense of words such as "revolution, Mexico, Freedom, Che Guevara, disalienation, 'People, Unite!' "[103] To some extent, the question of *cognitive democracy* is linked to various ways of perceiving spatiality, temporality, and optics of language with which an entire system of property, appropriation, and a sense of ownership are expressed.

As one of the first fictionalizations of '68, *The Apando* could be read as recasting the same problem addressed by theoretical action, approaching the question regarding freedom *in* history, but now from a different angle. If theoretical action refers to a present that stirs the layers of past moments that had previously been repressed and raises their emancipatory struggles anew, *The Apando* emerges as a reflection on the complexity of liberation amid sustained and repeated waves of state repression, now suffered by the movement itself. That is, just as theoretical action illuminated zones that had been expunged from the emancipatory calendar, *The Apando* sheds light on the question of what kind of freedom surfaces almost as an interval between moments of oppression. What once resembled the great motor of a subterranean history is now obscured by the frustration and powerlessness that comes with slaughter and imprisonment. Yet it is interesting to note that the exploration of these '68 acts of freedom emerges as a reflection on words and the field of literary imagination. There is a materiality of the word that Revueltas explores, almost as though he were *undergoing* the process of signification, which, in his pamphlets on self-management, he refers to as the transformation of the communication of knowledge. This relates to what was said above: it is not the transmission of knowledge as a given and eternal truth but rather the notion that the very communicability of knowledge implies the collective journey of a process.

Imprisoned Words

Weary of the legal limbo in which they had been placed, the political prisoners at Lecumberri started with a hunger strike from the end of December to the end of January (one thousand hours without eating). In a peculiar, sinister fashion, the story narrated in *The Apando* seems to have been filtered through the reality of the precinct several months after its creation. On January 1, 1970, after thirty days on the hunger strike, the political prisoners were approached and assaulted by a group of common prisoners, under the monkeys' orders. Just as in the story, they used metal bars to imprison the protesters even further. The most detailed description of this event can be found in a letter that Revueltas sent to Arthur Miller, then the director of the International Pen Club. He also summarizes it in conversation.

> That was terrible. By all appearances, it was going to be a massacre, but I think they had orders not to kill us. If they had wanted to, they would have, and in that moment I thought they would. I said to myself: well, it's a shame to die in such conditions—like St. Bartholomew—but no matter. Everybody has to die somehow. They came in drugged with hands unshackled, ready to plunder: they took radios, typewriters, books. I've told this story before: I didn't want to even see my cell, which would have been deserted, stripped of its books; and yet I found it full of my manuscripts. I always staple them, so that saved them. I went in and as I did so, I stepped on something hard; I leaned down and it was my fountain pen. I said to myself, "They couldn't conquer it."[104]

This joke, which bridges the magnitude of the repression he survived in prison and the successful survival of his pen, confronts us with the distinct incommensurability between the experience of captivity and the freedom to rely on intellectual life. After this repressive episode took place inside the prison, Revueltas wrote a series of texts reflecting on the relevance of language and the meaning of words in the middle of a political struggle. On the very day when freedom of the press was established, Revueltas wrote a powerful text called "Imprisoned Words," published in February 1970 in *The Culture of Mexico*, the supplement of *Siempre!* Here we see that the materiality of this text constructs a bridge between interior and exterior, between Lecumberri and the press—a path out of prison.[105] The text responds to two issues: first, new iterations of state repression, now inside prison; and second, an article written by Martín Guzmán in honor of the official freedom of the press day in Mexico. The piece starts with a description of a workshop on words as a form of political struggle that takes place *in language* (in the same struggle for meaning): "Let us study language. Let us delve inside them and inhabit them to the greatest extent possible. Where we can, let us fill them with objects, with relationships between things and tasks, with the comings and goings of common people, just as we would in a house that we are about to occupy and belong in forever: the house of language."[106] Language becomes spatialized, instituting new ways of inhabiting an ever more precarious world, and words become a place of resistance within and against prison. In explaining them, Revueltas brings attention back to the problem he highlighted in *The Apando* in regard to dichotomies like productivity-unproductivity and useful-useless. He seems to draw parallels to allotropic negation, now equipped with key words that Revueltas previously used to define the student movement: self-management and cognitive democracy (confronting ideas and meanings, procuring education, generating a common language that transcends specializations). He writes that in the house of language,

> we would place our objects of knowing, our signs and meanings, our own pieces of understanding and those that we will soon regain (*the necessary and the fortuitous*), useless things and useful ones (useful [*útiles*] almost in the schoolchild sense of the word: notebooks, pencils, erasers), our tools: the wisdom of saying something and knowing why it has been said; words and their ordinations, love for them and their deciphering. It is the work of the literary workshop we have founded in Cellblock M: teachers and students from the '68 Movement, now prisoners of almost one year in Lecumberri Prison. Rather, it is the work of pursuing our academic activities—at least some aspects of them—despite the prison conditions in which we find ourselves and *beyond the particular specializations* of each member. Founding the Workshop began with a meeting of political prisoners housed in Cellblock M; and with the sole act of meeting, we have already confronted the meaning of the words just uttered: *cellblock, prisoners, political prisoners.* We are prison inmates occupying our respective cells in Cellblock M of Lecumberri Prison. But are we really? No, but it depends on your point of view. Officially those words—*cellblock, prisoners, political*

prisoners—do not exist. Bureaucratic language has replaced them with more benign, neutral alternatives: *dormitories* for "cellblocks," *internees* for "inmates." Besides, we know that political prisoners don't exist in Mexico. Yet words haven't yet replaced the actual things. A cellblock is a cellblock and a prison is a prison and we are political prisoners, before and after these new baptisms: same walls, same cells, same bars.[107]

This quote is fascinating yet difficult. In it, Revueltas exposes words to many different meanings that address the same key question raised in *The Apando*— *what for?* (*¿Ya para qué?*)—the question of dubious usefulness, the different meanings of "carajo," and the fact that the word *shit* is itself a form of registering loss in language. When we say, "I don't give a shit" (*no me importa un carajo*) or "that's not worth shit" (*no vale un carajo*), we are saying it is nothing: "it doesn't matter to me" or "it's worthless." Linguistically, "shit" (*carajo*) is an expression of uselessness. In this passage, this is evident from the use of the word *útiles*, as in Spanish this word refers not only to that which is productive but also to the tools we use to learn and write: notebooks, pencils, and erasers are all included in *útiles*. In this context, the Spanish word *útiles* means both "useful" and the concrete materials that enable writing and thinking in school. The great utility of those *útiles* is that they *make things possible* without being concerned with *productivity*, or producing something useful, as such tools can easily generate useless products as well.

Disentangling all that is implicit in this extensive quote and in the surrounding text poses a significant challenge, for it is perhaps one of the most synthetic and interesting reflections on language to be found in Revueltas's entire body of work. Language is revealed to be a common space that is created, inhabited, and redesigned. The text sets various languages and systems of meaning against one another: the state's monopoly on words, which refuses to designate political prisoners as such, and a language that enacts a new existence through its opposition to the former language. In his texts on poetry and dwelling, Martin Heidegger elucidates the relationship between them in an intriguing and no less fascinating manner: poetic dwelling relies on a singular form of measuring, one that does not have a quantitative sense. Rather, poetry involves ways of thinking about forms of measurement based on time of existence rather than time measured by a clock. The temporality that words create in poetry can help us to describe survival, which appears in one of Revueltas's poems as a way to preserve the memory of our existence. As we shall see, survival is constantly reinvented through words as they become the site of a struggle. In "Imprisoned Words," prison and freedom are locked in a verbal battle over the heterogeneous logic of state reasoning and the egalitarian demand of politics. The state replaces "cellblock" with "dormitory," "prisoners" with "internees," and "political prisoners" with "criminals." Before the hearings were fully processed, the word *political prisoner*, eliminated from the state's vocabulary, lacks a referent—it literally does not exist in an "official" capacity. Over nearly a year of existential limbo, the members of the movement of '68 resort to language to defend their own place, their own house: "They have sought to rob us of the freedom of these words, the freedom that people exercised by yelling them in the streets. *We are persecuted words*, isolated in cellblocks, filtered through cellblocks. *We now live them and study them* once more, shedding light on their true meanings. Just as the word 'dormitory' is nothing but a prison cellblock, 'freedom of speech' is nothing but its persecution."[108] In this text, the struggle over the meaning of words becomes the site of a struggle for freedom. Amid the repression that took place in prison, staging the end of the apando, what "remains" are words negated by the state but affirmed by political prisoners. Words assume the double meaning of "thinking and action," but they are also útiles: material conditions that make writing possible, without which content could not be set to paper: "Men were born with the Word, with their words, which are thought and action; to negate the use of words is to negate themselves. This constitutes our affirmation: imprisoned words, which we, imprisoned for them, set free in our workshop of words, our literary workshop. We have met in Cellblock M to found and organize it, designate teachers and integrate work groups. An assembly of prisoner students—future engineers, biologists, economists, mathematicians—with their old teachers, in the prison classroom, today's school."[109] In the final words of his text, Revueltas speaks of the creation of the workshop (or its intention) as an act of affirmation that lends freedom to words, to language *through* language. To return to an earlier reference to prison as a literary and philosophical dispositif of social analysis, the idea of "imprisoned words" emphasizes the political economy invisibly active in language. In sum, being able to think about everyday words becomes a way of continuing to imagine liberation, transforming language and history into contested spaces of dissent. For Revueltas, the struggle over language also becomes one over temporality as "imprisoned words" becomes part of an imprisoned history.

Imprisoned History

When public court hearings for the political prisoners of '68 began in September 1970, Revueltas stood accused of ten crimes. The hearings took place in the courtyard of Lecumberri Prison for forty hours straight. Revueltas was sentenced to sixteen years in prison, which was practically a life sentence considering the precarious state of his health after the hunger strike. The hearings mark the moment when the invisibility of their political imprisonment was made official, as their participation in the movement was officially declared a crime. With this legal and juridical act, the public prosecutor rendered the movement of '68 an act of vandalism. Revueltas wrote his defense in a meticulous and extremely philosophical style, combining many of the themes that were then at play—not merely his freedom and that of his comrades but also the freedom of a history that had been systematically *apandada* (confined to the punishment cell) in the way it was labeled and judged. By rendering the student movement a criminal act, the juridical process explicitly effected the criminalization of political dissidence (of what had remained after the massacre), judging the majority of convicted political prisoners on the basis of acts that the state had fabricated. Through his defense, Revueltas weaves a reflection on words and time, language and history, drawing close comparisons to "Imprisoned Words," which had now become "imprisoned histories." What he underlines in his defense is a discussion of the kind of relative and unilateral freedom that exists when the meaning of language and history are monopolized time and time again by a state-imposed order. Struggling for words and for a way of configuring the temporality of a political struggle, Revueltas wrote a defense of freedom in the face of monopoly, denouncing the way in which the state's semantic capture of the moment rendered '68 a criminal act.

The texts that remain to us from that moment are his impeccable defense and his response to the guilty verdict, "Last Words," published in *La Internacional* in October 1970 and in *La cultura de México*, a supplement to *Siempre!*, in April 1971.[110] Both his defense and his response function much like "Imprisoned Words" in that they open our eyes to the double life of words, time, and history in society. By double life I refer to the difference between the dominant regime, established and imposed by the state, and another meaning that critiques the former in the name of social transformation. It is perhaps in these texts that this duality is made sharper and more concrete, as if we are dealing with two separate worlds. The key or the point of contact between the two is the difference between common and political prisoners, which was an existential problem for the prisoners of '68, given that it also encapsulated the crucial drama of the moment; that is, how the state criminalized political dissidence, or how it elicited the critical thinking that opened up certain uses of language and certain ways of interpreting history, which were then made into criminal acts.

In giving his defense, Revueltas achieves a profoundly interesting eccentric act: he delivers a lesson on criminality as an artifice created and sustained by the state. Through a series of close readings of Marx, he offers an analysis of the diagram that constitutes prison in society, calling attention to the relationship between criminality and the functioning of the state. Once again, the prison appears as a site to which Revueltas directs our gaze so that we can imagine the system of relationships that comprise the world we live in, casting off social invisibilization. Revueltas begins by addressing his harsh sentences. "The Public Prosecutor, charged with abolishing delinquency, creates delinquents," he writes. "Notwithstanding the total and absolute ignorance shown by this gentleman representative of the Public Prosecutor's office regarding Marx and Marxism, it would appear that, at the very least, he has read the page of Marx that I will now take the liberty of reading."[111] He proceeds to recite a long and well-known passage in which Marx identifies the mechanism of the criminal world, linking it to the way in which

> a philosopher produces ideas, a poet, poems. . . . A criminal produces crimes. . . . The criminal produces not only crimes but also criminal law, and with this also the professor who gives lectures on criminal law and in addition to this the inevitable compendium in which this same professor throws his lectures onto the general market as "commodities." This brings with it augmentation of national wealth, quite apart from the personal enjoyment that . . . the manuscript of the compendium brings to its originator himself. The criminal moreover produces the whole of the police and of criminal justice, constables, judges, hangmen, juries, et cetera; and all these different lines of business, which form equally many categories of the social division of labor, develop different capacities of the human spirit, create new needs and new ways of satisfying them.[112]

Having read this passage, Revueltas goes on to interpret how it corresponds to the nation's reality, connecting it to Gustavo Díaz Ordaz's invisibilization of political prisoners: "Surely this gentleman representative of the Public Prosecutor's office read this page by Karl Marx and, being thus inspired, sought to keep pace with President Díaz Ordaz's last State of the Union address and contribute, in his own small way, to advancing the country's current stage of economic development? At least this undoubtedly explains why he is moved to create *common delinquents* out of what are really and truly *political prisoners*."[113] Revueltas gave this reading of Marx in an effort to trace a critical genealogy of the situation that the political prisoners of '68 were living. By converting political acts into criminal acts, the state translated the useless or apparently unproductive entity that is political dissidence (that which denies, resists, criticizes) into something that is productive within the logic of its own development:

more criminals. On the other hand, if he who commits a crime is a criminal, that would mean that the state—having made it a crime to think differently—ought to be subject to the same penal apparatus that it constructed to deal with crime. This affirms what the political prisoners already knew: the Mexican state held an absolute monopoly over the signification, words, life, and death of dissenters. From there, both the defense and response center on an intensification of what we saw in "Imprisoned Words" as language and signification, now applied to the history and temporality imprisoned by the PRI.

Imprisoned words here take the form of an imprisoned history in which the revolutionary component influences a determined language, one that demands time—its possibility, outside the universe of debt and condemnation: "We are *in* history, but not in the way that philistines and the naïve-minded think we are: to appear, to underscore. No. The false and empty 'grandeur' belonging to heroes or so-called historical figures matters very little to us. We are a small and barely significant part of the *imprisoned history* of Mexico, that is, in a country that lacks a real history."[114] That imprisoned history puts us once again in a familiar zone in which the geology of subterranean currents, always repressed, seems once more to emphasize the clash between the state monopoly and the struggle to reinvent the political. Through these trials we witness, in their naked form, the arbitrariness and weight of the authority the state exercises over speech. Clearly Revueltas did not mean to defend himself with this intervention, even though he had been subjected to what was almost a life sentence. This is shown at the end of the text, when he writes that everyone knows that the sentences that would be handed down had been written *before* the legal process even began, independent of that legal process, and would be applied to the defendants no matter what they said. The storyline had already been written, and yet Revueltas's criticism makes for a thorough defense.

The philosophical-critical defense introduces a new way of understanding the trial and the length of the sentence that the legal apparatus imposed. It defends a historical moment that the legal apparatus sought to invisibilize and detain, and does so from outside the arithmetic count by which the state translates the debt that the individual must pay with the privation of his freedom (sentence). With this, he alludes to a form of freedom that differs from how the state counts time (years of a sentence) and refers to the possibility of *making* history. In other words, as with words, Revueltas configures a similar move in which freedom connects to an improper form of inhabiting language and history, opening and expanding them, instead of caging or confining them to a punishment cell. In this defense—which is a defense of freedom—Revueltas proposes cognitive democracy and autonomy as the right to a language and a time *apart from* that which is measured by the state.

The question that emerges is: what kind of measurement does this freedom entail, since it is in conflict with state time and no common system of measurement exists outside the conflict or antagonism between metrics? In "Last Words," Revueltas's response to the sentence of sixteen years in prison, he goes directly to that point: the struggle between various temporalities and their incidence in the form of conceiving and living freedom. He speaks of the individual sentences that fell to each prisoner, each one an excuse for a sentence that really referred to something else.

> Gentlemen judges, or you who appear to be such in this country, have sentenced this legal object, this person, but *not their spirit, not their thoughts.* Against those spirits and thoughts, you, gentlemen judge, can do nothing; you, Mr. President of the Republic, can do nothing, and nor will you ever. Who can prevent what it is we're struggling for, from prison, armed with criticism and thoughts? Herein lies the inconsequence of those who have convicted us. They have been unable to sentence us to death, not because such a penalty is not inscribed in the legal code, nor because it is outside of their power to murder us—as demonstrated by the Vandalic assault we suffered on January 1 of this year—but because they cannot murder what we represent. *You can neither kill nor invalidate our minds, no matter how many years you add to our prison sentences.* Certainly our minds are not immortal, and nor is the work we have created in the past and will continue in future years. But *as long as our minds and thoughts are alive and active, you will be helpless to prevent our action.*[115]

This long response unfolds personal and historical reality, condemnation, and the certainty that words can be put to the defense of freedom of thought, criticism, and transformation. Here we detect some of the same ideas discussed at the end of the introduction: his only remaining freedom is intellectual freedom (or "the survival of the pen" that he found after the assault on political prisoners in Lecumberri). This passage raises the crucial theme of measurement, in that political freedom is not measured by the established patron of the criminal code and the sentences that afflict the lives of individuals but rather by an alternative way of measuring, through a different way of experiencing time. It is a moment in which the duality between free and imprisoned worlds becomes so powerfully visible that we must adapt it to a critique of the present. Roberta Avendaño would later allude to this in her text on the women's prison: where can we escape if all of society is a prison? The film *History of a Document* would ask the same question visually from Lecumberri. There is undeniably a struggle here for the existential conceptualization of a freedom negated by the state. The freedom that emerges as both an act and a mode of existence, something not measured with the alienated space and time demarcated by the state and capital. A radical heterogeneity exists between the length of a prison sentence and the duration of the freedom that Revueltas configures through the words of his defense. In fact, the very defense embodied a form of freedom that Eduardo Valle (El búho, or "The Owl") recalls in these terms: "The best moment in Lecumberri was the wonderful evening of our constitutional prior hearing, when Revueltas and I defended the student movement politically and intellectually. . . . Revueltas ended up yelling down the cellblock, 'Look, you bastards, we're political prisoners!' That was one of the best nights of my life."[116] It seems that the freedom defended here is measured in a different way, one that Revueltas thoroughly explores, perhaps less affirmatively, in his final novel, *Time and Number*, where he recasts this problem in literary language.

Time and Number

If you can't bear the desperation of prison, it's because you can't bear the desperation of freedom, either. (I'll come back to this.) —JOSÉ REVUELTAS, *México 68*

On February 8, 1970, Revueltas wrote in his prison notebook:

> The expected, the inevitable has arrived, naked, concrete, real, with its precise limits: time and my hearing before it, with a response that I myself should formulate and to which I should subject myself unextendably, lucidly, firmly, and mercilessly, for the first time in my life, until the end, since this is also the last time. . . . Time is presented to me now as *my last time*, I attend my hearing *for the last time*, and nothing, no information, no reasoning can alter the objective, inexorable fact of it. If I weren't in prison, things would obviously happen differently. If I were free, I wouldn't have to confront the problem of what I want that last time to be like; for the essence of freedom lies precisely in the richness of its options, a richness that, explained in abstract terms, is reduced to its most extreme limits only when faced with the imminence of death. The problem here is that unfreedom represents a kind of death, a constant imminence of death, that renews itself each day for years, which, seeing as the number of options made possible in prison is enormously reduced, such that all that remains to a person summoned to die within a week or a month, proceed from the *final warning*. (Continue tomorrow, February 9).[117]

Revueltas wrote this note in his Lecumberri diary months before receiving a prison sentence. Within this legal limbo in which time kept passing, and after the attempt of the hunger strike was repressed in the attack they suffered on New Year's Eve, a sense of imminent death was hovering above his head. Time and (un)freedom became a recurrent obsession where the key questions covered by the theoretical act and the apando were now posed within the frame of his own history of struggle and repression. In this context, the project of a novel that he had stopped writing when the 1968 movement started, and which he subsequently resumed, becomes a stage for continuing his reflections about temporality and freedom in forms that would avoid the figure of a teleological line. His obsession now is with the cycles, the waves of emancipation and repression, posing the question that characterized the theoretical act in a new figure.

Time and Number is the draft of a novel that Revueltas started to develop in 1967, only to be interrupted by the struggle of the student movement and his subsequent captivity in Lecumberri, when he wrote many crucial texts of the moment (*The Apando*, "Ezequiel, or the Massacre of Innocents," and "Hegel and I," among others). Reading the notes in his journal, however, we perceive that the project of the novel continued in his head, particularly because the novel's thematic obsession with temporality was ever-present in that moment of his life in prison and in the questions left by '68. An unpublished poem and two chapters are all that remain to us from this project. The first piece was published in *Casa de las Américas* in May 1968, no less, and the second was published in *Eros* magazine, in two installments in July and August 1975, when Revueltas was released, retaining criminal charges but outside of Lecumberri, shortly before his death. Four years later, in November 1979, the first chapter, which had been published in Cuba in May 1968, reappeared in *Estela cultural* in the city of Xalapa, Veracruz. These published materials are supplemented by reflections that Revueltas shares in various conversations, interviews, and personal notes on his project that seem to represent, as Edith Negrín proposes, a synthesis of what the problem of freedom meant to Revueltas.[118]

The novel initiates an interesting spatial trajectory in Revueltas's work: the scene is not Lecumberri but a punishment camp on Islas Marías, a kind of open-air apando on a prison island whose invisible gates are the sea, metaphorized as sea time. With this, Revueltas seems to trace an almost poetic path through his entire body of work, as this is his last, incomplete literary project, which involves a return to Islas Marías, the site of his first captivity (at the age of sixteen) and the scene of his first published novel, *Walls of Water*, 1941. In his first novel, the prison is problematized as a space that produces monstrosity and madness, that is, as the effectuation of a form of degradation that the author dramatizes alongside the problem of how to put together a political collective. Revueltas develops this idea through a group of Communist political prisoners who are sent to the island's punishment camp. Revisiting this memory feels symptomatic at first, but then Revueltas introduces a prisoner accused of homicide through whom he attempts to frame the problem of alienated freedom in which the existence of the political as a differential act is dismantled. Just as in *The Apando*, this novel has no political prisoners, only common prisoners, as if reflecting the state's world of social signification that made the militancy of '68 a crime punishable by lengthy prison sentences.

Thus, we can see how—just as *The Apando* offers an example of a "gargantuan defeat of freedom at the hands of geometry,"[119] expressed through the idea of the prison as a society-prison—the draft of *Time and Number* is presented as a reflection on alienated time in calculation, a thematic that gives rise to the title, which refers to the length of the sentence and to the number that stands in for the name of the prisoner from the moment he enters prison. In an interview, Revueltas explains the title in relation to the everyday: " 'Time' and 'number' do not encapsulate abstract concepts that would like to have pretensions to philosophy. They describe a group of common prisoners in Islas Marías. 'Time' is the collective sentence they bear, and the 'number' substitutes for their names."[120] The choice of title is undeniably crucial and poses something abstract and quotidian: time and the everyday circumstance of living out a sentence. Before broaching the theme of the role that quotidian temporality plays in the text, it is important to examine how the question of freedom within the prison emerges in this incomplete novel, whose central plot is liberation. Revueltas summarizes the idea behind this literary project as follows:

> Since the central theme of this novel is that of freedom, I have taken it to the opposite extreme: men who lose their freedom, *the ultimate loss of freedom in our immediate understanding*, the fact of being imprisoned, being sentenced to X years of prison. One of the main characters discovers a kind of savage, primitive, and hallucinatory entertainment, which is to run across a rocky outcrop that the sea strikes at fixed intervals. Running to the edge of the abyss and back before the sea can sweep him away. Thus, in those minutes, in those seconds he spends performing this intrepid and foolish action, he encounters a sense of freedom: those three minutes make him feel freer. . . . His fight against the thirty years of his sentence lies in those three minutes of freedom.[121]

In this game of come and go, the prisoner, whose name is Evodio, feels freer; as if in those three minutes, the twenty-five years that remain on his sentence were made lighter. At the same time, through daily repetition of this exercise, the prisoner challenges his sentence by engaging in another struggle: a struggle against death.

The entire theme of the novel is realized in this site between life (like that itinerary) and the abyss, that brings that to-and-fro up against the waves of the sea (time) and, according to Negrín, against the metaphorical prison (walls of water) that forms the paradoxical structure of the narration: "The prisoner *escapes, without escaping* the prison. The sea is at once the prison—walls of water—and the possibility, however illusory, of liberation. *The prisoner combats his captivity, "objective" time, the infinite, and death all at once.* He reaches the limits, *but he never achieves the opposite extreme.* This action is completed each day only to start again, the following day, in virtually the same place where the game began. *The prisoner's movement is incessant and paradoxical, not unlike the struggle of the narrator against reason and for freedom.*"[122] The interminable paradox that Negrín describes is suggested by the almost cyclical nature of the exercise, namely, reaching an endpoint and returning to the start without being able to go *further*, similar to the allotropic element of *The Apando*: that change that does not fundamentally change anything, a change without evident *transformation*. In both texts, Revueltas uses a cyclical structure to express a form of alienated freedom—the "small, ephemeral pleasure, the serenity produced by the drug" in El Carajo, and the "three minutes" of freedom in Evodio's game. At their core, Revueltas's literary texts delve deeply into the question of the meaning of freedom in political action within the context created by each crushing sense of failure. How can one feel free within a cyclical mechanism of repression, within the sequence of apandos that punctuate twentieth-century Mexican politics? I am interested in searching for how these literary meditations enable us to shed light on a crucial problem that has already emerged in the theorization of the '68 movement as a theoretical act but that now permits us to observe the projection of one characteristic of social movements in general: the fleeting yet intense temporality that produces uncertainty once it gains a foothold in the narrative. In some sense, here we must confront the temporal correlate to the philosophical problem assumed by the theoretical act: a history made of fragments of moments of freedom; a history of three minutes of freedom before waves of repression.

Within the narrative outline of a novel about time and freedom (and perhaps about the incommensurable time expressed by certain acts of freedom), the heart of the problem lies in narrating the disproportion that emerges between the intensity of a few minutes of lived freedom versus three vast moments of two greater temporalities: the sea time (nature's finite time) and the state's disciplinary clock time, expressed by a thirty-year sentence (of which Evodio has *paid* five). The speeches that open the first published chapter exemplify this disproportion: "Evodio watched the sea with a *choleric and impotent* hatred, despite his happiness. No matter what, he'll never defeat it, it is immortal, it is eternal, *it is time*, yet he returns to the fray. Returns and returns."[123] Here is the affective composition of the game that the novel lays out: happiness brings that feeling of freedom and a feeling of a radical impotence to match, what would be freedom and condemnation, repeating the same exercise with the certainty that it is *nothing* compared to what you are attempting to combat (the sea as time, as a cycle, as death). There is a task of observation and calculation by which Evodio constructs his game, his exercise in liberation, with the faith of a regularity that nevertheless could be suspended at any moment by the sea or by the death threatened by the boss of a criminal mafia of people within Islas Marías (other prisoners and guards). The distance measured by this game for his freedom is replicated in the second chapter through the work of navigating the distance between past and present, life and death. This is implied by the flashbacks that accompany the description of his sensation of freedom: dislocated images of various memories of torture and pain in which the mafia threatened to kill him if he didn't "sing" them the information they were looking for. Everything follows in a chaotic stream in which freedom emerges, juxtaposed to various times of life and death, remembrances of instances that sweep through without a common thread or explicit causality. It would appear that this game of freedom is duplicated in the present and past of the story: the pleasure of running toward the wave and returning, the pain of the torture session in which Evodio does not give up the information—profiling a peculiar kind of freedom associated with the risk of death and the happiness of surviving *each time*.

We might say that Evodio operates as a generic character or conceptual figure through which Revueltas visualizes a line of thought that had fascinated him since the hunger strike in Lecumberri: that of the risk that alters the distance between dying and the actual arrival of death. At the same time, it is significant that he has made a game of it, a playful exercise that becomes quotidian and allows him to defend a practice of freedom that is not expressed in relation to the years remaining on his sentence but rather refers to a different experience of time. The novel operates as a cipher or key to an imprisoned history in a time that is foreign to that of his freedom, a history marked by the insistent exercise of opening another space of freedom that always runs the risk of being systematically repressed, murdered. The disproportion of those three minutes compared to thirty years can be read alongside Revueltas's reflections on the theoretical act: moments of eruption of an alternate time in politics, a time that is different from clock time but nonetheless elicits deep changes. What if we interpret this prisoner's game and his feeling of freedom as a figure that expresses the moment of freedom offered by each political struggle to forge a new possibility of a life of equity and redistribution (peasants, railroad workers, students) and is abruptly censored, repressed, invisibilized by the state—struggles that are criminalized so as not to be legitimated as political? The text leaves us with the question of how to transform stories of prisons into stories of freedom and how to conceive of a type of freedom capable of negating and transforming (not allotropically negating) that social horizon. If each attempt to destroy the prison is subsequently imprisoned, repressed, massacred, how can a new story emerge from this context? Do such projects of self-management constitute attempts to seize those three minutes of freedom? To sketch out an answer, it will be necessary to return to a crucial element of the purpose of the work, which is the coexistence of temporalities and their links to the experience of a freedom that is heterogeneous to the distribution of the sensible imposed by the state.

Considering the Temporality of '68

Understanding the transformation that unfolded in '68 in the everyday and historical perception of politics means raising a series of questions about the relationships between temporality, politics, and historicization that are often left to the side. The exercise that Revueltas imagines the prisoner performing dramatizes a freedom and a time that is incalculable by clock time. On a broader level, we might say that the text stages an apparent problem: How can the movement of '68 generate in only a few months—or, as has also been calculated, about 136 days—a destabilization incomparable to the years or decades in which one feels that *nothing politically and existentially relevant is happening?* In various accounts of '68, participants in the movement emphasize the difficulty of putting into language the effect those few months had on their personal and political lives. The temporality of the feeling of freedom they experienced over the course of a few months becomes incommensurable with the metric usually used to count time, particularly when considering widespread changes. There is something ungraspable about that experience, and therein lies a portion of its potential.

In their classic work, *Antisystemic Movements*, Giovanni Arrighi, Terence Hopkins, and Immanuel Wallerstein maintain that '68 shaped one of the two global revolutions that transformed the world, emerging as something unplanned and ending with a sense of failure and defeat.[124] The brevity and intensity characteristic of such moments means that they carry an element of impropriety and untranslatability from the viewpoint of realpolitik, since their "achievements" cannot be defined in terms of specific "successes."[125] Rather, their demands imply a change in the political system itself, the aperture of the possibility of transformation: the demand for a different kind of politics and different kind of time. As Lefebvre explains when discussing the role of self-management as an element of political strategy, this should not be seen as a goal in the teleological sense but as a medial element. It has to do with an "opening toward the possible" that gives access to the present moment's automatized mechanisms of reproduction, thus consolidating the idea of a circumstance in which the people can take control of their destiny and time.[126] This illuminates another facet of the problem I pointed out in the introduction, demonstrating how the focus on self-management and on mechanisms of direct democracy practiced at that near-utopic moment of freedom led to a substantial rupture with the traditional dynamic of representative politics and with the narrative mechanisms of official history. The historicization that Revueltas achieved with the theoretical act raises questions about the style in which we might narrate such brief and essential episodes in history, when the notion of transformation lies at the very core of political life in its present moment. The demands of self-management imply a fundamental pivot in ways of narrating the trajectory of political transformation, since, instead of adhering to the traditional teleological framework, it raised questions about the transformation of politics through the everyday practice of the present. In '68, time was no longer seen through the teleological lens of a productive development automatized "toward" (perpetual waiting for a miracle); rather, the possibility of rethinking a new form of democratic participation erupted through the *here and now* of participatory experimentation. Moments of freedom are unusually brief in duration but produce a feeling of transformation and joy in participation that seems to overcome decades of living out *the same*. This kind of discussion can arise more naturally in the field of testimony (the sensation of lived time), but it becomes more difficult to explain in the historical field, which generally needs to narrate within a logic more akin to calculus, entailing the need to explain the gains, successes, and failures of a political movement. I propose to forge another exploratory path toward alternative ways of answering the question of how to write these histories of incalculable freedom while respecting the multiplicity of heterogeneous times in which they coexisted. Here, freedom and temporality become crucial problematic sites from which to approach the experience of '68, furthermore permitting us to project certain reflections over other, similar moments of political aperture, of the possibility of transforming the social order. It strikes me as important to understand the reflections made in this latter part of Revueltas's thought so as to propose some coordinates for reading social movements.

The prisoner's game provides not only a key for understanding the fleeting intensity of these laboratories for change but also the opportunity to delve deeper into the kind of political movement that results from their radical demand for democracy. We might say that the never-finished project that he titled *Time and Number* provided Revueltas a place for visualizing alternative temporal images that manifest the "shadowy figure" of a synthesis that implies neither advance nor regression. The literary space allowed him to explore the problem of freedom in relation to a time that is heterogeneous to state calculation and, therefore, to the alienated form of freedom subjected to the state's clock. How can we configure a history capable of honoring the repetition of each one of those *three-minute* segments of freedom that occur *within* history over the course of years, decades, centuries? In part, we can see that in these literary texts, Revueltas finds a more subjective and existential way of posing a question that, in philosophical and historiographical texts on '68, would take the form of a theoretical act: how can we liberate each remnant of *imprisoned history*, a fragmented prose of emancipatory acts that are terminated and censored by a state that only accepts the logos of its own narrative? In other words: how can we express the incommensurability of radically heterogeneous times in a language that does not belong to the state, in which the duration of those three minutes of lived freedom becomes laughable, if not grotesque, when compared to a nearly lifelong sentence? The theme of freedom developed in this unfinished novel brings us to the problem of how to accept a time that does not belong to the narrative of development and productivity (where time is understood as wealth and capital). How do we comprehend a vital social and political freedom that is incommensurable with the language of earnings?

This brings us to a reflection on life that is inextricable from everyday life, something utterly absent from a heroic and idealized view of history in which key moments arise almost magically, thereby invisibilizing their arduous processes, conflicts, and contradictions (irresolvable instances). That is, it primarily erases the radical and absolute contingency of a present that has not yet been assigned historical significance: radical uncertainty and error as crucial components of dialectical thought. This is particularly evident in the wake of '68, when, as Bosteels observes, the majority of Revueltas's work is dedicated to reformulating the sketches of dialectics as "conceptualization of the non-conceptual" or "representation of the nonrepresentable."[127] One component underemphasized in "epic" tales of '68 is the way in which the quotidian truly affected ways of thinking dialectically about life and death. As Peter Osborne indicates, it is in the everyday that the coexistence of multiple temporalities and sensibilities—lived time, social time, historical time—are made visible.[128] From the complex plot wrought by this compound temporality emerges another way of signifying freedom and historical acts. Perhaps for someone like Revueltas, this problem is vital because *he himself is living that question*: as he is writing these works, he remains a prisoner even though he is outside the prison. While experiencing "freedom under protest" (*libertad bajo protesta*), Revueltas remains a prisoner even in freedom and dies completing his sentence, which means perpetually facing the possibility of being sent back to prison. His life is filled with a multitude of ways of experiencing time and freedom in their complex relationship with possibility and the proximity of death. This is evident from a poem found in his drafts of *Time and Number* as an outline or sketch of the novel.

> Things fall, cease to be, disappear.
> Something halts them in their shadow,
> where they lie, snuffed out, alive only
> by the urge to not yet be nothing.

> Love itself is something
> on which new things are layered
> each time, a palimpsest where
> memories differ from what they remember
> and seem beautiful, though they were not,
> because death retouches them, tenderly
> and disguises them as encounters, though they were not.[129]

In this poem, Revueltas points to a distance between personal death and its afterlife in language—a space of re-signification of what no longer exists—thereby tracing a counterpoint between that which no longer exists and ways of narrating and signifying it through memory. Death and love make us refigure things in ways that differ from how they looked in the present, become something different, retouched by a sense of continuation. The poem, also unfinished, works within his obsession with exploring temporality out of unity in progression, playing with the contrast between the sense of things within a present, and the labor of memory in re-creating them once they have passed. He explores the paradoxes between memory and experience, looking into a *here and now* in which to reconsider the politics of the everyday and the communal as something that is created, made, enabled—like history.

In the critical Marxism of the seventies we find an insistence on a critique of the teleological component of the classical politics of vulgar or dogmatic Marxism. Confronting developmentalism required acknowledging the emergence of a certain limit within thought. During this period, Revueltas's fiction focuses on representing, in literary form, a dialectical process with neither an endpoint nor an ascent. If his obsession was to critique the developmentalist view that conceives of development as the growth of "productivity" (the urge for "more" as an economic imperative) instead of thinking of development as growing through apprenticeship and transformation, then the problem with this arithmetic notion of development is that it has dominated conceptualization of the history of Marxism itself.[130] What remains is to commence a study of temporality capable of decentralizing the primacy of development as the focus, one that will illuminate our understanding of historical imagination. At the same time, it is easier to criticize developmentalism than to truly reflect on and articulate the consequences of suspending the role it plays in the *political* imagination of the twentieth century. As Osborne notes, it is a matter of deciding *what type of time* (of *politics of time*) can support this critical line of thought while striking chords with Sartre, Benjamin, Althusser, and Lefebvre.[131] How do we count the time of difference, of the coexistence of a multiplicity of varied temporalities? How do we bring them *together* without reducing them to a mere union of unrelated differences or restricting them to a single site, time, or place? How can we arrive at a new way of contemplating a motley temporality of difference?

In Latin America in the late 1960s and early 1970s, the possibility of inventing a politics of temporality that did not adhere to the paradigm of homogeneous development and progress was crucial, since it hinted at the possibility of situating less predictable, less calculable struggles within a then-dogmatic Marxist tradition. Revueltas seeks to devise a dialectic that includes neither progress nor development (that is, a nonanthropomorphic dialectic), one that we can address in the same tone as the ideas raised around the same time by José Aricó in the Argentine interior (during events in Córdoba)[132] and René Zavaleta Mercado in Bolivia, regarding several revolutionary strains, but more specifically the varied temporalities pertaining to the Aymaran and Quechuan cultures, the industrial bourgeoisie, and the oligarchy of La Paz. In diverse ways, depending on each context and situation, all three propose a historical temporality in which time is neither single nor homogeneous, thereby dismantling the notion of a privileged conscience that operates as the engine of history. From this follows a problematization of how to conceive of the historical formation of a social class when its "stages" of development do not advance linearly and successively—instead, we detect the simultaneity of incommensurable processes, generating the need to address and think through a motley social consciousness.

This motley consciousness (*lo abigarrado*) originates in Zavaleta Mercado's text on dual power and continues in other works he wrote in exile in Mexico while endeavouring to radically rethink moments of social movements and their temporalities.[133] Through his efforts to interpret dual power in Bolivia, where the interpretive framework derives more from orthodox Leninist Marxism, he hit upon the notion of motley time as a heterodox shift that could be key to identifying another kind of illegibility inherent in the possibilities and tensions at play at a time of social transformation. A motley society entails the multiplicity and coexistence of various modes of production and life *without integration or assimilation*.[134] Therefore, the principal theme is: what sort of time can we devise to imagine revolutionary change or transformation by which a temporal multiplicity becomes perceptible? This is the vital problem that materializes during the seventies, connecting diverse ways of displacing the matrix of a more homogeneous and teleological dialectic in favor of a complex multiplicity of times—of modes of production and our existence within them.

A philosophical strain emerges that relates to a form of thought that attempts to deal with this irresolvable tension or contradiction by seeking modes of thought and action that do not adhere to the dichotomy between theory and practice, between alienation and nonalienated miracle. It hopes to attend to both sides without *synthesizing them or resolving them in unity*. I find that the thinkers who tend toward this line of thought are those who were obsessed with reflecting on self-management and the possibility of conceiving of a dialectic that assumes *nonresolution* as a form of thought that is not only *valid* but essential to redefine a nondevelopmentalist dialectic, a dialectic that I will call *improper* and that manifests itself in many different forms and registers. The problem does not pertain to the dialectics of nature, which renders history to an applied pattern that predicts facts, but rather to the possibility of opening up our thinking about history to include new temporalities and inquire into the consequences that this insertion provokes.[135] On this point, I am interested in studying this curious encounter between dialectics and '68—curious in that the event of '68 is, almost by definition, a moment of radical questioning of developmentalist, finalistic dialectics. With this, I do not mean to say that this political form has disappeared but rather that the novelty of '68 lay in its expression of exasperation with traditional politics at that time: dogmatic Marxism and liberalism. From here stems the question of the possibility of developing a new way of thinking and staging changes that do not fit into the idea of revolution as the arrival of a magical solution but rather seek ways of thinking about the transformability of life by focusing on its most quotidian, miniscule, intimate, contradictory elements. It is perhaps in this sense that the figure of an irresolvable contradiction presents itself as a model by which to understand the moment: rejecting the notion of "moving toward" revolution (the teleology of progress), of preparing "for" (productivism), in favor of an opening and circulation of the possibility of a different politics, one that babbles in almost untranslatable languages most of the time. In this moment, a new form of politics crystallizes, one that does not hang on the notion of the temporality of movement. It represents a rupture with a certain spatialized version of time. In this sense, it precipitates the formation of a philosophical obsession with thinking events.

It is a zone of impropriety in which the eruption of '68s relates to an experience of the political that contrasts with a political system organized in fixed units (such as party or revolution) in that it appears to lack a defined goal toward which it moves—state takeover, staging revolution. It is a moment of a radical questioning of the very logic by which the political operates—its conditions of production and reproduction—and therefore, it is the moment in which the central figure becomes, paradoxically, democracy: its reconceptualization and redefinition in order to establish freedom as a mode of existence. However, here we detect a new shadowy, difficult figure: a way of de-auratizing the political (taking the miracle out of revolution) that transforms freedom into something else entirely: inhabiting a process that has no finality (understood as "end") can likewise be unbearable. Freedom appears as an act that focuses on untying (spacing out) connections that had imprisoned Marxism, but it is an uncomfortable freedom; for instead of bringing a new "good"—the miracle of resolution—*it inserts uncertainty* in the most empowering (everything is possible from now on) and most desperate (but *nothing* might happen) senses of the word. Here is the essence of the liberation of philosophy that occurred in that moment: it entails a disalienation that neither assumes nor supposes goodness. In this sense, freedom refers to an abysmal circumstance, since without legislation, we are merely left with a series of contingent events—that is, a history that can only be understood retrospectively, as it is essentially a fiction produced ex post facto.

THE EFFECTS OF '68 ON CINEMA

The Image as a Place of Political Intervention

How is the change that '68 entails expressed in the production and circulation of images? How would the project of emancipating the image connect to the discussion that this book organizes in terms of redefining or experiencing a freedom that distinguishes itself from forms of property, teleology, and development, instead addressing itself to issues of the everyday? In other words, in what form do political reconceptualization and its different practices have a correlate in cinema? Film allows us to enter into the first afterlife closest to the movement, following the strong state repression of October 2. Collective Super 8 film production, which began occurring intensely in the early 1970s, materialized a singular form of continuing the open and experimental character of the moment. The world of Super 8 linked to militant cinema opens two areas of analysis. On the one hand, it presses us to address the forms in which collective and cooperative experiences are translated to the cinematic field, modifying the notion of auteurist and commercial filmmaking that still prevails in conceptualizations of independent film. On the other hand, it involves investigating the transformation that these practices entail in the world of film production, something that is at the heart of discussions of militant cinema, and that is also related to different film interventions within the disciplinary spaces of modernity, such as the factory or the prison.

In the volume he recently edited, *Ruptures of '68 in Latin American Cinema*, Mariano Mestman proposes to analyze the effects of '68 on Latin American cinema in terms of a two-dimensional break, the political and the counter-cultural, and to look for the different forms that this rupture took in different regions.[1] As Álvaro Vázquez Mantecón analyzes in his chapter devoted to Mexico, the movement of '68 was "key for the transformation of cultural practices in the country."[2] This transformation, he argues, involved not only a shift in the "modernizing artistic projects" that had characterized the developmental impulse of the 1950s and 1960s but also produced a radical change in the relationship that artists had had with the state until then. After '68, "independence would play an important role in cultural creation, and a new displacement in the role of politics in art would be the object of experimentation."[3] In this chapter, I explore this displacement in terms of the question of self-management and cognitive democracy, searching for the ways in which they were expressed in the world of filmmaking. That is, just like the question that Revueltas set forth about self-management as transformative autonomy, the expression of the movement emerges in the field of cinema in terms of a problematization of what the word *independent* means when speaking of a cinema that remained affected by the obligation to comply with and reproduce the rules imposed by the state. From this angle, the question that emerges is: how do we address the idea of film's autonomy, and moreover, of the ways in which this would involve a process of socializing cinematic experience? As one more link in the chain of experiments in social self-management, the autonomy in/ of film would involve an emphasis on the process more than on the product, thereby decentering or destabilizing the category of the work. Thus, in various cinematic experiments after '68, the film is conceived as a multifaceted process in which the subjects involved in the problem that the film addresses will also be the actors and narrators of their story. As we will see with regard to the Cooperative of Marginal Cinema (Cooperativa de Cine Marginal), films emerge as mechanisms for visualizing fragments of everyday political life—material that is usually not treated as filmable—while at the same time comprising a singular experience amid other forms of political action. For example, for striking workers, the possibility of thinking of the strike as a form of making cinema, whether through searching for background music, performing, or making an announcement, entails an unusual form of political experimentation. That is, the creative dimension becomes a constitutive component of the political experience, and vice versa. If the crux of the movement was the word *freedom* as a form of dismantling the farce of supposed independence—the permanent capture of that which dissents—the cinema produced in the first years of the seventies was an intense labor of *elaborating the meaning of autonomy in the world of the image.* Instead of reproducing an autonomy governed by the idea of "art for art's sake" in its modernist sense, what it created was a singular form of relating the autonomous and the political. Critical not only of the state and the market but also of the forms of traditional political struggles, the experiences on which I focus my analysis relate to the figure of the strike after the end of the big university strike—strikes by workers asking for autonomy from the co-opted trade unions, and the aftermath of the strike of political prisoners from the '68 movement at the Lecumberri Prison. At a figurative level, the strike will help me to also shed light on the ways in which '68 affected the artistic realm, producing an interruption regarding the forms and roles of artistic production. Thus, I am interested in delving into an analysis of the different forms of linking cinema and politics based on the new styles of militancy that became possible after the experience of '68. I set out to illustrate ways in which the crucial points comprising self-management were continued in the experience of making films, above all in the moment following the great demobilization produced by the massacre in October and the end of the big university strike in December.

In the Mexican visual realm, a first experimentation related to the movement came out of the University Center for Film Studies (Centro Universitario de Estudios Cinematográficos, CUEC), and consolidated with the collective elaboration of the images for the first great documentary about the movement, *El grito* (*The Shout*). A second part emerged at the beginning of the seventies, when film began to generate new questions about how to continue the experience of '68 in the midst of an environment different from the months of July to December.[4] I have chosen to focus on two Super 8 experiments produced in Mexico after Tlatelolco: the Cooperative of Marginal Cinema (1971–75) and the process of making and editing *History of a Document* (1971), the film that was made clandestinely in Lecumberri Prison. In the case of the Cooperative of Marginal Cinema—focused on the world of workers and, more than anything else, on intervening in strikes of small and large independent unions—we delve into the issue of a political aesthetics of connectivity or encounter, typical of Mexico '68. In addition to the creation of the *Communiqués of Labor Insurgency*, and of films made among students and workers, the cooperative places us at the heart of a struggle at the level of the factory. This is a component that connects to one of the movement's crucial points in its petition for justice for the struggles of union democratization that had always been repressed and imprisoned, as in the closest case of the railway workers. As Vázquez Mantecón explains: "The emergence of the Cooperative coincided with labor mobilizations that sought independence for the unions. From the end of Adolfo Ruiz Cortines's regime, different trade organizations (railway workers, telegraphers, teachers) were fighting intensely to separate from the control of the Confederation of Mexican Workers [Confederación de Trabajadores de México, CTM], which was integrated to the official party and aligned with the government administrations in power. Throughout the sixties and seventies union insurgency was harshly repressed."[5]

With *History of a Document*, we delve into another paradigmatic disciplinary space: from the factory or the university we shift to the prison and to the transformation of the prisoners into producers of a film about their everyday situation and geography of the condition of confinement. The film is a continuation of the struggle against the repression that took place within the prison in order to put an end to the hunger strike that many political prisoners had begun in December 1969. Directed by Óscar Menéndez, the film was edited in France with the support of the Groupe de Recherches Technologiques— Atelier d'expérimentation Super 8, created with the goal of converting this experiment to 16mm. *History of a Document* allows us to question the category of work through its emphasis on visualizing the process of the production of what was filmed. This is connected to the form that we saw that characterized the role of self-management as the transformation of the material of knowledge itself—its communication. I have chosen these interventions to reflect on the transformation that occurs in the cinema of '68, because both function as extremely interesting and apt ways to explore what it meant to try modes of doing politics through the image after '68. They function as afterlives or modes of continuing the movement by other means and outside the university, and they also allow me to trace a map of the international context of militant cinema in Latin America with the emergence of "new cinema" (later called "third cinema") and to discuss the project of a "fourth cinema" that arose in relation to the Super 8 experiments in Mexico.

This chapter repeats two figures from Revueltas that I analyzed earlier— self-management and prison—now by problematizing the field of the image's action. In both cases, the strike by factory workers and of prisoners after the end of the big university strike plays a central role and allows me to outline a subsequent assessment of these practices of militant art. Through these materials I address the question of how *the movement was put into images*; that is, in what way the movement continued after the general sensation of defeat left by the Tlatelolco massacre and mass imprisonment. In an experimental and somewhat chaotic way, a cinema formed that set out to *intervene* in the political process no longer as an agent that would observe from outside and record what was happening politically but rather as a mechanism capable of acting politically with and from the image. The medium was also the place of political intervention, thus expressing the problem of a social emancipation of the image with respect to the dominant forms of cinematic creation and circulation. The questions that join these visual experiments are: How are politics possible from and in film without assuming a kind of propagandistic logic?

How can one translate the political transformation of '68 into the world of moving images?

In her classic *Avant-Garde, Internationalism, and Politics*, Andrea Giunta states that a novel feature of the relationship between art and politics in the 1960s should not be understood as the typical operation of the political avant-garde that uses art to transmit an already made message but that it instead resides in the possibility of converting art into a space of political experience.[6] This difference is important because it implies a desire to link art with a process of intervening in the world that is filmed. The strength of the work as a space that generates situations that unleash unforeseeable processes (the work as action-intervention) implies a destabilization of the supposed unquestioned unity of the work as a film and of the spectatorial situation that goes along with it. The majority of the productions of *superocheros* (Super 8 films) from Mexico, as well as those from other parts of the world, allow us to see that the productions are small interventions with multiple functions. These range from communicating struggles that occur in different areas through communiqués, to visualizing alienating spaces, or narrating and contextualizing specific strikes within a larger framework, and so on. The communiqués produced by the Cooperative of Marginal Cinema connected workers' struggles (strikes) that occurred in different parts of the country; *History of a Document* visualized the existence of a world that the state denied (the political prison). Just as we saw that the everyday emerged as a problematic point in the way of redefining freedom and the experience of the political in '68, it should be noted that it was in film more than literature that this same shift occurred, from the choice of technology (Super 8) and the subject matter. In this sense, the use of Super 8 is a tool that not only puts the movement into images but also implies a manifest form of political intervention of the image. This does not have to do with filming about, but rather with making a change of and in the image as a place of transformation of aesthetic habits. In short, it has to do with a shift not only in the type of cinema that begins to be prioritized within the political movement but also, and fundamentally, in the type of subjects that become its agents and mobilizers: anyone could use the Super 8 without much training. As we will see, small-gauge film facilitates the possibility that anyone can film, introducing a totally different type of production, use, and circulation of the image, which also modifies the meaning of the artistic work. Cooperatives, groups, and projects emerge that go beyond the notion of producing a "great film" and open another type of role for the image in connection to the everyday nature of the spaces, times, and subjects that become visible.

Through the development of a different cinema, a *desire* for emancipation is produced through artistic practice. The emergence of the political in these visual experiments is linked to the possibility of destabilizing and influencing the naturalized and hierarchical distribution of roles and functions; in this respect, we could say that the visual experiments that continue '68 constitute specific modes of emancipation that destabilize not only the logic of bodies and words but also the rules established by artistic practice itself, with its producers and spectators. Something that had begun in the work of the brigades and in the creative development of the movement emerges in the seventies in a very interesting way in the field of the image. Film becomes a place where this gesture of dislocation is explored and manifested in unusual ways. In one of the most complete volumes on France '68 in cinema, Amador Fernández-Savater and David Cortés say something that also explains the Mexican experience: "Cinema around May '68 is political not only because it documents, serves as a mouthpiece, or denounces situations of oppression or struggle, but rather because the conception, production, and circulation of the films appear magnetized, in their fracture, by the essential questions that the movement set forth: autonomy, overcoming social boundaries, the emergence of new subjectivities, the denial of all forms of representation (political, union, intellectual)."[7]

The decision that many cinema collectives make to use Super 8 facilitates one of the most innovative aspects of militant cinema, since it allows mobility in various senses: from the most literal, to move easily among sites, to the modification of roles in that anyone could learn to film in small gauge without cinematographic training. This makes it possible to use Super 8 to cut through different spaces of life that go from filming the daily life of the student movement in its marches, brigades, and meetings (material that makes the documentary *The Shout* possible) to the possibility of taking the camera to labor strikes to intervene in the struggle against the monopoly of unions and project what was filmed, and finally, the case of taking the Super 8 to the prison itself, in order to film a paradigmatic space of repression in the image. As in the factory, filming in the prison was not permitted, and Super 8 made it possible. One could think that just as '68 in Mexico is a great event against the monopolization of a type of politics that even today threatens everything that puts its power at risk, Super 8 filmmaking was the strategy that produced this critique from the image as a result of the high level of control and repression. This transformation that occurred in the field of the image is related to what had already begun to be questioned in the domain of Latin American cinema since the fifties and that, following the Cuban Revolution, acquired a singular force.

Super 8 in Mexico: Toward a Fourth Cinema

Let us now examine some specific ways of putting '68 into images. Within the modes of visualizing the Mexican '68, it seems that there were two fields: on the one hand, we find a series of films whose goal is to thematize '68 and, above all, the traumatic experience of the massacre. This category contains films that are disparate among themselves, such as *Red Dawn* (1989), directed by Jorge Fons; *Erase from Your Memory* (2011), directed by Alfredo Gurrola; *Tlatelolco: Summer of '68* (2012), directed by Carlos Bolado; and *Neither Forget Nor Forgive* (2004), directed by Richard Dindo.[8] On the other hand, there is the practice of visual experimentation generated in '68, which afterward keeps repeating this gesture: that is, not addressing '68 as a thematic object but rather expressing the transformation that '68 produced through cinema.[9] In this area, we find the multiplicity of projects on Super 8 that arose after Tlatelolco, and that became timely forms of continuing the movement amid the sensation of defeat left by mass repression and the massacre. Through publications and events, we can observe a growing interest in historicizing and narrating the history of the whole Super 8 circuit, a necessary task given the marginality and underground nature typical of small-gauge production, which makes access to the works difficult. Key texts that address this moment are the special "Superocheros" issue of the journal *Wide Angle* edited by Jesse Lerner in 1999; the compilation of texts about and from the cinematographic insurgency in the book *Independent Cinema, Where To?* published by the Mexican Association of Documentarians (Asociación de Documentalistas de México) in 2007; and most recently, Álvaro Vázquez Mantecón's book *The Super 8 in Mexico*, which represents the broadest study of the Super 8 experience given that it traces its history in the political and artistic field.[10]

Super 8 implies a before and an after in the articulation of cinema and politics insofar as it brings to cinema the change that had occurred in political organization during the intense climactic months of the student movement, operating almost like a translator for a fundamental concern: *how can the image modify the perceptibility of the political?* The small format became popularized in Mexico at the end of the sixties, above all for family use, given that it entered the market with the function of filming everyday scenes of the family in its private environment (a child's first steps, birthdays, etc.). As Jesse Lerner analyzes, even though Super 8 was introduced "as a middle-class hobby," it soon became an instrument of alternative cinema that countered the so-called new cinema that was financed by the state and semiprivate ventures with the idea of promoting a quality Mexican "new cinema." Nevertheless, by conferring the advantage of being able to make films in a simple way and without the filters of censorship, it became the most widely used technology in the development of young militant cinema. Its advantage was that, with its low cost and high accessibility, it offered a true alternative with which to create a new art, because its size enabled it to easily avoid the filters of police surveillance and censorship. Unlike other formats, Super 8 created a possibility that fit very well with the character of the moment: anyone could take the camera and learn how to use it quickly.

Coinciding with the state's attempt to create a new Mexican cinema capable of improving the quality of cinematic production, the Super 8 appeared in order to dismantle the fantasy of independence in film, first attacking the idea of quality cinema (something that went hand in hand with Julio García Espinosa's proposal of imperfect cinema).[11] Under the pretense of quality cinema, the supposedly independent cinema continued to depend on patterns imposed by the state.[12] It can be said that the terrain of the image expressed the same problem of independence and of the possibilities of political alternatives, given the monopoly on the idea of revolution that the PRI had established since the beginning of the century. At the same time, in the cinematographic field, the possibility of thinking of the image itself as the place where another politics is expressed implies a radical redefinition of the units of the practice: film work, director, spectator. As Sergio García mentions, a lot of proposals that included cooperative forms of filmmaking emerged in these years, such as the Cooperative of Marginal Cinema, the Cinematographic Workshop of the Casa del Lago, the Experimental Workshop of Cinema, the Popular Workshop of Experimental Cinema, the Workshop of Juárez University of the State of Durango, the Group 8 Filmmakers, and the Cinema 8 Video Cooperative, among others.[13]

In one of the few remaining records from the experience of the Cooperative of Marginal Cinema, "Toward a Political Cinema: The Cooperative of Marginal Cinema," José Carlos Méndez holds that the strategy of cooperative cinema in Super 8 gains strength after the demobilization of the student movement following the massacre. In the midst of this panorama, in 1971 the second contest of experimental film in 8mm was held, the theme of which was "Our Chief Problem" (the first contest's theme was "Our Country"). The proposals came from The Muses (Las Musas) group, composed of different artists and filmmakers such as Óscar Menéndez, Rubén Gámez, Víctor Fosado, Armando

Zayas, Juan de la Cabada, and Leopoldo Ayala. Along these lines, the relevance of Super 8 as a continuation of the movement of '68 by means of the image was attested to in the organization of the Second Contest of Experimental Cinema in 8mm in 1971, for which the Luis Buñuel prize for independent cinema was redefined and awarded in this format. The award situated the terrible "demobilization created after October 2" as the guiding theme. The contest was inspired by the idea of giving the tone of an alternative character to the notion of independent cinema. In July 1972 Méndez writes that this contest of experimental cinema in Super 8 format was put forward as an initiative to transform the idea of independent cinema. It was a form of protest against the film industry and the hypocrisy of the notion of independent cinema that was co-opted just as the workers' unions were.[14]

The majority of the proposals presented for the contest were linked to the experience of '68 from different perspectives, generating the environment in which experiences of cooperatives and workshops emerged, including the appearance of the Cooperative of Marginal Cinema, which tried to go against the notion of "auteurist cinema" in order to affirm the marginality of collective production. It is also relevant that taking the Luis Buñuel contest to small gauge was inspired by ideas that Óscar Menéndez had had during '68, because attempts to record acts of authoritarianism in larger formats were under constant persecution and investigation of the documentary materials. As part of the team of the University Center for Film Studies, led by Leobardo López, Menéndez used his 16mm camera and equipment to film the events comprising the protests of '68, exhibiting his materials in different places at the Polytechnic Institute (Instituto Politécnico), classrooms of the UNAM, and different schools. As repression, and with it the confiscation of materials, increased, he began to carry only a Super 8, which was easier to hide and use surreptitiously, insisting on the need to have a documentary record of images of the struggle and the massacres. In this way, it was possible to construct a foundation of images of different sequences from the massacre of Tlatelolco and, afterward, of life in Lecumberri Prison, where Menéndez smuggled in different Super 8 cameras and film so that the prisoners could film the continuation of '68 in the prison. According to Sergio García, this experience of clandestine filming is what "gave rise to the 8mm movement in Mexico" and what was then denominated the project-promise of a fourth cinema.[15] This project of a fourth cinema was proposed in close relation to the Super 8 experiments, because it was a simple and economical technique from which another cinematic language could be created, one differentiated from commercial cinema (named as first cinema), art cinema (second cinema), and political cinema (third cinema).[16] I will return to the idea of a fourth cinema linked to the continuation of '68 in the visual realm at the end of this chapter.

Even though the focal point of this proliferation of small-gauge images speaks to the essential role of counterinformation, there is also something more that this medium is introduced as a message and political action. We have a blurry image that introduces the everyday, with its nuances, compressing the images of the goings-on of the political organization (pamphlets, protests, marches in *The Shout*), the different forms of repression (images from the military interventions on centers of study, the Tlatelolco massacre, the Corpus Christi massacre, and so on), the tedium of the carceral everyday of *History of a Document*, or the day-to-day of the workers' strikes throughout the country (shown in the works of the Cooperative of Marginal Cinema that focused on the struggles for autonomy in the labor world). All this work of visualization of the everyday enables entering '68 from angles that were not just those that fit in with the official image, which reduced the movement to the historical punctuation of a strike that culminated in massacre. It also helps to shed light on other forms that the figure of the encounter took and that were registered in visual works, again, not understood as an "object"—that is, as a film *on* the encounter—but the encounter as that which made these works possible. As we will see, it is the encounter of students and workers that made the whole work of the Cooperative of Marginal Cinema possible, a process of working together that took the language of film as a communicative chain with multiple purposes; or, rather, forms of cooperation among prisoners as well as among artists and intellectuals from different countries constitute the encounter, as we will now see in the case of *History of a Document*.[17]

The Cooperative of Marginal Cinema

Among different collectives, I am interested in exploring the experience of the Cooperative of Marginal Cinema because it implies a form of approaching the demand for democracy that came from the student movement with the demand for union democracy that was systematically repressed in the labor world. That is, its interest in taking cinema to and making cinema in the labor world brings us one of the most relevant strands of the '68 moment: the notion of autonomy in organization (union democratization), the establishment of a large-scale struggle that the search for a common language involves, and the possibility of dislocating the order and logic of social places, questioning the role of art and opening a different form of experimenting with artistic practices.

Guadalupe Ferrer, then a student at the School of Sociology and Political Science, recalls that one day a colleague asked her if she wanted to participate in making a film.[18] In spite of the fact that she had never thought of making a film—although since childhood she had been a devoted fan of cinema—she joined the project. This experience explains a little bit about what the cooperative would later become: a form of making collectively, which is far from what was considered professional in the film world. With the participation of people who had different abilities, the initial group of the cooperative was formed by Gabriel Retes, José Carlos Méndez, Carlos de Hoyos and Paco Ignacio Taibo II, Víctor Sanén, Jorge Belarmino, Enrique Escalona and Eduardo Carrasco Zanini, Guadalupe Ferrer, and Paloma Sáiz.[19]

At the beginning of the seventies, the world of small-gauge film was born in an environment of experimental ambition, which was then directed to two fields: more artistic cinema or the possibility of a different political cinema. In keeping with the latter, the cooperative proposed a practice focused on the labor world, which involved multiple forms of doing: not only making films but also creating communiqués that could travel to different parts of the country, putting independent strikes in contact with one another, in addition to helping the striking workers to mimeograph leaflets, circulate them, and so on. As Ferrer tells it, everything began with the proposal that the *superocheros* would make to the striking workers, regardless of whether the strike was large or small: to play a film while on guard at night, followed by a discussion. The form in which they operated was truly collective: its materials for intervening in the labor world had neither the signature of an author nor an individual director; at the same time, Ferrer recalls that even if they did not have resources to leave cameras with the workers (as some similar groups in France could), the workers were the creators of their narrative or of the music or of the direction of the film.[20] As Méndez remembers,

> During this time, in the student milieu of Mexico City, mainly of high schools as well as in some universities of the provinces, it became commonplace to see the figure of the Cooperativa member carrying the projector, adapting it to the existing conditions to project on a sheet or on a wall, starting the debate which changed in its form and approach according to the audience. For example, a film such as *Jueves de Corpus* (*Corpus Christi*), on June 10, unaccomplished both in its form and content (as a political view of the facts), gave rise to different types and levels of discussion. In the Mexico City high schools, the emotional factor prevailed over the analysis. . . . In [workers'] circles, repression did not cause the

same astonishment, though this did not mean less indignation. . . . The debates largely depended on the level and experience of the Cooperativa member present, especially because the film itself, beyond the testimony, is limited in its elements, and to a great extent the questions posed lay outside its purview.[21]

Through these memories, we can observe that there is a total decentering of the unity and autonomy supposed by the work: the film operates as a bridge that connects experiences and as a trigger for situations (dialogues, discussions, commentaries). There is a decentering of the typical objective of finality in a film, since in the cooperative the dimension and framing of filmmaking was radically modified: the film starts from the moment in which there is a projection that generates dialogue, or in the case of processing language and script in step with the action of a strike, and so forth. After 1971, the cooperative began to produce the *Communiqués of Labor Insurgency*, which documented different union actions and strikes. Vázquez Mantecón notes that "their principle objective was to report on the efforts for union independence to different trade organizations of the country to establish the effectiveness of the movement."[22] The communiqués begin in December 1971, when a fight for union independence erupted in the Union of Electric Industry Workers of Mexico (Sindicato de Trabajadores Electricistas de la República Mexicana, STERM) after the corrupt (as usual) negotiation of the Confederation of Mexican Workers (Confederación de Trabajadores de México, CTM). After this moment, the cooperative decided to film the labor uprisings taking place in any part of the country. In this way, they are able to make around twenty communiqués, which, as Ayala Blanco argues, served to unify scattered fights for union independence throughout the country through the Super 8 cameras, "which recorded it, to later introduce it to other workers, peasants, and students who are potentially sympathetic to this fight, which is also theirs."[23]

Inspired by the *Communiqués of the National Strike Committee* (*Comunicados del Consejo Nacional de Huelga*) that Paul Leduc, Óscar Menéndez, and Leobardo López Aretche developed in '68, the function of the shorts and the communiqués responded to something more than the desire to produce information and record events. According to Ayala Blanco, these were put forward to record and impact an immediate present, to which we could add that they also operated as spaces of *putting into communication* different struggles through the image: both to communicate a situation and to place many situations on a *common plane*. As we will also see with regard to the elaboration of *History of a Document*, the image emerges as a bridge that puts into communication different situations, spaces, and people that were not only made invisible but also disconnected as a common experience. *Thus, in an almost immediate way, the image functioned to organize a common language of struggle that was able to trace the polyphonic language of the protests that resisted the union monopolies.* In this way, in very little time, the cooperative became a *transmitting and connecting chain* between small trade unions. As Ferrer recounts, at its highest point of action, up to seventy people participated in the cooperative, and the circulation of materials through different provinces caused experiences to begin to duplicate, an example of which was the creation of a section of the cooperative in Cuernavaca. At the same time, it also became a form of life in which many members lived communally in a house that was also a seat of operations for editing and postproduction.

Little remains of the materials produced by the cooperative, which in part expresses the functional character of the films as interventions in situations, as well as the marginal character they have in the history of cinema. In one of the few short films available, titled *Otro país* (*Another Country*) (1972), included in the selection of Super 8 films published on DVD and compiled by Vázquez Mantecón, we can observe the type of material produced by the cooperative. Made in conjunction with the Student Democratic Labor Front (Frente Democrático Obrero Estudiantil), *Another Country* expresses the desire to connect different struggles that allow us to see the same dynamic of the cooperative in action: strikes in Monterrey and Nuevo León, which share the space of a short and visualize a fight for union democratization that had always been marginalized and repressed. The short is divided into various sections regulated by the calendar. We begin with "the morning of November 20" in Monterrey, when an official parade in which the governor is participating is interrupted and transformed into a demonstration. In the midst of the typical little Mexican flags of the official parade, a voice-over gives a colloquial explanation of the action that students, workers, teachers, and residents from the neighborhood kept on joining, in addition to the reaction of many people in the street clapping in time, leaving Governor Luis M. Farías in silence. To the succession of signs held by marching students and workers, another marker of time follows; we move to another area the same day: "the afternoon of November 20 in Topo Chico." What follows are images of the working-class neighborhood of Topo Chico in its everyday routine. A voice-over describes the episodic history of how inhabitants took the lands in order to live in "a part of what was left over from the owners of the country" (*una parte de los que les sobró a los dueños del país*). To the rhythm of images of the terrain in Topo Chico, we listen to a story that reiterates the continuous expropriation that the population has suffered in its history: "This is not the first time; before, there were other plots of land but the police kicked us out." To the repetition of this cycle of struggling to have a place, a right to their land, and the police repression that expropriates it, there is a kind of accompanying *ritornello*, which declares "But we stay here."

After this, we move to the next day: "November 21. The Dead of the Foundry." Constant expropriation of the land is followed by the precariousness in which bodies live at work. This part is about the funeral of workers who died in accidents in the steel factory. Images of people carrying wreaths of flowers appear on screen, and it is explained that the steel factory workers died because of the intransigence of the owners, who let them die "so that money could keep flowing into the coffers of Monterrey's oligarchy." The pain of the constant death of workers and the funeral ritual underway in this particular case fits within a demand for the right to live and work with dignity. The images show us the encounter of the workers and their families where the homage to the dead is accomplished from political action: they hand out leaflets, they outline readings, and they wonder: "How many more will have to die in this absurdity? How many more, goddammit?" From here, two sections follow that are much shorter than the rest. "The Morning of November 24: The Old Flags of the CTM" shows the sign for "La Victoria Sawmill Co.," while the voice of a woman announces that the flags of the CTM are old, thereby denouncing the systematic betrayal of strikes and stating that "new flags" must arrive. Next, we move to "The Afternoon of November 23: Colonia Díaz Ordaz. October 2nd Group," in which the camera eventually stops on the flag of the "Independent Front of Popular Organizations. October 2nd Group, San Nicolas, Nuevo León," surrounded by humble people who look at the camera, as if posing in a family portrait, without moving. The group portrait is followed by a panorama of the settlement and the precariousness of the housing and the neighborhood—a precariousness that at moments is also expressed in the filming, with typical scratches that continuously interrupt the small-gauge image. The name of the neighborhood, "Colonia Díaz Ordaz," followed by the name of the group, traces a struggle through language, as people show their repudiation of the Tlatelolco massacre orchestrated by Díaz Ordaz. By playing with the names, a tension between the author of the massacre and the "October 2nd Group" is visualized and continued from the space of a settlement that is constantly massacred. From here we move to "The Morning of November 24: Bakery Strike," which again connects to the issue of the co-optation of the strikes by CTM leaders. The Revolutionary Confederation of Workers and Farmers (Confederación Revolucionaria de Obreros y Campesinos, CROC) strike of the Nopal Industrial Bakery is filmed and the voice-over offers to relate this strike "exactly as they told it to me," commenting on the effort that this involved and the betrayal of the CTM, which ended the strike in exchange for five thousand pesos, which it divided among its leaders. Here, the short ends, somewhat abruptly.

This material serves as an example of the role played by the Super 8 cinematic intervention: to put all the struggles in the same space, juxtaposing the problem of land, of the life and death of the workers, and of the union co-optation that the system of inequality reproduces with the fraud in which the union leaders surrender for a little money. The counterpoint that the images and texts outline from their precariousness makes visible an entire world that had been marginalized from the realm of images: this is "another country" that exists and whose visualization opens up another order of the sensible. Almost expressing the crucial problem of political autonomy that started '68 in a country monopolized in word, image, and body by the PRI, this short leaves us with a question that had also emerged in the work of Revueltas: how is a struggle amid cyclical repressive blockage possible? The images connect different attempts, visualizing a common desire that runs through different geographies—the desire for a life with dignity. Both the precariousness of production and the role played by showing films in order to discuss them as a group express a different type of aesthetics that replies to the problem analyzed earlier with regard to university self-management through an emphasis on the process, more than on the ennoblement of the value of the film as a closed product. In this short, it seems as if the strike, which connects all the different struggles, leaned over the institution of art itself, resulting in an art based on the interruption of the contemplative enjoyment of the viewer. At the same time, by moving the image to an environment in which it participates, this experience of doing cinema transforms the relationship between work and action into part of a single process of intervention. The camera and image functioned as communicators of experiences and facilitators of a common language. In this sense, cinema became a medium for continuing the cognitive democracy sparked by the student movement of '68.

The question that the conceptualization of self-management sustains in Revueltas emerges in the cinematographic field in a similar form: to be able to conceive a type of production and circulation of films able to disalienate the senses from the sensation of the spectacular and private enjoyment. In the shorts and communiqués, the value of the material would seem to come from the experience itself that was involved in the possibility of creating the work to be watched. That is, its value stemmed from the connection that was established among students and workers and the visualization of an entire world that had been made invisible in the official visual narrative, because they had to do with small or large unions that confronted the co-optation of the CTM. The collaborative form of preparing communiqués or films expressed the singular event of together doing something that, for a brief period of time, opened the possibility of weaving a common language. The work became a site or place for the communication of a repressed language, and the striking workers became actors and narrators of their own situation in such a way that the experience of their political struggle itself also became a different process of apprenticeship. At the same time, this impure experience of practice and art as place of encounter, among people who would not otherwise meet, lasted for a limited time. As Ferrer explains, a first break in the cooperative began when some of the members decided to leave the group in order to make more traditional cinema, given that the artistic cinematic component had been waning while support of and participation with the labor movement was gaining predominance. On the other hand, after so many years, the experience of filmmaking began to be displaced by the experience of truly political militancy. In this collaboration, the needs of the labor struggle relegated aesthetic experience on the plane of enjoyment to a lesser position, given the urgency of the situation. In an interview with Vázquez Mantecón, Ferrer explains: "One of the things that led us to abandon cinema a little and to finish with much more direct support was that people said to you 'yes, well, we already saw a bunch of films, and you even filmed us, but we need more help, help us . . .' Why don't you stay with us? Why don't you make us a leaflet? Why don't you take us to see a lawyer? Why don't you come with us to the meeting?"[24] We can see here that a closure occurs that culminates in the heterogeneous practice of politics-cinema but in a way that is different from what happened in the project of the Liberation Cinema Group, in which the struggle of cinema became a medium for transmitting the party's message (a point I will return to later). What happened here is that cinema stopped being a useful tool for the workers' struggle because other tools, which the students could facilitate, were needed—access to lawyers, petitioning to be heard in meetings, instruction on how to use mimeographs for producing leaflets, and so on. Something similar happened in the experience at Topilejo, where the students began to participate using the kinds of knowledge that were needed and that enabled them to contribute, so that the voice of those who never counted before could be heard. Years after the pinnacle actions of '68, and throughout the cinematic field, a form of trust and connection developed between people who had no other link.

The nonspecificity of a collective form of art seemed to have operated in that time as a kind of scaffolding: it connected political struggles, it built a form of trust, and the pleasure of students and workers learning together was possible, but it became unnecessary after a time when the artwork and the process of learning was put aside. For the group of students and participants, the experience of this nonspecific cinema as art also seemed to have created a suspension of the established order, of the place occupied in society, *a kind of strike in the system of roles and social functions*. Something of this was proposed in the spirit of the cooperative, with its interest in problematizing the role of cinema at its core, its social function, and its possibility to be a tool of action far from the experience of spectatorship. One of the communiqués says: "We learned that cinema is beyond the camera. It is exactly on the screen and in the debate. And together with our people, we continue learning what this cinema can serve to do. *We are not artists* (Cooperative of Marginal Cinema, February 1973)."[25]

Now, where does this leave us? The sixties express this pattern in the field of the new intellectual artistic and political avant-garde: a moment of experimentation that has a specific duration. However, to look at this and see failure would be to impose on innovative experiences a nearly neoliberal logic of success and failure. As we saw in the case of Revueltas, a distinctive character of the experience of disalienating freedom is that it cannot be conceived as a permanent or constant attribute but rather as temporary, episodic, and heterogeneous to the time of the clock and the calendar of history. We return here to the same problem that we confronted in the previous chapter with regard to the duration of these experimental practices of freedom and the type of transformation that it entailed in the lives of many people and groups. This kind of experience becomes incalculable with regard to the usual patterns for measuring political success in multiparty and numerical democracies: winning an election, having the majority of votes, and so forth. To give an example of this, I offer the image of a memory that Ferrer shares about the notion of failure in the labor strikes and the reflection about this that the bakers made in the film *Con la venda en los ojos* (*With Blindfolded Eyes*), one of the films that she recalled as the most intense and beautiful in the experience of the cooperative, whose reels were lost. *With Blindfolded Eyes* was made with the workers from the striking industrial bakery, who created the script and music, as well as the report of the conflict. Ferrer says that defeat of their strike emerged as an issue at the end of the film, when two workers were walking and talking about the experience.

"Hey, we lost . . ."
"Well, yeah . . ."
"So, what good did any of this do?"
"What do you mean what good did any of this do? The blindfold fell from our eyes."[26]

The blindfolded eyes that can begin to see do so through the singular experience of a strike that was also an artistic experience of learning. Undoubtedly this final dialogue again affirms a transformative component of the experience, where liberation cannot be measured by terms of gain or loss, nor in terms of property (a possession won), but rather as the intensity of an experience that cannot last forever. When approaching the image as a site for political action, the complexity lay in the fact that freedom is expressed as an intervention in the political itself—in the act of those people who are not assumed to have a right to design or modify the order of the visible and enunciable, and who dare to do so, thereby modifying the experience of democratic participation in the distribution of equalities and inequalities itself. This process, in which students and workers unite in order to make visible this field of those who have no part in what we see socially, refers not only to the type of revolution that involves workers who, lacking access to art, are usually seen as not competent to intervene (in this case, in cinema). It also refers to the students themselves who, instead of profiting with their films for their future careers, unleash an entire cooperative process of redefining the practice.

The political emerges *in and from* the field of the image through the destabilization and opening of another field of vision and discourse. That is to say, the capacity that the political occasions in art would not reside in the more traditional idea of militancy as "transmission" of a message in which art would be an unquestioned medium but rather refers to the capacity to transform experience through its roles and places. By producing a rupture with the idea of art as a sphere separate from political life, this reorganization of the common influences the question about the institutionalism itself of art, its specificity as practice. Here, a political event in art or an artistic event in the political is produced: instead of shutting oneself away to make their work, artists go out to encounter a specific situation, connect their work with the work of nonartists, and this encounter produces a singular experience in the production of a work. A film that generates a dialogue is transmitted and leads to the question about the possibility of filming the strike, while students begin to participate politically through the production of bulletins, circulation, and so on. In a way, everyone "does" everything—the division between spheres is suspended and the strike becomes a space for producing innovative practices. According to this dynamic, the type of work that is done varies, since it can be a communiqué that will circulate through other states and will work as a space for building a common language of alternative strikes, or it can be a short that participates in the political struggle as a pretext to generate a common language, a common music.

In the case of the Cooperative of Marginal Cinema, the situation was the strike of workers who sought what the university strike and the rail workers' movement also sought: a form of dissidence that distanced them from the unions co-opted by the parties. Once this encounter was produced, they began to work together at a basic level, which consists of sharing abilities: from teaching others how to use a mimeograph, to filming communiqués that connected the strikes, or filming a short in which the striking workers themselves became creators of the script, music, and message. The particular situation of each group or action (each strike) emerges as a singular instance from which a resonance is created with respect to other instances that form a political struggle of the twentieth century. What becomes difficult to analyze is how this instance of democratization of the practices in which the political erupts as destabilization can only last *a short and intense, determined period*. In almost all the experiences of militant cinema, this political and aesthetic opening (aperture) is followed by a form of specialization: the artist becomes strictly militant, the worker returns to the factory, the student returns to class. This return to the situation that had been interrupted, whether the return to the purely artistic field or to militancy in a party or union, puts us before an unanswered question at the moment of theorizing these great historic events that last so little time and that, nevertheless, following the idea of the theoretical act, operate as fundamental instances for understanding a historicity always erased by the logic of the state and the market. What happens is that the universe of dissensus that suspends the typical forms of inhabiting the political disappears, replaced by a common sense in which practices follow a course of specificity more than experimentation. The freedom that this incommensurable instant generates for the usual logic of social (re)production—the fact of breaking the barriers of places and specificities, the freedom of inhabiting differently the common as that is permanently becoming—cannot be transformed into a permanent way of life.

It could be stated that the impossibility of maintaining the heterogeneity of the sensible that characterizes the moment of opening and the ambiguity over what art is speaks to a triumph of the logic of work, of the capture of the idea of a politics that moves as a goal, as a telos. After all, the road that many militants followed was to leave their lives as students or artists to go live in the workers' neighborhoods, to enter into the world of the factory and organize it, which implies abandoning this intoxication between art and politics, between strike and film, to decide to enter a form of politics that is more definite and less ambiguous, both at the level of finality and at the level of temporality.[27] As we saw earlier, the heterogeneous experience of an impure art gives way to merely political activity, as if time could no longer be wasted with the impurity or ambiguity of art given the urgency of managing a different union structure. We might think that this crucial problem of politics after '68 would again confront us with the core of the account of '68 that is perhaps most complete: *El apando* and its honest question about how we can address freedom in an alienated society that forms it, that thinks about it, that seeks it. In this return to a more defined politics, does that crucial component of self-management as an instance of nonspecialization dissolve? That is, does the fight against the technocracy of a society of specialists and professionals at different levels (university, artistic, political, unionist) disappear? The key that we can set forth as a strategy of analysis is to be able to rescue these episodic images of freedom, which speak to a certain effort to disalienate the way in which types of knowledge and struggle are compartmentalized in society. At the same time, the key to freedom as a process and not as a goal-ideal brings up the core of the philosophy that Revueltas proposed in the "theoretical act," in that it demands that we are able to address these instances of freedom without projecting on them the notion of achieving an end. For this reason, to say that the experience of militant cinema failed because it was temporally limited would almost be a myopic evaluation, given that it would project the idea of freedom as an eternal achievement.

Filming the Invisible: History of a Document

History of a Document is a work that also achieves the gesture of opening and dislocation that we saw earlier, but now in the prison, where the prisoners visualize the everyday routine of life there and write the script to accompany it—a script that exits the prison in order to spatialize it as *history.* The project, which was carried out in 1970 and completed a year later, takes Revueltas's idea of the prison as a situation and as a symbol of a *society-prison* to the visual realm. In *History of a Document,* images move from between the cells and the situation of prison to the history of the struggles for union democratization and the persistent repression of those struggles. This is something that is expressed in the history itself of Lecumberri Prison, which housed those who were systematically repressed for participating in those struggles. I have chosen to analyze this work for various reasons. On the one hand, it is a documentary that is remembered as an essential component marking a beginning in the practice of Super 8 cinema in Mexico in relation to '68, together with *The Shout* by Leobardo López. On the other hand, it carries out an important dislocation that was central to the use of small-gauge film as a visual weapon of '68: taking the camera to places that historically remained outside the horizon of the filmable—the prison. In this way, it was a gesture similar to that of the workers' cinema cooperatives in France, above all the Medvedkine group, which carried out their work within the factories, where, as inside the prisons, filming was forbidden.

These spaces change the form of construction of the work given that the act of filming was carried out clandestinely, thus converting space itself (its prohibited visualization) into a central axis of the material. By being situated in these spaces that are denied by the social gaze, the image becomes a form of expressing and reflecting on sites and situations within the order of the sensible that excludes them. In this context, something different is produced; the situation of filming itself becomes an essential part of the film that speaks to what is socially accepted and tolerated as an "object" of cinema, as an image "passable" to enter the cinematographic sphere, producing a different way of looking at the idea of artwork and of characters. Therefore, *History of a Document* refers to a double gesture. On the one hand, it visualizes what official language left clandestine, that is, the existence of political prisoners who had been erased from the sphere of the public after the Tlatelolco massacre and Díaz Ordaz's official declaration that there were no political prisoners in Mexico. On the other hand, it creates a film-document that intervenes or interrupts the official realm of the visible, visualizing that which had been denied. Nevertheless, just as in the works of the Cooperative of Marginal Cinema, the purpose was not to show victim-subjects; by participating in the creation of the film itself, workers and prisoners intervened in this interruption of the order of the visible in an active and transformative way: they resisted through the image. In *History of a Document*, it is the prisoners themselves from within the prison who make us look differently at the outside that we are inhabiting, by proposing—as one of its prisoners, Revueltas, had done—a metonymical way of looking at the prison as the social whole. What becomes visible from the prison? In what way does the film make us think of the prison as a situation and a social diagram?

History of a Document was directed by Óscar Menéndez from outside Lecumberri with material recorded mostly within it. The project emerged as a visual experiment that aimed to document the invisibilized zones that continued the movement after the Tlatelolco massacre, above all in the moment of the political prisoners' hunger strike in Lecumberri.[28] The idea consisted of taking Super 8 cameras to the prison and filming the everyday world of the political prisoners. In an interview, Menéndez says, "The massacre leaves us traumatized but we think of the comrades who are in the prisons. The only way to say 'alright, they are there' was to make a film."[29] To do this, during their visits, the prisoners began learning, in theory, how to use a Super 8 camera—in theory because cameras were not allowed. Over the course of several months, the visits functioned as training workshops, in which the prisoners learned the necessary tools to begin to film. After three months, they were able to smuggle in cameras during the women's visits, and filming began. Menéndez says in the same interview: "It was the best kept secret in the prison; two hundred people from the movement knew that they were making a film and no one said anything. In a hostile environment, nobody informed on them." There were also prisoners who had begun to write the text that would go with the images. Thus, the film begins explaining that "in prison, political prisoners learn that the government will not allow the practice of democratic freedoms and rights, but rather the people should struggle in order to obtain their own independence in order to achieve democracy. So, we had to *tear out of the prison the voice and the image* of these men: students, workers, researchers, employees, professors, peasants, unionists."[30] The idea of "tear[ing] out of the prison the voice and the image" of those who had been silenced sets forth, from the beginning, the role of the work as an intervention in the discursive and visual field. After filming multiple rolls, and as the situation became more dangerous, the struggle to remove the material from the prison began. Once outside, the rolls were taken to be developed as though they were videos of weddings and birthdays, in this way attempting to avoid them being seen and censored. According to Menéndez, the film helped to remind people what was still happening politically and also made many students begin to go to the prison again to visit the prisoners. As with the communiqués of the cooperative, this intervention did not just serve to "record" a situation, making it visible, but worked as a communicative bridge connecting the inside and outside of the prison.

Once the filming stage finished, the second part of the story began, and it did not lack epic details: Menéndez traveled to England with the materials in a suitcase, but it was still difficult to find places that had the technology to transfer Super 8 to 16mm. He traveled to Italy, where all the materials were seized, and he fell into a depression given that everything that had been achieved was confiscated by Italian customs. The filmmaker Renzo Rossellini helped Menéndez, giving him support and housing and intervening in customs, saying that they were materials intended for Rossellini himself. Once the reels were recovered, Menéndez traveled to Paris, where with Sartre's support, they contacted the director of the "Recherche," who liked the idea for the project because it used film as a means to communicate with people who could not be reached. Menéndez recalls that the director had created a clandestine radio for the Maquis in their resistance against the Nazis, and he expressed his solidarity with the project, but months passed and there was no news or money—"we went hungry." After a time, they were informed that a special working group called Groupe de Recherches Technologiques—Atelier d'expérimentation Super 8 would be formed and would be dedicated to the conversion of the Super 8 film reels so that they could be broadcast by the Office de Radiodiffusion-Télévision Française (ORTF). It was then a joint French-Mexican effort, which would also edit and copy the material. The context of works that the Recherche put out that year went along with the themes of the new material, since of the four films made that year, the other three were about Vietnam, the Indochina War, and Algeria. The collaboration and the urgency of the specific situation (to get the material out of the country and disseminate it outside Mexico) was sealed in the bilingual form of the work, since the voice-over accompanying the images speaks in French, to which Spanish subtitles were later added. Making the script was a problem since the French participants in the project wanted recognizable writers like Octavio Paz or Carlos Fuentes to do the narration, but Menéndez recalls that his group refused this because they believed that the script should come from the prisoners themselves. The writer Rodolfo Alcaraz convinced the French and served as the scriptwriter who narrates the images in French. Once this stage was completed, the problem was then broadcasting the film, with which another detail in the epic arose: the prisoners in Mexico had given Menéndez letters for Sartre, who spoke with people from the ORTF in order to support the documentary. *History of a Document* (referred to in the archives by the French title, *Histoire d'un document*) was slated for broadcast on Channel 1 on July 23, 1971. Having begun with clandestine filming, now a hundred million people throughout Europe would be able to see the film. Researching in the broadcast records of the ORTF in the Inathèque in Paris, one can see the file card that verified the film's future broadcast, while the reason that it was never actually put on air remains unknown. The act of censorship from Mexico is kept outside the records, which only verifies the fact that it was going to be transmitted July 23, 1971, and after this date, the records show that it was not (there is no confirmation of broadcast). In spite of this, in a symbolic way the documentary had its release in France, at the Recherche office, with functionaries and members of the French intelligentsia, and later it was clandestinely broadcast in Mexico. Clandestine once again, the film returned to Latin America with Óscar Menéndez, who tried to show it in Chile, where the Spanish subtitles were added, but the possibility of broadcast does not take hold, given that Salvador Allende's government had good diplomatic relations with Luis Echeverría's government. The whole struggle that made this documentary possible allows us to visualize a political and cultural map of the moment, one in which the weight of censorship also marks the importance that some fifty minutes of images were able to have.

History of a Document was an urgent attempt to make visible the political character of what was denied at the official level. By saying that in Mexico there were no political prisoners, the president was making a statement whose ambiguity was alarming. On the one hand, it was a naturalization of state authoritarianism and an invisibilization of the imprisonment of dissidents and activists. On the other hand, this same statement criminalized dissidents and activists given that the phrase can be read as "there are no political prisoners" only "common criminals" because dissidence was itself naturalized as a crime against the ownership of language and a way of understanding politics. In this moment, the struggle became how to visualize in language and image what the state made invisible, to make visible the inappropriate, which in the state's distribution did not count as political, and to illustrate from there an entire layer of history that, likewise, had been denied and made invisible. This is the framework of almost the entire first part of the text of the film, which begins by invoking the censorship of the material we are watching. At the beginning of the documentary itself, we are informed that the film that we are going to see and that had been a struggle to make because of censorship remained censored for three decades: "The editing of this film was possible in 1971 thanks to the support and solidarity of French Television [ORTF]. Nevertheless, due to diplomatic demands made by Luis Echeverría, then the president of Mexico, the television broadcast in France that had been promised was forbidden. We trust that now, after 33 years of condemnation, it will now be freed. We will never forget October 2nd!"[31] Right after, the camera passes through a row of cells until we arrive at the central tower of the Panopticon, which, because of the perspective from which it is filmed, is presented in a disproportionate size in comparison to the rest. The image of surveillance serves as a counterpoint to the text that explains the clandestine character of the work:

PRETRIAL PRISON OF MEXICO, MAY 1970
(PRISIÓN PREVENTIVA DE MÉXICO, MAYO DE 1970)
We are in the pretrial prison of Mexico City. In May 1970, we began clandestine filming, whose results would be this exceptional documentary: the political prisoners film themselves.

From the tower, we move again to the series or row of cells from the next corridor, where nothing more is seen than the door with the small closed window (through which food can be passed). While the camera travels through the prison—showing the rows of cells, the bars, and the security operating from the tower, the roofs and the patios of the cellblocks—the drama of how the film was carried out is added. The space is supplemented by the explanation of the process of making the film: "How do we get a camera into this prison? How to get past the surveillance of the guards? How many and which of the prisoners could film? How to teach them to use a film camera? How, where, what?"[32] The script does not connect to what we see in an explanatory or descriptive sense but rather it connects to the operational drama that was faced in order to make the film. The space is described through discussing how to modify its function: in the midst of a Panopticon, how does one slip past security? The only instant in which text and image coincide in their descriptive character is when for the first time a thread appears that will be observed in many images, like a line that divides the image in two: it is part of the clothing of the prisoner who carries the camera hidden in his clothes: "This thread that appears is a testimony of the obstacles that had to be overcome." The persistent appearance of the thread interrupts the homogenous vision of the image and robs us of our condition as passive viewers and, perhaps, of our expectation as viewers. It fissures the image, doubling the gaze that, in addition to seeing the scene, makes us see the thread of the clothes of the prisoner who carries the hidden camera. This interruption makes the image become expressive of its condition, and prompts us to think of the conditions of (im)possibility in which art can be made in the prison, operating as a reminder of the condition of the prisoner.

The visual documents that comprise *History of a Document* generate a collage of different image-fragments composed of scenes filmed by the prisoners within the prison, as well as of takes shot by those who were outside. It should be noted that those on the outside were also filming in precarious, clandestine conditions, thus introducing the idea of a population that was also imprisoned, but outside the prison. This summarizes the contrast between the two optical regimes that comprise almost the whole film: that of the architectonic complex of the Panopticon (the tower, the walls) and that of the creation of the image within the cellblock that shows us everything at too close a distance, in moments, crossed by the thread that traverses the image and the fissure. The images of the outside (taken from outside the prison) and the images from inside (with the thread and the lack of definition) produce a contrast between the more encompassing gaze that communicates spaces (it takes us to the cells, the tower, Mexico City) and the other image that makes it almost impossible to define what is being seen and expresses the difficulty itself of the condition of creating this image that we see: the clandestine nature of filming within the prison.

The documentary not only proposes a visualization of the figure of the political prisoner that was made invisible by the presidential-state language following the Tlatelolco massacre; it also incorporates political imprisonment into a broader history of criminalization of political dissidence. The first part of the film is the pure visual form of the spatialization of power through architecture. As only rarely occurs in the cinematic world, what we see is pure architecture functioning as a form of expressing control: cells, bars, surveillance tower, guards. This part is continued in the first scene outside the prison and the capital city, passing though rings of poverty, and arriving at the peasant world where the failure of agrarian reform is narrated, as is the misery of the peasantry and the end of their struggle with the murder of peasant leader Rubén Jaramillo and his family in 1962. In order to visualize the architectonics of a century of political history that reiterates a cycle of dissidence-massacre-prison, the team working on the outside takes the camera (also clandestinely) out of the prison, and uses images that show the repetition of the history of dissidents, histories that all end in this prison (peasantry, railway workers, students). A series of photographs is introduced that shows murdered bodies that outline the history of the accumulation of capital in which the peasant's only option is to abandon the land to emigrate "to sell himself in the United States or in the big cities. The absolute control of the unions is fundamental for the continuity of the State apparatus and to protect the interests of foreign investors, particularly Americans." This entire interlude of historicization, narrating history from 1957 to 1968, upsets the expectation created at the beginning of the documentary: that the crux of the documentary is the possibility of expressing the prisoners' situation, requiring them to film their situation *from inside* the prison. Nevertheless, after establishing the contrast between the central tower and the cells, the view of Lecumberri is "taken away" from us; we are taken to "see" a history that only at the end seems to create a visual document (perhaps the first) of this prison as the end of the blockage of state authoritarianism. In an almost cyclical form, it shows a history of the reproduction of a mechanism that criminalizes protest against the state monopoly of dissidence. Thus, images become the site for connecting a history of political struggles that had taken place throughout time, all of which were systematically imprisoned at Lecumberri. The camera flies away from the prison and visualizes a history of struggles that take us back to the same place. As in the shorts made by the Co-operative of Marginal Cinema, the image works as a bridge that puts together fragments of a history of active resistance against different forms of monopoly. In *History of a Document*, this is made visible from another angle, one facilitated by the Lecumberri Prison, where the visual history of the movement is expressed by means of a long-term memory of struggles and repression.[33] The film-document represents an estrangement from what is officially held in common through the play of its visual field—its spatialization of history, its temporality drawn from the accumulation of histories of liberation that are censored and repressed.

Images become the site for multiple connections among different territories and temporalities: the struggles from 1957 to 1970 operate as a form of historicizing the prison since all the dissidents were deposited in it. This visual document makes us think about this architectonic as a diagram of the politics of the century, almost metonymically taking the prison to the society kept under surveillance by this tower every time this political technology is questioned or problematized. Nevertheless, this passage that takes us from the prison to an open carceral society is also problematized by the image itself in its constitution, given that the scenes produced inside the cells are fissured and fragmented in a way that the images from the outside are not. The counterpoint with which the documentary begins—which takes us inside the bars, the cells, and the central tower's supervision ideal of the Panopticon—doubles itself in the narrative that structures the documentary of a history of struggles that have been kept under surveillance or erased in the official narrative. All these struggles recurrently lead to the same space, the bars of Lecumberri, in each decade of the century, as if the prison were a funnel in which the state's repression and impunity ends.

In a modest form, the documentary experiments with visualizing a history of political movements resisting state (PRI) monopoly from one space: the prison. The narrative of the peasant struggles of 1957 and their culmination in the Tlatelolco massacre, which appears in speech but not in images, returns to Lecumberri, but in silence, again establishing a contrast or discrepancy between what we see and what we are told, between the visualization generated by speech and the mute visualization brought by the return to prison—a black hole in which the state resolves the demands for social justice. The return to the prison is made with images that pass by rapidly, as if from a train, through the bars that separate the inside and the sky, arriving at Cellblock C, where the political prisoners were held. We can see the faces of some prisoners who walk through the cramped space, and a prisoner appears writing in chalk on the floor: "Here Mexico" (*Aquí México*), the title of the documentary that would recycle images from *History of a Document*. This is *History*'s script: to visualize the architectonics of a century of political history that reiterates the cycles of dissidence-massacre-imprisonment—a document about the condition of possibility of the history of the Mexican state, made by those who were its condition of impossibility, its invisibilized source of discomfort, the struggles that were looking for an outside.

It should be noted that the contrast made between prison and the outside refers to the Olympic Games and the 1970 elections when the presidency was won by Luis Echeverría, who had been the Interior Minister and gave the order for the October 2 massacre. While this information is given in a voice-over, a prisoner films one of the doors that we have seen throughout the film, but now with its window open. Political prisoners pass by the window, and we see only their faces framed by the window's edges. This creates the shape of the civil identification card, the photo that matches and registers citizens, now framed by the door of the cell, juxtaposing the idea of similarity between citizen and prisoner and again opening the question about the political freedom of the citizenry when the status of political prisoner is erased from the ambiguity of this framing (the bars). Simultaneously, in addition to the earlier contrast of the bars and sky, now the bars are shown to us as a shadow reflected on the floor, and from there we see another graffiti: *Freedom*, inscribed on the wall of the prison, ends the film.

In *History of a Document*, there is a double articulation of the image from which we can define the polyvocal sense of the word *document* in the title (in place of *documentary*, which is what the work is). On the one hand, the image operates in the sense that Roland Barthes accorded to the photographic image in his classic *Camera Lucida:* it certifies an existence (in the case of *History*, one that was systematically invisibilized by the state).[34] In this act of certification, something else emerges that opens up a way of thinking about art and history that have to do with the gaps between the histories recorded on the bodies and spaces that were filmed and the discourse that attempts to explain it through a sequence that shows the architectonics of a century composed by the almost cyclical recurrence of dissidence-repression, struggle-massacre. On the other hand, the existence of this film itself works as a certificate of collective acts of resistance, which expresses the possibility of a flight from the spatial and optical system embodied by the Panopticon as a spatial and optical system of power. The film embodies a collective desire located in the cracks of such ideals and opens up a different visualization of the space, communicating a powerful message as it smashes one of the most subtle assumptions of the carceral imagination that gave rise to the Panopticon as a technology of power: the introjection of the system of control on which the whole system is based. It is the idea that Foucault emphasizes in his classic *Discipline and Punish* regarding the novelty of this technology of power in which forms of subjection are produced by an architectural and optical situation: "He who is subjected to a field of visibility, and who knows it, assumes responsibility for the constraints of power; he makes them play spontaneously upon himself; he inscribes in himself the power relation in which he simultaneously plays both roles; he becomes the principle of his own subjection."[35] In *History*, from the very start, this principle is interrupted as the goal is to collectively film the inside without being caught by surveillance, thus assuming that the ideal of absolute control does not work as such. There are moments of the film that express this in visual terms, as happens when we see the all-seeing surveillance tower of the Panopticon in an image taken clandestinely by the hidden camera that the prisoner wears in his clothes; or, when we see the image of the armed prison guards surveilling the prison and listen to an off-screen voice saying, "How can we get past the surveillance guards?" In both moments, the images of surveillance that we see had been taken clandestinely with the camera hidden in clothes, showing a form of acting from within the blind spots of the panoptic dream of total control. Itself a certificate of collective resistance against a prison-state, the film produces a double effect. On the one hand, it awakens us to a social diagram that comprises a history of cycles of resistance-massacre-imprisonment. On the other hand, it provokes a sense of spatial and temporal claustrophobia, while it challenges us to search for an alternative form of seeing and experiencing the political. However, this is not posed in terms of a "recipe" for a different political regime but in the form in which the camera operates, from the interstices where this project was made possible.

This form of visual resistance connects with the idea that lay at the center of García's proposal to conceptualize Super 8 experiments in Mexico as a path *toward* a fourth cinema. As I mentioned earlier, this was a form of envisioning an artistic intervention that did not work in terms of a political indoctrination but as a form of awakening. It was also an explicit commentary on the destiny of some forms of third cinema and a desire for a different form of visual intervention. Before moving onto a conclusion, I will briefly analyze the proposal of a fourth cinema within broader history and map multiple forms of articulating the liberation of the image in Latin America at this moment.

Positions in Militant Cinema:
Cinema and Liberation in Latin America

We have seen that '68 is a fundamental moment of reflection and variation in Latin American cinema, proposing the problem of liberation and dependency, and debating questions connected to a series of proposals that had begun at the end of the fifties within the map of what is called "new Latin American cinema." The "new cinema" emerged as an alternative to the empire of Hollywood and as a form of articulating a new cinematographic language able to tie in with a larger process of liberation and disalienation. As Javier de Taboada explains, "new Latin American cinema" begins to be called "third cinema" when it becomes internationalized as a form that is tied not only to Latin America but also to everything called "Third World" in that moment.[36] Ramón Gil Olivo finds that a shared concern for different vertices of new cinema in Bolivia, Brazil, Argentina, or Chile comes from a desire to create a language that gets close to people: "Confronted with a cinema that backs, hides, or maintains a moralizing attitude about the conditions of overexploitation, what is necessary is a cinema that immerses itself in reality, that expresses the miseries of the real man, and that, in short, speaks in their same language, beginning, as Jorge Sanjinés affirms, by denouncing the mechanisms of their oppression."[37] Within this context, the proposal of a third cinema emerges as a strategy of moving cinematographic production closer to the specific problems of liberation. Linked to different liberation movements, it also became a field of struggle for the signification of different practices and conceptualizations of politics on the basis of basic components such as collective production instead of individual, the opening of the work to dialogue made possible by the projection of the films with conversations and discussions, and the almost clandestine circulation of the materials, in part because of censorship but also because of the decision not to commercialize these materials. The Liberation Cinema Group (Grupo Cine Liberación) led by Argentine directors Fernando Solanas and Octavio Getino expressed the need to think of cinema as a front to activate processes of disalienation, beginning with their own mechanism of image, language, and technology. In the classic "Report by the Liberation Cinema Group," they state that "information does not exist" in neocolonial countries, which makes it necessary for a liberation cinema "to provoke information, spark testimonies that lead to the discovery of our reality."[38] Along these lines, the manifesto "Towards a Third Cinema," published in 1969, delves into the idea that, in the midst of the anti-imperialist struggle, the "*Third Cinema* is, in our opinion, the cinema that *recognizes in that struggle the most gigantic cultural, scientific, and artistic manifestation of our time*, the great possibility of constructing a liberated personality with each people as the starting point—in a word, the *decolonization of culture*."[39] For them, third cinema emerges as a form of introducing an alternative to the dialectic between dominant (commercial) cinema and the cinema that was called independent but was still seen as a tool of dependency through which both the state and the market controlled the framework of what could circulate. In the case of Mexico, the interest of the state in promoting an independent, quality cinema was seen by its critics as an invisible mechanism of censorship: under the idea of quality control, the state exercised control over content and what was deemed "passable" and could be shown.

The definition itself of militant cinema implies a multiplicity of meanings that vary according to how each practice is connected; within it, "third cinema" becomes a category where various roads or tendencies of militancy emerge, with more rigid or more experimental structures coexisting. As a political cinema that expresses the politics of national liberation in the moment, it becomes a minefield of distinctions in which views on the pedagogy and function of the image are in play. A quite direct way of manifesting a desire of categorical differentiation emerges in Sergio García's proposal to situate the Mexican superochero world as a road toward a fourth cinema. With this, García proposed to distance filmmaking from the third cinema and moreover to the way in which it monopolized the characterization of militant cinema.[40] In setting itself out as the road toward (a fourth) cinema, it brings up a critical tension with a political cinema that "has become a cinema of propaganda," and indicates a direction: "I believe, without claiming to establish a rule, that 8mm cinema must be brief, concise, and impactful; something like a poster."[41] The goal would be to find "a cinema that awakens consciousness, not that forms it."[42] The contrast between awakening and forming consciousness is important since it helps to explain the difference between militant cinema that aims to transmit a message and cinema that resolves to "provoke" something (awaken to another reality). In the first case, we have a type of vertical militancy that assumes artistic practice as a medium through which to communicate decisions, information, and ways of looking produced by the vanguard of the party. In the second, it is about addressing an artistic practice as an open medium of a more participatory or innovative type, in that the message is what the experience itself of making film and discussing it generates.

We can approach García's proposal to move beyond the third cinema in relation to (and as a reaction against) the progressive semantic closure that emerged within militant cinema after the publication of Getino and Solanas's "Militant Cinema: An Internal Category of Third Cinema" in 1971, where they define it as a cinema that maintains an engagement with the beliefs of the party to which the filmmakers belong.[43] According to Mariano Mestman, this text functioned as a discursive instance that showed the change in direction of third cinema toward a more direct instrumentalization of cinema.[44] What had been the basis of third cinema as an open category able to group Latin American filmmakers with different perspectives and political positions began to be questioned as something dangerous in its possible ambiguity. Its heterogeneity became a threat as state repression increased and militant structures became more closed. Mestman writes that, at the end of 1970, the members of the Liberation Cinema Group "questioned the political vagueness and lack of commitment on the part of the Realizadores de Mayo group in the process of instrumentalization of the collective film and spoke of the difficulty of maintaining a common front between filmmakers with different political positions: the Peronism of Cine Liberación contrasting with the Nueva Izquierda (New Left) position."[45] Within this context, we can note that the proposal of a fourth cinema as an intervention in the politics of the image implied the necessity of not converting cinema into a visual pamphlet of a political line, that is, to avoid the mere instrumentalization of the image, to be able to transform the form of politics implicit in the image. This introduced a distinction in what would be understood as political cinema in terms of a form of experimenting with and of making the image generate another type of political process. Through this we can note that the problematization that is crucial in certain modes of '68 militancy is replicated within cinema: for instance, the counterpoint between ends-oriented forms of political change and the most process-oriented forms of political change, thought of as modes of miniscule self-management able to produce a social transformation. The question that Revueltas set forth from his reflections about self-management and cognitive democracy emerged in the seventies in these small visual laboratories. In fact, the manifesto "Toward a Fourth Cinema" posed the challenge of imagining a cinema that would be thought of as a "cultural action for freedom, seeking to achieve this by way of dialogue, reflection and action."[46] The idea of avoiding propagandistic cinema that offered a prescription for change opened a totally different field for making and conceiving the role of the image in a nontraditional politics from a less traditional cinema. Lerner argues that the project of a fourth cinema did not differ significantly from "third cinema" as seen from the ideals of liberation, but it did have significant distinctions if we consider "a stance toward an imported youth culture."[47] Fine-tuning this, I would say that even if they comprise an ideal of liberation, the project of the Mexican superocheros brought a less stuffy form of change than Solanas and Getino's proposal. A not insignificant difference in some cases is that the Super 8 groups did not belong to the same political sector, which made the idea of communicating a message different. For example, participants who belonged to diverse movements coexisted in the cooperative, and the key was the possibility of not imposing one tendency onto the rest. In a sense, it is in the diversity of movements that coexisted in the different forms of participation that one can find the most salient characteristics of '68 in something that was also translated onto the cinematographic experience sometime later.

Through the visual experiences filmed in Super 8 analyzed in this chapter, we can see that certain crucial points, with which Revueltas characterized the movement of '68, acquire new forms of expression. Self-management, encounters among nonequals, and communicability among different temporalities of political struggle that had always been made invisible function as axes from which to redefine a practice of disalienation of the senses and of language. In the midst of the strong waves of repression that circumscribed the movement—not only in the months that the strike lasted but also continuing in new forms of extreme violence (the Corpus Christi Massacre [el Halconazo], the intra-carceral assault at Lecumberri at the end of the year)—it is remarkable that these microrevolutions in the work of production and circulation of the cinematic image became a crucial mode of "continuing" '68 in another medium. The gesture of '68 can be perceived in the interest in redefining artistic and political practice from the image, linking it with the problematic core of self-management as transformation in the form of practicing and communicating a knowledge. This great work of re-elaborating the image could even be read as a correlate to what we saw in relation to the word in the prison's workshop of words and its thematization in Revueltas's "Imprisoned Words." Word and image transform into ways of continuing a struggle in the field of the distribution of the sensible, a form in which politics becomes visible and enunciable when it leaves the order established by the state. As I said earlier, the logic of the inappropriate can only last a very short time. The innovative and experimental key of '68, consisting of the disarray of practices and the opening of a political dimension different from that of the parties, fades *without disappearing*. Certainly, as time has passed, memories return to this moment of the political—a moment that did not come to pass in a similar form in the subsequent decades. If we address this dynamic from Revueltas's reflections examined in the earlier chapters, it would perhaps be too simple to think that, as the practice disappears, its effect in the social field disappears as well. What disappears remains in this subterranean memory, and its fragments will be reactivated (reactualized) when a new situation comes into contact with this and makes it newly clear in its differentiation. Nevertheless, in the aesthetic field, it is perhaps important to examine the type of relationships between art and politics implied by these experiments, to attend to the ways in which this destabilization takes place within the works themselves.

In Sergio García's texts, a fourth cinema would emerge from the subtle distinction between forming consciousness and the experience of provoking an awakening. But how does this provocation take place? We can find the key to this historic moment in the fact that not just an artistic practice in cinema is defined but also a way of addressing politics, where even if the university and the production of knowledge occupy an essential center of the political mobilization of the moment, it is the possibility of reconfiguring the idea and the property of knowledge (as effect) that the image takes as key. In other words, it is not about education as forming (imposing a form) on the masses with the image but rather an education by means of generating forms of awakening the gaze to what we do not see when we look, which has to do with a social diagram being both visualized and questioned. In the shorts that '68 made possible, we see images that seem neither to begin nor to end. I am interested here with the idea of a paradoxical aesthetic efficiency that comes from the *interruption* itself of the mechanisms expected from cause-effect; that is, from the determinism of the work as a recognizable, acceptable, and enjoyable work in the frame of its institutional definition (the institution as a frame contains it in the field of its practice).[48] Instead of playing with the development of an idea, this exposes us to another way of exhibiting the reflexive process. Here, 1968 cinema expresses a similar gesture to that of nondevelopmentalist thought analyzed in the previous chapter, but now from visual experience: a cinema without development of the plot, without defined, clear spaces. The idea of filming as a weapon of social struggle implies a transformation of cinema itself, an intensely reflexive moment of the image that does not necessarily mean to say that a lot of theory about cinema was produced. More than "theory about," the reflexivity of the image emerges from its becoming, from its practices themselves. When the prisoners learn to use Super 8 cameras in Lecumberri, or when the workers of Besançon did something similar in France, taking the camera to the factory, questions emerge from both the medium and the practice. For instance, when the camera enters Lecumberri Prison, prisoners learn how to use it at first, but later, it is necessary to see what can be done in an everyday carceral space, where not much really happens. Transforming cinema into a critical weapon means delving into the possibilities of the medium and of the situation through doing, in order to create more possibilities from there.

By considering Super 8 filmmaking in the cinematographic period following the great massacre of October 2 at Tlatelolco, I have attempted to carry out a double task: to think a cinematographic event that proposes to open a notion and a circulation of the image and, on the other hand, to turn this event into a more abstract questioning of the ways in which the image can become critical. That is, even if Super 8 filmmaking was used as an essential tool to continue '68 by other means (other means of communication, a different production of the image that countered the official monopoly of the image) and was used as a kind of witness (its character as testimony and document), what most interests me now is outlining a question about the type of revelation that the projects I have analyzed imply: What is a revelation in this specific historic moment, one that echoes the present, not only in the sense of the university actions but also in the sense of a revelation that resolves to deprivatize knowledge *from* the image? What is a revelation that, instead of revealing mere information, reveals a situation? This implies delving into the core of '68 as a transformation having to do with a demand for democracy more than for a specific petition of the resolution of a political problem. It is a moment in which asking means asking about the conditions of possibility of politics, as an experience of transformation, a constant process that never ends.

WHERE ARE THE WOMEN OF '68?

Fernanda Navarro and the Materialism
of Uncomfortable Encounters

Emancipating Memory: Where Are the Women of '68?

The current notion of '68 in which women's roles are discounted is completely patriarchal and forces me to conclude what I had never sensed back then. . . . I think that in
'68 the theme of discrimination against women was absent. Never did I sense what is
being said now about the scarce participation of women. *In what was truly a democratic
atmosphere, all men and women played an incredible role within the movement. Each person
participated in accordance with his or her ability and to the extent that they desired. Perhaps
for that reason it would be worthwhile to reimagine '68 as a political movement that was
inclusive, tolerant, and guided by a truly representative leadership, all of which generated
a sense of euphoria and filled us with hope. I have not seen a similar movement in the last
thirty years. . . .* It was a marvelous era imbued with a sense of profound democracy. In
the Manifesto of October 2, there is a line that reads, "We demand democracy because we
practice it." And effectively, this was one of the things that we truly did accomplish in
'68. —EUGENIA ESPINOSA CARBAJAL, quoted in "la visión actual del 68 es totalmente
machista," by Sonia Del Valle

The words of Eugenia Espinosa Carbajal in her interview with Sonia Del Valle
echo the sentiments of many women who participated in '68 and who remember it as a moment of experimentation toward a sense of democratic equality. This liberatory narrative contrasts greatly with the biases that seem to have
dominated the process of memorialization of the movement's history through
the frameworks of its male leaders, generating an intriguing paradox in which
the moment of emancipation is followed by a fictional memory that is framed
by invisible forms of inequality. In one of the few yet most significant studies
regarding this subject, Gloria Tirado Villegas suggests that upon reading the
vast textual corpus of the movement's history, written mainly by "participants,

members of the National Strike Council, social activists (some while incarcerated), by proclaimed journalists, by academics . . . I thus ask myself, where are the women of '68? The question arises each time that the subject of women within the movement is suddenly deployed in diverse lectures, where women's roles are hardly even mentioned."[1] If we then affirm with Espinosa Carbajal that "women might as well not have participated at all," their absence in the grand corpus of narrativized contentions suddenly evolves alarmingly into its liberatory parallel: *How are we to eradicate the strong inequality and imbalance within the use and circulation of a memory regarding a time that was deeply characterized by a feeling of equality in the participation and form of experimenting the political?*

Without a doubt, it does not cease to strike the curiosity that in regard to a historically crucial moment within the dislocation of roles and the encounter among those who had not crossed paths, the very same bibliography that crystalizes modes of articulating this experience actualizes this promise very poorly. One gets the impression that, instead of actualizing a moment profoundly open to the destabilization of conventional roles, the liberatory potential of the moment was superseded by a memory that was consummated in reproducing the same system of hierarchy that they had previously contested, in terms of both social class and sexual difference. I trace here the various compositions of '68 that appear in multiple textual margins written by women in the decades that followed, from the seventies to the present.

It is clear that there is a tension between the *equality* that operated as the basic force and engine of popular participation in the movement and the inequality that has traversed the processes of memorialization and attestation within the narrative. My main interest is to illuminate the heterogeneity that constitutes '68 as a revolutionary moment in terms of participation and political organization, in contrast to the homogeneity that during subsequent decades has composed its dominant form of memorialization. In this manner, I am interested in generating a sort of guideline of the marginalized yet potent interventions by women who participated in different modes in '68. At the same time, my goal is to *go beyond* the typical attestation of the presence of female militants so as to move toward the philosophical and political dimensions in which certain interventions took place in the map of memories of the eighties, nineties, and the present. That is, I am interested in attending to how dominant frames and figures of '68 analyzed in the previous two chapters—such as the encounter and dislocation of fixed social roles and places—are recomposed and enriched from other angles.

Some precisions are in place here. When I pose the question about the participation of women in the construction of a memory of the movement of '68, I take the word *women* as a space of open signification. That is to say, I do not want *woman* to be understood as a fixed identity that responds to a series of roles and social functions; nor do I want it to become a new identity that comes to replace the traditional forms of social construction. On the contrary, I take the word to refer to different acts of political intervention and participation in the movement that radically questioned the form of identification that froze women in a certain place. In the few memories from women who participated in the movement, the remembrance of a sense of equality in the forms of doing politics and changing traditional habits, at home and in the streets, in dialogue with their peers in the movement or with their parents at home, talk about the ability of *not being where they were expected to be and of doing what they were socially not expected to do.* Needless to say, this was a powerful component for the many collectives that emerged since '68 or that had already existed but became more visible in the decade after, with the foundation of groups for women and homosexual liberation (with many nuances, distinctions, and struggles between heterosexual and lesbian feminisms). However, I would say that a distinctive component of women's participation in the movement of '68 comes from *an irreverent and profound break* involved in their participation, a form of "strike" within the everyday repetition of habits and pressures. Not responding clearly to the play of interpellation, and facing and/or living through all the contradictions involved in moments of break and transformation, the words *women of '68* become here the space for a struggle of signification, the opening of a space for an experimentation with different forms of subjectivation. The sense of an irreverent, *forced equality* is based on the possibility of being a woman in ways that did not respond to fixed social spaces and roles. It was through different forms of participation that the social construction of "women" was transformed.

It is fair to say that the masculine monopoly over the memory of the moment is not something that only occurs in Mexico's '68; if we attend to the different perspectives on '68 in the world, we find that it concerns a generalized problem. Ross analyzes this in detail in the French case, focusing on the masculine style of leadership and the erasure of social class in the different memorializations that compose the official landscape of the French May (a category that Ross also questions). Sheila Rowbotham expresses this sentiment in relation to the stereotypical phrases that are manifested within the self-historicization of England's political left, wherein "amidst all the words expended on the sixties, women make limited entrances"—and when they are mentioned, their presence is reduced to "legs in miniskirts."[2] The publication in 1988 of Luisa Passerini's *Autobiography of a Generation: Italy, 1968* picks up the preoccupation of how to write a collective memory of that moment from a personal experience and, simultaneously, to address the situation of a woman in the midst of a process of liberation, something that the hybrid composition of the text achieves in an extremely complex and interesting manner. Passerini also wrote the introduction to the compilation of texts that make up Lessie Jo Frazier and Deborah Cohen's *Gender and Sexuality in 1968*, which presents an international panorama in which the same problem is manifested throughout many places (Sub-Saharan Africa, Czechoslovakia, Cuba, the United States, France, and Mexico).[3]

Over the decades in Mexico, as in a variety of countries, a discomfort has begun to appear with respect to the collective lack of knowledge about the massive participation of women within the movement and, subsequently, in regard to the necessity of recuperating a memory of their participation. Even though the decade after the movement saw the publication of Elena Poniatowska's key work, *Massacre in Mexico*, a text that documents the voices of various women who participated in the movement from a truly diverse set of social backgrounds, there has nevertheless remained a masculine dominance of the bibliography of the movement's historical memorization. Following the ongoing creation of an archival memory concerning '68, in the nineties Frazier and Cohen opened a path of research with the publication of their essay "We Didn't Just Cook . . . The Unedited Story of the Other Half of '68." In one of the first interventions concerning gender bias in the memorialization of '68, the authors argue against the way in which women enter the historical register simply as the bearers of food for the movement's political prisoners. Their work marks the beginning of a particular desacralization of the form in which dominant memory had constructed women participation; that construction is indeed one in which, in the very same moment that the woman enters in a mass form into the public space of politics (the streets, educational institutions, buses used for public transportation), the memory of her participation resituates her within the site of the domestic and its corresponding tasks (cooking, cleaning, child care).

Pushing against the dominant view, Tirado Villegas reveals how women participated in different tasks,

> from booting, to leafleting, to organizing lightning rallies, painting signs, canvassing information, making flyers, and even cooking duties. The ma-

jority preferred to go to into the streets and express their opinions, while others preferred to work within the internal organization of the brigades. Yet as difficult, dangerous, or arduous as the tasks were, the majority of women avoided extending domestic work into the movement; this kind of sexual division of labor was unobserved as such a commitment was assumed by both genders. This experience was fundamental for the female participants, who felt just as capable as the men.[4]

This passage illustrates how the sexual division of labor in the daily organization of the movement was a sort of implicit struggle that was forged by both men and women. In various conversations I had with women who participated in these tasks, this sentiment of *equality of participation* in which the tasks were divided in an egalitarian manner emerged as a common tone. Nevertheless, once the moment had passed, it appeared as though political inertia had overwhelmed women in spite of that impulse, leaving the memory of the movement monopolized by men, and particularly members and leaders of the National Strike Council. *What would it mean to democratize the memory of '68? How does one construct a history of the moment that is polyphonic and complex, as well as able to attend to the voices that were marginalized within the field of the improper?* In a certain form, the questions would be, rather: *How can we bring the impulse of '68 into its own memory? How are we to repeat its gesture?*

In 2005 Elaine Carey's *Plaza of Sacrifices: Gender, Power, and Terror in 1968* was published, proposing a study of '68 from a gendered perspective capable of observing and introducing the agency of those who were marginalized. The book also aims to address the double transgression of women who, along with going against the established order, also broke with a series of implicit rules of patriarchal society with the mere act of participating and confronting the authority inside their homes.[5] In 2007 Cohen and Frazier published *Gender and Sexuality in 1968* with the purpose of bringing to light this problem in many countries and emphasizing how the primacy of masculine voices not only reproduces the schema of inequality within gender but also influences the kind of memory that is constructed. In focusing on movement leaders, the most horizontal forms of grassroots participation were left at the margins. That is, along with the massive participation of women, the movement counted on major participation from people who had never acted within the political sphere and who therefore took to the streets in creative forms, establishing dialogues, creating situations that promoted discourse; in sum: performing the small quotidian acts that began to win the massive support of a whole population outside the sphere of universities.[6] As Marcia Gutiérrez expressed, "the brigade is the alive element of the movement," its societal vessel of communication.[7] Reynoso remembers something similar when she appeals to the creativity of the brigades: the use of street dogs as messengers that functioned as a sort of Twitter within the movement, the climax of an event that Topilejo became in regard to experience in social encounter and collaboration, and the work of men and women within the kitchens—later reduced to the memory of the women who brought food to Lecumberri Prison, thereby erasing the joint labor carried out throughout multiple mobilizations before and after Tlatelolco. It can be said that the most "singular" formative political experiences of the moment of '68 (although they have perhaps been less frequently thematized) were the daily collective actions within the brigades, the mutual participation in the popular elementary schools project, and the work in Topilejo as a grand laboratory of an alternative egalitarian politics.[8] Part of Reynoso's effort in rethinking Memorial 68 lies in constructing a dynamic and inclusive space in which memory can operate as a social activity in a constant process of elaboration. In fact, many of the events that commemorate the movement have been devoted to discussing the poor representation of women in the dominant narrative of the space, which relates almost metonymically to the absence of voices in the social memory of the movement. Along these lines, in October 2015 the Memorial 68 at the University Cultural Center in Tlatelolco proposed a roundtable following the theme "The Women of 1968" within which various women who researched and wrote on this topic participated, including Renate Marsiske, Gloria Tirado Villegas, Beatriz Argelia González, and Mónica García Contreras.[9] A short time after, a roundtable was held for a discussion of the book *Ovarimonio: ¿Yo guerrillera?*, by Gladys López Hernández, published in 2013, a view of '68 based on the experience of the Popular Preparatory and the repression of the seventies. During that time, López Hernández was arrested and then incarcerated for three years on charges of guerilla participation.[10]

As mentioned above, I find it of crucial importance that decades after the moment of '68 we can move beyond the mere contestation of women's participation into an analysis of the forms in which this activity has taken place at different levels and in various registers, whether philosophical, literary, testimonial, or visual. It is worth noting that the significance of '68 is that it brought about the participation of women who were themselves diverse (students, mothers, workers) and also generated a series of questionings of authority, traditional politics, and the hierarchies of traditional political parties. I am referring to a moment prior to what would later consist of the logic of reclaiming more specific rights through fashioning of a more declaredly feminist idiom in the succeeding decade. Even if we were to reduce the sixties to mere preamble, it is nevertheless relevant to note the way in which women's participation takes a less-articulated and perhaps more brazen approach in a variety of aspects, perhaps caused by the reality of encountering and confronting the patriarchal order in its minute, everyday forms, including the so-called protection of "young girls" at stake in the home, in the streets, and in the movement. The possibility of confronting patriarchal structures to a massive degree is perhaps what most characterizes this unique instance of assuming an egalitarian space.

In almost all historicization of the emergence of new feminisms, '68 appears as a crucial instant in which the mass participation of women acted as a force of further transformation. As Francesca Gargallo writes,

> It is not true that the global revolutions of 1968 originated feminist liberation, nor was it true that feminists were the biggest benefactors of that period. Nevertheless, between the movement of women's liberation and the questioning of everyday life, as well as the questioning of the notion of the political left, of sexuality, of the relation between the individual and the political party, between the revindication of the streets and the dethroning of the nuclear family and the patriarchal state, between the assault on fantasy and the affirmation that "this body is mine" that broke out in 1968, there exists an inescapable nexus.[11]

In tune with this, Márgara Millán notes that the feminism of the seventies "synthesized the libertarian spirit of the sixties";[12] and Teresita Barbieri expresses that the movement of '68 worked as a "broth of cultivation" of feminism; that is, of a movement whose demands were both conscious and specific. She notes, "Even as Mexican women were an important part of the student protests of 1968, they did not do so in a manner that was organized as a current of demands for themselves as women. Rather, their participation as a feminist movement was gestated soon after."[13]

There are many positions in terms of explaining and narrating the relation between the movement of '68 and the emergence of second-wave feminism in Mexico; most of them see '68 as the opening of a field of transformation for modes of thinking of culture, politics, and democracy.[14] In this sense, I find it important to pay attention to the different temporalities that indeed were distinct from the feminism(s) that emerged more publicly and distinctively in the 1970s and 1980s. In suggesting a notion of previous temporalities, I refer to what Julie Mitchell suggests in her classic, *Woman's Estate* (1971), where she poses the question of how to differentiate the feminist movements that emerged in the seventies with respect to the events of the previous decades.[15] As I mentioned earlier, one salient distinction that emerges between the memories of

'68 and what would happen soon after within feminist discourses is that in the former there is an emphasis on a sense of equality, a sort of momentary suspension of the logic of proper place in which women and men participated in whichever way they could. By this, I do not mean that the irruption of an equality would erase the logic of (sexual or class) difference but that these differences took a secondary role in light of what were demands for a total democratization of society.[16] This distinction is important because it indicates a form of equality that is linked with a differential mode of acting collectively from the suspension of fixed places and social roles; it also relates to the creation of spaces of encounter where women from different places (including the same home, as with mothers and daughters) shared problems and forms of doing together, while also confronting the inertia of some roles (like always being responsible for cooking, to mention one gendered task among many). Of course, this suspension of inequality was not absolute and it was full of frictions; however, it also involved the opening of a new form of acting politically in a broad sense. As a key component of '68, it refers to a demand for democracy and equality through the suspension of fixed social categories and roles, where the participation of women and the reactions that emerged upon remembering them express a right to stand precisely where they were not envisioned: *to share that space which has been denied to them for decades and to do so in an egalitarian manner.* Alma Rosa Sánchez Olvera explains, in the Mexican context, that the passage toward a more conscious feminism has sometimes been framed within a narrative of blame, accusing feminists for having divided the big political struggle into a struggle between men and women.[17] Leaving the narratives of blame aside, I would like to once again recall the trope of duration that emerged in the two previous chapters and say that the intensity of the instants of encounter and equality lasted for a brief time, but they made possible forms of continuing the movement by other means as well. Here it should also be fair to say that feminism was just one among many other forms of intensifying struggles of gender equality.

Considered a "broth of cultivation," a mumbling, a laboratory of what would become the language of the second wave of feminism, '68 is ultimately expressed in the necessity of questioning certain bases of patriarchal society, in radically practicing forms of political participation that destabilize the spaces allocated for each person and that furthermore generate consciousness of a persistent grand inequality. In many of the testimonials of students, mothers, and housekeepers published in *Massacre in Mexico*, a common emphasis (upheld in the analyses of Cohen and Frazier and in various interviews with the female participants of the movement) is the experience of a kind of *equality* that movement participants had never previously encountered—something that had effects on different spheres and affects, such as the domestic interactions of the family, the modes of living in relationships, the politics of the word, and the relations of the body. Various passages stress how political participation resonated in different spheres, especially in the passages concerning the transition from the home to the streets and from the streets back to the home. In cases such as Gladys López Hernández's, it is not only participation in politics but the unprecedented opportunity to study (even as she did so in a rather clandestine manner) that marked this growth, since as a woman, the fate that her parents conceived for her consisted of a simple elementary education and the expectation of marriage. Her divergence from this fate therefore implicated her in a double life due to her decision to both participate in politics and pursue her studies.[18]

In other cases, the dislocation of roles affected the notion of the family in confrontations that young daughters began to have with their parents and the emotions that such changing relations provoked in the latter. Two of the participants in the testimonies gathered by Poniatowska, mothers Luz Fernanda Carmona Ochoa and Yvonne Huitrón de Gutiérrez, speak about their emerging consciousness of the kind of life their daughters sought to lead, which was therefore a consciousness of the necessarily changing relations brought about by unfamiliar affections and their daughters' novel language: what they noticed was an "absence of hypocrisy" in the manner in which their daughters "involved themselves in love and experienced love," which caused these mothers to reflect on the features that had guaranteed for them a life of deceit. The mothers of these revolutionary daughters therefore began to realize a sentiment similar to what we find in Gutiérrez's testimony: "We did everything on the sly and it seems to me that's how I lived my whole life, on the sly."[19] Other cases suggest the confrontation between revolutionary daughters and their fathers, such as the story that we encounter in the testimony of Ferrer, who remarks that, as the authoritative repression of the movement became more and more massive, her father asked her to remove herself from a life of militancy, to which she responded by questioning how someone who had taught her that civic values were the most important in life could ask her to remove herself from militancy. From that moment on, her father never again insisted on such things. These memories forcefully emphasize that the political struggle of the movement began in the home, that is, that the possibility of participating in public space was something that women themselves needed to make available through the dialogues they initiated and maintained with their parents. The reports of women, unlike those of the men, speak to the significant amount of micropolitical ruptures that women experienced in '68, and they furthermore speak to the abuses that many women faced by virtue of the "post-'68" affect, whereby the intensification of the movement brought about an increase of assaults on women's bodies, including sexual violation, systematic torture, and incarceration, all at a very young age.

In contrast to other masculine memories of the moment wherein the theme of egalitarian gender relations is completely absent, Eduardo Valle and Paco Ignacio Taibo II rescue the sentiment of an unusual sense of equality that was beginning to take place in quotidian practices. Valle provides an anecdote in which the theme of egalitarian participation demanded that men actually modify their quotidian lives. He remembers that, following the silent march (*manifestación silenciosa*), he said: "Let us not shed tears like women for what we were unable to defend like men." The next day two brigades of women waited for him outside his classroom and insisted on the injustice of such a phrase.[20] Taibo tells a similar story in his book *'68,* where he points to the somehow camouflaged struggle that used to take place between the empowerment of women as equal participants in the movement and the inertia of the traditional gender roles that many men haughtily held on to: "We were so damn equal—and so damn different. Sure enough, there was always some dope who wanted the women to run the kitchen of the department café; but there would always be someone slightly less dopey to say that that was everybody's job."[21]

This is an idea that is present in many of the memories of women who participated in the movement and whose testimonies were collected by Cohen and Frazier: a sentiment of openness to an egalitarian participation that had not existed until then, accompanied by a necessary quotidian struggle that functioned on many levels. "Women took on a very important role because we participated on par with the men," said Rosa. "We shared serious risks in entering buses to proliferate information; even speaking to people on the street implicated the risk of arrest or possibly being followed. Men as well as women share the risk equally. The men were therefore forced to change."[22] The very notion of an egalitarian participation incited what were permanent struggles between the men of the movement and the society that demanded that women become subservient in the roles that patriarchal society prescribed for men (the kitchen, the home) as well as a society that simultaneously permitted these stereotypes to take on a confrontational tone with novel forms of entry into public space. It should be noted that in both personal interviews and in the very few memories that have been written, the singularity of the moment is described in terms of the possibility of sharing an egalitarian space, a totally new experience. More than emerging with the generally resentful conscience of an identity that reclaims itself, the polyphony of memories held by the female participants of '68 better yet emphasizes a form of emancipation that appeared to follow the tone of what Rancière refers to as "a mode of experiencing inequality according to the mode of equality," a very uncommon and extremely difficult exercise to even conceptualize.[23] This is important to emphasize as it differs from the logic of identity in which some demands tend to fall in reinforcing the identity created by such rejection. As Sofía Argüeyo Pazmiño argues, framing the struggles in terms of fixed identities tends to freeze an always changing process in forms that "leave little space for paradoxes and limits," which constitute relational processes of identification.[24] In contrast to a logic of identity, it is curious to hear a similar tone in memories from women who participated in such various forms, in the brigades, in the National Strike Council, in the committees, at the rallies, and who together carry the rhythm of a form of *equality in difference*. In this same vein, Eugenia Espinosa expresses that it is paradoxical that the dominant patriarchal view would have prevailed not much in '68 but rather in the subsequent memorializations of the event, generating the image of an *equality that is remembered from the point of view of inequality*. Such equality indeed destabilizes the figure of identity that marks women in a social role and fixed locality within society and furthermore opens other processes of subjectivation and becoming. As Rancière observes, the subjectivity that generates the eruption of the political involves a form of *disidentification*, a "removal from the naturalness of a place, the opening up of a subject space where anyone can be counted since it is the space where those of no account are counted, where a connection is made between having a part and having no part."[25] This is important as it erases the fixed notion of "woman" as a frozen site of subscribed roles and furthermore implies the creation of other forms of being and doing through the practices that are assumed as egalitarian even as they fail to achieve this universally. In this sense, a striking feature in the texts I analyze in this section is that women's appeal for an *encounter between the non-analogous* is made not from the position of an identity claim (such as being a woman) but rather from an insistence on the conditions of possibility of the encounter with forms of otherness that are not analogous and by the memory of specific situations of such encounters in the internalization of inequality itself.

The figure of the encounter was also a central knot in the texts written by women who in one way or another participated in '68. For Revueltas, the theoretical act referred to an encounter among ideas that brings the strata that are most subterranean and most distanced from history to the surface. The connector among negated moments is the very idea-force of a *cognitive democracy*, the specter of an unfulfilled promise of emancipation and democracy that endlessly returns, connecting fragments of the past and the present. In Louis Althusser's aleatory materialism, the encounter that takes place in divergence (*clinamen*) relies on a certain concordance that makes possible the permanence required for the encounter to configure a world. This kaleidoscope generated around the figure of the encounter appearing within critical Marxism as a form of thinking freedom in history—an alternative to the positivist notion of materialism dominated by strict legal rulings—emerges in the texts written by '68 women from a different angle: *the question of freedom still relates to the figure of the encounter, but an uncomfortable or less harmonious one.* Freedom emerges as a form of (violent) spacing of "normal" life in a way that makes possible the construction of a commonality based on the approach between those who are not equal, non-analogous, but who nevertheless converse and share a quotidian space. Thus, based on three women who designed different crucial interventions with regard to the forms of understanding freedom in the encounter (or the freedom of the encounter), I am interested in examining the forms in which the memories of the moment begin to transmutate from the very insistence on a question concerning equality to the reconceptualization of the political that this implies. I approach the interventions of Fernanda Navarro from the philosophy of the eighties; Roberta "La Tita" Avendaño and Gladys López Hernández from testimony in the nineties; and ovarimony in the new century.[26] Each of these interventions urges us to confront a difficulty that had not emerged in the previous two chapters: a preoccupation with the sui generis forms of equality that emerge in the memory of women who remember this moment in order to understand, from that point, a central key in what would become an active consciousness of the need for political and economic social transformation.

In these textual interventions, whether from a philosophical framework, from testimony (Avendaño), or from ovarimony (López Hernández), these women did not conceptually limit their participation in the movement as a form of affirming identity. Rather, their way of denoting difference emerged out of a form of opening and *widening* the memory of the moment toward modes of encounter with that which was utterly unlike them. This produces an interesting gesture that makes us look at the encounter in a more complicated way: it is as though a single memory opened multiple others, illuminating the tensions and paradoxes that remained in their thoughts as unfulfilled promises or as instances capable of speaking to a present where such inequalities continued to operate. *The crucial point in '68, seen as a grand instant and art of encounters, is here reconfigured from the standpoint of a philosophical poetics that cultivates such encounter into an ethical questioning of the alterity of the non-*

analogous to the self, the other who does not resemble me—an encounter in whose subsequent set of relations resides the very culmination of an ethics. This relates to a figure of the encounter that insists on the non-analogous; we find this in the figure of the encounter with an alterity in Fernanda Navarro and as the encounter among people from different social classes in the memories written by Avendaño and López Hernández. The insistence on the conditions of possibility for an encounter with alterity that emerges in texts written by the women of '68 becomes a form of questioning the structure of invisible universalities assumed within the notion of subject or citizen, when these imply *particular conditions and situations.* The point that Navarro will trace through articulating a feminist materialism of the encounter therefore allows us to challenge and deconstruct the "properties" of the political subject assumed as universal, therefore daring to ask about the conditions of those who are not qualified to occupy its position. If her philosophical intervention is one in which the woman is always the alterity of the universal (masculine) subject of modern thought, her insistence on the encounter does not direct itself at a feminism of the female but rather *at the deconstruction of patriarchy as a formula of identities.* In this sense, she refers to the encounter between that which is analogous to my person and threatens the integrity of every fixed locality through which determined order settles.

As in the first two chapters, I depart here from the idea of '68 as an instant of destabilization of prescribed and fixed social roles where an active redefinition of freedom is at play. The *impropriety and creativity* of this "forced equality" provokes figures and reflections in various registers: philosophical, testimonial, and ovarimonial, destabilizing tropes that later became primary elements of the dominant masculine narrative. As a guide to my reflection, I take an argument postulated by Christine Delphy that the materialist feminist gaze allows us to propose a new perspective, a mode of observing from another angle rather than contemplating the creation of a whole new objective or new identity.[27] Thus, I am interested in connecting with questions that emerged previously but are now presented from a different angle in materials made by the women who participated in '68 and continued their militancy in other ways: what kind of imagination and what kind of language does freedom take in the texts of the women who participated in '68 but who write about it after the fact? Relying on the differential component of '68 as an instant of disorganization of social spaces, it is the figure of the *encounter between the disparate or unequal* that will play a central role in these last chapters. It is curious that something that had helped define the theoretical act in Revueltas's work reappears here as a central trope from which a reflection on an unusual form of learning emerges, one that does not take place in the classroom and that furthermore suggests for us an uncomfortable form of encounter with alterity. This moreover indicates an obsession with the idea of the encounter—of its possibility—as problematic center as well as a reflexive indicator of the insistence of democratization, freedom, and space for the communal. In their focus on this encounter among disparate, asymmetrical beings, these texts urge us to contemplate the very idea of the encounter in its emphasis, on the one hand, on something incalculable that causes the destabilization of an ordered, fixed positionality for every being. On the other hand, they emphasize the disorder that the encounter suggests as an entirely new ethics that allows us to understand, even if in abstract terms, the relevance of '68 as a grand moment of social connectivity. Intending to avoid an idealized gaze, I examine the modes in which the writings of these women would come to treat the subject of the encounter more profoundly as a fundamental ethical moment of a new form of politicization.

Focusing on the figure of the encounter allows me to explore in more depth the form in which connectivity works in memories of the movement. At the same time, far from taking an idealized form, the encounter also emerges in these texts as a problem and an uncomfortable or disturbing zone that allows us to see some of the limits and limitations of the movement in terms of sexual and gender divisions. In fact, it is becoming more common to see reflections on the memories of women who participated in the movement, but there is a disturbing silence with regard to homosexuality within the movement, significantly at such a moment of sexual opening. This is an area that needs further investigation as, along with the beginning of a more consistent movement for women's liberation in the years that followed '68, there was the beginning of the movements of lesbian feminism and homosexual liberation.[28] By focusing on the figure of the encounter as an instant of forced equality, I will focus here on the powerful sense of social connectivity that existed for a brief moment before a new wave of struggles regarding sexual freedom emerged on the horizon.

The Critique of the Domesticated Sovereign Subject

Truncated Eros, besieged Eros, eroded Eros. Centuries of history have mourned centuries of hysteria as a pathology that remained registered in the annals of History, in the parameters of normality. —FERNANDA NAVARRO, "ETHOS versus EROS ... y el silencio de la filosofía"

Fernanda Navarro positions us in the field of feminism that emerged from the halls of the university where she collaborated toward the creation of a feminist network that would facilitate the encounter between women from the Federal

District and Michoacán, Morelia. Her life is full of encounters with key political and philosophical figures at different moments (José Revueltas in the sixties, Hortensia Bussi de Allende in the seventies, Louis Althusser in the eighties), all of them leaving marks on her work while urging her to conceptualize a freedom within concrete and situated actions.[29] Her participation in the events of 1968 does not emerge in the form of the publication of memories or testimonies but rather permeates a certain philosophical path. In 1977 she began to teach philosophy at the University of Michoacán of San Nicolás de Hidalgo and concurrently, starting in 1980, she studied for a master's in philosophy in the School of Philosophy and Letters at UNAM. Her thesis was titled "Of Intersubjectivity" and was later published by the University of Michoacán with the title *Existence, Encounter, and Chance* in 1995.[30]

In May 1982 she participated in chartering a feminist collective called VenSeremos, a name that invokes a plurality of meanings, the closest being a play on the word *venceremos* (meaning "we will win"), but broken down to imply in its first half "Come" (*Ven*), and in its second "We will be" (*seremos*): Come, we will be, come *to* be. The initiative came from some women who studied philosophy at UNAM and who found it of great importance to "organize themselves as women in a population that until then was lacking any organizations of women."[31] The practice of the collective became characterized by this ambiguity, and therefore a sense of openness, allying itself with the radio show "Nosotras las mujeres" ("We the Women"), as well as the column "Marginalia" in the journal *La Voz de Michoacán* (*The Voice of Michoacán*), and furthermore assuming the leadership of *La Boletina* (*The Bulletin*) of the city of Morelia beginning in 1983. In the words of Nathalie Ludec, who conducted a detailed analysis of *La Boletina* and its relevance in the history of feminism: "This mimeographed, modest, alternative was proposed as an organ of internal information and communication among different organizations of women that now shape the Red Nacional de Mujeres de México [National Network of Women in Mexico]."[32] In 1982 this network of twenty-one groups from around the country was created. Through these movements that helped connect feminists from various parts of the country, Navarro's participation is characterized by an obsession for the word—*language as a site of a struggle from which to conceive liberation*, an emphasis that would permanently become the center of her attention.[33]

"Asfixiata (A Feminist Theatrical Sketch)" is a brief piece in which Navarro displays the relevance of language in the struggle for liberation, attending in diverse manners to the words that appear to imprison women in fixed roles and places.[34] Prolific in its humor, the sketch dramatizes a dialogue between a reporter and a woman by the name of Asfixiata ("she who is suffocated"), and through that dialogue examines a series of linguistic turns that demonstrate the naturalization of her subalternity in regard to quotidian life.

R[eporter]: Your civil state?

A[sfixiata]: Wifed [*esposada*, from the word *esposa*, which means "wife" and "handcuff"].

R: Do you mean married?

A: Yes, I'm a wife, a wife to my husband. Do you know what wives/handcuffs [*esposas*] are?

...

R: What do you dedicate yourself to in your personal life?

A: To *domestic* labor. Yes, I am a *domesticated* woman, so that you may understand me better.

R: Are you in . . . ?

A: [*interrupting*] . . . In the reserve army of *unpaid labor*, that is, along with those programmed to not expect wages.

This short dialogue reenacts another crucial aspect of the distribution of the sensible in relation to language and also comes closer to a particular relation that we analyzed in "Imprisoned Words," now concentrated on the problem of the situation of women in a language that in those times connoted imprisonment.

In 1983 Navarro flew to Paris to dedicate her sabbatical year to attend Michel Foucault's seminar "History of Systems of Thought" at the Collège de France. While in France, Navarro visited Louis Althusser with a letter of introduction from Mauricio Malamud and began a fraternal relationship with the thinker during what were for him times of great pain and isolation due to his recent release from the psychiatric hospital. Althusser gave Navarro access to his unpublished works, and Navarro proposed to establish a series of conversations with him regarding these materials, which would later be published as *Philosophy and Marxism*, published in Mexico in 1988 and six years later in France with another title, *Sur la philosophie* (*On Philosophy*), in which Navarro's name does not appear.[35] It should be noted that, outside feminist circles, her participation in second-wave feminism after '68 has been displaced by the role she played in the introduction of Althusser's late work to Latin America, mostly through the publication of *Filosofía y marxismo* and later, her permanent and continuous participation in the Zapatista movement.[36] There is something quite uncomfortable about the fact that Navarro's name has been commonly linked to Althusser's without the development of any interest in analyzing how such a partnership impacted her later work on both materialism and Zapatismo. Perhaps the fact that she had always been in close relation to prestigious philosophers such as Revueltas, Althusser, and Villoro was simply unremarkable to the typically lethargic criticism that instrumentalizes women as the vehicles and muses of "famous" men rather than as thinkers who created their own works. Intending to rupture the form in which Navarro's work has been fetishized by her encounter with the "French thinker," I am interested in bringing forward here an alternate route from the form in which the seeds of '68 subsequently emerge in the field of philosophy. Instead of looking for signs of '68 as a theme or object in her work, I would like to examine the way in which the force of '68—its gesture—is projected onto a revision of materialist philosophy. Considering such a motive, in this chapter I do not analyze Navarro's role in introducing Althusser to Mexico, as such efforts often generate a certain type of injustice toward other authors (including, among many others, Alberto Híjar and Oralba Castillo Nájera) who also facilitated the readership and discussion of Althusser in the post-'68 moment at UNAM. Rather, I am interested in addressing the form in which Navarro intervenes in aleatory materialism from a distinctive angle that relates with her feminist militancy and her readings of '68.

I focus on her master's thesis, which, as stated previously, was published by the University of Michoacán with the title *Existence, Encounter, and Chance* (1995) and combines her feminist philosophy with aleatory materialism, questioning the latter from an alternative standpoint. I investigate how Navarro intervenes in the discussion on the encounter, which we saw in Revueltas's theoretical act and which became the central form of aleatory materialism as posed in Althusser's post-'68 works. In this manner, certain themes that were essential to Navarro's conversations with Althusser about philosophy and Marxism are resituated in *Existence, Encounter, and Chance* from a different perspective, one that supplements and questions their exchanges in subtle ways. In the end, what Navarro criticizes is not only the rigid gaze of a dialectical materialism that destroys emancipatory liberation in its legislation of a history of necessity, something that both Revueltas and Althusser criticized. Rather, this same criticism is then applied to a struggle against the dominant patterns that compose the idea of a universal (heterosexual masculine) sovereign subject, through which the encounter is nonetheless thought (through the metonymic universality of the dominant and the masculine).

Before entering into a discussion of the text, it is necessary to ask: Why bring up the question of the emergence of women in philosophy? In what ways did women begin to intervene in the philosophy that followed '68, insofar as until then they had remained in the margins (if we look beyond the figure of Simone de Beauvoir, who was always referenced at the international level and who was a key figure in Mexico)?[37] Grace Lee Boggs, Angela Davis, Silvia Federici, and Rossana Rosanda are only some of the names that usually come to mind when one thinks about militant women's articulation of philosophy. In the cases of Davis and Boggs, their interest in Marxist philosophy was expressed in the sixties through their timely and unhesitant participation within the movement of black liberation, which both women articulate differently in their writings. What happens in Mexico at this same moment? While it can be taken as irrelevant, this question about the sustained intervention of women in philosophy is fundamental since it is connected to an effort to relate the democracy of thought to an emancipatory praxis.

In *Existence, Encounter, and Chance*, Navarro incorporates the most important themes of her previous works, such as intersubjectivity and the silencing of the body in the philosophies of reason, in order to investigate the necessity of connecting the insistence on liberation with the possibility of conceiving a space for the encounter with alterity. The text departs from the centrality that the figure of the encounter has within the aleatory materialism of the late Althusser, yet it approaches the topic from various theories in the history of modern philosophy. The question that recurs in the text emphasizes the ways in which modern forms of conceiving subjectivity do not make an encounter with alterity possible, "but rather they speak to the figure of a domesticated subject protected within and from his sovereignty."[38] Thus, we are urged to wonder up to which point does the figure of the encounter demand a reflection as well as an ethics capable of widening itself in order to meet an alterity that is not analogous or symmetrical—as though the history of philosophical idealism had been led by a paradigm of immunity, a protection against the arrival of the unexpected. The domestication of the subject in its proper place within the distribution of the sensible in the modern philosophical order reduces the very field of experience, making impossible the encounter between disparate beings. In this way, the underlying proposal suggests that we contemplate the figure of the encounter as a form of destabilizing the constitution of existential and political subjectivity.

Navarro takes the proposal of aleatory materialism to the site of a question that is directed at the possibility of contemplating the grand philosophical turn that occurs after '68 from the investigation of new processes of subjectivation. As expressed by Enrique González Rojo, "In Mexico and in France, Althusserianism revolved around '68" and emerged in Mexican universities as a language that made possible a conceptual opening within the tradition of orthodox Marxism and materialism. Similarly, Híjar expresses that "the works of

Althusser were the alternative to Stalinist manuals as well as to the necessities of solving the continuity and ruptures of the practical demands that followed '68."[39] The insistence on engaging in this exploration from the philosophical horizon, the primordial masculine space, already provokes an intervention that doubly deviates from a common course—in the marginalization of women and in the takeover of a word within a masculine space without this being limited to what would later be known as "gender studies," which in some cases function as a ghettoization of difference while also sustaining certain established hierarchies: the man philosophizes, the woman studies her gender.[40] A dominant, indeed masculine, space is inhabited, but with the supposed insistence on *occupying it and modifying it* from a type of questioning that inscribes itself in the most crucial trope of '68 (the figure of the encounter), provoking a brief deviation from that singular point. Navarro's distinctive component within the philosophy of the encounter is that in her questioning she stops thinking about the perspective from which the encounter *is observed and configured as an idea*, questioning instead what is being assumed as given and what this presupposition excludes. In addition, we could say that Navarro's entire philosophical work is obsessed with the figure of the *encounter* with alterity; that is, *with that which destabilizes the site of the occidental subject as something determined or enclosed in a fixed place.*[41]

The introduction of aleatory materialism in *Existence, Encounter, and Chance* is important given that it takes the questions that invoked a nondogmatic line of thought concerning the political to a quite different zone: the existential processes and the implicit ethics of the encounter with what is not assimilable to the subject that is immunized in its dream of selfhood. The book begins with a preface about the clinamen, a crucial figure within Althusserian aleatory materialism, where freedom is associated with the encounter that occurs in deviation. As a minimal form of diversion that occurs in the parallel fall of a rain of atoms, the clinamen operates as an act in which freedom is expressed as indeterminable encounter: "If the atoms of Epicurus, which fall into the vacuum in a parallel shower, encounter (escaping the determinism of Democritus), it is so that we can recognize the random eruption of freedom in the senseless backdrop of an endless falling of particles. *It is a freedom born out of the encounter.*"[42] For Navarro, the encounter involves a "displacement, *from the substantial to the relational*, from structure to modality. Hence, the imperative of a change of perspective directed toward a vision of the universe that would permit another orientation of being, no longer as a foundation; a vision of a world inhabited not by essences bur rather by actors, situations, and singularities."[43] The encounter refers to a desubstantialization of the world in order to address the singularity of situated actors. In questioning the space that dominated the philosophical imagination of subjectivity, Navarro proposes to establish a displacement from the intrasubjective to the intersubjective: this implies introducing the body to thought, not quite as "object" but rather as part of what constitutes the experience of a situated and ever-changing being.[44] Navarro's reflection combines the imagination of the encounter as a crucial component of a materialism that is open to the incalculable as well as to the existentialist question that she picks up from Sartre and Beauvoir. From this perspective, the book insists on the necessity of transforming philosophy into a space that is fundamental for imagining liberation in relation to an ethics of alterity instead of maintaining the privileged subject of reason in its designated place.

The discovery of the aleatory and contingent is one of the effects that '68 had on philosophy, invoking an entire corpus that critiques representation in all its forms, principally in the matrix that constitutes the sovereignty of the subject of Western metaphysics in its different aspects. As in Williams's analysis of one of the classic works of Lecumberri, *Los días y los años* (*The Days and the Years*) by Luis González de Alba, '68 is an event that comes to imply the suspension of the determinism that constitutes the sovereign subject and furthermore opens the very space of the contingency of the indeterminable.[45] Breaking with the structure of a political monopoly implies also breaking with the kind of subject that it implies, and with the fiction of "choice" that sustains it. In this way, the reflections that are reproduced during and after '68 regarding the figure of radical contingency (a matter that Revueltas's theoretical act had intended to configure at the historical level) invoke the modes of thinking about the indeterminable components that give constituency to the new within history. It is important to emphasize that Navarro's philosophy can be seen as a site in which a double gesture takes place. On the one hand, her philosophical intervention in *Existence, Encounter, and Chance* can be located within the tradition of poststructuralist rupture, displacing the ideal of the sovereign subject as it appears to always be immune to the encounter with alterity.[46] On the other hand, she introduces, simultaneously, an attempt to think together the dimensions of historicity and subjectivity that are produced in the encounter between sexed and situated beings that meet up in their deviation. In speaking of the subjective dimension, it is necessary to clarify that I am not referring here to the emergence of a novel "subject" that would come to replace the one that had been criticized. Instead of keeping her discourse in this zone, Navarro honestly inquired into how the radical destabilization of the idea of freedom based on the will of a subject (substance) who can decide and choose generates processes of subjectivation to which it is truly incommensurable.

Freedom is problematized not only as a philosophical matter that concerns the critique of the sovereign subject, of simple causality, and legislative determinism, and so on; it also is a problem that concerns itself with subjectivities situated in a place, in a social class, in a kind of ethnic and sexual difference. Navarro's work also produces something with which Gayatri Chakravorty Spivak would perhaps agree in her affirmation from the classic essay "Can the Subaltern Speak?" when analyzing the forms in which postrepresentationalist thought can fall into particular essentialisms when attempting to establish a critique of representation, assuming certain capacities or agencies as given, without putting them in question.[47] I consider this to be a crucial point when developing an honest analysis of the critiques of representation that derive from '68 and from the forms in which its language maintains a type of dominant unquestioned structure. It is therefore not strange that it is women philosophers who bring such dissonance to language and furthermore expose it; in the case of Navarro, it does not suffice to talk about a philosophy capable of conceiving the encounter with the radically other, but rather it becomes necessary to give a body to that alterity.

Situated Experience and Freedom

In effect, the crisis of the subject is not only an epistemological break nor a residual ideological schism for conceiving new forms of human community. It is fundamentally an experience, a constitutive fact of intersubjectivity. It is the phenomenon itself that is given in the contact with the other—an encounter that is not foreseeable—and thus, in the return to the self, this one adopts another figure, different from the one at which it first departed, since the metamorphosis of the I implies the encounter with an other and supposes the fracture of the self, that is, its crisis. —FERNANDA NAVARRO, *Existencia, encuentro y azar*

Aleatory materialism ultimately emerged in the heterodox Marxist thought of the sixties (on both sides of the Atlantic) as a form of breaking with the notion of legislating history, thus opening up the possibility of thinking transformation within politics. As Balibar expresses it in a talk he gave in Mexico about Althusser's late work and his entailments with Latin America, the theme of encounter invoked a "modality of contingency, of fragility."[48] However, it is perhaps crucial to add that such contingency always continues to be traversed by the interest in encounters between unities (students, working class, modes of production, political organization, and epistemology) without thereby having to address the various undertones present in concrete situations and the indelible inequalities between unities. It is perhaps in this aspect that Navarro's writings work to supplement these ponderings, especially as she attends to the figure of alterity and therein poses the necessity of incorporating the existential and situational sphere in which the encounter becomes textured—in other words: the necessity of adhering *bodies to the encounter.* To this end, Navarro sustains the relevance of two figures who had been crucial both in '68 and after, Sartre and Beauvoir, noting: "I decided to incorporate Sartrean existentialism within the interpretive line that traverses this text for considering it one of the contemporary views that has managed to lucidly and zealously capture the problem of existence . . . *ultimately in its interest in the conditions of possibility of others' experience, in alterity—a fundamental category for our theme of the Encounter.*"[49] It would seem that the insistence on the encounter with alterity, its possibility, is posed in both abstract and situated terms, in the passage from existence as "primary act," freedom as the "first condition for action," and action itself as the modification of "the figure of the world . . . always in a *situation that is given.*"[50] At the beginning of her section on Beauvoir, Navarro points directly to this: "The woman has been constituted in the absolute alterity through the millenary gaze of patriarchy. This fact has impeded the development of an ethical theory that is constitutive of the person: vindicating itself as subject. Never had they shared the world *as equals.* The man, the sovereign, has defined the woman not in herself as a self that is autonomous, but rather in relation to him, positioning himself as the point of reference."[51]

The role that situated existence acquires in the text is important in that, for Navarro, this position is conducive of a certain level of honesty or nakedness of a thought confronted by its limitations. Alterity is generally an abstract category, distanced from its existential and everyday concreteness, which paradoxically sutures it onto an otherness that one can call "comfortable." For Sartre, however, the encounter with alterity suggests a conflictive instant in that it implies a threat to the security of the self in its hypothetical sameness—otherness therefore implies the decay of whoever looks at it: "According to the philosopher, we are therefore witnesses to a paradoxical and conflictive relation in anticipating the emergence of the subject as the subject is intent at the negation of the other—that other who I am not—and, simultaneously, capturing the other within his own self as another subject, the authentic other."[52] This section of her book poses a theme that positions us in the zone of '68 that is linked to philosophies of liberation and ultimately to the problem of the violence that the emergence of alterity into the dominant Western conceptual space provokes. This emergence refers not only to the fact that the dominant subject (the philosopher) attempts to conceive alterity but also to the fact that what used to function as alterity (the woman, for example) not only enters and occupies this space but also attempts to intervene in it (in that very violent equality mentioned by Taibo).

Navarro dedicates many pages to the contemplation of how alterity indelibly implies an instant of the destabilization of the self, of comfortability, of establishment. Returning to Sartre, she writes:

> In the origin of the problem of the existence of alterity there is a fundamental and threatening supposition: the other is s/he for whom I am not a subject but rather an object, an obstacle. My response will therefore be to make an effort toward reducing the other to object as well, insofar as he is a subject that denies my character as subject: While I try to liberate myself from his dominion, he intends the same. My project of recovering the subject of my self cannot be met without me taking power of the freedom of the other and submit his will to mine . . . and thus his freedom is a foundation to my being.[53]

This is nevertheless only a small component, because—for the other to be found within one's gaze—one is already assuming the other's interiority: "The desire or impulse of reducing the other to object is impossible. Freedom, taken as gaze (*hecha mirada*), can only be assumed by a subject."[54] Returning to thinking about the condition of possibility of the encounter with alterity is thus crucial since it figures the other as a substance that is in many ways less harmonious, and it furthermore addresses the agonizing and conflictive component that is at play in the encounter.

I emphasize this form of conceiving the uncomfortable and conflictive aspect of the encounter (threatening insofar as it poses a crisis of stability) since it drastically changes the way in which we can conceptualize the freedom that it expresses. This is a question that is not just about the plenitude of the encounter among singularities within a space incommensurable with freedom, as Jean-Luc Nancy expresses in *Experience of Freedom*, but rather about the space and the very situation in which it takes place—the conditions of possibility and impossibility of the exposition of uncomfortable alterities.[55] The emphasis on the not-so-idyllic forms of encounter among singularities in deviation furthermore connotes the violence of the act of cohabiting a place that is uncommon yet ferociously communized. Turning to concrete cases of fundamental value for understanding this, such discomfort and violence are expressed within the forms in which the few participants of '68 who categorize women's participation as novel remember the complexity of this moment as all the inertias of masculinity began to be exposed as part of an invisible struggle. Such a struggle was nothing less than the possibility of treating the participation of women in a field of equality that was undermined by macho positions. Thus, a violence that was not previously perceived as such gradually begins to become visible, making itself an important component of change in the comprehension not merely of politics but also of the space that makes politics possible—that is, of a space of assumptions from which a world or a plane of coexistence and participation emerges among those who do not usually share these existential and situational planes. Navarro's texts take this complexity to the philosophical field.

I tend to think that the discomfort of this non-idyllic encounter, one that maintains a certain conflict instead of creating a new subject, is figured in Althusser's aleatory materialism as a missed encounter. This idea emerges within his text "The Underground Current of the Materialism of the Encounter" in a moment that invokes nothing less than the events of '68, especially toward the end of its highly poetic reflections of historical encounters, where he names the missed encounter between workers and students.

> This is where their *surprise* lies (*there can be no taking-hold without surprise*). This is what strikes everyone so forcefully during the great commencements, turns or suspensions of history, whether of individuals (for example, madness) or of the world.... No one will balk at the idea that this is one of the basic features of the history of individuals or the world, of the revelation that makes an unknown individual an author or a madman, or both at once ... when the French Revolution breaks out and triumphs down to the march of Napoleon ... when the Commune bursts forth from treason ... when 1917 explodes in Russia, or, *a fortiori*, when the "Cultural Revolution" does, a revolution in which, truly, almost all the "elements" were unloosed over vast spaces, although the lasting encounter did not occur—like the 13th of May, when the workers and students, who ought to have "joined up" (what a result would have resulted from that!), saw their long parallel demonstrations cross, but *without joining up*, avoiding, at all costs, joining up, conjoining, uniting in a unity that is, no doubt, still forever unprecedented (the rain in its *avoided* effects).[56]

This extensive paragraph reads like the photographic negative of what Revueltas proposed in his notion of the theoretical act through his reading of similar moments, looking for encounters that a present moment is able to produce by simultaneously removing and linking truncated pasts. In contrast, Althusser traces an encounter that could not take place, yet one that nevertheless is worthy of the question: how would the "joining up," "conjoining," "uniting in a unity" of students and workers function? There are perhaps two things at play in this crucial passage that describe the encounters. On the one hand, there is the fact that, without permanence, the encounter is not able to form a world. On the other hand, we have the idea that the encounter implies a "joining" in unity, something that Navarro questions in her *Existence, Encounter, and Chance* in proposing a different conceptualization of the encounter. While for Althusser the *union in unity* appears to synthetize the idea of the enduring encounter, this is made more complicated if we read it from the framework of instants/events that are crucial but are full of encounters that did not last in terms of a continuous, unbroken permanence; that is, in the sense that the contingent and transient seem to leave behind seeds that are capable of being cultivated in a future moment, thereby modifying what we understand by the notion of duration. We are facing here the same problem that Revueltas pointed to when analyzing the temporality of revolutionary situations and moments that do not last but continue their existence in an underground mode of existence (something that was posed in *Time and Number* as the struggle between three minutes of freedom and the giant weight of years of sentence). In chapter 2, dedicated to cinema, we saw the emergence of forms of collaboration that, although they did not endure, were nevertheless crucial in a moment of urgency. The questions that Navarro poses here are: How can an encounter that does not imply gathering in a "unity" last? How can we think of a duration that does not invoke calendarization and therefore exists as a nonchronological temporality? Here we find a particular partition in Navarro's reflections on aleatory materialism, one that perhaps brings us philosophically very close to what Revueltas poses in his *Time and Number*. What happens when a fleeting but nevertheless intense encounter occurs and makes possible, perhaps for the first time, the visualization of something that had always been politically purged? Such was the encounter among students, workers, and artists, between women and men that for *a very short instant* (yet gigantic as a singularity) proceeds in a crossing of gazes and a cohabitation of the space of communication as equals. To an extent, this is part of a problem that needs to be revisited, especially as the gaze that has prevailed over the moment is one that annuls, almost in an a priori way, this very instant in the past through its intention to measure and evaluate it with the standard of the linear time of a historical continuum. At the end of the book, Navarro discusses the temporality of the encounter and the mode in which this encounter is to be associated with different forms of subjectivation; she thus titles the last section with an idea that destabilizes the notion of permanence as union in unity: "*Today is always.*"

Today Is Always

Yet there is another facet of Time: *that which concerns the duration (of the relation).* Consistent with the uncertain and unsubstantial condition of the "subject" thus maneuvered, the subject *incapable of coinciding with itself: how could we then ask it to coincide with alterity?* It appears thus as a multiplicity, inhabited by a multiplicity of selves, and *we could indeed venture very poorly into the shape of such calendarization.* This congruency impedes us from speaking, for the meantime, of an a priori duration. Since the self and the other do not arrive at the same Time, there is no synchrony in the relation, and thus, they are not contemporaries. *Prior to such asymmetry, the conventional forms of entailment that appeal to artifices such as the Law or to Language—in order that they assure an illusory permanence or duration—result to be quite unfounded, if not pathetic, or even, "against nature"* . . . as in the case of the lifetime contracts consecrated through ceremonies. In this I concord with the proposal of two philosophers in their appeal to the "invitation of the two lonelinesses" (De Beauvoir), "to a sharing of a temporality" (Luce Irigaray). A temporality, of course, whose duration can range anywhere between weeks, decades and lustrums. A temporality that furthermore does not guard any relation with the same degree of intensity and plenitude that it could potentially reach. In any case, it is manifested as that which is limited more through the signs of life than though its regulations. —FERNANDA NAVARRO, *Existencia, encuentro y azar*

This extensive passage from the end of Navarro's text signifies the crucial point in *Existence, Encounter, and Chance* where Navarro destabilizes the form through which we have come to conceptualize the permanence of encounter, an effort I find important in light of the forms in which it speaks to the temporality of social movements, which is usually of great intensity and fleetingness. The question that follows would be, once more: in what form of thought does the philosophical figure of permanence fall once we arrive at a desubstantialization of the form of existing and conceiving the free? By appealing to a permanence that measures temporarily in terms of the calendar, are we not committing the error of reintroducing the linear logic and teleology of the historicization that we had aimed to disrupt? Is there a way to exit this dilemma? How does something live even as it is chronologically dead as substantial unity?

In chapter 1, on Revueltas, some of this was at play when I approached the paradoxical role of the disproportion between three minutes of freedom and the fifteen-year sentence. In other words, this freedom does not adhere to the properties of linearity but instead follows a form that is much closer to the spiral: it could be the image of the freedom of the prisoner (abandoned as nameless) that runs toward the cliff and then returns—as he experiments with a novel form of sensing freedom, one that is radically other and *heterogeneous* to the time of the sentence, postulating, perhaps, a problem similar to that which Navarro postulates toward the end of her book. In Navarro's text, the present is read as multiplicity: it does not exist as a reference for the purpose of regulating the past and the future in the mode of projection but rather is a motley present time composed of many temporalities that are not symmetrical within themselves, nor are they reducible to a single unity (they are asymmetrical temporalities). Every singularity, every time that is reunited in an encounter, cannot therefore encounter the other in a matter of summation. The regulation of encounters through temporal measure invokes the intention to legislate a multiple life that resists this very thing (duration here appears to be close to the Bergsonian notion of duration). A crucial example in this case is the form in which the Zapatista movement introduces this theme with the intention of addressing a differential politics that is not made rigid by the markers of an electoral calendar nor by the times demarcated by the state and its register. Instead, the Zapatista movement appeals to another temporality: that of the heteronomous alterity found in a life based on community, in its agony, in its becoming, in its metamorphosis.[57] From this perspective, what is at stake is not the fact of submitting to temporal trials the events that are marked by encounters that, in one moment within the history of the world, traced a different course. This would implicate a continuation of that which was previously denied: the notion of a possible revolutionary "success"—one that would be nothing less than the end of history (if by "success" we suppose an absolute transcendence brought by a final unity). Navarro expresses it best:

> The notion of Time that is here required: alien to any notion of ultimate end and of Hegelian "superation." It now seems clear to me that interpersonal experience is not a question of evolution. It does not refer to progress nor to the advent of a Messianic Era, nor does it refer to the fantasy of changing the world. It does not refer to a nostalgic return to a mythical Golden Age either. . . . Simply, it refers to a distinct modality of residing in the world. *Today is Always. The Time of the encounter is and has always been a permanent event, already-here, embodied and manifested in an incontestable omnipresence that encompasses and embraces a contemporary anachronism.* The relation between people is given by way of an intuitive and immediate re/cognition that exists in the TODAY *with its multiplicity of dimensions . . .* in the fortuitous and aleatory encounter that can take place in any intersection of time and space . . . in

an always-already-here, under the particular luminosities and silences of every epoch and of each particular encounter—in all of its necessity and contingency.[58]

"Today" therefore emerges as a reflection on change from the standpoint of life rather than from an already-established plan. Furthermore, it constitutes the conceptualization of history as an anachronistic system in which a multiplicity of dimensions exists at every moment (every moment habituated by many moments past). In part, Navarro poses a complete radicalization of the gaze onto a time that is at a loss for chronology, a time at a loss for linearity: "The I and the other do not live in the same Time. There is no synchrony in our relations, and thus, they are not contemporaries."[59] Even as this is a case, they seemingly share a now (a now that is nevertheless different for both of them).

At the end of her book, Navarro takes the insistence on the aleatory encounter to the question of love and the introduction of what therefore presupposes an encounter that does not reduce or *assimilate* but is capable of being conceptualized with the care of an anachronistic temporal notion: I refer here to inhabiting a heterogeneous multiplicity of times while *sharing* a mode (a piece) of present time in everydayness. The radicalization of the conceptualization of time within events (outside the time imposed by the logic of developmentalism) in situated examples takes us to a reflection on the everyday that makes possible life *in common* within such anachronism through the repetition of each day, each time, and the freedom found in an encounter that does not necessarily head toward a "forever." That which is free invokes a repetition rather than a substantial permanence:

> It will not be the belief in an evolutionary process that will permit us to speak about an authentic relation of love, of an encounter between two subjectivities that share a space and respect each other in the recognition of their alterity, of their freedom, and are furthermore willing to engage in adventure in their duality. It will be precisely in the heat and the noise within the repetition of each day, where we will find the ties that suppose a relation between two people as continually integrating . . . both unexpected and intuitively, through the medium of gazes and heartbeats: more powerful and defiant than all Decalogue, vigilance, or prohibition.[60]

In bringing forward everyday life as a crucial element of an affect that is woven into its very process of existence, it appears that the theme we saw in Revueltas's preoccupation with language and imagination is now part and parcel of an alterity that is not determined or protected by the notion of the assimilable or the analogous. Jacques Derrida traces this question in terms of an insistence on what he calls a "pure ethics" and poses that, through its existence, it "begins with the respectable dignity of the others as the absolute unlike, recognized as nonrecognizable, indeed as unrecognizable, beyond all knowledge, all cognition and all recognition: far from being the beginning of pure ethics, the neighbor as like or as resembling, as looking like, spells the end or the ruin of such an ethics, if there is any."[61] In a certain way, this indicates the ability to trace the uncertain frontier between ethics and the kind of politics that is generally based on "electing and preferring the most seeming, that which is knowable, that which is familiar and recognizable, the technique and the right of calculation that seek to know and recognize the seeming and the same as a unity of measurement)."[62] The insistence on alterity emerges within Navarro's work through her dialogue with Foucault, Derrida, and Emmanuel Levinas, wherein she concentrates on the figure of the encounter as a mode of asking for a certain widening of what could appear to be ungovernable—that is, of what exceeds the technicality of government in their arrangement of domesticated and predictable subjects. The difficulty with this ethical insistence is that, as Judith Butler argues, it places us at the limits of our own schemas of intelligibility and urges us to contemplate the meaning of being able to establish a dialogue "at the limit of what one knows."[63] I will now take this reflection to other sites of language associated with the memories of women that bring about '68 through a similar insistence, yet this time in contexts through which the laboratory of liberation emerges in experiences of the opening and coexistence of difference.

REMEMBRANCES FROM THE WOMEN'S PRISON
AND THE POPULAR PREPARATORY

Of Freedom and Imprisonment by Roberta "La Tita"
Avendaño and *Ovarimony* by Gladys López Hernández

In the nineties, the memory of '68 began to expand through new questions
and obstacles in which—in addition to a series of mostly investigative texts
about the massacre and the reflections of some spokespeople who had written
several volumes over the decades—a series of different and disparate proposals
emerged.[1] If we pay attention to studies such as *1968: El fuego de la esperanza*
by Raúl Jardón (1998), the new testimonies gathered in *1968: Más allá del mito*
by Esteban Ascencio (1998) and in *De la libertad y el encierro* (*Of Freedom and
Imprisonment*) by Roberta "La Tita" Avendaño (1998), or the fictionalization
of the era in *Amulet* by Roberto Bolaño (1999), we find that whether in essay,
testimonial form, or fiction, '68 emerges from a gesture of multiple decenter-
ings with respect to the usual ways it is thought about.[2] Here, imagination plays
a singular role in the ways of thinking of the movement above and beyond
the massacre. These publications have in common the fact that they avoid the
semantic closure of '68 as "Tlatelolco" while sharing the desire to open the
memory of its temporality as a way of re-signifying aspects that had remained
somewhat closed off. As Ascencio affirms in the prologue to his collection of
testimonies, "reducing the movement of '68 to what occurred on October 2nd,
to confine an entire process of struggle to a single day, on the one hand min-
imizes the multiplicity of expressions, and on the other hand worships a
very basic necrophilia."[3] The same question that Ascencio puts forth initiates
Jardón's meticulous study, but now in relation to a return to the historicity of
the moment that attempts to avoid the idea of '68 as a "spontaneous explosion
in which, as if by magic, the students suddenly became politicized and threw
themselves into the streets," and to propose ways that "take into consideration
the social situations that fermented the explosion, and the previous struggles

and organizational experiences that constituted the grounds for the mobilization."[4] It has to do with a desire to do the movement justice with a memory that can decenter what has come to be known as the myth of '68 in order to put together other points of view, times, and ways of reimagining the event with a plurality of colors.

Two of the interventions that appeared on the thirtieth anniversary connect to this field with the presence of women: as a character in Roberto Bolaño's *Amulet*, and as the narrator in Roberta "La Tita" Avendaño's *Of Freedom and Imprisonment*. From the space of literature, *Amulet* reconstructs a polemical image of '68 from the re-creation of Alcira Sanst-Scaffo (as the character Auxilio Lacoutoure in Bolaño's novel), the Uruguayan poet and teacher who lived undocumented in Mexico. Centered on a character who does not have anything to do with the typical subjects of the '68 repertoire, the novel imaginatively reconstructs a history that circulated orally through the School of Philosophy and Letters: at the moment when the riot police took the school, violating the university's right to autonomy, Alcira decides to remain in a stall in the women's bathroom for several days, without eating or drinking anything. At the beginning of Poniatowska's *Massacre in Mexico*, Carolina Pérez Cicero tells the story of Alcira, who could not escape, or who did not want to, and whom a worker found lying on the bathroom floor fifteen days later. Following this oral reconstruction almost exactly—"It must have been terrible staying in there *hour after hour*, with nothing but water from the faucet in the washroom"—Bolaño's novel imagines these days from the work of imagination of this character, who was paradoxically so crucial and so marginal in the memories of the time.[5] The text is organized around Auxilio's obsession with remembering hypothetical encounters, encounters that never took place. Instead of outlining a testimonial fictionalization, it sets forth the question of building a memory from a counterfactual question: *what does it mean to imagine what did not take place yet could have all the same?*[6] In this way, the story emerges as a labor of imagination, linked to the possibilities that await when we open the potentiality of "what was," delving into its unfulfilled promises— a history written in the "future perfect."[7] The question that Auxilio asks expresses her obsession with imagining encounters that never happened. It generates a double that continues in a different form, what Revueltas's theoretical act proposed. In this case, it has to do with provoking with an act of the imagination, a continuation of instants from a truncated past, almost following the idea of the Paris graffito that was so representative of the moment: "Be realistic, demand the impossible," only changing "demand the impossible" for "imagine the impossible."

Avendaño's *Of Freedom and Imprisonment* was published in 1998 and to date has been very poorly circulated, which has resulted in scant critical reception. Instead of bringing out a more conventional memory of the movement, almost all the remembrances from the time center on lived experience in the women's prison. This re-created memory becomes a small theater that dramatizes a crucial component for the analysis of the encounter that prevailed in '68, through questions that open up a moral and political zone, where the prison appears not only as this large blockage of political dissidence but also as this great space where a difficult and also unique solidarity among women from different social classes can be tested. This generates a type of memory that does not exist in the vast testimonial complex of the male prisoners at Lecumberri, who were in a special cellblock for political prisoners. In contrast, the female political prisoners of the movement did not have this spatial differentiation and shared the everyday prison space with the common prisoners. In this way, the crucial figure of encounter that, as we saw, traces an entire zone of memories about the time, appears here presented in relation to *the difference in social class* staged through the distance between political and common prisoners. This makes it possible to ask interesting questions that up to this point had not been put forward: In what way is the figure of the encounter, until now advanced in mostly abstract terms, intersected by the question of social class? In what way does this reconfigure parts of the memory of '68 that had not appeared? In the women's prison, the coexistence of political and common prisoners makes class difference a problem and a crucial point of the experience that follows '68. We can read this problem as a form of staging of the core of the movement, whose most notable feature as a "student and popular" movement had been its ability to connect. We saw in the case of the Cooperative of Marginal Cinema that the project visualized a type of communication between students and striking workers. Nevertheless, in these memories from prison such communication is linked to everyday life, given that it has to do with the management of a common space that was not chosen as such.

The prison appears as a space in which basic principles of the movement are put to the test through an everyday exercise in which the encounter begins from something that Navarro refers to as the exposition of an alterity that emerges as a threat to the stability of the self. In Avendaño this alterity opens up a double register, since it is not only a sustained contact with women of a different social class that is marked by the difference of class and the division of labor within the prison but also the clash of morals that exposes the foundations of prejudices that continued to operate within the sexual revolution and that in the prison collide with the presence of issues such as lesbianism and prostitution.

In this sense, even if this text typifies the issue rather than analyzing it, *Of Freedom and Imprisonment* elaborates on this confrontation of social class in a way that makes it possible for us to interpret the passage from the initial fear of the world of prison to the development of communication and affection toward "the common prisoners" that Avendaño begins to experience. This generates a series of reflections that presses us to think about *how the political emerges* in this singular and uncomfortable encounter and how this form of encounter forces us, as readers, to question the lenses that we use to approach what we see in the texts by women imprisoned during and after '68. As we will see, the recollection that Avendaño makes as a teacher and law student who was a member of the National Strike Council differs from the one offered by Gladys López Hernández, a student at the Popular Preparatory, who was also imprisoned at Santa Martha. Each text allows us to look at different ways in which the political is signified when the environment being written about refers to the primacy of what we call "common" prison, which is generally discredited by revolutionary politics' forms of legibility. A distinctive component of these memories is that they open up the possibility of establishing networks and words that enable us to think in intersectional ways and to attend to the transformation that the encounters and interactions among women from different social classes and cultural backgrounds made possible.[8] The advantage of an intersectional approach is that it produces "a shift in the analytical framework of categories from one of centers and margins to a conceptualization of 'interlocking' (or 'interacting') categories of difference."[9] As Ange-Marie Hancock states, intersectionality allows one to "no longer self-locate as *either* on a margin *or* in a center. . . . Conceptually shifting in this way includes moving away from additive models of inequality."[10] This implies a different political and epistemological understanding of the situations that the texts dramatize, allowing us to connect each singular experience with the complexity of the social system and diagram in which inequality is produced. For instance, at the beginning of the text, when Avendaño describes her entrance into the prison and mentions her fear of the "criminal" women, configured as abject, she does not address the process of social composition that situates some women in the university and others in the prison: the systematic injustice of the prison as a particular space for the seclusion of what does not assimilate or what is not assimilable to the dominant order. I approach the text from this angle, in terms of a *process* through which we can see an instance of learning through reading the context, conversations, and lives of the women prisoners. By taking the lives of others as the main corpus of her text, Avendaño displaces both herself and a "proper" memory of '68, allowing us to ask about the connection this memory makes to the movement in which she participated and of which she says little.

Avendaño was a teacher who was studying at the UNAM School of Law when the student strike began. Her militancy had begun a decade before when she participated in the teachers' movement led by Othón Salazar and afterward was vice president of the Generation Committee of the Movement of Student Teachers (Comité de Generación del Movimiento de Normalistas).[11] In the formation of the National Strike Council, she was one of the few women delegates in her school, and in January 1969 she was detained for her participation in the movement. After passing through detention centers and Lecumberri, she was transferred to the Santa Martha Acatitla Women's Prison, where her trial began. She was sentenced to sixteen years in prison, along with the other detained students. Published in 1998, *Of Freedom and Imprisonment* is the only text of this length that Avendaño has ever written about '68.[12] The way the narrative is structured is radically different from all other accounts published by National Strike Council members that have appeared over the decades, in part because the account is not so much about the movement as it is about the common prisoners among whom she lived at Santa Martha. As Aurelia de Gómez Unamuno writes, the text "centers on injustice and prison life more than on the student movement," becoming a denunciation of the entire prison complex.[13] In this way, the text sets itself out as an intervention that attempts not only to outline a story "lived at one time in our country" but also to link it with a present in which the demand for unfulfilled democratization persists. Avendaño opens the book by stating: "The struggle continues and the spirit is still not tamed, the beast continues to roar, let's contribute to the roar being heard until total triumph arrives."[14] The lack of mention of '68 in the book's title is explained by the fact that the text does not limit itself to the year 1968. Instead, it addresses '68 from the limitations of the present in which it is written, the nineties and the lack of economic and legal justice that affects those who do not count as privileged citizens.[15] It is as if the text were attempting to connect two temporalities (sixties and nineties) through this thread, which introduces a completely different image of '68 by focusing on the arbitrariness of the criminal justice system and shedding light on the lives of those who remain invisible behind bars.

The text begins at the moment Avendaño was detained together with other compañeras and sent to clandestine detention centers, then to Lecumberri, and finally to the Santa Martha Women's Prison, where she was held between 1969 and 1971, when she was finally released under amnesty, although without having the charges against her removed (*libertad bajo protesta*). The student movement returns at the end of the story, when the list of demands is mentioned and its validity is analyzed in light of life in prison and the view that this situation allows her to construct. This speaks to the limited notion of democracy that is upheld in Mexico and the continued validity of the movement's demands. Curiously, there is almost no mention of the other female political prisoners; their names are mentioned at the beginning, but almost the entire text is dedicated to narrating the stories of the lives of the common prisoners with whom she was imprisoned.[16]

At the beginning of the text, the student movement, full of the ideals of democracy and sociocultural change, is confronted with its internal prejudices and moral foundations as issues of class and sexual difference arise in a conversation the political prisoners have with another prisoner before being transferred to the Santa Martha Women's Prison. Symptomatically, the two pertinent issues that they are warned about have to do with cleaning (something that the "political" prisoners found insulting) and homosexuality (the fear of being sexually abused by common prisoners). As the "political prisoners" enter the women's prison and pass inspection, Avendaño narrates her first encounter with "a common prisoner" who seems to synthesize all her fears. She takes this common prisoner to be a man, but it turns out to be Martha ("Martín") Maldonado, a mustachioed woman dressed as a man, who is in charge of organizing the cleaning. The political prisoners presume that they will not clean, but Martha Maldonado could not care less about their presumption, "so we had to make an arrangement, I don't remember if it was for 15 or 20 pesos a week, to pay someone to do the cleaning for us."[17] This first "encounter" explicitly marks the class difference that would continue to operate in the prison: domestic work, seen as an insulting task for "political prisoners" who ironically could not read the politics behind this division. Although this position changes throughout time, as Avendaño starts to connect with the women she was afraid of and faces the need to start working in prison for lack of income, it should be noted how symptomatic the comment is as an assumption about the division of labor in the prison.[18] Among other things, it puts before us a paradox that emerged in the experience of prison more than in the life of the movement, as domestic tasks (especially cooking) were something in which all the participants contributed, even when the memories of the moment only stigmatize women as the ones who took primary responsibility for it. Just as the men expected meals from the women political activists, the women "political" prisoners expected the cleaning to be done by the "poor" prisoners, the "common" ones—those who had done the same work outside the prison, in the political prisoners' homes. On the other hand, we can see a similar operation in the field of sexuality: in a radical change in the way Avendaño thinks about sexual politics, the ghosts of lesbianism in the prison shows how sexual liberation upholds a heteronormative framework, where the opening taking place still did not lead to the dismantling of this framework. The blinding fear of lesbianism appears in Avendaño's description of the first encounter she had with a prisoner who was screaming, and that given the warnings, Ignacia ("La Nacha") Rodríguez told Avendaño "she must be a lesbian, defend me."[19]

It is important to note how these differences are named at the beginning of the text, in an honest testimony that enables us to see the frameworks and limitations made perceivable by this more extreme situation. It offers a map of micropolitical affects that facilitate the vision of the binaries that remained in operation in certain zones of the movement. In Avendaño's text, sexual and class differences, and, more specifically, lesbianism and criminality, mark a border of the text that she gradually learns to narrate, as if she were confronting some of the biases that constitute heteronormativity. Social patterns that were being questioned in a more radical form at the beginning of the sexual liberation taking place become frames for her first memories of the prison experience, reiterating social stereotypes of lesbianism as pathological or antinatural.[20] Even though the movement of '68 is regarded as a crucial space for the possibility of liberation movements that were to explode in the early seventies, such as the homosexual liberation movement, the fear of being approached by lesbian common prisoners haunts the first pages of the prison memory. Outside, the encounter among classes had a common language of struggle: we saw this in the case of the practices of the Cooperative of Marginal Cinema, or in the case of Topilejo, where the differences were not fraught with fear but rather imbued with a common language of struggle. In the prison this common language did not exist and was what they needed to construct another way of looking that, as we will see, entailed transformation and becoming. One could say that '68's equality had an excess of fraternity among brothers, but what happens with what is not similar or brotherly? What Navarro focuses on in the philosophical field emerges again in this text, which recalls the prison as a form of thinking an uncomfortable freedom based in a situation of exposure to an encounter with that which is not the same or symmetrical: for Avendaño, that which is non-alike is crystalized in the figure of the common prisoner. From this point of view, the memory of prison that *Of Freedom and Imprisonment* sets forth outlines an interesting trajectory that we could almost take as a lens to understand what the movement entailed: the passage from the feeling of distance toward the common prisoners, seen as abject in the eyes of the young, middle-class, educated women who arrive at the prison, to becoming nearer to this world as time goes by and their situation becomes precarious.

Guadalupe Díaz emphasizes that the prison became a place of learning and organization for Avendaño; this can be seen when Avendaño dedicates her first paragraph to provoking different readings of what prison can signify: "Prison, I don't have its dictionary definition, but there are so many and they are so varied, there is someone who spends his life imprisoned by his prejudices, by his habits, by his economic situation, by his affection, by things and by people; there are also clandestine prisons, those that no one declares and that all the authorities deny."[21] This reflection connects with the small prison of prejudices in which some of the "political" prisoners are already incarcerated when they enter the actual prison and where the process of learning through cohabitation generates a form of understanding freedom. That is, it would seem that the text itself is the site of a reflection on the forms of equality and encounter that after '68 become possible from uncomfortable places of learning. This is related to the idea from Navarro where the encounter is not just seen in the more romantic sense, which appears in Revueltas or Althusser as an encounter that generates something from a certain sympathy with what is found. Instead, the relevance of the figure of the encounter in relation to freedom is also seen from the perspective of forms of micropolitical violence that fear generates when an encounter with alterity threatens the stability of the subject and destabilizes its existential comfort. It is in this zone of thought that the most interesting part of Avendaño's testimony and reflection of freedom is located, in an honest and profound reflection about the tensions between equality and inequality seen from a complex and multifaceted field in which the woman is also a problematic multiplicity and not a homogenous subject. I will address the text as a process or space of interpretation of what it meant for her to live in prison, especially as a law student punished for a whole series of crimes related to the practice of politics. We might think that the prison operates throughout the entire book as *a complex system of signs* with which Avendaño attempts to compose different meanings.

Of Freedom and Imprisonment is organized around the stories of the women prisoners whom Avendaño knew and the friendships she established based on this encounter between women she would never meet in any other context. Rather than idealizing the prison, I am interested in analyzing and bringing out the conceptual figures of freedom that emerge from the uncomfortable, difficult cohabitation of women of different social classes and educational backgrounds. The exposure to alterity triggers a reflection on the form of the unpredictable encounter with the world that remains distant from the university, no longer in the sense of the distance between the capital city and the rest of the country, or the urban and the rural, but rather the distance of class and the realities that this implies. A complex perspective arises that governs the textuality of the women's prison: the university student is confined in the same place as women who were socially denigrated and excluded (the world of poverty and its drifts into prostitution, homicide, etc.). In one of the testimonies reproduced by Poniatowska in her *Massacre in Mexico*, Avendaño stresses the shock her parents experienced when they visited her in prison for the first time. She recalls the difficulty of the conversation that she had with her father, who was angry to see his daughter held as a criminal when she was the first person (and, moreover, a woman) from the family who was able to attend university.

The perception of the prison as an apparatus that reproduces this system and the abuse of women (the use of the women prisoners as prostitutes, drug mules, etc.) causes Avendaño to address the prison as a school where she can learn about systemic injustice and ethics. This perception is not about transforming the prison into an extension of the university but rather, in Avendaño's text, the learning process comes out of the possibility of communication among people of different social classes who have little in common outside the fact of living in the same place. Just as we saw in Revueltas and in the cinema of '68, this transforms the prison into a different vantage point on society in its entirety and on the rules that govern the inclusion and exclusion of people in an order. The text proposes a reading that underscores what is socially discriminated and invisibilized, something that Avendaño poses throughout the text in relation to poverty and the processes of criminalization that prevail over lives that do not have access to another future. Through the history that Avendaño constructs about several prison compañeras, she shows the destiny of a social class that is locked in a cycle based in the injustice of the system, which is difficult to break: prison-freedom-prison-freedom. This opens up the notion of a social freedom that progressively becomes enclosed and relativized: When we speak of freedom, who are its subjects? Is it the freedom of one social class and the invisibility of another layer of society that is systematically marginalized? From here, the memory of the encounter between nonequals deepens but also is enriched, since an entire micropolitical reading emerges when the text begins to operate as the *construction of a process* that re-creates *in words* a form of passage, the desire of a bridge of communication between totally asymmetrical but shared situations. This is a memory that has to do with different affects of life in common (fear, anger, love, solidarity) from where an entire zone is visualized, one that, little by little, moves from the place of opposition between the political consciousness of the educated woman and the border she confronts when she lives with an until then almost abject "otherness," marked by the fear of the "common" prisoners with whom she begins to develop a close link and a zone of exchange in language, histories, and life together.

The text begins in fear, where the prison figures as a "pandemonium" until the routine and tedium is broken by nothing less than the escape of a common prisoner named Sharon. The event modifies the routine and everyone gets up to look, generating a change in the tone of the narration, as if the jailbreak were replicated in the text itself, escaping the monotony of binaries and the separations created by the division between political and common prisoners. These latter begin to intermingle, creating a passage between experiences that modifies the place in which speech is produced. Following the escape, the text becomes decentered and weaves a common space among the different prisoners from a "moment of diversion" that eases the separations between the "political" and the "common" prisoners, distracting them from the monotony of the everyday life of the prison.[22] The text begins to flow in another direction: a dialogue with common prisoners begins to displace the political prisoners' old life to the extent that from this point on, the entire text will be about the common prisoners. Playing with the figure of a border that has begun to be crossed, the narration of the escape that wakes them up and entertains them is followed by a memory that is curious because of the ambiguity of the situation that begins to blur this categorical division of the political and the common. It has to do with an encounter with a common prisoner who was isolated from the rest in the area for the "disturbed." As Avendaño and her fellow prisoners approach this woman, they hear her ask,

> "Are you the students?" Yes, we responded, to which she said "and you haven't seen my daughter? She is dark-skinned, with short, straight hair, she studies in the university. You haven't seen her? No? You must have seen her! She went to the demonstration and she hasn't come back, tell her to come back already." . . . I could not give an affirmative response to her question, I could not help this poor mother get her daughter back, I could not give her news of her daughter, I could not, I could never console her and tell her where her daughter was. Might someone know? Perhaps those people who massacred her on October 2, 1968, might know? The mother went crazy from pain of the loss of her daughter; when she was able to escape from the house of the family members who were caring for her, she threw rocks and insulted the causes of her disgrace, politics and the military, for which she was immediately detained and sent to prison.[23]

Because of the very ambivalence of this woman, a mother who was detained and kept in prison as "disturbed," the distinction between political and common begins to become less strict and more intriguing. Tlatelolco emerges at this point in the text through the desperation of a mother who continued to search for her daughter until she was transformed into a crazy woman and then a prisoner. This story, which introduces something familiar to the political prisoners but from someone whom the system did not consider "political," causes the text to begin to regard the histories of so many other women in a different way. Thus, a certain ethic begins to emerge, displacing the dividing line that was so pronounced at the beginning. How is politics understood from the prison and the injustice that it expresses and represents?

Avendaño speaks of the passing of time and distance since the end of the university strike as increasingly greater. Visits from her compañeras and compañeros from the student movement become less frequent and money is scarce, which generates a change in her situation and the beginning of a new routine of work and exchange. The time of normality returned for many who progressively distanced themselves, and a breakdown began between the life of the movement and the time of life in the prison. In *Massacre in Mexico*, this is mentioned in a passage by Avendaño:

> Many of my friends have gotten married and gone back to their hometowns—now that there's nothing left of the Movement; they've made new friends and have new interests, and I feel very far away from all of them now. When they come to visit me, we get to talking about some mutual friend or other, but it isn't the same any more. 'I haven't seen him for ages . . .' 'I wonder what's happened to so-and-so . . .' People have lost contact with each other. What's Enrique up to? What happened to Pedro? And Clemente? And Lisandro? Nobody knows. . . . It just isn't the same. It's as though the whole thing happened years and years ago.[24]

This double temporality reverberates in prison life as their privileges as "political prisoners" begin to disappear and they must work in order to survive the everyday experience of prison.

> At the beginning of our confinement we had many visitors, some money that they collected at the School used to arrive for us and with it we covered the expenses of washing clothes, or a treat, or to buy something for my mom. As time passed I began to make loaves of bread on Saturdays, which I sold to compañeras and earned some money; I made stuffed animals that always ended up a little lopsided and poorly made, but they

were a big hit, also slippers with pompoms, beaded necklaces, all to make a few pesos.[25]

With the passage of time, the initial privileges disappear and Avendaño begins to speak of the friendships she has made with some common prisoners. She says that, before prison, her friends were people like her, but now in prison she discovers friendship among people who were not so similar: "There were many compañeras I met in the prison, for me it was a new world," she writes, and adds the formation of bonds of solidarity that break the stereotype that "given the characteristics of the people who live there one could think that indifference or not-giving-a-shit pervade, but this wasn't the case, and on multiple occasions support was given for different problems that arose."[26] In a way, this description of the lives and friendships she established emerges from the surprise that Avendaño experiences when she negotiates the web of prejudices through which she previously saw the other prisoners. Little by little, this distance grows shorter, and the woman who goes free is not the same one who entered the prison. In a way, this marks the broadening of a certain sense of the political in which the democratic demands of '68 were taken toward a zone that still remained outside the specter of the political for those lives destined to the common prison.

Freedom?

The entirety of Avendaño's text deals with confinement. But how is freedom, the other word in the title, configured? Avendaño remembers that when her mother died and they released her from the prison to attend the funeral, some of her colleagues from the School of Political Science proposed the possibility of fleeing. She comments that she told them no, because "we live in a country that is like a large prison. Where would I go?"[27] This sensation that the idea of a society-prison awakens is strengthened over the course of many moments in the text in which freedom emerges as a reflection of the false idea of "getting out" of prison. She narrates the feelings that she experienced every time a common compañera was released: Avendaño felt happy for her but she also felt a strong sadness, given that, in spite of the fact that the person being released promised to keep in touch with those who remained inside the prison, this was almost impossible given the harshness of the outside world and the daily struggle to survive. Many of those who went "free" returned shortly thereafter, charged with recidivist crimes, creating the notion of an always enclosed and relative freedom in which the prison refers not only to confinement but also to society itself. The text also plays with the idea of freedom and leaving the prison in an ambiguous way in another moment in which Avendaño describes the death of an elderly fellow prisoner, who had been imprisoned there for decades. This case replicates the question and the impotence that emerged in the case of the mother of the student who disappeared in Tlatelolco: this woman lived in a shantytown and had an altar with candles for Our Lady of Guadalupe. One night, the flame of a candle set the altar, and her ranch, on fire. She was accused of the crime of "damage to property of the nation" because the fire reached government electricity poles, and she died years later in prison. When her coffin was taken away, the prisoners shouted, "She goes free!" leaving a bitter image of freedom that would seem to coincide with death.[28]

As time goes by, freedom's spatial and temporal meaning is lost in order to connect to a problem of justice and equality. Avendaño narrates the experience of the prison as the exposure to a sense of unreality of her earlier perception about education and knowledge. This leads her to speak of two kinds of knowledge: one is imposed in schools as a form of skeletal truth that has little to do with what she has lived; another is generated through certain experiences that enrich but also involve a painful awakening to something that had previously gone unseen, a reality that radically differs from what is taught in the institutions and questions this knowledge. Avendaño describes it in the last pages of the book as a learning process that was hard, but real, based on experience: "You live it and it breaks you and it knocks you down."[29] The text culminates with the comparison between these two schools: education that teaches a world that seems unreal and the experience lived in the prison that emerges from a counterknowledge, a destabilization of what was learned. In leaving the prison, she asks herself, "Which [school] do I go with? . . . with the one that they give me or the one that I seek?" as a way of inquiring about the form of learning that differed from formal education. And she responds, "And your life is decided, and what in a moment they give you as punishment to discourage you, transforms into your greatest support . . . here are the poor, those who suffer, those who because they do not have anything to pay with are hit and humiliated, here close to injustice I have gotten stronger, although I have also given up hope when I have not heard people echo that this should not be allowed."[30] With these last words, the text that recalls '68 in 1998 brings up what had been at the core of one of the fundamental issues of self-management: the articulation of the knowledge of the world, learning as social interaction and not as an imposition of abstract solutions to distant problems. The prison transforms into a brutal form of school that nevertheless brings to the fore this component of '68 that generally is mentioned in different testimonies: the awakening to another Mexico, to another reality that had been invisible through the different modernizing phases. In Avendaño's text, it is reality and the lived experience from the site and social place adjudicated to those who *do not count* and who were, even for her at the moment she entered the prison, the abject who made her feel afraid. Throughout the years she spent in prison, Avendaño's experience of awakening to another reality came from learning about the context and situation of all these "lives that are lost without knowing it, without even recognizing it, only going along with the lot they were given."[31]

Although the months of the movement's greatest intensity produced a singular encounter among people of different social classes and groups, what emerges in the experience of prison is the problem of how to connect with those who are situated on an almost apolitical edge. To put it in other words, this is the problem of how to relate to realities and lives that would seem to have their destiny in the prison without political or militant organization being a component of it. In these situations, what is essential is not to see how these others who seem reluctant to participate in politics can be converted but rather to configure an approach to transformation that implicates both sides, thus posing a different way of thinking of politics. It is the world of the lumpen, so difficult for Marxism and liberalism to read and understand given that it consists of a radically asymmetrical otherness, which appears in this text in a different way from the typical reaction to the abject.[32] However, *lumpen* also works as a category that serves to stabilize the anxiety produced by the illegibility of the situation. This tension that emerges in *Of Freedom and Imprisonment* reminds me of Gareth Williams's analysis of a crucial passage of Carlos Montemayor's *War in Paradise*, which compares two types of knowledge: the knowledge of theoretical Marxism learned in the city and the knowledge of the peasants who fight with Lucio Cabañas in the Party of the Poor (using the context of the rich and the poor instead of the bourgeoisie and the proletariat). Williams interprets this difference as a struggle that "presents politics in practice," the great theater of the inequalities that surface within the languages of liberation and remain as limit-sites in university knowledge.[33] If '68 made a radical heterogeneity of language possible in a few months, the decades that followed involved a return to the specific languages of each sector and of each party. The insistence on being able to maintain that polyphonic multiplicity implies also being able to question the knowledge that is produced from urban centers and their elites, something that emerges in the memories of the women's prison and has appeared in the interior of the capital itself. This is a key point of Avendaño's memoir, and we will see a similar point in Gladys López Hernández's work: it is not only a struggle between the logics of the urban lettered elites and the logics of the rural environment that generally take on their mechanisms of legibility within political militancy where it becomes a form of recognizable other. Rather, what is at stake emerges from the two "schools" that Avendaño conceptualizes as the knowledge produced by institutions and all the languages that speak of situations that are differentiated and excluded in the constitution of this dominant pattern.

The small school that emerges from the prison opens up something that does not frequently appear in texts about or from Lecumberri insofar as it has to do with a knowledge in which an ethical question emerges about the invisible border that divides the world of those who can choose certain futures and those who seem condemned to a destiny of poverty and prison. The freedom to which the title of Avendaño's text refers takes on an enigmatic character when it is linked to the learning process that emerges from the encounter with a world of alterities that are not easily recognizable as fraternal. This uncomfortable but essential situation enables her to visualize a world that is kept *invisible* behind the walls, where inequality and injustice are eternal for a certain social class and where the prison is not an unusual and exceptional moment but rather the life itself of a destiny. In this sense, the memory of '68 from its carceral afterlife poses freedom in close relation to this encounter among nonequals in which an ethics occurs. From here, the memory of the student movement of '68 is narrated in a curious way, in that, instead of operating as a site of memorialization, it generates a question about the demand for democratization, which is still valid from another time and place. The text culminates with an assessment of the list of demands of the student movement, observing the validity of every one of the points. Nevertheless, the text does not end here: from the democratic demands of the movement, the text moves to the situation of the prisons and their multiplication: "Things in the prisons have gotten worse, now there are multiple buildings to 'contain' the criminals, how many more will they have to construct? . . . They pompously call them Rehabilitation Centers, but rehabilitation to what, if the prisons are nothing more than universities of crime and of ignominy, where humiliation is the daily bread?"[34] From here, the passage through the prison emerges, three decades later, as a way of bringing the knowledge and memory of '68 to bear on one of the key issues in the petition for freedom and the possibility of thinking about it beyond the narrow limitation of a state that reproduces exclusion and discrimination.

The encounter with the "common" population in the prison demands another type of reading of the political in which categorical knowledge gives way to a type of situational learning, recalling that, in this gesture, the experience itself of '68 is condensed as a moment of suspension of the languages "proper to" politics. Through the journey that occurs in *Of Freedom and Imprisonment*, the person who goes into and later leaves the prison is not the same. However, it is not a matter of establishing a heroic imaginary; on the contrary, it is an event throughout Avendaño's experience that modifies her ways of seeing and thinking. The entire journey through the women's prison, which would seem not to have much to do with a memory of '68, enables us to visualize the idea of social transformation that we saw at the beginning in Revueltas's texts from another angle: there can be no freedom without equality. Freedom emerges affixed to the problem of equality, as if the prison made visible a problem that extended the demands the student movement made in the field of legal injustice to the field of economic injustice. The accumulation of histories of existences and situations in which the common denominator is poverty and inequality before the law leads to the emergence of this crux of democratic demand in the political and economic field, thus projecting the key words/ideas of '68 onto this problematic: freedom, democracy, and equality. This enables us to illustrate the zone that Balibar calls "equaliberty," referring to his hypothesis that modern democracy, in which the form of citizenship as universal right to politics is instituted, is based on a principle of equality and liberty in which it is assumed that there is not one without the other, and vice versa.[35] What interests Balibar is the ability to insist on the notion that equality and liberty are not assumed to be incompatible, as occurs in the liberal frame in which economic and social equality are considered a threat to liberty, based on the notion of the individual-proprietor. The situations that the prison made visible to Avendaño lead to this problematic in which the poor women described in this memoir never go free (even when they leave prison), which transforms the notions of freedom and imprisonment into co-implicated relational instances, putting into practice what this great revolution of '68 posited as a divergence from the official languages of liberation. Of all the critiques that can been made of the text (for example, its reproduction of moral clichés), it is still relevant to note the honesty that it generates as a memoir of '68 insofar as it is not a monument that is redecorated with new wreaths of flowers every decade, praised and linked to real democratization. Here, '68 opens and closes a form of remembering that reiterates a process of learning that made it possible to understand that the demand for democratization continued to be as valid as before. Instead of closing its voice in the sphere of an old memory, the text opens the need to connect '68 with the present through poverty, humiliation, and the radical inequality of the world that the university resolved to understand and transform.

Ovarimony: Me, a Guerrilla Fighter? *by Gladys López Hernández: Memories of Self-Management from Below*

In 2013 the publication of *Ovarimony: Me, a Guerrilla Fighter?* by Gladys López Hernández provided another text written by a woman who participated in the student popular movement. It is the first text of '68 that addresses a constellation of experiences in which the common rhythm of the moment emerges through a singular learning process entailed by the project of academic and social self-management embodied by the Popular Preparatory. This collection of memories configures a way of looking at the '68 moment as an instance of liberation with regard to predetermined places and social roles, which in López Hernández's text arises from her situation as a woman from a working-class family, who was not allowed even to think of continuing her education, as her father set out her destiny as one of acquiring the necessary skills to perform domestic tasks and prepare for marriage. Silently subverting her father's expectations, López Hernández began living a double life, participating in the Popular Preparatory, one of the most incredible laboratories of self-management of the movement of '68. The impression the text leaves is the product of the memories of this experience, which promoted a different type of pedagogical horizontality based on the equal participation and organization of all students and faculty at the school. From this angle, the temporality of the movement is signified differently, as the foundations of the movement of '68 are linked with this dream of a pedagogical laboratory. Here, the figure of the encounter emerges as an experiment in popular education established between UNAM students and faculty and those who were systematically excluded from it: the rejected students who, belonging to the classes with the lowest incomes, saw themselves disqualified from a future in the world of higher education. Thus, '68 emerges in *Ovarimony* as a liberating learning process connected to the possibility of breaking with the predestination of class and gender, thus opening a whole set of micropolitical memories.

The Popular Preparatory has received very little attention in the histories of '68, putting us once again before a certain class limitation that marks the dominant that has signified the movement for the past five decades. In spite of this, in the last few years several texts have emerged that reconstruct this history, opening an entirely new layer of meaning for '68, especially from the remembrances of those who participated in this experience. In *Ovarimony*, the dominant myth of '68 is desecrated, not because the text is an "ovary-mony" (a testimony postulated from a site marked by gender) but rather because it introduces what '68 meant to many of the students from the popular classes. For those who were part of it, the "first international student movement of 1968" begins here, with an experiment that was made possible by the protest and organization that arose from the Miguel Hernández group of the School of Philosophy and Letters at UNAM. In this unusual text, one of the very few written by a woman who was not a university student, the history of the movement is told from the perspective of multiple dislocations.

When answering the question of what '68 was for her, López Hernández said: " '68 was like an awakening, not only for me, but for the young people of this time here in Mexico: to see other horizons, other paths, other ways of thinking, of living, of knowing, like an awakening to a *real* reality, pardon the redundancy, not what they put on television, in the family."[36] From her perspective, the history of the movement is organized around different points of dislocation that altered what she saw as a fixed destiny. That is to say, from López Hernández's view, '68 looks like a moment of awareness and disruption with regard to the predestination of social positions, the normative processes of subjectivization, and the experience of temporality marked as destiny. Equality and inequality emerge in complex ways as the text describes and explains not only what it implied for a sixteen-year-old young woman to get involved in a movement that radically changed her life; it also makes visible the forms in which the difference of social class manifested in the difficulty of entering higher levels of education and the consequent (in)ability to choose future(s) different from what had already been established. Thus, the experience of the Popular Preparatory opens up a broader question about the social temporality that education implies by playing a fundamental role in refiguring destiny according to class and gender.

The text, which begins in the '68 movement, illustrates an instant in which it becomes possible to rethink freedom from the situated and concrete experience of the self-management of the Popular Preparatory. As a laboratory of popular education for different social classes, this key experience in López Hernández's life allowed her to endure years of imprisonment in Santa Martha, where she spent three years after being charged with being a guerilla fighter and accused of common and federal crimes. In contrast to Avendaño, whose testimony starts with participation in the student movement, López Hernández's ovarimony narrates injustice as part of her own biography and of the history of her struggle as a woman who had to fight against a destiny rooted in her gender and her social position.

Before outlining a brief history of the Popular Preparatory, it is necessary to give a brief survey of the text, beginning with its title: why *Ovarimony*? What does an "ovarimony" speak to? In an epigraph, López Hernández recalls that a male friend once told her that the word *testimony* sounded too much like "testicle," so she decided to (somewhat jokingly) counter-title her text as an ovarimony in an attempt to break the gender imbalance in the memoirs and testimonies of '68. The joke takes on a larger meaning when we read the text and note that it contains a persistent view toward gender inequality in the forms of remembering '68:

> Throughout history, we women have been considered *adelitas* who always follow their husband, not thinking beings but only as procreators of sons, as maids, escorts, cooks, washerwomen, housewives, etcetera.... We women have been minimized in the publications about the movement and the student repression of '68, as well as in films and documentaries that have been made about this topic. The only participation of women that is mentioned is as being in charge of making food for the student comrades who were active in the struggle. However, I remember that during this movement the first brigades to inform about the State's aggressions were those exclusively made up of women students from Preparatory 8, denominated "Max." This is the brigade that Diana, one of the compañeras of one of my brothers, was in, along with many other women students from different schools, Roberta Avendaño and Ana Ignacia Rodríguez, who were in prison for many years for their participation in the movement. There were other women who painted murals on walls, made pamphlets, flyers, and propaganda in general to raise awareness about this movement.[37]

The marginalization of women's participation emerges out of the field of the gender inequalities that mark the memories of the moment but also from the greater context of lived inequalities that were preponderant at all social levels. In the first pages, López Hernández contextualizes the role that '68 had in rupturing a number of social habits and in the numerous struggles that this rupture ignited in many young women who began to live double lives behind their families' backs.

Ovarimony sets forth a temporality and a punctuation of events that differ from the usual: the beginning of the '68 student movement, understood as an international popular movement, is outlined from the beginning of the Popular Preparatory and the school's subsequent opening in Tacuba. *Ovarimony* then takes us through Tlatelolco, up to the increase in repressive forces that escalated with the Corpus Christi massacre of June 1971. The student popular movement is described from the lens of the Popular Preparatory as a unique laboratory of collective self-management, something that is repeated in her memories of prison, where López Hernández created a small secretarial school. The book is organized around four axes: the environment of '68; the beginning of López Hernández's participation in the Popular Preparatory and the Corpus Christi massacre of June 10, 1971; her visits to political prisoners in Lecumberri, where in addition to her relationship with Pablo Alvarado, she facilitates the prisoners' communication with the outside; and her detention and imprisonment in the women's prison over the course of three years, her release on bail, and the challenges of "reintegration" into a macho environment after prison, in which those who had been accused were a cause for family and public shame.

The entire first part of the text is titled "Family Environment," and it allows us to visualize an entire network of relationships of inequality that explain the relevance of '68 in López Hernández's life: "There were not enough spaces to study, much less for women. We adolescents who wanted to free ourselves through education did not have alternatives, so some of us analyzed the way to create openings, since all the paths were closed."[38] In addition to the lack of spaces, López Hernández explains that her father did not want or permit her to continue studying; he instead wanted her to learn domestic tasks so she could eventually get married. With her mother's support, she was able to get a secretarial degree when she was fourteen and began to work in a law firm, something that her father disapproved of as he thought this route was for women of loose morals. In 1967 her family was shaken by her brother's arrest alongside others from the Movement of the Revolutionary Student Left (Movimiento de Izquierda Revolucionaria Estudiantil), and López Hernández began to visit her arrested brother's compañeros in Lecumberri, where she started a relationship with Pedro Alvarado. A rural teacher and member of Arturo Gámiz's popular guerrilla group in the Chihuahua mountains who was linked to the teachers' struggle in Guerrero, Alvarado was murdered in Lecumberri years later, while López Hernández was being held in the women's prison.

Almost the entire first part of *Ovarimony* centers on the experience of the Popular Preparatory, configured as a space of freedom for the construction of a collective experience in which the rejected students could seek alternatives for their future. López Hernández emphasizes the fact that, unlike the accepted preparatory students, "our situation as *rechazados* [rejected students] was totally different, since we had to organize to obtain everything that was being denied to us. We didn't want to get discouraged, but there was a lot that needed to be tackled. The space had already been awarded; now only the necessary tools to take classes were missing, like blackboards, chalk, trained teachers, syllabi, tutors, etcetera. It was our obligation to do everything humanly possible to eventually win a place at the UNAM."[39] Upon entering this project, López Hernández began to inhabit a double life: the one her parents knew of, which included her secretarial work; and her clandestine life, which was her education in the preparatory and her participation in the movement. Unlike Avendaño, for whom the relationship between '68 and the problem of social justice was centered in the prison system as an expression of an injustice that is almost invisible for those who do not share this experience, López Hernández's text operates as a diagram that illuminates different forms of inequality and the way they formed a search for alternatives. The text problematizes something that almost no other memoir of '68 emphasizes: the question of the privileged subjects of education; that is, the question of who qualifies for and who is excluded from the right to postsecondary education, which largely determines the different futures available to the productive life of the country, its professionals, and its laborers. This places before us the central problem of self-management that we also saw in the chapter on Revueltas, insofar as it questions the complex plot that is woven between the state and epistemology and that has to do with validated forms of knowledge and the pedagogy itself that reproduces them. The state achieves stability through the repetition and reproduction of a series of social relations that uphold an implicit division of knowledge and class.[40] The great university mobilization that had been forming in the years leading up to '68 involved the emergence of a radical questioning of this division and its invisible reproduction, wagering on a radical transformation that can be seen on different levels throughout the different moments of the movement.

The Popular Preparatory

One effect López Hernández's text has is that it addresses '68 in relation to the laboratory of self-management embodied by the Popular Preparatory, situating it within a greater historical political process in which the new high schools (the Tacuba school, used as a model that is taken to other states) arose. In illuminating this entire process, from both personal and collective perspectives, the question about education that was central to the movement of '68 emerges here as a theoretical and practical question. Due to the fact that the dominant memory of this moment is expressed through the figures of university leadership, the world of the self-managed high schools that were founded at the time is not commonly noted in remembrances of '68. Among the few existing fragments of memory of these self-managed high schools written by UNAM students, Eugenia Espinosa Carbajal mentions the Popular Preparatory as an example of the concrete and highly ambitious struggle of the movement. This not only demonstrates the significance of the achievement but also marks the beginning of the student movement in the years preceding 1968.

> At that time, we were fighting for very concrete things, like we were demanding job placement for graduates or the recognition for professions, because at this time historians, philosophers, geographers did not have a federal professional license [*cédula profesional*], we also joined the movement of rejected students. In 1967 there were 13,000 students who did not get into the UNAM and we embarked on the project of the Popular Preparatory.... *The Popular Preparatory, which was successfully authorized by the Ministry of Public Education on July 13, 1968, is the first student movement in the world.*[41]

In another of the few key discussions about self-management during this time, Alberto Híjar discusses the constellation of collective experiences that put fundamental points of the movement into practice: "There was the pride of the first brigade composed of workers, professors, and students and the relatively successful support to the town of Topilejo, which had been attacked by a public transportation vehicle that ran over a resident."[42] At the same time, those rejected from the high school had organized an assembly with the parents of the excluded students. He recalls: "With the support of the Miguel Hernández group, they founded the Popular Preparatory in the unoccupied classrooms of the School of Philosophy [and Letters] and with the teaching support of dozens of student teachers. In February 1968, the self-management of public education, with the critical exercise of autonomy, began in this way. Years later the University Council would approve the incorporation and revalidation of studies at the Popular Prep, just before accepting the Self-Government of the School of Architecture."[43] With the exception of these interventions, most memories of the preparatory's importance are limited to those produced by its graduates, among which we find "La escuela imposible" ("The Impossible School") by Fernando Castillo Bolaños and Jorge Maza, as well as *Voces de la Preparatoria Popular* (*Voices of the Popular Preparatory*) by graduates of the second class: Esperanza Lili Aparicio Hoyo, José Manuel Galván Leguízamo, Rubén Dac Pérez, and Abraham Manuel Vidales Abrego. Among academic studies of the experience is the undergraduate thesis of Carlos Muñoz López, "La preparatoria popular 'Mártires de Tlatelolco': A. C. orígenes y desarrollo y desincorporación de la UNAM" ("The 'Martyrs of Tlatelolco' Popular Preparatory: Origins, Development, and Disincorporation").[44] This is an investigation that aims to analyze the history of the first Popular Preparatory, filling a vacuum of academic disinterest in the topic. As Muñoz López points out, the origin of the Popular Preparatory goes back to 1966, when the struggle of the rejected students and protest against university rector Ignacio Chávez began. Chávez's subsequent resignation made possible the election of Javier Barros Sierra, a figure who will be crucial in understanding an important change that took place in Mexican higher education at the same time as the student movement. In 1967 an inordinate number of rejected students initiated the protest struggle along with their families and the support of the Miguel Hernández group from the School of Philosophy and Letters at UNAM. This organization played a fundamental role in drawing attention to the petition for an education that would give options to the sectors denied access to higher education. In February 1968 Popular Preparatory classes began to be held in the School of Philosophy and Letters at UNAM, using empty classrooms, patios, stairs, or the auditorium.[45] In mid-July, the university announced that it would allocate the building located at 66 Liverpool Street for use as the Popular Preparatory's headquarters.[46] In his brief essay "The Hour of Self-Management," Híjar writes that "the appearance of the Popular Prep's great disorder in reality gave rise to a powerful self-management that had a great influence on the popular movements that took the project on, and that reproduced it."[47]

The "Declaration of the Principles of the Popular Preparatory," written by a coalition of groups, articulates how those who were rejected students were mostly from the low-income sectors of the population.[48] The document relates the creation of the Popular Preparatory to a larger problem: that of the meaning and reach of education, the conditions of its possibility, and the subjects who qualify for it. The declaration clarifies that the Popular Preparatory was created in the heart of UNAM, and that the preparatory's student body does not see its connection to UNAM as "one more part, another bureaucratic organism"; instead, the Popular Preparatory is conceived as the "most dynamic and advanced" sector of the university, "both because of its origin as well as its social composition and its political orientation." The democratic proposal that governs the form of self-management in this educational experiment puts together two of the forms in which Revueltas spoke of cognitive democracy: first, its arithmetic sense, as access to education for many people; and second, its fundamental qualitative sense, as a different organization of the transmission of knowledge and of the learning process in general. This had to do with thinking about a kind of education that, although within the parameters of the curriculum demanded by UNAM, proposed a different learning process: a key element of the preparatory was that its subject matter was taught in constant connection to and interaction with what was happening in society at large. López Hernández recalls that the classes were always theory in practice, insofar as they learned about the issues of the day and visited the sites where they could think about what they learned in another form.[49] This experience illuminates an entire problematic zone that refers to the relationship between state, education, and epistemology that we saw at the beginning of the book in more abstract terms, and that is rarely mentioned in the dominant memories of '68. By the relationship between state and epistemology, I mean that a memory is created not only of a struggle around how certain class relations were reproduced at the level of education (i.e., who qualified for higher education as a basic right and who did not) but also of the mode in which the struggle to transform this system of privileges also implied a transformation of pedagogy itself. It was a laboratory of educational self-management by those who were systematically excluded from the right to knowledge and instruction. In the memories of the moment that this social and pedagogical laboratory allows us to reconstruct, education cannot be separated from politics, as if this form of education were already a political intervention but put forward from the polyphonic opening of positions and gazes.

As with the rest of the movement, the Tlatelolco massacre produced a drop in participation and different cells were created, but according to López Hernández, the Popular Preparatory continued to maintain itself as a "space open to plurality," including all types of representatives of different factions.[50] Her memory of this pedagogical and political experience appears as a sort of utopian instant: "Little by little, without us realizing it, thanks to daily coexistence and to our accomplishments, we initiated an indestructible friendship through the years based on support and trust, it was like a sensitive and democratic socialism. We constructed a humanitarian utopia. Although we attended classes every day, we were always available to take a collection jar and go and hand out propaganda soliciting money, and in this way cover the most basic requirements, like paint, paper, soap."[51] The utopia achieved here had a rotating organization in "coed groups in which men and women performed the same tasks, like painting the classrooms or the building itself, the light, the benches, etcetera. In the same way, we learned to make our own 'artisanal mimeographs' looking for teachers in the different schools . . . or to publicize the origin and the objectives of the preparatory."[52] At the end of the text, López Hernández tells us that the Popular Preparatory had more than seventy thousand graduates in a period of approximately twenty years, and that "great professionals emerged," "representative leaders of the people in the countryside, in the city, in unions, in big businesses," but above all else, the preparatory was a funda-mental link in questioning the inequality implicit in the law and in access to education.[53] The existence of the preparatory was a way of visualizing the predestination of each class, suspending it on the basis of a collective labora-tory that expanded the horizons of what education meant. In almost all the memories of preparatory graduates, what prevails is a feeling of pride for hav-ing belonged to this experience and the joy of having constructed a space that made the future possible for those who, from such a young age, were excluded from all the preparation that would form a new class of university students.[54] Esperanza Lili Aparicio Hoyo remembers the Popular Preparatory as a form of searching and doing through the encounter with women from different social classes, all *inconformes* and rebels like her. The experience of popular education allowed her to inhabit the question of what kind of woman she wanted to be-come, confronting her inherited ideas of femininity, and sharing a sense of rup-ture with traditional ideas and social roles: "It was a period to pose questions about the decision to create bridges to go who knows where, but bridges based in the respect of collective work . . . of social and political explorations . . . that would allow me to understand that living in a better world was possible!"[55]

This experience proposed a form of democratization that gave a place to those who did not have the means to access higher education. However, it was not just about creating a type of parallel school that opposed a form of subal-tern knowledge to official knowledge, creating two types of graduates who, in this way, maintained two social spheres (higher and marginalized). Instead, the agreement that was reached with the rector was that those who graduated from the Popular Preparatory would have the credentials to be able to enter the university without class distinction. Nevertheless, the educational process was very different: the same teachers taught in both facilities, but in the prepara-tory, horizontality took precedence as a daily practice. López Hernández states that something unique from this moment was that "all the agreements were dis-cussed in general assemblies and resolved by democratic voting."[56] In line with this, Híjar recalls that "in one of the commemorative round tables, a professor narrated how he was worried because, arriving late, he was sure that he would not find the group. But to his surprise, the group was seated in a circle, reading and discussing, without needing supervision at all."[57] There were teachers and there were students, but there was no imposed verticality or authority; the learn-ing process came out of dialogue and debate but also from the entire horizon of tasks necessary for the school to continue operating (cleaning, organizing the curriculum, procuring materials, etc.). It was an education on many levels that generated an active feeling of belonging that became perceptible in daily life.

In this sense, self-management emerged as a daily practice that questioned the relationships between the organization of institutional knowledge and participation (epistemology and state, university): we could say that the Popular Preparatory was for education and epistemology what Topilejo was for solidarity among classes. Its principle was one of horizontal participation, something that was based on dialogue, since it was not about learning eternal truths but rather a matter of going through knowledge as a process, and the classes engaged in practice in the areas of society that required support. José Manuel Galván Leguízamo remembers: "There was always debate and confrontation between ideas, some of them well grounded, others more hormonal . . . but all of them had the intention of building a common dream: popular education. What does it mean, exactly? I am not sure, yet, but for me, it was a very moving learning period. We lived theory in the daily practices of the classrooms."[58] Aparicio Hoyo connects this sense of embodying theories in practices with the ability that these experiences gave her to go through the myths of socialism in relation to popular education, asking herself how it could impact her dreams of becoming a revolutionary practitioner of the performing arts.[59]

The growth of participation in the first Popular Preparatory prompted the opening of another preparatory on Tacuba Street, and interest in replicating the experience in other parts of the country, such as Puebla, Sinaloa, and Veracruz as well as in parts of the United States, through the Chicano movement, began to increase. It is also important to note that the Popular Preparatory was a crucial site for connecting with the Chicano movement, mostly through choral poetry and theater groups such as Mascarones and Emiliano Zapata.[60] López Hernández's experience of the preparatory did not end when she was arrested and imprisoned; once in the women's facility at Santa Martha, she found a way to take the experience to the prison, where she founded a secretarial school.

Fragments of Self-Management in the Women's Prison

Ovarimony recounts the rising infiltration, repression, and radicalization in both the movement and the high schools. Taking us through the Avándaro concert, the rest of the book covers the memory of López Hernández's detention, hours of abuse and torture, followed by her transfer to Santa Martha. Her arrival at the prison is similar to Avendaño's in the importance she places on the prisoners' gaze and on the fear she experiences, which is followed by a sensation of respect and solidarity that López Hernández feels for the common prisoners and for her compañeras and compañeros from the high schools. In López Hernández's memory of the prison, she expresses a close relationship to the experience of self-management she previously lived, a sense of collective doing that is key to finding a process of freedom within the framework of a prepared destiny. The life of the common prisoners does not emerge here in the same way as in *Of Freedom and Imprisonment*, where the life of each woman is narrated. Instead, the life of the common prisoners emerges as a situation of social punishment in which "many of the common prisoners are prisoners because of the lack of economic resources, since they committed crimes out of economic necessity, like the woman who, desperate at seeing her children dying of hunger stole a bag of sugar. . . . Other women are in prison because they didn't have money to pay a lawyer who could defend them. . . . Imprisonment is always for the low social classes."[61]

This is followed by López Hernández taking on an active role in her own education as well as in organizing a small secretarial school in the prison. Her compañeros from the preparatory contribute to this by bringing educational and other useful materials to the prison, thereby putting into motion a work of education that now found another situation of "the rejected," the women destined for prison.

> My coexistence with the common prisoners was always very cordial and respectful. . . . Within the rules of the penitentiary, we were obligated to do the cleaning of a determined area once a week. There were those who had the luxury of paying money in order not to do it. However, I enjoyed it; together with my students I applied to do the cleaning of the sports field every Thursday and Saturday, and among all of us we swept, and when we finished we started playing tennis, basketball, or any other athletic activity, since we did not have guards nearby.[62]

The moments of solidarity and cooperation are also supplemented by moments of pain and frustration, as when the news of Pablo Alvarado's murder arrives and López Hernández is denied permission to attend his burial.

López Hernández's memory of her years in prison always emerges in two voices: the internal life of the prison with the common prisoners, whom she teaches and for whom she creates a school that completely modifies the carceral routine; and the life that "arrives" from outside, with the flow of visits and letters she receives from her classmates and militant friends who remain present in spite of the walls that separate them. López Hernández remembers the constant influx of people and letters as something that kept her alive and helped her to continue building a sense of national and international solidarity, as she got letters from abroad, including one from another key woman of the sixties, Angela Davis.

The creation of the secretarial school replicates the problem of self-management that López Hernández had lived in the Popular Preparatory: they received approval and space but lacked the materials that would make its practice or material operation possible. Nevertheless, the problem is immediately resolved through her compañeras and compañeros at the preparatory who begin to facilitate materials for pedagogical support needed for educational training, as well as basic supplies, the blackboard, paper, and so on. Because of this, the memory of the moment is curious: López Hernández remembers prison as a highly political moment, not in the traditional sense of a kind of "evangelization" of the poor but rather in the sense she learned in '68 with its form of empowerment through collective self-management.

The practical and affective process of learning at the Popular Preparatory translated not only to a way to endure the years in prison but also to a means of communicating with the women for whom prison was almost a destiny prepared by the state and the patriarchal society. This generates a powerful image: the inequality and class difference that marked the rehearsal of self-management in the preparatory is followed by a tension with greater social differentiation regarding the common prisoners, women from the lower classes who have been excluded from a right to education and at the same time to a different future. The figure that in the world outside of the prison referred to the rejected students had its asymmetrical parallel in the prison in the type of exclusion that affected the common prisoners who were included in society only through their destiny in imprisonment. However, unlike Avendaño's narrative, which centers on conferring subjectivity to the prisoners and generating life stories, in López Hernández's text the experience of living with the common prisoners emerges through the collectivity that is assembled in daily management, through such tasks as the cleaning and the attempt to convert the prison into a space of transformation to which the experience of the preparatory is fundamental. This generates a unique political memory in which López Hernández sets out the same questions that Avendaño posed at the end of her text, about the social farce of thinking of prison as "rehabilitation" when it was a school in abuse and humiliation. But López Hernández goes a step further, proposing a training program that enables the women to have a daily routine in prison and a working life after they are released.

Ovarimony introduces an uncommon memory: one of the practice of self-management at different levels and across different social classes and spaces that also finds a certain continuity of practices from the '68 moment and afterward. It seems as if in this text, the "class" as a space of learning becomes a space of encounter and communication among social classes and different forms of knowledge. The differences that the state uses to reproduce itself at various levels that comprise the social whole—that is, differences in gender, in manual or intellectual forms of knowledge, in normal or pathological subjects, free or criminal—permeate the text and form an image of '68 and its aftermath. López Hernández enables us to discuss the social reach of this revolutionary instant at many levels. She was a student of the Popular Preparatory and a participant in its self-managing process. She was one of the women who visited Lecumberri and was accused of being a guerrilla fighter and subsequently imprisoned in Santa Martha, where she resisted prison, torture, and abuse before even turning twenty years old. And she confronted the conflict that all this entailed with her family, losing connections and spending years before being able to speak of the past. Her book narrates the entire process of these experiences through the horizontal education that operates in her memory as a crucial place for making the encounter among classes and forms of knowledge possible. It is as if it were there that the wake of the movement and its political revolution of self-management is expressed, now in a strange form that is complex to read. It is as if the role that the useful (útiles) fulfill in the text "Imprisoned Words" were replaced here by the role of class: *to transform the prison into a school of self-management that disarms it as a prison.* This creates or opens the expectation of a time, of a future denied to the segments of society that spend their lives between prison and recidivism. In López Hernández's text, the encounter between nonequals connects to the desire and practice of transformation of what is given, making equality the motor of a transformative force and promise that '68 emerges from as a vital lesson, a beam of light that is projected to different sites at different moments of learning, education, and equality.

Freed from Prison, and Then . . . ?

After three years in prison, López Hernández was released thanks to bail money raised by friends from the Popular Preparatory. The return to the social world outside the prison is narrated as a complex process that is further complicated by gender difference: "The fact of being a woman and being in prison has many disadvantages compared to what happens to men. Having been in prison, a man becomes the idol, the hero, very manly for having been incarcerated, and other men even respect and fear him. They are never forgotten: they receive visits from their wives, their children, their mothers, etcetera. However, when the prisoners are women the situation changes. Some compañeras were abandoned by their husbands, who influenced their children to reject the mothers."[63] It is important that this difference is narrated since memories of '68 do not usually include the history of what happened to the participants in the murky years that followed prison and repression. That is, memory is frozen in an instant and leaves its characters outside the uncertainty of the present in which it is difficult to speak naturally about the movement in the midst of a society highly punished by state repression.

The texts written by some of the women who participated in the movement emphasize the pain and difficulty of this process of demobilization and "return to a world" that has remained the same as always. Reynoso mentions it in an interview, explaining the traumatic process that followed her participation in the movement, when she was excluded from the educational system. Her entire student record had been burned by someone in the preparatory, leaving her unable to continue her studies, with the wounds left by demobilization still open.[64] The possibility of remembering this difficult moment of return to a false social "normalcy" also appears in López Hernández' text as an instance of highly naturalized violence in which the double life narrated at the beginning rises again. While she was in prison, her family made up a story about her, claiming that her absence was due to the fact that she had gotten married abroad, to avoid being shamed by neighbors and friends. They also moved away from their old neighborhood, cutting off connections and obligating López Hernández to reassemble a life that had almost no history, erasing the past and remaining in a world in which "class consciousness did not exist, and [she] didn't discuss anything having to do with [her] way of thinking and feeling."[65] She expresses that she began to feel once again as if she were living two different lives, and that she started to avoid social gatherings as she could not keep up with the stories that her mother made up to cover her years in prison. Two decades passed until López Hernández was able to start talking openly about her past and to begin reconnecting with her friends.

In the previous chapters, the texts (like Avendaño's) I examined move toward a series of assessments and readings that contrast the struggles that began with the '68 student movement, in the decades that followed, at the level of official politics and of other kinds of changes that impacted people—such as women's rights or the belief in education as a civic right instead of as a privilege. As Oralba Castillo Nájera writes of López Hernández, "Her memories do not remain arrested in time, petrified as objects of archaeology, but rather they illuminate present events," manifesting the continued need for a democratization that never arrived.[66] This illumination generates a singular image in which past and present communicate the demand for justice and a still unfulfilled democracy within a fragmented and divided political map.

The disappeared of the '70s still have not appeared, and those responsible for the massacres of October 2nd, 1968, June 10, 1971, for the dirty war, Aguas Blancas, Acteal, Atenco, etcetera, have not been tried or punished under the law. On the contrary, they are protected by the government itself. Those engaged in social struggle continue to be sent to prison, with various crimes invented against them; many continue to be disappeared. The inequality of rights continues. The indigenous remain as marginalized and in extreme poverty. The poor are increasingly so. The prisons remain full of victims of poverty. The mass media remain controlled by the State. Or, the reverse? Is the State controlled by the mass media? The Church continues on the side of the powerful, influencing and threatening the people. The "Mexican left" is unable to unify and each sect continues to fight for its own interests.[67]

Undoubtedly, as we have seen, the memory of a process of liberation does not only refer to remembrance as something fixed and frozen in time; it also refers to a form of activating an entire process in the present in which this act takes place. The memory of the revolutionary process of '68, which many accounts activate, creates questions about a troubling present motivated by recollections of that process of personal and collective emancipation.

In *The Arcades Project*, Walter Benjamin expresses his intellectual desire as a concern for finding a constellation of memories that would make possible an awakening in which mythology dissolves in the "space of history."[68] This dissolution implies breaking the eternity of its mythology in order to politicize the present in another way. Similarly, the memory that *Ovarimony* activates opens a space in which finitude emerges from the nonpresence of heroines or heroes, opening the possibility of introducing the memory of the political as that instant in which those who did not count began to struggle and create a collective mode of learning, forging the possibility of a future free from the myth of education as a privilege. What is important about this layer of the past that Lopez Hernández's text activates is that it introduces the problem of class and gender inequality in terms of social time, that is, of the right and the nonright to a different future. The dislocation of the fixed places in the dominant order of the sensible is put forth in its connection to education and to the alternative experiences that arose from those who did not accept their place as "rejected students" (*rechazados*) and began to create a collective possibility to forge another time. Nevertheless, this past does not appear closed in on itself but rather tells us that, with the passage of time, the high schools ceased to include the component of self-management and have transformed into more traditional schools that charge students fees. Again, we find the problem of the ephemerality of the projects and the return to a certain inertia once the moment of struggle passes and groups are blocked by divisions and the meticulous work of state repression, which should not be minimized. In spite of this, *Ovarimony* generates an open memory, one in which the past and the present connect from the call to transform a moment still plagued by inequality and injustice.

Resituating Class and Gender in Their Place: Tlatelolco: Summer of '68

I conclude this chapter by making a somewhat arbitrary contrast between forms of portraying the difference in social class in the memory of '68. In the same year that López Hernández's text was published by a minor press, the issue was also configured at the level of mass cinema in a film, *Tlatelolco: Verano del 68* (*Tlatelolco: Summer of '68*), directed by Carlos Bolado, which deals with the problem of difference in social class seen from a Romeo and Juliet–style romance, in which it is impossible for the relationship to flourish. The months from July to October are addressed from the romance between Ana María, a preppy (*fresa*) student at Universidad Autónoma Metropolitana, and Félix, a lower-class student from the Architecture School at UNAM. Alongside images that show us students mobilizing, two parallel stories are outlined at the level of the repressive apparatus, and following a difference in class: Ana María's father works for the Federal Security Directorate (Dirección Federal de Seguridad, DFS), while Félix's brother works for the Olympia Battalion. We learn practically nothing about the student movement in terms of content: we know that students mobilized and that characters participate in protests and rallies; we see signs of repression in the photographs that Ana María takes behind her father's back. However, there is hardly any more detail regarding the content of the struggle; almost all of the most concrete information comes when Ana María reads the newspaper to her grandfather, who sympathizes with the movement, and who is in the hospital seriously ill. The conflict between Ana María and her parents comes from two sides: they do not want her to become involved in the movement, and they certainly do not want her to carry on a romantic relationship with a student from a lower social class. However, she systematically puts off her parents, continues participating in the protests and rallies, and continues seeing Félix. When a friend of Félix is detained and tortured in Military Camp Number 1, Ana María sees that her father enters and leaves the facility, thereby confirming his participation in the hell of so many, and opening the eyes of Ana María's mother, a female character who seems to live in another world in which she cannot figure out anything that is going on in her house or in her country. Afterward, Félix is detained under the orders of Ana María's father, with the goal of separating the couple, but Félix's brother, who works in the clandestine center, is able to get Félix out. Following the fixed forms of melodrama that portray the impossible love between poor and rich, the movie repeats the typical prescription of class difference employed by soap operas to reinforce it through the ending that each class receives: the poor man dies, murdered in the Tlatelolco massacre, while the rich woman saves herself and is overwhelmed by sadness as she attends the official inauguration of the Olympic Games. This is the end of the film, where '68 is framed as an intense summer love story that ends in a tragedy.

The poor boy does not have a future; the rich girl saves herself and continues her life. By inscribing itself in the simple format of the predetermined destiny for each person, nothing in the story digs into the meaning of this social inter-section. It is as if the memory of one of the most open and critical moments for the destiny of roles and social places was tamed in this movie through its official resolution. The predetermined destiny also corresponds to a mode of organizing the story that centers on the repressive staging that directs the history we are watching. This results in an emptying of the mobilizations' political content, which appears as a kind of "backstage" to the drama carried out by the state.

The *Ovarimony* of Gladys López Hernández, together with other texts about the Popular Preparatory, brings us a radically different memory in which class difference emerges from the radical modification of roles that occurred for some at that moment. The emphasis does not arise from the possibility of an intersection between classes based on romance but instead on a project of self-management as the mechanism of social and subjective transformation. This has certain repercussions for how history decenters the role of the repressive apparatuses of the state, since these latter are not the "motor" that govern López Hernández's memory (as occurs in the movie). Instead, history is seen from the processes of transformation within which the repressive apparatuses unleash their strategies of paralysis and division. This act of memory allows us to read '68 and its aftermath from the effect of the transformation that it entailed in the lives of many people who, after this moment, were never the same. López Hernández's text emerges as a gesture of opening and destabilization in which the effect of '68 does not appear as the memory of that singular instant in her life but rather as a process in which memory itself is expressed—as a becoming that marked her life. As a postscript, this contrast between stories is important because it takes us to the problem that I mentioned in the introduction, through the question about the form in which history is punctuated and framed, facilitating or preventing looking toward the zones of intersection and transformation that were crucial.

'68 AFTER AYOTZINAPA

When I began writing this book in earnest, '68 had surfaced in the political imaginary through the emergence of #YoSoy132, which produced hope in the game of political cycles. Inscribing itself within the "new global culture of protest," and in tune with other movements of the moment, #YoSoy132 exposed "power relations between the political system and private communications industries" and advanced the need to dismantle a script written in advance.[1] When I was finishing the book, '68 again appeared in the political imaginary. This time it was through the figure of Tlatelolco and the necrological apparatuses of the state, owing to the disappearance in 2014 of the Escuela Normal de Ayotzinapa students. In the blink of an eye, '68 once again emerged in the frame in which it usually returns: with #YoSoy132, its originality in mobilizing and connection to an environment of global protest evoked the sixties; what appeared with Ayotzinapa was the figure of the crimes and the disappearances committed by a state that always remains in impunity. Even if this new aggression on the student body maintains a clear link to the memory and history of the struggle of Guerrero's *normalista* teachers—in the sixties and in the subsequent creation of the Party of the Poor—the connection to Tlatelolco is marked in the itinerary during which the kidnapping took place: the students were preparing, as they usually did, to attend the annual march in Mexico City commemorating the Tlatelolco massacre, collecting money and taking possession of the buses that provided them transportation. The murky and clandestine character of the state crimes generated connections between Tlatelolco and Ayotzinapa, in which the disappeared and murdered are young people and students engaged in protest and committed to their present. The recent book by Sergio Aguayo attests to this, using the state crimes in Ayotzinapa to again shed light on the facts of the Tlatelolco massacre.[2] A series of articles published in the press further link together the moments within the context of the historical repetition of violence and the figure of circularity.[3] In "Tlatelolco: 48 Years Later," published in *La Jornada*, Elena Poniatowska ties the commemoration of the massacre to the commemoration of the two years since the disappearance of the forty-three Ayotzinapa students, writing:

> Despite temporal and geographic distance, not only are they united by tragedy but also by forgetting. It must be remembered that the normalistas sought to take over buses (as is their custom) and travel the area in search of donations that would fund a trip to the capital to commemorate October 2nd. What a cruel twist of fate that they themselves disappeared a week before the 46th anniversary of Tlatelolco, and two years later we still do not know anything. Today, the Plaza de las Tres Culturas takes on a new meaning.[4]

The October 2, 2016, march was led by the parents of the newly disappeared. The next day, the *La Jornada* declared: "Search for justice unites the movements." The text traces a chain of student murders that goes from the Tlatelolco massacre in '68, to the Corpus Christi massacre of 1971, to Acteal, Aguas Blancas, El Charco, Tanhuato, Nochixtlán, and Ayotzinapa: "Impunity is a ghost that gallops over us."[5] With Ayotzinapa, the total impunity of the Mexican state once again gains visibility, now through the new logic of the accumulation of capital, one of whose links is the narco (drug trafficker), the "war against drugs," and the formation of what is called the "narco-state." As Ivonne del Valle and Estelle Tarica affirm:

> From Acteal to Atenco, Oaxaca to Wirikuta, from the drug war to the neoliberal transfer of wealth up the social ladder—a reality that becomes more firmly enshrined in law with each passing day—the desires and interests of the strong prevail. The case of Ayotzinapa, which unfolded over the last months of 2014, has confirmed what many of those in Mexico and the international community already knew: that "the emperor has no clothes," that the Mexican state carries out a double violence against the citizens it is supposed to protect, first by participating in their killing and disappearance, then by refusing properly to investigate these crimes.[6]

Ayotzinapa not only raises the issue of impunity but also displays, once again, Gareth Williams's hypothesis that the sovereign exception is a constitutive form of modern Mexican history. Yuri Herrera analyzes this in detail, seeing impunity as the machinery within the engineering of illegal businesses of the state.[7]

The new forms of articulating politics from social networks made it possible for the protests against the killing and disappearing of students to spread throughout the world. This facilitated new forms of international solidarity that also made use of platforms created through #YoSoy132. Once again, countless cries of ENOUGH! traveled far and wide. This established, as Rossana Reguillo puts it, a before and an after with regard to the denunciation of the narco-state as "a deep relationship between political powers, economic powers, and the forces of organized crime."[8] The faces of the murdered normalista students, and those who remain disappeared, prevent "indifference."[9] Ayotzinapa became a force that crosses borders and continues to make demands, resembling '68 in its characterization as having a before and an after.

These two figures, marking the beginning and the end of writing this book, affirm how '68 traverses Mexican history to the rhythm of mobilization and to the constant of state oppression. Relevant here is the figure of Evodio's coming and going from Revueltas's unfinished novel. With this figure, Revueltas asks how to live the intensity of the tempo of freedom—a freedom that appears as fragments, instants, or episodes that resemble almost nothing, if viewed from the quantitative and cumulative zeal that governs the fantasy of development. The figures of circuits, of ebbs and flows, of waves that come and go, are crucial when we address the question of social transformation and freedom, outside the usual paradigms of the social sciences, governed by the linearity of development. In her analysis of the intensity of the mobilizations against the privatization of water in Cochabamba, Raquel Gutiérrez proposes a musical figure to speak of the "rhythms" of the Pachakuti, raising what the Colectivo Situaciones, in the introduction to Gutiérrez's book, highlights as the virtues of anachronism: "That which reveals time as a dimension that is *multiplied, complicated, and disjointed* from historical experience." In this way, an "anachronistic sensibility offers the alternative of jumping out of chronological time toward another type of processuality, one that is rhythmic: a processuality that is long-term but that moves by jumping."[10] The rhythms indicate moments of complication, of brief and intense syncopation that produce a transformation in everyday life. Pachakuti is the rhythm of the disruption of the order, generally followed by the emergence of a new form of regularity.

In the epigraph to the preface of this book, Rancière's words refer to the temporality of the moments of irruption and interruption that characterize these smaller revolutions as instants that produce a modification of the ways of living and perceiving life, the seeable and the sayable. After this moment, another wave appears that disrupts these minutes of freedom and demands that freedom be posed again.

Throughout this book, the figure of the encounter flashes in different ways and styles, all while sharing a sense of brevity if the encounter is measured by the time of the clock and the intensity of its ability to survive the instant that it marks. "Today is always," Navarro writes about the form the encounter takes when it is conceived in terms of a de-idealization time, from the present of its happening. Against the notion of duration in the encounter, which Althusser proposes to measure the creation of a world, it is in the capacity of the past to be rekindled by a new present that this past continues in time from the syncopated figure of instants that thus acquire their long duration. That is, instead of thinking of the enduring encounter as what is world-making, perhaps instants of collective freedom are what arm the history of emancipation. In her brilliant study of the Paris Commune, Kristin Ross refers to "a mode of being intensely in the present made possible by mobilizing figures and phrases from the past." This is what led to the word *commune* "exceed[ing] everything it was supposed to designate."[11]

This historicity is marked by a different understanding of the creation of critical thought. Just as the logic of time is turned back, a different way of thinking of reflexivity is generated. As I explained when analyzing Revueltas, a moment becomes critical of its own present through *collective participation in the making of history.* The singular temporality of self-management, the polyphony of voices, and the practice of equality—all collude to interrupt linear time and chronology: "Although we cannot say in absolute terms that a fairly high level of theoretical understanding existed within the Movement of '68, we *can* say with total certainty that *all* protesters participated in making history— all of them, free of hierarchical distinctions."[12] In other words, this moment becomes one of Mexico's first great democratic events, one that destabilizes the notion of democracy as partyocracy and enables common action. Here, Ross's reflection on the way that the commune *affected* Marx's notion of theorization expresses more clearly what I mean: "His shift from the history of theory to the history of the class struggles at the point of production *becomes the theory.* He thus moves away from a concept of theory as a debate between theorists, and away from the idea that it is *that* history that matters, to a concept of theory as the history of production of relations."[13]

Appealing to the figure of the encounter as this light that flashes in different memories of '68, I have examined the social connectivity that came to light and created relationships among people who otherwise rarely connected *to act in common.* Connectivity does not emerge as a "project" to achieve but rather is what constitutes the movement itself. As Esmeralda Reynoso shows when she narrates how she remembered the day-to-day of the movement, what was most incredible was having everyday experiences with people who were not necessarily from the same school or the same group as always.[14] This connects to Revueltas's sense of surprise about the singularity of the movement, in that the movement was a space in which the conflicts between different political positions could coexist without the logic of purges; Revueltas called this cognitive democracy, or at other times, socialist democracy, referring to an instant of the confrontation of ideas, of political positions, of ideologies. This confrontation was made possible by the force of a desire for transformation that began in the everyday practice and thought of the brigades, in the logic of the assembly. The sovereign verticality of "with me or against me" that usually governs confrontations with divergence, through a multiplication of divisions, is suspended. This capacity to do and to transform collectively has its most powerful expression in the first of the popular preparatories at 66 Liverpool Street; paradoxically, even today this experience exists on the margins of the more official memories of '68. Nevertheless, here self-management is the impulse marking the encounter among different kinds of people who had been "rejected." The division of labor broke down to such an extent that all participants cleaned, collected funds, created syllabi, and engaged in thinking.

In different ways, these unusual instances of the encounter have a force that the state cannot stand given that one of its foundations is the inability to label *what* is happening. At the same time, the instant of encounter makes visible the distances that comprise the social, from the force of the heterogeneous, from the ability to shout "no" or "enough," but also, and above all, from the *desire* to generate another form of reproducing everyday life. This is the component that stammers in these microsettings of collective self-management that narratives based in the logic of the police (repression, death) are usually able to erase. This is something that connects recent incursions on the figure of the "commune" as a distillation of this desire for transformability and practicality. In the commune, as Ross emphasizes, the motor impulse comes from cooperation and association that suspend divisions that mark the reproduction of everyday life. This makes possible a "capacity to think together domains of the social formation that the bourgeoisie devotes itself to keeping apart."[15]

Perhaps we can say that at a historical level this same division or separation takes place, and that the figure of these moments of collective emancipation are brief flashes that help remind us of a capacity that is anaesthetized by the neoliberal way of life, with individualism, precaritization, and the general atomization of life and of knowledge, which is increasingly segmented. This capacity, numbed in the rush of our neoliberal existence, receives through new movements and positions a new light that generates an interest in constructing other histories. In "The Mexican Commune," Bosteels sets out to shed light on "an underground current of mass mobilizations around the notion of the commune," a figure capable of representing a "common ground" among anarchists, socialists, and those who do not identify as one or the other.[16] As the figure of the commune emerges in these new mobilizations, it is necessary to think about the brief instants of freedom in the encounter. They become forms that remind us of a peculiar kind of memory, one related to the improper, in the sense of that which comes from attempts to interrupt the logic of private ownership in its most quotidian expressions; this form contains the possibility of reminding us of a different way of doing that cancels so many of the divisions promoted by capital according to the old idea of "divide and conquer," divisions that mark the permanent structures of doing.

Here I want to raise a contrast or a distinction, in dialogue with a recent publication from this same series, George Ciccariello-Maher's *Decolonizing Dialectics*. He approaches dialectics in a way that questions the role of unity, something that had appeared in the form of understanding the encounter in Revueltas and in Navarro. Ciccariello-Maher proposes to

> approach the task of decolonizing dialectics by excavating a largely sub-terranean current of thought, what I call a *counterdiscourse*, that I argue constitutes a radicalization of the dialectical tradition while also opening outward toward its decolonization. This is a dialectical counterdiscourse that, *by foregrounding rupture and shunning the lure of unity, makes its home in the center of the dialectic and revels in the spirit of combat*, the indeterminacies of political identities slamming against one another, transforming themselves and their worlds unpredictably in the process.[17]

Ciccariello-Maher mentions the risks of Occupy Wall Street's use of the figure of the 99 percent to appeal to a unity that sought to conceal differences that were left unproblematized. That is, for Ciccariello-Maher, the issue is how the 99 percent can become a unit that covers up difference, internal violence, and division. This argument forced me to think about how encounter and connectivity in my own work can be read and critiqued as camouflaged forms of unity. However, I think it is important to maintain the figure of these moments of encounter that do not necessarily imply or indicate a unity (in the same sense in which Althusser, for example, considered it a requirement of "world-making"). When the encounter is seen and written through the textual reconstructions of the women of Mexico '68, nuances and distinctions become crucial: in Navarro with the encounter that is not "in unity," in Avendaño with the discomfort felt in the encounter, and in López Hernández with the encounter between those who are rejected by the false "universality" of the university. A possible challenge that remains is how the encounter can operate as a form of differentiation that is not another attempt to conceal differences under a false mantle of harmonious unity. In the case of OWS, even though it is true that the 99 percent encompasses a broad spectrum that includes people in a situation of total precariousness and others in a situation of extremely high income, the force of the division between the 1 percent and the 99 percent also comes from the way it appeals to the interruption of the problematic logic of essentialized identities, above all in a country in which culturalist identitarian politics are effectively able to divide any struggle against capital. The figure of the 99 percent created a possible language to name a common denominator of a large part of the population through debt, through the indebted subject. For example, in a country in which an extraordinary multiplicity of cultures coexists, in which approximately 800 different languages are spoken (138 in Queens, New York, alone), the possibility of joining together with those who do not come from the same circuits, neighborhoods, or groups is a major challenge. Something as simple as being able to converse with others, to do together, to think together is difficult.[18]

In Revueltas's writings, the figure of cognitive democracy helps to differentiate the encounter from the form of an unproblematic unity, because it leads to the possibility of thinking about and shaping a common, collective consciousness. This consciousness is made of *tensions, struggles, debates*—the controversial character of a moment in which people from different political groups, as well as people who had never participated in politics before, shared the space of making the movement and came together. Grace Lee Boggs and James Boggs emphasize the need to think about connectivity between groups, people, and struggles in order to avoid falling into the trap of identitarian politics that began to deepen in the seventies. In one of the last chapters of *Revolution and Evolution in the Twentieth Century*, titled "Changing Concepts for Changing Realities," they write of the lack of imagination that led to the inability to resist identitarian isolation. The great instant of the encounter was progressively captured by the logic of receiving a "share" in politics as usual. A long passage explains this:

> In the last ten years various liberation movements have come into being. Some of these are still concerned chiefly with the question of redistribution of the cake—how blacks or chicanos or women or young people should share in it. Others claim that their values should be the values of the entire society. But few, if any, of these groups think in terms of their commitment to the whole of society. A kind of absenteeism has developed. Liberation has come to mean separation. . . . None of these groups seems to have thought about how all of this is to come together or converge at any point. . . . Each group is going to become more negative,

and the possibility of bringing them together on any basis is going to become harder. All these groups talk about freedom. *What do they mean by freedom?*[19]

The freedom that flashes in these instants of encounter derives from the urgency to open another time in the present of the reproduction of everyday life, in everyday time, crossing a geography of imagination that, as Ross writes in the French case, is not "that of a national republican middle class nor that of a state-managed collectivism."[20] The role that this had in the new modes of articulating the collective since 2011 also came from the force that the commons acquired as a horizon of this moment. At the beginning of the first ows Forum on the Commons, Silvia Federici said something that has stayed with me to this day. She reminded us that *history is, perhaps, our first commons.*[21] In this sense, it is important to address the ways that the ravages of neoliberalism affect how we narrate and link pasts and presents, usually displacing the role that imagination and invention play in them. By this, I mean the capacity for collective emancipation, not only in the sense of great irruptions but in the smaller acts in which there is a "takeover" of words, of images, of bodies.

Notes

Preface

1 Roberto Bolaño, *Amulet*, trans. Chris Andrews (New York: New Directions, 2008), 32; originally published as *Amuleto* (Barcelona: Anagrama, 1999).

2 Bolaño, *Amulet*, 33, 55.

3 José Revueltas, "Las palabras prisioneras," *México 68: Juventud y revolución* (Mexico City: Era, 1978), 245–47.

4 Susana Draper and Vicente Rubio-Pueyo, *México 68: Modelo para armar; Archivo de memorias desde los márgenes*; Héctor Aguilar Camín, "68, modelo para armar," in *Pensar el 68*, edited by Héctor Aguilar Camín and Hermann Bellinghausen (Mexico City: Cal y Arena, 1988), 13–14; Julio Cortázar, *62. Modelo para armar* (Buenos Aires: Editorial Sudamericana, 1968).

Introduction

1 See Eric Hobsbawm, "1968: A Retrospective," *Marxism Today* 22, no. 5 (1978): 130–38; George Katsiaficas, *The Imagination of the New Left: A Global Analysis of 1968* (Boston: South End Press, 1999); and Luisa Passerini, *Autobiography of a Generation: Italy, 1968*, trans. Lisa Erdberg (Hanover, NH: University Press of New England, 1996).

2 Daniel Bensaïd and Henri Weber, *Mai 1968: Une répétition générale* (Paris: F. Maspero, 1968).

3 Giovanni Arrighi, Terrence K. Hopkins, and Immanuel Wallerstein, *Antisystemic Movements* (London: Verso, 2012).

4 John Holloway, *Change the World without Taking Power* (London: Pluto, 2002).

5 See Kostis Kornetis, "Introduction: 1968–2008: The Inheritance of Utopia," *Historein* 9 (2009): 7–20. In Mexico, '68 became a political referent for understanding #YoSoy132: see Oswaldo Zavala, "Del '68 al 132," *Proceso*, July 13, 2012, http://www.proceso.com.mx/314002/314002-del-68-al-132; Georgina Howard, "El 68 es un pendiente que retoma el YoSoy132," *Reporte indigno*, October 3, 2011, http://m.reporteindigo.com/reporte/mexico/el-68-es-un-pendiente-que-retoma-el-yosoy132; Daniel Casillas, "Siguen vigentes demandas del 68 ahora con #YoSoy132," *Animal político*, October 3, 2012, http://www.animalpolitico.com/2012/10/siguen-vigentes-demandas-del-68-ahora-con-yosoy132-comite-68/; Óscar Martín Álvarez Jiménez, "Del movimiento del 68 al YoSoy 132," *Zócalo*, October 15, 2012, http://www.zocalo.com.mx/seccion/opinion-articulo/del-movimiento-del-68-al-yo-soy-132; Itzel Castañares, "Del 68 al YoSOY 132, caras de los movimientos," *24 horas*, October 7, 2012,

http://www.24-horas.mx/del-68-al-yosoy132-caras-de-los-movimientos-estudiantiles
-video/.

6   Daniel Sherman et al., "Introduction," in *The Long 1968: Revisions and New Perspectives*, ed. Daniel Sherman et al. (Bloomington: Indiana University Press, 2013), 16–17;
Elaine Carey, "The Streets Speak, 1968 and Today," in *Protests in the Streets: 1968
across the Globe*, ed. Elaine Carey (Indianapolis: Hackett, 2016), 120–32.

7   Katherine Hite, *Politics and the Art of Commemoration: Memorials to Struggle in
Latin America and Spain* (London: Routledge, 2013), 1–2.

8   Kostis Kornetis explores this point in greater detail in " 'Everything Links'? Temporality, Territoriality and Cultural Transfer in the '68 Protest Movements," *Historein*
9 (2009): 34–45. Regarding the analysis of various aspects of the new movements
mentioned above, see Marina Sitrin and Dario Azzelini, *They Can't Represent Us!
Reinventing Democracy from Greece to Occupy* (London: Verso, 2014); Michael Gould-
Wartofsky, *The Occupiers: The Making of the 99 Percent Movement* (New York: Oxford
University Press, 2015); Luis Moreno-Caballud, *Cultures of Anyone: Studies on Cultural
Democratization in the Spanish Neoliberal Ciruit* (Liverpool: University of Liverpool
Press, 2015); Raúl Diego Rivera Hernández, *Del Internet a las calles: #YoSoy132, una
opción alternativa de hacer política* (Raleigh, NC: Editorial A Contracorriente, 2016).

9   Kristin Ross, *May '68 and Its Afterlives* (Chicago: University of Chicago Press,
2002), 1–2.

10 Bruno Bosteels, "Mexico 1968: The Revolution of Shame," *Radical Philosophy* 149
(May–June 2008): 11, emphasis mine.

11 Alain Badiou, "May 68 Revisited, 40 Years On," in *The Communist Hypothesis*
(London: Verso, 2010), 62–63.

12 Luisa Passerini, "The Problematic Intellectual Repercussions of '68: Reflections in a
Jump-cut Style," *Historein* 9 (2009): 24.

13 See Andreas Huyssen's analysis in *Present Pasts: Urban Palimpsests and the Politics of
Memory* (Stanford, CA: Stanford University Press, 2003), along with various texts
on consumption and memory in Latin America found in Ksenija Bilbija and Leigh
Payne, eds., *Accounting for Violence: Marketing Memory in Latin America* (Durham,
NC: Duke University Press, 2011).

14 Samantha Christiansen and Zachary A. Scarlett, eds., *The Third World in the Global
Sixties* (New York: Berghahn Books, 2013). There are lessons to be learned from a
whole genre of creation in the 1960s—lessons that make the sharp division now
in fashion (Global South vs. Global North) sound a bit problematic. I think, for
instance, of Agnes Varda's collaboration with the Black Panthers in California, which
resulted in the censored film *The Black Panthers*, in which she learns to question
what it means to be a woman artist, thus cultivating a feminist gaze; or Jean Genet's
clandestine visit to the United States to raise money for the Panthers.

15 Karen Dubinsky et al., "Introduction: The Global Sixties," in *New World Coming: The Sixties and the Shaping of Global Consciousness*, ed. Karen Dubinsky et al.
(Toronto: Between the Lines, 2009), 2.

16 Kornetis, " 'Everything Links'?," 34.

17 Katsiaficas, *The Imagination of the New Left*, 3.

18 Within the field of Latin American studies, the national-international character of 1968 and the 1960s has been studied from many angles. Some studies address the internationalism of the sixties by focusing on specific local processes—here I refer to Andrea Giunta's *Avant-Garde, Internationalism, and Politics* (Durham, NC: Duke University Press, 2007), Vania Markarian's *Uruguay 1968: Student Activism from Global Counterculture to Molotov Cocktails* (Berkeley: University of California Press, 2016), and Eric Zolov's *Refried Elvis: The Rise of the Mexican Counterculture* (Berkeley: University of California Press, 1999). Others map out the Latin American landscape by connecting various regional sites and events, as Diana Sorensen does in *A Turbulent Decade Remembered: Scenes from the Latin American Sixties* (Stanford, CA: Stanford University Press, 2007).

19 It is worth emphasizing the anti-imperialist and anti-colonialist lens that enables us to see each "national" history in an entirely different light. As Fredric Jameson demonstrates, there is a whole "beginning" to '68 rooted in the so-called Third World and its struggles for freedom. Likewise, we must acknowledge this same phenomenon in great centers of culture and consumption such as France (i.e., fighting over Algeria) and the United States (i.e., the civil rights movement). See Fredric Jameson, "Periodizing the 60s," in *The 60s without Apology*, ed. Sohnya Sayres et al. (Minneapolis: University of Minnesota Press, 1985), 178–209.

20 Along with Ross's statements on the connection between the French '68 and decolonization, Rancière states that "'68 was not a youth revolt. '68 did not represent the emergence of a new way of life. '68 was an event inscribed within a certain type of political memory, and that memory was bound up with decolonization. The 'German Jew' of '68 would have been unthinkable were it not for a certain mode of including the Other. *And that mode of inclusion was inscribed within the after-effects of mobilization against the Algerian War.* It was bound up with the way in which the figure of the colonized and their War of liberation replaced the figure of the proletarian as the form that allowed a wrong to be universalized and as a way of espousing the cause of the Other." Jacques Rancière, "Democracy Means Equality: Jacques Rancière Interviewed by *Passages*," *Radical Philosophy* 82 (March/April 1997): 33, emphasis mine.

21 Topilejo is a town located twenty-one kilometers south of the UNAM campus where, at the very beginning of the movement, on September 3, 1968, a bus accident occurred due to poor road conditions and vehicle malfunction. Learning of the ten dead and thirty-four wounded, the people of Topilejo—mostly from rural settings— began to organize a demonstration. Student brigades came to the neighborhood to stand in solidarity with the protesters, who demanded improvement in the conditions of the roads and public transport vehicles, compensation for the families of the dead, and economic assistance for the medical treatment of the wounded. As Sergio Zermeño observes, they organized three different types of brigades to provide political, technical, and direct action support. Sergio Zermeño, *México: Una democracia utópica; El movimiento estudiantil del 68* (Mexico City: Siglo XXI, 1978), 226–32. The resulting cooperation between the student movement and the people exceeded a mere list of demands—which, by the way, were awarded. Many of the slogans stemming from this encounter emphasize how important this moment was to the

imaginary of the movement: "Let's make two, three, many Topilejos." In 2008 *La Jornada* published a series of testimonies of the experience: "Topilejo, primer territorio libre de México" by Antonio Vera Martínez and "Las campanas de Topilejo convocan al pueblo" by Lourdes Edith Rudiño. Interviews with townspeople who participated were recorded in "Testimonios del 68 Topilejo," YouTube, January 28, 2014, https://www.youtube.com/watch?v=pqM77CUSCzA.

22 For an analysis of the Olympic Games, see Luis Castañeda, *Spectacular Mexico: Design, Propaganda, and the 1968 Olympics* (Minneapolis: University of Minnesota Press, 2014); and Celeste González de Bustamante, "Olympic Dreams and Tlatelolco Nightmares: Imagining and Imaging Modernity in Television," *Mexican Studies / Estudios Mexicanos* 26, no. 1 (2010): 1–30; for an analysis of the movement and the preparation for the Olympic Games, see Elaine Carey, "Mexico's 1968 Olympic Dream," in *Protests in the Streets: 1968 across the Globe*, ed. Elaine Carey (Indianapolis, IN: Hackett, 2016), 91–119. For a creative work that sets the massacre alongside the Olympics, see Brian Holmes, "1968 Olympic Dreams and Tlatelolco Nightmares: Imagining and Imaging Modernity on Television," November 18, 2015, https://prezi .com/47wxztjxocr6/1968-olympic-dreams-and-tlatelolco-nightmares-imagining -and/. For an unusual perspective on how the student movement appropriated the creative design of the Olympics, see the compilation by Grupo Mira, *The Graphics of 68: Honoring the Student Movement* (Mexico City: Ediciones Zurda, 1993).

23 Ross, *May '68 and Its Afterlives*, 2–3.

24 Ross, *May '68 and Its Afterlives*, 6.

25 Samuel Steinberg, *Photopoetics at Tlatelolco: Afterimages of Mexico, 1968* (Austin: University of Texas Press, 2016), 9.

26 See Francisco Medina, "El 68 un cambio social y no democrático: Esmeralda Reynoso," *almomento noticias*, October 10, 2013, http://www.almomento.mx/el-68 -un-cambio-social-y-no-democratico-esmeralda-reynoso/.

27 He states, "What Ayotzinapa reveals is more radical: it is not that the transition was truncated, but that there had not been a transition at all," going through the aperture of the PRI and the emergence of PAN as reforms instead of a form of democratization. Rafael Lemus, "Ayotzinapa, la multitud y el antiguo régimen," *Política común* 7 (2015), http://quod.lib.umich.edu/p/pc/12322227.0007.010/—ayotzinapa-la-multitud-y-el -antiguo-regimen?rgn=main;view=fulltext. Translations throughout the book are mine unless otherwise noted.

28 Bruno Bosteels, *Marx and Freud in Latin America: Politics, Psychoanalysis, and Religion in Times of Terror* (New York: Verso, 2012), 163, emphasis mine.

29 Passerini draws attention to similar issues when she states, "My definition of 1968 poses a general problem of temporality, or rather of the series of temporal sequences in which 1968 is situated," pointing to the brevity of the events, the life of the movements, and the cultural changes that they provoked and still mark the present. Luisa Passerini, *Memory and Utopia: The Primacy of Intersubjectivity* (London: Routledge, 2007), 55.

30 Elizabeth Jelin, *State Repression and the Labors of Memory*, trans. Judy Rein and Marcial Godoy-Anativia (Minneapolis: University of Minnesota Press, 2003), 4–5.

31 Eugenia Allier Montaño, "Presentes-pasados del 68 mexicano," *Revista Mexicana de Sociología* 71, no. 2 (2009): 302. I also refer to Allier-Montaño's further development of the analysis of how the memories and accounts of 1968 varied throughout the decades ("Memory and History of Mexico '68," *European Review of Latin American and Caribbean Studies,* Revista Europea de Estudios Latinoamericanos y del Caribe 102 (2016): 7–25. See also Vania Markarian's analysis of how narratives have transformed over time: "Debating Tlatelolco: Thirty Years of Public Debates about the Mexican Student Movement of 1968," in *Taking Back the Academy! History of Activism, History as Activism*, ed. Jim Downs and Jennifer Manion (New York: Routledge, 2004), 25–34. Steinberg's recent book *Photopoetics at Tlatelolco* examines the legacy of Tlatelolco in greater depth over time and through different media.

32 Elena Poniatowska, *Massacre in Mexico*, trans. Helen R. Lane (New York: Viking Press, 1975); Allier Montaño, "Presentes-pasados," 311.

33 Esmeralda Reynoso, interview with Susana Draper and Vicente Rubio-Pueyo, *México 68: Modelo para armar; Archivo de memorias desde los márgenes,* 2015, https://www.mexico68conversaciones.com/.

34 José Ramón Ruisánchez Serra explains how the voices that predominate in the tour are those of well-known people in the cultural sphere yet again telling their version of events. Besides noting the silencing of voices that have not been adopted by the establishment, Ruisánchez Serra highlights the absence of more contemporary views that have disputed the construction of this kind of monument. José Ramón Ruisánchez Serra, "Reading '68: The Tlatelolco Memorial and Gentrification in Mexico City," in *Accounting for Violence: Marketing Memory in Latin America*, ed. Leigh A. Payne and Ksenija Bilbija (Durham, NC: Duke University Press, 2011), 179–206.

35 Daniel Bensaïd, *Marx for Our Times: Adventures and Misadventures of a Critique* (New York: Verso, 2002), 10.

36 Aguilar Camín, "68, modelo para armar," 13.

37 For instance, it seems odd how "Tlatelolco" is often used as a kind of shorthand for the Mexican '68 movement in the recent wave of studies about the sixties in the Global South. In this context, Claire Brewster argues that on the international level, the Tlatelolco massacre receives the most emphasis, diverting relevance away from the movement that preceded and followed it. Claire Brewster, "The Student Movement of 1968 and the Mexican Press: The Cases of *Excélsior* and *Siempre!*," *Bulletin of Latin American Research* 21, no. 2 (2002): 150.

38 Esteban Ascencio, ed., *1968: Más allá del mito* (Mexico City: Ediciones del Milenio, 1998), 9.

39 Bosteels, "Mexico 1968."

40 Gareth Williams, *The Mexican Exception: Sovereignty, Police, and Democracy* (New York: Palgrave Macmillan, 2011), 133.

41 Steinberg, *Photopoetics at Tlatelolco*, 25.

42 Gastón Martínez, "Todo el mundo era protagonista," in Ascencio, *1968: Más allá del mito*, 99.

43 David Vega, "Una vida del Politécnico: entrevista con Hermann Bellinghausen," in Aguilar Camín and Bellinghausen, *Pensar el 68*, 43.

44 Pablo Gómez Alvarez, "Las enseñanzas: entrevista con Víctor Avilés," in Aguilar Camín and Bellinghausen, *Pensar el 68*, 216.

45 Deborah Cohen and Lessie Jo Frazier, "'No sólo cocinábamos...': Historia inédita de la otra mitad del 68," in *La transición interrumpida: México 1968–1998*, ed. Ilán Semo (Mexico City: Departamento de Historia, Universidad Iberoamericana, 1993), 75–105.

46 Gloria Tirado Villegas, *La otra historia: Voces de mujeres del 68, Puebla* (Puebla: Benemérita Universidad Autónoma de Puebla, Instituto Poblano de la Mujer, 2004), 13.

47 Blanche Petrich, "Entrevista a Ana Ignacia Rodríguez, *La Nacha*," *La Jornada*, July 22, 2002, http://www.jornada.unam.mx/2002/07/22/009n1pol.php?origen =politica.html.

48 Paco Ignacio Taibo II, *'68*, trans. Donald Nicholson Smith (New York: Seven Stories Press, 2004); Eduardo Valle, *Escritos sobre el movimiento del 68* (Sinaloa: Universidad Autónoma de Sinaloa, 1984).

49 Sally Alexander, *Becoming a Woman: And Other Essays in 19th and 20th Century Feminist Theory* (London: Virago, 1994), 19; Passerini, *Memory and Utopia*, 9.

50 Reynoso, interview with Susana Draper and Vicente Rubio-Pueyo, *México 68: Modelo para armar*.

51 Taibo, *'68*, 51, emphasis mine.

52 In interviews with Guadalupe Ferrer, Esmeralda Reynoso, and Gladys López Hernández, it should be noted how, for each of them, equality in everyday practices felt like a singular characteristic of the moment (all the interviews are part of *México 68: Modelo para armar*, https://www.mexico68conversaciones.com).

53 In *The Political Thought of Jacques Rancière: Creating Equality* (Edinburgh: Edinburgh University Press, 2008), Todd May distinguishes between passive and active cquality in order to emphasize the difference.

54 Among a long list of titles narrating this passage, I refer here to bell hooks, *Feminism Is for Everybody* (Cambridge, MA: South End Press, 2000); Nancy Fraser, *Fortunes of Feminism: From State-Managed Capitalism to Neoliberal Crisis* (New York: Verso, 2013); Nancy Fraser and Axel Honnett, *Redistribution or Recognition? A Political Philosophical Exchange*, trans. Joel Golb (New York: Verso, 2003).

55 Judith Butler, *Notes toward a Performative Theory of Assembly* (Cambridge, MA: Harvard University Press, 2015), 5.

56 If we track the key works that have been published nearly every decade as if to mark the anniversary of the event, it is alarming to observe the powerful, almost exclusively masculine presence in the field of speaking and making the movement legible. In the 1970s: Raúl Álvarez Garín, *Los procesos de México 1968: Acusaciones y defensa* (Mexico City: Editorial Estudiantes, 1970), Luis González de Alba, *Los días y los años* (Mexico City: Era, 1971); Elena Poniatowska, *La noche de Tlatelolco: Testimonios de historia oral* (Mexico City: Era, 1971); José Revueltas, *México 68: Juventud y revolución* (Mexico City: Era, 1978); Sergio Zermeño, *México: Una democracia utópica; El movimiento estudiantil de 1968* (Mexico City: Siglo XXI, 1978). In the 1980s: Eduardo Valle, *Escritos sobre el movimiento del 68* (1984); Héctor Aguilar Camín and Hermann Belling-

hausen, eds., *Pensar el 68* (1988); Gilberto Guevara Niebla, *La democracia en la calle: crónica del movimiento estudiantil mexicano* (Mexico City: Siglo XXI, 1988); Heberto Castillo, *Si te agarran, te van a matar* (Mexico City: Océano, 1983); Leopoldo Ayala, *Nuestra Verdad: Memorial popular del movimiento estudiantil popular y el dos de octubre de 1968* (Mexico City: Porrúa, 1989). In the 1990s: Raúl Álvarez Garín, *La estela de Tlatelolco: Una reconstrucción histórica del movimiento estudiantil del 68* (Mexico City: Grijalbo, 1998); Sergio Aguayo, *1968: Los archivos de la violencia* (Mexico City: Grijalbo, 1998); Esteban Ascencio, *1968: Más allá del mito* (1998); Paco Ignacio Taibo II, *'68* (1991); Roberta Avendaño, *De la libertad y el encierro* (Mexico City: La idea dorada, 1998); Julio Scherer García and Carlos Monsiváis, *Parte de guerra, Tlatelolco 1968: Documentos del general Marcelino García Barragán; Los hechos y la historia* (Mexico City: Nuevo Siglo/Aguilar, 1999). In the first decade of the twenty-first century: Gilberto Guevara Niebla, *La libertad nunca se olvida: Memoria del 68* (Mexico City: Cal y Arena, 2004), and *1968: Largo camino a la democracia* (Mexico City: Cal y Arena, 2008); Gladys López Hernández, *Ovarimonio: ¿Yo guerrillera?* (Mexico City: Itaca, 2013).

57 I take the line from his song "Samba da Bênção." Vinícius de Moraes, Odete Lara, and Baden Powell. *Vinicius De Moraes.* [S.l.]: Folha de S. Paulo, 2008.

58 Heidrun Hozfeind, "Entrevista a Mercedes Perelló," *México 68: Entrevistas con activistas del movimiento estudiantil.* http://www.mexico68.net/files/mex68spanishrz.pdf.

59 I use the notion of climate that Amador Fernández-Savater proposes to explain the movements that emerged in 2011 in their displacement of the forms of naming traditional politics. A climate implies an environment that is progressively modified and in which a multiplicity of projects, expectations, and desires coexist and are linked under the umbrella or sign of a name (15-M, Occupy Wall Street, etc.) instead of following the logic of a "party" or a specific petition (a project with a beginning and an end). Amador Fernández-Savater, "How to Organize a Climate?," *Making Worlds: A Commons Coalition*, https://makingworlds.wikispaces.com/How+to+Organize+a+Climate.

60 For a discussion of the popular character of the movement, see Zermeño, *México: Una democracia utópica*; and Ayala, *Nuestra verdad*.

61 Zermeño, *México: Una democracia utópica*, 51.

62 César Gilabert, *El hábito de la utopía: Análisis del imaginario sociopolítico en el movimiento estudiantil de México, 1968* (Mexico City: Porrúa, 1993).

63 Luis Villoro, *Tres retos de la sociedad por venir: Justicia, democracia, pluralidad* (Mexico City: Siglo XXI, 2009).

64 Gilabert, *El hábito de la utopía*, 138.

65 Adolfo Gilly, "1968: La ruptura en los bordes," *Nexos*, November 1, 1993, http://www.nexos.com.mx/?p=6916.

66 Álvarez Garín, *La estela de Tlatelolco*, 30.

67 Guevara Niebla, *La democracia en la calle*, 49. The student movements began years before in Puebla, Morelia, Sonora, and Tabasco as more localized struggles that elicited acts of solidarity from the rest of the student population.

68 Also contained in the petition is a denunciation of the harsh repression of the 1958 railroad workers' strike, where the state put an end to the struggle for union independence (up to that point, the struggle had been co-opted by the PRI), and of the repression of the peasant struggle, whose critical event was the assassination of the peasant leader Rubén Jaramillo and his family in Morelos.

69 Zermeño, *México: Una democracia utópica*, 35.

70 Álvarez Garín, *La estela de Tlatelolco*, 47.

71 Álvarez Garín, *La estela de Tlatelolco*, 77.

72 Gilabert, *El hábito de la utopía*, 184–85.

73 Esmeralda Reynoso, interview with Susana Draper and Vicente Rubio-Pueyo, *México 68: Modelo para armar*.

74 Gilabert, *El hábito de la utopía*, 170.

75 On this point, besides Gilabert and Zermeño, see Enrique de la Garza, Tomás Ejea Mendoza, and Luis Fernando Macías García, *El otro movimiento estudiantil* (Mexico City: Universidad Autónoma Metropolitana–Azcapotzalco, 2014).

76 Guevara Niebla, *La democracia en la calle*, 57.

77 For a comprehensive analysis of the ways in which authority cuts across political, cultural, and subjective boundaries, see Zolov, *Refried Elvis*.

78 Carlos Monsiváis, "1968: Dramatis Personae," in *México: Una democracia utópica; El movimiento estudiantil del 68*, by Sergio Zermeño (Mexico City: Siglo XXI, 1978), xviii. For a fresh and detailed characterization of 1968, I refer to Monsiváis's classic *El 68: La tradición de la resistencia* (Mexico City: Era, 2008).

79 Guevara Niebla, *La democracia en la calle*, 47–48.

80 Williams, *The Mexican Exception*, 12.

81 Gustavo Díaz Ordaz, quoted in Jorge Volpi, *La imaginación y el poder: Una historia intelectual de 1968* (Mexico City: Era, 1998), 234.

82 Volpi, *La imaginación y el poder*, 238–39.

83 Jacques Rancière, *Disagreement: Politics and Philosophy*, trans. Julie Rose (Minneapolis: University of Minnesota Press, 1999), 29.

84 Gilabert, *El hábito de la utopía*, 173, 175. In relation to the relevance of words, see also Monsiváis, *El 68: La tradición de la resistencia*.

85 José Revueltas, "Las palabras prisioneras," in *México 68*, 246, emphasis mine.

86 José Revueltas, *El apando* (Mexico City: Era, 1978); José Revueltas, *El tiempo y el número*, in José Revueltas, *Las cenizas* (Mexico City: Era, 1988), 127–54.

87 Óscar Menéndez, *Historia de un documento / Histoire d'un document* (Mexico City: Ediciones Pentagrama, 2004).

88 Fernanda Navarro, *Existencia, encuentro y azar* (Mexico City: Universidad Michoacana, Secretaría de Difusión Cultural, Editorial Universitaria, 1995).

89 Roberta Avendaño, *De la libertad y el encierro* (Mexico City: La idea dorada, 1998).

90 Glady López Hernández coins the term *ovarimony* to refer to a testimony postulated from a site marked by gender. *Ovarimonio: ¿Yo guerrillera?* (Mexico City: Itaca, 2013).

91 Michelle Zancarini-Fournel, *Le moment 68: Une histoire contestée* (Paris, Seuil, 2008).

1 Volpi, *La imaginación y el poder*, 349.

2 J. Revueltas, "Prohibido prohibir la revolutión," *México 68*, 25.

3 J. Revueltas, "Nuestra revolución de mayo en México," *México 68*, 39.

4 José Revueltas, *Las evocaciones requeridas*, vol. 2 (Mexico City: Era, 1987), 184.

5 Roberto Escudero, "Prólogo," in J. Revueltas, *México 68*, 11.

6 We must also remember that Revueltas put his body into this immersion as well—not simply in the act of moving to occupy the university but also in his awareness of the risk involved in joining the Lecumberri political prisoners in their hunger strike even as his health was becoming increasingly fragile (the onset of diabetes was aggravated by the thousand hours of the strike they organized).

7 José Revueltas, "Ezequiel o la matanza de los inocentes," in *El material de los sueños*, 115–128 (Mexico City: Era, 1974); Martín Dozal, interview with Susana Draper and Vicente Rubio-Pueyo, *México 68: Modelo para armar; Archivo de memorias desde los márgenes*, 2012, https://www.mexico68conversaciones.com/martin-dozal.

8 Dozal, interview with Draper and Rubio-Pueyo.

9 Alberto Híjar, interview with Susana Draper and Vicente Rubio-Pueyo, *México 68: Modelo para armar; Archivo de memorias desde los márgenes*, 2015, https://www.mexico68conversaciones.com/alberto-hijar.

10 Andrea Revueltas, "Aproximaciones a la obra teórico-política de J. Revueltas," in *Revueltas en la mira*, ed. Emmanuel Carballo et al. (Mexico City: Dirección de Difusión Cultural, 1984), 86.

11 Álvarez Garín, *La estela de Tlatelolco*, 152–53.

12 Revueltas's formal incarceration began on November 22. He was accused of "incitement to rebellion, conspiracy, sedition, damage to property, assault on general lines of communication, theft, plunder, possession of firearms, homicide, and assault" (Aguilar Camín and Bellinghausen, *Pensar el 68*, 272). This sparked profound indignation among many writers on the international stage, who drew up a letter of protest. "En defensa de José Revueltas" ("In Defense of José Revueltas"), was published by *La Cultura en México* on December 3. It was signed by Julio Cortázar, Carlos Fuentes, Gabriel García Márquez, Adriano González León, Juan Goytisolo, Jorge Semprún, Mario Vargas Llosa from París, and subsequently acquired by Arthur Miller and the International Pen Club. For the full content of the letter, see Volpi, *La imaginación y el poder*, 351–52.

13 Gilabert, *El hábito de la utopía*, 173.

14 Gilabert, *El hábito de la utopía*, 173.

15 J. Revueltas, *Las evocaciones requeridas*, 185, emphasis mine.

16 J. Revueltas, *México 68*, 21.

17 Bosteels, *Marx and Freud in Latin America*, 70.

18 J. Revueltas, "Un movimiento, una bandera, una revolución," *México 68*, 142, emphasis mine.

19 There is a great deal of background to be discussed here, since the trope of young people spontaneously waking up feeling rebellious threatens the same kind of dehistoricization latent in the contemporaneous narrative of the so-called Mexican

miracle. These fetishes stymie the possibility of even conceiving a present within a greater history. Moreover, describing the events of '68 in other regions as "spontaneous youth rebellions" serves to legitimate Díaz Ordaz's ideal of progressive development, which he attempted to manifest during the Olympics. Reducing '68 to a "spontaneous youth rebellion" perpetuates the myth of Mexico's "miraculous progress"; after all, France too had its moment of madness.

20 Walter Benjamin, *The Arcades Project*, trans. Howard Eiland and Kevin McLaughlin (Cambridge, MA: Harvard University Press, 2002), 460. This problematic doubtless also refers to the international renovation of materialism and dialectics happening at that time (in the works of Lefebvre, Marcuse, Sartre), leading Revueltas to reread and rethink some of young Marx's crucial themes, particularly "a political economy 'beyond' *Das Kapital*; that is, an 'ignored' Marxism, a Marxism that languished in an *epojé* for over fifty years—and not just because of Stalinism." J. Revueltas, *Las evocaciones requeridas*, 244.

21 José Revueltas, "Autogestión académica y universidad crítica," *México 68*, 152, emphasis mine.

22 J. Revueltas, "Autogestión académica," *México 68*, 151.

23 I borrow the word from Luis Villoro's argument that liberal democracy in Mexico takes the form of a "partyocracy." Villoro, *Tres retos de la sociedad porvenir*, 117–29.

24 Peng Cheah, "Non-Dialectical Materialism," in *New Materialisms: Ontology, Agency, and Politics*, ed. Diana Coole and Samantha Frost (Durham, NC: Duke University Press, 2010), 71–72.

25 J. Revueltas, "Autogestión académica," *México 68*, 151.

26 J. Revueltas, "Autogestión académica," *México 68*, 151, emphasis mine.

27 J. Revueltas, "Autogestión académica," *México 68*, 149–51.

28 J. Revueltas, "Significación actual de la revolución rusa de octubre," *Dialéctica de la conciencia* (Mexico City: Era, 1982), 227–28.

29 José Revueltas, *Dialéctica de la conciencia* (Mexico City: Era, 1982), 228, emphasis mine.

30 J. Revueltas, "Clase y partido: los nuevos contenidos de la realidad en la segunda mitad del siglo XX," *Dialéctica de la conciencia*, 233.

31 J. Revueltas, "Un movimiento," *México 68*, 140.

32 J. Revueltas, "A la generación 1965–1969 de sociología," *México 68*, 253, emphasis mine.

33 For a critique of Eurocommunism, see Étienne Balibar's *On the Dictatorship of the Proletariat* (London: NLB, 1977).

34 Adolfo Sánchez Vázquez, "La estética terrenal de José Revueltas," in Carballo et al., *Revueltas en la mira*, 228.

35 Sánchez Vázquez, "La estética terrenal," 229, emphasis mine.

36 Sánchez Vázquez, "La estética terrenal," 229.

37 A few years later, Bolivian thinker René Zavaleta Mercado would speak of a dual power that seeks to deliver the same message. See René Zavaleta Mercado, *El poder dual en América Latina* (Mexico City: Siglo XXI, 1979).

38 J. Revueltas, *México 68*, 139. Many of Villoro's reflections on democracy in *Tres retos de la sociedad por venir* expand on these same ideas by placing them in a modern context.

39 Bosteels, *Marx and Freud in Latin America*, 59.

40 J. Revueltas, *México, una democracia bárbara; y escritos acerca de Lombardo Toledano* (Mexico City: Era, 1983).

41 J. Revueltas, *Ensayo sobre un proletariado sin cabeza* (Mexico City: Era, 1980).

42 Gilabert, *El hábito de la utopía*, 138.

43 Guadalupe Ferrer, interview with Susana Draper and Vicente Rubio-Pueyo, *México 68: Modelo para armar; Archivo de memorias desde los márgenes*, 2015, https://www.mexico68conversaciones.com/guadalupe-ferrer.

44 J. Revueltas, "Un movimiento," *México 68*, 137, emphasis mine.

45 Sánchez Vázquez explains the conceptual modifications Revueltas made: "His contributions to this field are not casual or incidental. Rather, they were informed by real-life problems, both political and literary. Truthfully, these reflections deal with his own practice; thus, José Revueltas remained faithful to one of the medullary demands of Marx's thinking: the rationality of praxis." Sánchez Vázquez, "La estética terrenal," 227. In the same text, the thinker notes that in his final texts, Revueltas seems to have returned to his interest in the figure of the party.

46 J. Revueltas, "Esquema para conferencia sobre autogestión académica," *México 68*, 101.

47 J. Revueltas, "Esquema para conferencia," *México 68*, 97.

48 J. Revueltas, "Esquema para conferencia," *México 68*, 97.

49 Enrique González Rojo, "Las últimas concepciones teórico-políticas de J. Revueltas," in Carballo et al., *Revueltas en la mira*, 102.

50 José Joaquín Blanco, *José Revueltas* (Mexico City: Ed. Terra Nova, 1985), 91.

51 J. Revueltas, "Consideraciones sobre la autogestión académica," *México 68*, 112.

52 With this, Revueltas develops a crucial theme that was also analyzed by Luc Boltanski and Eve Chiapello by pointing out the risk inherent in self-management: namely, that it may become a mere change of hands without modifying the ruling capitalist logic whatsoever. Luc Boltanski and Eve Chiapello, *The New Spirit of Capitalism*, trans. Gregory Elliott (London: Verso, 2005).

53 J. Revueltas, "¿Qué es la autogestión académica?," 107.

54 J. Revueltas, "¿Qué es la autogestión académica?," 108.

55 Valle, *Escritos sobre el movimiento del 68*, 72.

56 J. Revueltas, "Consideraciones," *México 68*, 119.

57 J. Revueltas, "Esquema para conferencia," *México 68*, 102.

58 Híjar explains that on the one hand, there was José Gaos, who insisted on a standardization of the philosophy program with the introduction of Heidegger. On the other hand, Sánchez Vázquez began his professorship on the young Marx and invited key contemporary figures such as Herbert Marcuse to the university (Híjar, interview with Draper and Rubio-Pueyo). This 1966 visit not only complicated the philosophical reorganization happening at UNAM but also drew the hatred of President Díaz Ordaz—who, in his fourth State of the Union address, called Marcuse "The Philosopher of Destruction" (as Volpi reminds us in *La imaginación y el poder*, 152). For a more detailed analysis of this visit in the context of Adolfo Sánchez Vázquez's work, see Stefan Gandler, *Marxismo crítico en México: Adolfo Sánchez Vázquez y Bolívar Echeverría* (Mexico City: Fondo de Cultura Económica, 2007). A concise history

of the actions and relevance of the "Miguel Hernández" group, particularly its contributions to the configuration of critical Marxism at the university level, remains to be written. Some commentary on the subject may be found in Alberto Híjar, "Autonomía, autogestión, autogobierno," *Izquierda Revolucionaria Internacionalista Buenaventura Durruti* (blog), http://colectivobuenaventuradurruti.weebly.com /autonomia-autogestion-autogobierno.html.

59 For more on this experience, see the work of Rafael Reygadas, *Universidad, autogestión y modernidad: Estudio comparado de la formación de arquitectos (1968–1996)* (Mexico City: Centro de Estudios Superiores Universitarios, Universidad Nacional Autónoma de México, 1998); and Javier Mendoza Rojas, *Los conflictos de la UNAM en el siglo XX* (Mexico City: Plaza y Valdés, 2001).

60 As Abraham Guillén points out, "Under State capitalism, although private property and capital would be abolished, the worker would remain alienated unless he came into direct possession of the State's means of production and change. How else can we explain why the USSR has not become a self-managing, debureaucratized society after fifty years of . . . 'socialism'?" Abraham Guillén, *Democracia directa: Autogestión y socialismo* (Montevideo: Editorial Aconcagua, 1972), 99.

61 Henri Lefebvre, *Dialectical Materialism*, trans. John Sturrock (Minneapolis: University of Minnesota Press, 2009), 19.

62 J. Revueltas, "¿Qué es la autogestión académica?," *México 68*, 108.

63 J. Revueltas, "Consideraciones," *México 68*, 112.

64 J. Revueltas, "Algunos puntos programáticos sobre la autogestión académica," *México 68*, 155.

65 J. Revueltas, "Esquema para conferencia," *México 68*, 101–2.

66 J. Revueltas, "Consideraciones," *México 68*, 119–20.

67 Theodore Roszak, *The Making of a Counter Culture: Reflections on the Technocratic Society and its Youthful Opposition* (Garden City: Doubleday, 1969).

68 J. Revueltas, "¿Qué es la autogestión académica?," *México 68*, 109.

69 See Frank Georgi, "Construire l'autogestion," in *Autogestion: La dernière utopie?* (Paris: Publications de la Sorbonne, 2003), 11–28.

70 J. Revueltas, "Autogestión académica," *México 68*, 154.

71 Luis González de Alba begins *Los días y los años* by referencing the apando that provided him a hiding place during the common prisoners' attack on the political prisoners in December 1969 during their hunger strike. During an interview, Martín Dozal, Revueltas's cellmate, showed us the apando that he had kept from those years at Lecumberri (see https://www.mexico68conversaciones.com/martin-dozal).

72 Gustavo Sáinz, ed., *Conversaciones con José Revueltas* (Mexico City: Centro de Investigaciones Lingüístico-Literarias, Universidad Veracruzana, 1977), 39.

73 Sáinz, *Conversaciones con José Revueltas*, 17.

74 J. Revueltas, "Gris es toda teoría," *México 68*, 80, emphasis mine.

75 Jean-Paul Sartre, *No Exit, and Three Other Plays* (New York: Vintage International, 1989).

76 Ignacio Trejo Fuentes, "Las novelas de José Revueltas," in Carballo et al., *Revueltas en la mira*, 23, emphasis mine.

77 Jaime Ramírez Garrido, *Dialéctica de lo terrenal: Ensayo sobre la obra de José Revueltas* (Mexico City: Consejo Nacional para la Cultura y las Artes, 1991), 16.

78 J. Revueltas, *El apando*, 45–46.

79 Guards are called *los monos*, or "monkeys," in Mexican prison jargon.

80 J. Revueltas, *El apando*, 52.

81 J. Revueltas, *El apando*, 40.

82 J. Revueltas, *El apando*, 54–55.

83 J. Revueltas, *El apando*, 56.

84 J. Revueltas, *El apando*, 56.

85 J. Revueltas, *El apando*, 11.

86 J. Revueltas, *El apando*, 34, emphasis mine.

87 Sáinz, *Conversaciones con José Revueltas*, 38, emphasis mine.

88 In his *Critique of Everyday Life*, Lefebvre suggests the possibility of making way for new forms of feeling and imagining not conditional upon magic. He uses the case of Bertolt Brecht to illustrate "art liberated from magic." Henri Lefebvre, *Critique of Everyday Life*, trans. John Moore (New York: Verso, 2014), 43.

89 Sáinz, *Conversaciones con José Revueltas*, 10.

90 Sáinz, *Conversaciones con José Revueltas*, 10.

91 Sáinz, *Conversaciones con José Revueltas*, 71, emphasis mine.

92 Lessie Jo Frazier and Deborah Cohen, "Talking Back to '68: Gendered Narratives, Participatory Spaces, and Political Cultures," in *Gender and Sexuality in 1968: Transformative Politics in the Cultural Imagination*, ed. Lessie Jo Frazier and Deborah Cohen (New York: Palgrave, 2009), 149. For an analysis of masculinity in a broader context, see Elaine Carey, "Los Dueños de México: Power and Masculinity in '68," in Frazier and Cohen, *Gender and Sexuality in 1968: Transformative Politics in the Cultural Imagination*, 59–83.

93 J. Revueltas, *Los muros del agua* (Mexico City: Era, 1973).

94 J. Revueltas, *Dialéctica de la conciencia*, 37.

95 J. Revueltas, "Hegel y yo" in *El material de los sueños*, 9–24; J. Revueltas, *El tiempo y el número*.

96 Ramírez Garrido, *Dialéctica de lo terrenal*, 16.

97 During his visit to Cuba two years after the revolution, in the happiness of those first years Revueltas confesses his fascination with that almost Edenic moment in a letter: "A revolution in an Edenic state, which before always began with naming things: this is water, this is wind, this is a mountain, this is socialism. The best part is that things proceed, and a splendid, awakened youth surges up all around, carrying things, pushing them." J. Revueltas, *Las evocaciones requeridas*, 89. Julio Cortázar articulated this phenomenon most powerfully in his debate with Óscar Collazos in the Casa de las Américas, where they discussed the role of authors and literature in times of revolution: "We're missing 'Che' Guevaras of language," Cortázar, *Literatura en la revolución y revolución en la literatura* (Mexico City: Siglo XXI, 1970), 76. During his stay in Lecumberri, Revueltas became obsessed with words and attempted to create a workshop of words that, according to Martín Dozal (Interview with Susana Draper and Vicente Rubio-Pueyo) was largely unsuccessful but nonetheless shed light on the

importance of language, words, and materiality in Revueltas's work. (I will return to this at the end of the chapter.)

98 Sáinz, *Conversaciones con José Revueltas*, 57, emphasis mine.

99 J. Revueltas, "Apuntes para un ensayo sobre la dialéctica de la conciencia," *Dialéctica de la conciencia*, 31.

100 John Kraniauskas, *Políticas literarias: Poder y acumulación en la literatura y el cine latinoamericanos* (Mexico City: Facultad Latinoamericana de Ciencias Sociales, 2012), 139, emphasis mine.

101 J. Revueltas, *El apando*, 34–35.

102 In "A Life Without Object(s)," Carlos Liscano—a Uruguayan political prisoner during the last military dictatorship—reflects on language in prison, underscoring how words start to empty of concrete referents in the simplicity of the space. From this emptying emerges a materiality of meaning that itself becomes a struggle. Like Revueltas, Liscano makes an argument for the necessity of defending words, fighting for them and their meanings—and perhaps also for the freedom inherent in performative acts of language that unveil the Constitution and penal codes as acts of language that operate on bodies. Life in captivity begins with a word and a number, a passage from free citizen to bound prisoner whose freedom is replaced by the number of words that make up his sentence. Even so, the word *freedom*—even in Revueltas's remark about freedom of consciousness—implies a curious split between body and consciousness (see endnote 70). Carlos Liscano, "A Life Without Object(s)," in *Truck of Fools* (Nashville, TN: Vanderbilt University Press, 2004), 1–14.

103 J. Revueltas, "Las palabras prisioneras," *México 68*, 246.

104 Sáinz, *Conversaciones con José Revueltas*, 43.

105 J. Revueltas, "Las palabras prisioneras," *México 68*, 245–247.

106 J. Revueltas, "Las palabras prisioneras," *México 68*, 245.

107 J. Revueltas, "Las palabras prisioneras," *México 68*, 245–246.

108 J. Revueltas, "Las palabras prisioneras," *México 68*, 246, emphasis mine.

109 J. Revueltas, "Las palabras prisioneras," *México 68*, 247.

110 J. Revueltas, "Palabras finales," *México 68*, 282–283.

111 J. Revueltas, "Intervención de José Revueltas en la audiencia de derecho de la vista de sentencia, Audiencia celebrada en la cárcel preventiva de la ciudad, del 17 al 18 de setiembre de 1970," *México 68*, 273.

112 J. Revueltas takes the quotes from a selection from Karl Marx's *Theories of Surplus Value* (New York: International Publishers, 1952), published in translation by Fondo de Cultura Económica in 1945. Karl Marx, *Historia crítica de la teoría de la plusvalía: Adam Smith y la idea del trabajo productivo* (Mexico City: Fondo de Cultura Económica, 1945); also quoted in *México 68*, 274.

113 J. Revueltas, "Intervención," *México 68*, 273–74.

114 J. Revueltas, "Intervención," *México 68*, 278–79.

115 J. Revueltas, "Palabras finales," *México 68*, 282–83, emphasis mine.

116 Aguilar Camín and Bellinghausen, *Pensar el 68*, 243.

117 J. Revueltas, "Diario de Lecumberri," *Mexico 68*, 248–49.

118 Edith Negrín, *Entre la paradoja y la dialéctica: Una lectura de la narrativa de José Revueltas* (Mexico City: Universidad Nacional Autónoma de México, 1995), 205.

119 J. Revueltas, *El apando*, 55.

120 J. Revueltas, *El tiempo y el número*, endnote 14, in *Las cenizas*, 310.

121 J. Revueltas, *El tiempo y el* número, endnote 14, in *Las cenizas*, 311.

122 Edith Negrín, *Entre la paradoja*, 205, emphasis mine.

123 J. Revueltas, *El tiempo y el número*, in *Las cenizas*, 128, emphasis mine.

124 Arrighi, Hopkins, and Wallerstein, *Antisystemic Movements*, 98.

125 These moments define an epochal change along political and cultural dimensions. Hobsbawm, "1968: A Retrospective," 130.

126 Henri Lefebvre, "Theoretical Problems of Autogestion," in *State, Space, World: Selected Essays*, ed. Neil Brenner and Stuart Elden, trans. Gerald Moore, Neil Brenner, and Stuart Elden (Minneapolis: University of Minnesota Press, 2010), 150.

127 Bosteels, *Marx and Freud in Latin America*, 70.

128 Peter Osborne, *Politics of Time: Modernity and Avant-Garde* (London: Verso, 2007).

129 J. Revueltas, *El tiempo y el número*, in *Las cenizas*, 127.

130 J. Revueltas, "Reforma educativa," *México 68*, 170.

131 Osborne, *Politics of Time*, 3.

132 Aricó poses a whole host of questions that prompted intellectuals to embark on a sort of militant investigation of perception. In an article in *Pasado y presente*, he seeks to open many lines of inquiry into how manufacturing in Córdoba started to alter workers' perception of time. That is, having to think like a machine modified their way of viewing temporality. Although he never experienced this process, it seemed to him that intellectuals dedicated days to thinking about the world that was nevertheless completely unknown to them. José Aricó, "Algunas consideraciones preliminares sobre la condición obrera," *Pasado y presente* 3, no. 9 (1965): 46–55.

133 Dual power is a zone of reflection and debates about Latin American revolutionary processes in the early 1970s. According to José Harari, it was an alternative to emphasizing *foquismo* which came under fire during the same struggle. José Harari, *Contribución a la historia del ideario del M.L.N. Tupamaros: Análisis crítico* (Montevideo: Editorial MZ, 1986), 105–8. It reemerges as a theme of analysis (now of a more theoretical kind, poststruggle) among heterodox Marxist thinkers in exile after a series of coups and the subsequent dismantling of revolutionary groups. While this theme usually forms a crucial part of movements or parties that have armed factions, what interests me is the fact that dual power raises the possibility of decentralizing the idea of state takeover by proposing a zone in which this theme is a configuration of a culture divergent from the state as the very site of struggle (see Zavaleta Mercado, *El poder dual en América Latina*); Susana Draper, "Hegemonía, poder dual, post-hegemonía: Las derivas del concepto," in *Post-hegemonía: El final de un paradigma político de la filosofía en América Latina*, ed. Rodrigo Castro Orellana (Madrid: Editorial Biblioteca Nueva, 2015), 93–112.

134 The motley has been discussed in a series of deep readings of the social and political history of Bolivia. This concept has been applied in other fields in at least two

works: Luis Tapia, *La condición multisocietal: Multiculturalidad, pluralismo, modern-idad* (La Paz: Muela del Diablo, 2002); and Silvia Rivera Cusicansqui, *Ch'ixinacax utxiwa: Una reflexión sobre prácticas y discursos descolonizadores* (Buenos Aires: Tinta Limón, 2010). Abril Trigo's "Una lectura materialista de la colonialidad (segunda parte)," *Alter/nativas* 3 (autumn 2014), offers a profound and comprehensive analysis of the concept. https://alternativas.osu.edu/es/issues/autumn-2014/essays2/trigo2 .html.

135 As Fredric Jameson affirms, "It is now time to explore some other possibilities—the notion of a multiplicity of local dialectics on the one hand, and also some concep-tion of the radical break constituted by dialectical thinking as such." Fredric Jameson, *Valences of the Dialectic* (London: Verso, 2010), 10.

2. THE EFFECTS OF '68 ON CINEMA

1 Mariano Mestman, "Presentación. Las rupturas del 68 en el cine de América Latina. Contracultura, experimentación y política," in *Las rupturas del 68 en el cine de América Latina*, ed. Mariano Mestman (Buenos Aires: Akal, 2016), 8.

2 Álvaro Vázquez Mantecón, "El 68 cinematográfico," in Mestman, *Las rupturas del 68*, 307.

3 Vázquez Mantecón, "El 68 cinematográfico," 307.

4 *El grito* is made up of images that students gathered at the time of events of '68 (demonstrations, protests, brigades). In spite of the fact that many materials were confiscated on October 2, in 1969 almost eight hours of filming was edited down to a two-hour film, directed by Leobardo López Aretche and Roberto Sánchez Martínez. This was a project that López Aretche completed before his imprison-ment in Lecumberri and his subsequent suicide in July 1970. He had been the representative of the CUEC in the National Strike Council, and before his death he worked on the script for Alfredo Joskowicz's film *El cambio* (*The Change*), indirectly linked to '68. On the films that emerge after '68, see Jacqueline Bixler, "Mexico 1968 and the Art(s) of Memory," in *The Long 1968: Revisions and New Perspectives*, ed. Daniel J. Sherman, Ruud van Dijk, Jasmine Alinder, and A. Aneesh (Bloomington: Indiana University Press, 2000); and Álvaro Vázquez Mantecón, *El cine súper 8 en México 1970–1989* (Mexico City: Universidad Nacional Autónoma de México, 2012).

5 Vázquez Mantecón, *El cine súper 8 en México*, 199.

6 Andrea Giunta, *Avant-Garde, Internationalism, and Politics: Argentine Art in the Sixties*, trans. Peter Kahn (Durham, NC: Duke University Press, 2007).

7 Amador Fernández-Savater and David Cortés, "¿Qué vuelve política a una imagen?," in *Con y contra el cine: En torno a mayo del 68* (Seville: Universidad Internacional de Andalucía, 1999), 15.

8 Jorge Fons, dir., *Rojo amanecer* (Mexico City: Quality Films, 1989); Carlos Bolado, dir., *Tlatelolco: Verano del 68* (Mexico City: Eficine 226, Fidecine, Maíz Producciones, Producción corazones, Universidad Nacional Autónoma de México, 2013); Alfredo Gurrola, dir., *Borrar de la memoria* (Mexico City: Magenta Films,

2014); Richard Dindo, dir., *Ni olvido, ni perdón* (Zurich: Lea Produktion, Film Coopi, 2004).

9 For a reflection on cinema as the place where a process of interpretation of '68 takes place, I refer to Carolina Tolosa's excellent work: "Las memorias públicas del movimiento estudiantil de 1968 a través de *El grito* and *Tlatelolco, las claves de la massacre*" (presentation at the First University Colloquium of Film Analysis [Primer coloquio universitario de análisis cinematográfico], Mexico City, November 15–18, 2011).

10 Asociación de Documentalistas de México, *El cine independiente ¿hacia dónde?* (Mexico City: Asociación de Documentalistas de México, 2007); Vázquez Mantecón, *El cine súper 8 en México*.

11 Julio García Espinosa, "For an Imperfect Cinema," *Jump Cut* 20, no. 20 (1979): 24–26.

12 Jesse Lerner, "Superocheros," in "Superocheros," special issue, *Wide Angle: A Quarterly Journal of Film History, Theory, Criticism and Practice* 21, no. 3 (1999): 6. For a study and historicization of this project, see Gustavo García and José Felipe Coria, *Nuevo cine mexicano* (Mexico City: Clío, 1997).

13 Sergio García, "Toward a Fourth Cinema / Hacia un cuarto cine," in "Superocheros," special issue, *Wide Angle: A Quarterly Journal of Film History, Theory, Criticism and Practice* 21, no. 3 (1999): 135–61.

14 These points are explicitly set forth in Jaime Humberto Hermosillo et al., "Manifesto: 8 millimeters versus 8 millions / Manifiesto: 8 milímetros contra 8 millones," in "Superocheros," special issue, *Wide Angle: A Quarterly Journal of Film History, Theory, Criticism and Practice* 21, no. 3 (1999): 36–41, which states that a cinema cannot be denominated independent if in order to be made it must pass through various processes of censorship and contrasts this with a defense of Super 8 as an economical mechanism in which the possibility of creating a new and different cinema is affirmed.

15 S. García, "Toward a Fourth Cinema," 91.

16 S. García, "Toward a Fourth Cinema," 169–71.

17 For an analysis of similar forms of action and cooperation in 1968 Uruguay, see Cecilia Lacruz, "La comezón por el intercambio," in Mestman, *Las rupturas del 68*, 311–51.

18 Ferrer, interview with Draper and Rubio-Pueyo.

19 In his study of the cooperative, Jorge Ayala Blanco also mentions Paco Cantú, Ramón Vilar, and Jesús Dávila, and makes reference to "two housewives." Jorge Ayala Blanco, *La búsqueda del cine mexicano (1968–1972)* (Mexico City: Editorial Posada, 1986), 369. Although no one mentions the participation of women, both Guadalupe Ferrer and Paloma Sáiz were part of the project. I will cover this issue in the next chapter, but it should be noted here that the histories and memories of processes that had gender equality, perhaps for the first time in history, are narrated solely from the masculine perspective.

20 It should be noted that these experiments will contrast with the waves of neoliberalization of the image that started a decade afterward. For an excellent study of such processes, see Ignacio M. Sánchez Prado, *Screening Neoliberalism: Transforming Mexican Cinema, 1988–2012* (Nashville, TN: Vanderbilt University Press, 2014).

21 José Carlos Méndez, "Toward a Political Cinema: The Cooperative of Marginal Cinema / Hacia un cine político: La Cooperativa de Cine Marginal" in "Superocheros," special issue, *Wide Angle: A Quarterly Journal of Film History, Theory, Criticism and Practice* 21, no. 3 (1999): 47.

22 Vázquez Mantecón, *El cine súper 8 en México*, 205–6.

23 Ayala Blanco, *La búsqueda del cine mexicano*, 371.

24 Vázquez Mantecón, *El cine súper 8 en México*, 224.

25 Vázquez Mantecón, *El cine súper 8 en México*, 221, emphasis mine.

26 I excerpt this from Ferrer's memory in her interview (interview with Draper and Rubio-Pueyo).

27 On this point, I recommend Heidrun Holzfeind's interview of Mercedes Perelló, who speaks in detail of this afterlife of the movement in factories and working-class neighborhoods. See Mexico68, "Interview with Mercedes Perelló," 2007, https:// vimeo.com/77938520. To analyze a similar movement in the world of organizing teachers, I recommend the interview with Jesús Martín del Campo in *México 68: Modelo para armar*, in which he speaks of a process of communication between the struggles of the peasants and the teachers in different parts of the country, something that was central in the world of the image with the workers' strikes filmed by the Cooperative of Marginal Cinema. Jesús Martín del Campo, interview with Susana Draper and Vicente Rubio-Pueyo, *México 68: Modelo para armar; Archivo de memorias desde los márgenes*, 2012, https://www.mexico68conversaciones.com/jesus-martin -del-campo/.

28 Menéndez had filmed *Todos somos hermanos* (1965) before diving into the experience of '68 with his films *Únete Pueblo* (1968) and *Dos de octubre, aquí México* (1968), which include a number of materials filmed throughout the student movement, many of them during the Tlatelolco massacre.

29 Óscar Menéndez, interview with Susana Draper and Vicente Rubio-Pueyo, *México 68: Modelo para armar; Archivo de memorias desde los márgenes,* 2012, https://www .mexico68conversaciones.com/oscar-menendez/.

30 Óscar Menéndez, dir., *Historia de un documento / Histoire d'un document* (Mexico City: Ediciones Pentagrama, 2004), emphasis mine.

31 Menéndez, *Historia de un documento*, translation mine.

32 Menéndez, *Historia de un documento*.

33 I refer here to Ludmita Catela Da Silva's pioneering work on long-term and short-term memory, which explores the varied forms and formats memory takes when the history of human rights violation is narrated by people from outside the capital cities and for whom police violence is a constant threat instead of an exception. Ludmita Catela Da Silva, "Poder local y violencia: Memorias de la represión en el noroeste argentine," in *Inseguridad y violencia en el Cono Sur*, ed. Alejandro Isla (Buenos Aires: Paidós, 2007), 211–27.

34 Roland Barthes, *Camera Lucida: Reflections on Photography*, trans. Richard Howard (New York: Farrar, Straus and Giroux, 1981), 85.

35 Michel Foucault, *Discipline and Punish: The Birth of the Prison*, trans. Alan Sheridan (New York: Vintage Books, 1995), 202–3.

36 Javier de Taboada traces the different moments when the idea of a third cinema at the level of Latin America and the world is articulated, distinguishing between a first moment that corresponds to the publication of the different founding manifestos of this movement at the ends of the sixties in different countries: "Estetica da fome" ("Aesthetic of Hunger," 1965) by Glauber Rocha (Brazil), "Hacia un tercer cine" ("Towards a Third Cinema," 1969) by Fernando Solanas and Octavio Getino (Argentina), and "Por un cine imperfecto" ("For an Imperfect Cinema," 1969) by Julio García Espinosa (Cuba). A second moment corresponds to the internationalization of the phenomenon through African directors such as Ousmane Sembene and Ritwik Ghatak at the beginning of the eighties, articulating a broader notion of the phenomenon with the publication of *Third Cinema in the Third World. The Aesthetics of Liberation*, by Teshome Gabriel, in 1982; Javier de Taboada, "Tercer cine: Tres manifiestos," *Revista de crítica literaria latinoamericana* 37, no. 73 (2011): 37–60.

37 Ramón Gil Olivo, *Cine y liberación: El nuevo cine latinoamericano (1954–1973); Fuentes para un lenguaje* (Guadalajara: Centro Universitario de Arte, Arquitectura y Diseño, Universidad de Guadalajara, 2009), 20.

38 Fernando Solanas and Octavio Getino, "La hora de los hornos. Informe por el grupo Cine-Liberación," in *Cine del tercer mundo*, no. 1 (1969): 19, translation mine.

39 Fernando Solanas and Octavio Getino, "Towards a Third Cinema: Notes and Experiences for the Development of a Cinema of Liberation in the Third World," in *Film Manifestos and Global Cinema Cultures: A Critical Anthology*, ed. Scott MacKenzie (Berkeley: University of California Press, 2014), emphasis mine.

40 One of the most detailed analyses of the critical points of third cinema can be found in Alberto Híjar, "Introducción," in *Hacia un tercer cine: Antología*, ed. Alberto Híjar, Cuadernos de cine 20 (Mexico City: Universidad Nacional Autónoma de México, 1972), 7–27.

41 S. García, "Toward a Fourth Cinema," 171.

42 S. García, "Toward a Fourth Cinema," 170–71. I provide an alternative translation as I find it important to keep the word *awaken* that is used in the original and is lost in the translated article ("Un cine que despierte conciencia; no que la forme").

43 Mariano Mestman, "Third Cinema / Militant Cinema: At the Origins of the Argentinian Experience (1968–1971)," *Third Text* 25, no. 1 (2011): 29.

44 Mestman, "Third Cinema," 39.

45 Mestman, "Third Cinema," 33.

46 S. García, "Toward a Fourth Cinema," 169.

47 Lerner, "Superocheros," 23.

48 Rancière develops this argument in "The Paradoxes of Political Art," in *Dissensus: On Politics and Aesthetics*, trans. Steven Corcoran (New York: Continuum, 2015), 142–60.

3. WHERE ARE THE WOMEN OF '68?

1 Tirado Villegas, *La otra historia*, 13. The study conducted here is revolutionary not only in its approach to this vast and opaque silence in regard to women of '68 but

also in its interest to look for memories outside the Federal District. In addition to the discursive space of gender that holds a particular monopoly of the word and the memories of '68, it is necessary to insist on the investigation about the forms that this movement took on outside the capital. The work of Tirado Villegas sheds light on these points.

2 Sheila Rowbotham, *Promise of a Dream: Remembering the Sixties* (London: Verso, 2007), xii.

3 Luisa Passerini, *Autobiography of a Generation*; Luisa Passerini, "Foreword," in Frazier and Cohen, *Gender and Sexuality in 1968: Transformative Politics in the Cultural Imagination*, ix–xii.

4 Tirado Villegas, *La otra historia*, 25.

5 Elaine Carey, *Plaza of Sacrifices: Gender, Power, and Terror in 1968* (Albuquerque: University of New Mexico Press, 2005), 5–6.

6 Cohen and Frazier, "Talking Back to '68," 146.

7 Marcia Gutiérrez, "Éramos pocas las mujeres en el Consejo Nacional de Huelga," YouTube, September 29, 2011, https://www.youtube.com/watch?v=F6d1fL6lOUo.

8 Regarding the participation of women within the National Strike Council, I refer to the interviews with Esmeralda Reynoso and Marcia Gutiérrez, cited above.

9 It is worth mentioning that Beatriz Argelia González, one of the participants of the debate about the women of '68, wrote her doctoral thesis on the role of women in the movement of '68 and is currently working on a documentary that collected testimonies and memories, with the title *Las mujeres del 68: Mariposas en un mundo de palabras* (*The Women of '68: Butterflies in a World of Words*). Details on the forthcoming documentary project can be found in an interview of Argelia González by Mónica V. Delgado, "Las mujeres del 68: Mariposas en un mundo de palabras," *Vivir en Tlatelolco: Periodismo comunitario*, February 20, 2013, http://vivirtlatelolco.blogspot .com/2013/02/las-mujeres-del-68-mariposas-en-un.html. It should also be noted that in 2012, the annual march that the 68 Committee (Comité 68) organizes as a public commemoration of the massacre of Tlatelolco was dedicated to the memory of the women who were assassinated that day. For more information on the march of October 2, 2013, see "Marcharon mujeres del Comité 68 para conmemorar matanza en Tlatelolco," *Proyecto Diez*, October 3, 2013, http://www.proyectodiez.mx/nacional /marcharon-mujeres-del-comite-68-para-conmemorar-matanza-en-tlatelolco.

10 In regard to women and the guerillas, see Macrina Cárdenas Montaño, "La participación de las mujeres en los movimientos armados," in *Movimientos armados en México, siglo XX*, vol. 2, ed. Verónika Oikión and Marta Eugenia García (Mexico City: Centro de Investigación y Estudios Superiores en Antropología Social, 2006), 609–24.

11 Francesca Gargallo, "1968: Una revolución en la que se manifestó un nuevo feminismo," *La calle es de quien la camina, las fronteras son asesinas*, 2008. https:// francescagargallo.wordpress.com/ensayos/feminismo/feminismo-filosofia/1968 -una-revolucion-en-la-que-se-manifesto-un-nuevo-feminismo/. In her classic work, she affirms that "among all of the movements that converged in 1968, feminism was the one that had the longest-lasting resistance, while also the newest and the most

uncomfortable for the system. In fact, it was an outbreak of the commitment to life held by the majority of humanity. This indeed did not cushion the traditional forms of doing politics." Francesca Gargallo, *Las ideas feministas lationamericanas* (Mexico City: Universidad de la Ciudad de México, 2004), 16.

12 Márgara Millán, "Introducción: La construcción de la polivalencia del sujeto del feminismo," in *Cartografías del feminismo mexicano, 1970–2000*, ed. Nora Nínive García, Márgara Millán, and Cynthia Pech (Mexico City: Universidad Autónoma de la Ciudad de México, 2007), 17.

13 Quoted in Carolina Velázquez, "El 68, 'caldo de cultivo' para el movimiento de mujeres," *Cimac Noticias*, August 10, 2008, http://www.cimacnoticias.com.mx/node /46739. For a more detailed analysis of the specific groups that emerged in the early 1970s, see Rocío González Alvarado, "El espíritu de una época," in García, Millán, and Pech, *Cartografías del feminismo mexicano*, 65–116.

14 Ana Lau Jaiven relates the emergence of second-wave feminism to the cultural trans-formation that the sixties made possible. Ana Lau Jaiven, *La nueva ola del feminismo en México: Conciencia y acción de lucha de las mujeres* (Mexico City: Planeta, 1987), 11.

15 Juliet Mitchell, *Woman's Estate* (Harmondsworth: Penguin, 1971). For an analysis of the styles in which to *narrate* the different histories and discontinuities of women movements, I refer to Joan Wallach Scott's *Gender and the Politics of History*, rev. ed. (New York: Columbia University Press, 1999); and *Only Paradoxes to Offer: French Feminists and the Rights of Man* (Cambridge, MA: Harvard University Press, 1996).

16 As an aside, it is important to mention here that, just as many feminists express, the liberatory aspects of '68 were motivated by a specific geographical positioning and social class: the intellectual milieu and, more specifically, the university, made available mostly to middle-class women. As Nathalie Ludec writes, "The Federal District became the center of reception, production, and political debate by way of its creation of feminist groups and publications, especially *La Revuelta* (1976–1983), *Cihuat* (1975) and *Fem* (1976), publications that remain alive to this day. Yet femi-nist theories, adopted more for convenience than for necessity, were only of interest to a minority of intellectuals and women from the middle class." Nathalie Ludec, "*La Boletina* de Morelia: Órgano informativo de la Red Nacional de Mujeres, 1982–1985," *Comunicación y sociedad*, no. 5 (January–June 2006): 90. According to Milagros Peña, only after the First National Meeting of Women (Primer Encuen-tro Nacional de Mujeres) in the eighties did a dialogue emerge between women of different social sectors and various defining complexities within Mexico. Her work suggests that after this meeting, a matter that also emerged was the necessity of thinking about ethnicity and the difference implicated in the creation of a feminist language that attends to the racism perpetuated against the indigenous population. Milagros Peña, *Latina Activists across Borders: Women's Grassroots Organizing in Mexico and Texas* (Durham, NC: Duke University Press, 2007), 9. As this is the tone with which academic feminists would develop, we should also remember that for many women of working-class backgrounds, '68 represented an intense libera-tion, as we will see in the final part of this section through the memories of Gladys López Hernández.

17 Alma Rosa Sánchez Olvera, "El contenido del feminismo mexicano en los años setenta," in *El feminismo mexicano ante el movimiento urbano popular: Dos expresiones de lucha de género, 1970–1985* (Mexico City: Universidad Nacional Autónoma de México, 2002), 115.

18 Gladys López Hernández, interview with Susana Draper and Vicente Rubio-Pueyo, *México 68: Modelo para armar; Archivo de memorias desde los márgenes*, 2015, https://www.mexico68conversaciones.com/gladys-lopez-hernandez/.

19 Poniatowska, *Massacre in Mexico*, 17.

20 Poniatowska, *Massacre in Mexico*, 90.

21 Taibo, *'68*, 42, 43.

22 Cohen and Frazier, "Talking Back to '68," 165.

23 Rancière, "Desarrollar la temporalidad de los momentos de igualdad," 11.

24 Sofía Argüeyo Pazmiño, "Identidades en disputa: Discursos científicos, medios de comunicación y estrategias políticas del Movimiento de Liberación Homosexual mexicano, 1968–1984," in *La memoria y el deseo: Estudios gay y queer en México*, ed. Rodrigo Parrini and Alejandro Brito (Mexico City: Universidad Nacional Autónoma de México, Programa Universitario de Estudios de Género, 2014), 27.

25 Rancière, *Disagreement*, 36.

26 In choosing to focus on this issue, I am leaving behind part of a textual corpus of women writers whose emphasis resides in approaching through literature the trauma that the massacre of Tlatelolco left on the social imaginary (works such as María Luisa Puga, *Pánico o peligro* [Mexico City: Siglo XXI Editores, 1983]; Martha Robles, *Los octubres del otoño* [Mexico City: Ediciones Océano, 1982]; Emma Prieto, *Los testigos* [Mexico City: Porrúa, 2008]; or María Luisa Mendoza, *Con él, conmigo, con nosotros tres: Cronovela* [Mexico City: Joaquín Mortiz, 1971]). Michelle Joffroy analyzes the existence of a perspective that is both dominant and masculine in the literary field of what is called the "novel" of '68, in which the stories and testimonial narratives imagine the subject (the self) in '68 as a male-bodied figure, thereby reproducing, albeit indirectly, the state that they claimed to be critiquing. Michelle Joffroy, "Ambiguous Subjects: The Autobiographical Situation and the Disembodiment of '68," in Frazier and Cohen, *Gender and Sexuality in 1968*, 219–34. Although I take into account the conceptual images that emerge from these texts, I am also interested in reiterating the critical operation that lies behind this book as the proposal of opening up the memory of '68 to those sites that did not remain punctuated by the massacre of Tlatelolco.

27 Christine Delphy, "For a Materialist Feminism," in *A Materialist Feminism: A Reader in Class, Difference, and Women's Lives*, ed. Rosemary Hennessy and Chrys Ingraham (New York: Routledge, 1997), 62.

28 Sandra Emma Toledo Garibaldi offers a map of the different paths and the complexity of positions and divisions that were soon to take place between heterosexual and lesbian feminist groups. Sandra Emma Toledo Garibaldi, "La sexualidad disidente: El movimiento lésbico en México," in García, Millán, and Pech, *Cartografías del feminismo mexicano*, 161–91. Although 1968 is the year in which the histories of the movement for homosexual liberation started, there is a silence regarding homosexuality within the dominant narratives of 1968.

29 In 1967 Fernanda Navarro collaborated in the formation of the Bertrand Russell Peace Foundation and edited an anthology of Russell's works in 1971. Afterward, she wrote her thesis in relation to this experience ("Ethics and Politics in the Works of Bertrand Russell"). In 1972 she traveled to Chile to participate in the "democratic path to socialism" and served as a translator of English and French for the publisher Editorial Nacional Quimantú. After the coup, Navarro travelled with Hortensia Bussi de Allende (the widow of Salvador Allende) to continue her services as a translator.

30 Fernanda Navarro, *Existencia, encuentro y azar* (Mexico City: Universidad Michoacana, Secretaría de Difusión Cultural, Editorial Universitaria, 1995).

31 Ludec, "*La Boletina* de Morelia," 92.

32 Ludec, "*La Boletina* de Morelia," 93.

33 For more information on Navarro's philosophical trajectory, see the *Electronic Encyclopedia of Mexican Philosophy*. However, it is surprising that this text fails to mention Navarro's participation in feminist struggles, the establishment of VenSeremos, and the Michoacán *Bulletin*, as networks of cooperation and sites of circulation of the word for women as if these were not crucial components in her philosophical formation. "Fernanda Sylvia Navarro y Solares (1941)," *Enciclopedia Electrónica de Filosofía Mexicana. Centro de Documentación en Filosofía Latinoamericana e Ibérica* (Mexico City: Universidad Autónoma Metropolitana—Unidad Iztapalapa, 2014). http://dcsh .izt.uam.mx/cen_doc/cefilibe/images/banners/enciclopedia/Diccionario/Autores /FilosofosMexicanos/Navarro_Fernanda.pdf.

34 Fernanda Navarro, "Asfixiata (sketch teatral feminista en un acto)," *Lectura de la realidad en el aula. Textos de Fernanda Navarro*, 2010, http://www.lrealidad.filos.unam .mx/asfixiata.

35 Fernanda Navarro, *Filosofía y marxismo: Entrevista a Louis Althusser* (Mexico City: Siglo XXI, 1988); Louis Althusser, *Sur la Philosophie* (Paris: Gallimard, 1994).

36 With regard to the Zapatista uprising in 1994, Navarro published a series of texts about the movement in *La palabra andante: Revista de divulgación zapatista*, which records texts published from 1994 to 2001 in the *Jornada Michoacana*.

37 Regarding de Beauvoir's relevance to Navarro's work, I suggest a sui generis text by Oralba Castillo Nájera that permits us to also note the influence of her presence in the country, "Simone y yo," ("Simone and Me"), *Debate feminista* 38 (October 2008): 166–74.

38 Fernanda Navarro, *Existencia, encuentro y azar*, 24.

39 González Rojo and Híjar quoted in Gerardo Ochoa Sandy and Pascal Beltrán del Río, "Louis Althusser en México: La generación del 68 lo hizo suyo por radical y antidogmático," *Proceso*, October 27, 1990, http://www.proceso.com.mx/155935/sanchez -vazquez-gonzalez-rojo-luis-zavala-hijar.

40 It is worthwhile to note the problem of women's participation within the philosophical disciplines as well as within the very practices of programs and departments of philosophy in universities where, since the eighties, feminist struggles began to be integrated as comprehensible problems, and as such they were relegated to the position of *a female matter*. The recent volume *Women in Philosophy: What Needs to Change?* inquires about the ways in which the problem of women in philosophy was

relegated to the area of gender studies yet was not included as part of a questioning of the discipline itself. In the introduction to the volume, Fiona Jenkins and Katrina Hutchison ask themselves: "How would philosophy be today if feminist curriculums had transformed our comprehension of the discipline in its defiance to the norms of male authority?" Fiona Jenkins and Katrina Hutchison, "Introduction: Searching for Sofia: Gender and Philosophy in the 21st Century," in *Women in Philosophy: What Needs to Change?*, ed. Fiona Jenkins and Katrina Hutchison (Oxford: Oxford University Press, 2014), 9. They later argue that, even when feminist philosophy has been recognized as an important philosophical field, its presence is much stronger in "gender studies" departments rather than in departments of philosophy. How and why the questions that had been posed as philosophical problems and feminist inquiries end up being marginalized within fields of study indeed suggests an issue with the discipline in general. In line with this, Moira Gatens considers how philosophy can be transformed through a feminist perspective without being reduced to a separatist mode or to the passive acceptance of a singular dominant language. Moira Gatens, *Feminism and Philosophy: Perspectives on Difference and Equality* (Cambridge, MA: Polity Press, 1991). From the rise of feminist struggles and its contentious relation with the various philosophies of liberation, Carla Lonzi's classic work serves as a form of understanding a rejection of the most traditional form of establishing a link between liberation and recognition as a way to neutralize that which diverges from the logic that becomes primary with the Hegelian dialectic of the master and the slave. Carla Lonzi, *Escupamos sobre Hegel y otros escritos sobre liberación femenina* (Buenos Aires: La Pléyade, 1975).

41 This is an obsession also found in earlier texts; see in particular Fernanda Navarro, "ETHOS versus EROS . . . y el silencio de la filosofía," *Lecturas Filosóficas* 1 (1978): 17–19; and Fernanda Navarro, "La intersubjetividad en J. Sartre y Simone de Beauvoir," *Filósofos e ideas* (1990): 137–48.

42 Navarro, *Existencia, encuentro y azar*, 8–9.

43 Navarro, *Existencia, encuentro y azar*, 122.

44 For a very comprehensive reflection on the relevance of the body in the development of Mexican feminist thought, see Cynthia Pech, "La presencia del cuerpo en el discurso feminista," in *Cartografías del feminismo mexicano, 1970–2000*, ed. Nora Nínive García, Márgara Millán, and Cynthia Pech (Mexico City: Universidad Autónoma de la Ciudad de México, 2007), 327–43.

45 See Williams, *The Mexican Exception*, chapter 5.

46 In this sense, it enters within the preoccupation that emerges in that moment in connecting the works of Althusser with poststructuralist questioning, as Rafael Sebastián Guillén would do so in an exemplary fashion in his 1980 undergraduate thesis.

47 Gayatri Chakravorty Spivak, "Can the Subaltern Speak?" *Marxism and the Interpretation of Culture,* ed. Cary Nelson and Lawrence Grossberg, 271–313. Urbana: University of Illinois Press, 1988.

48 Étienne Balibar, "El infinito adiós al marxismo," *Revista metapolítica*, September 9, 2015, http://www.revistametapolitica.com/#!El-infinto-adi%C3%B3s-al-marxismo/c2oh6/55f0a72b0cf23d0fefffc695.

49 Navarro, *Existencia, encuentro y azar*, 88, emphasis mine.

50 Navarro, *Existencia, encuentro y azar*, 91.

51 Navarro, *Existencia, encuentro y azar*, 106, emphasis mine. It is worthwhile to bring in yet another zone of analysis of the late Althusser in respect to the urgency of feminism and his lectures on this matter within the unpublished papers found in the Althusser archive of L'Institut Mémoires de l'Édition Contemporaine, for example, "Texte (notes) sur le mouvement des femmes," along with the work that Balibar mentions regarding his analysis of Engels's partner ("El infinito").

52 Navarro, *Existencia, encuentro y azar*, 95.

53 Navarro, *Existencia, encuentro y azar*, 95–96.

54 Navarro, *Existencia, encuentro y azar*, 97.

55 Jean-Luc Nancy, *Experience of Freedom*, trans. Bridget McDonald (Stanford, CA: Stanford University Press, 1993).

56 Louis Althusser, "The Underground Current of the Materialism of the Encounter," in *Philosophy of the Encounter: Later Writings, 1978–1987*, ed. François Matheron and Oliver Corpet, trans. G. M. Goshgarian (London: Verso, 2006), 196.

57 See Fernanda Navarro, "A New Way of Thinking in Action: The Zapatistas in Mexico—A Postmodern Guerrilla Movement?," *Rethinking Marxism: A Journal of Economics, Culture and Society* 10, no. 4 (2009): 155–65.

58 Navarro, *Existencia, encuentro y azar*, 126.

59 Navarro, *Existencia, encuentro y azar*, 127.

60 Navarro, *Existencia, encuentro y azar*, 108.

61 Jacques Derrida, *Rogues: Two Essays on Reason*, trans. Pascale-Anne Brault and Michael Naas (Stanford, CA: Stanford University Press, 2005), 60.

62 Derrida, *Rogues*, 81.

63 Judith Butler, *Giving an Account of Oneself* (New York: Fordham University Press, 2005), 22.

4. REMEMBRANCES FROM THE WOMEN'S PRISON AND THE POPULAR PREPARATORY

1 Aguayo, *1968: Los archivos de la violencia* (1998), and Scherer García and Monsiváis, *Parte de guerra, Tlatelolco 1968* (1999), are published in this context.

2 Raúl Jardón, *1968: El fuego de la esperanza* (Mexico City: Siglo XXI, 1968); Ascencio, *1968: Más allá del mito*; Avendaño, *De la libertad y el encierro*; Roberto Bolaño, *Amuleto* (Barcelona: Anagrama, 1999).

3 Ascencio, "Presentación," *1968: Más allá del mito*, 9.

4 Jardón, *1968: El fuego de la esperanza*, 15.

5 Poniatowska, *Massacre in Mexico*, 65–66, emphasis mine.

6 I analyze the function of the hypothetical encounters in *Amulet* and the memory of '68 in "Fragmentos de futuro en los abismos del pasado: *Amuleto* (1968–1998)," in *Fuera de quicio: Sobre Roberto Bolaño en el tiempo de sus espectros*, ed. Raúl Rodríguez Freire (Santiago de Chile: Editorial Ripio, 2012), 53–76.

7 Gayatri Chakravorty Spivak has emphasized the role of the future perfect as a way of opening another type of narrative about the past that decenters the authority of "what was" as such and opens the past to a counterfactual knowledge that refers to its future. On this, see "Humanities" (Signature Series Talk, Princeton University, March 29, 2011), https://wilsoncollege.princeton.edu/college-events/signature -lecture-series/gayatri-spivak.

8 Joan Wallach Scott proposes this as a form of restructuring the vision of gender "in conjunction with a vision of political and social equality that includes not only sex but class and race." Scott, *Gender and the Politics of History*, 50.

9 Ange-Marie Hancock, *Intersectionality: An Intellectual History* (Oxford: Oxford University Press, 2016), 82.

10 Hancock, *Intersectionality*, 82.

11 Guadalupe Díaz recounts Avendaño's political life in "Roberta Avendaño: Entre Tlatelolco y Santa Martha Acatitla," *Fem: Publicación feminista mensual* 22, no. 187 (1998): 15–16.

12 The text was published by a very marginal publishing house, La idea dorada, with almost no circulation.

13 Aurelia de Gómez Unamuno, "Narrativas marginales y guerra sucia en México (1968–1994)" (PhD diss., University of Pittsburgh, 2008).

14 Avendaño, *De la libertad y el encierro*, 5.

15 As I was revising this manuscript, Juan Rojo's new book with a chapter on Avendaño's text was released. He approaches the temporal distance between '68 and the publica-tion of *Of Freedom and Imprisonment* in terms of a "memory of the memories of '68," as "the subject is remembering the events within a different political context than that of the subject from 1971." Juan Rojo, *Revisiting the Mexican Student Movement of 1968: Shifting Perspectives in Literature and Culture since Tlatelolco* (New York: Palgrave Macmillan, 2016), 86.

16 Among the women political prisoners mentioned are Teresa Confreta, Ana María Rico Galán, Marcué Padriñas, Adela Salazar de Castillejos, Amanda Velasco, and Ana Ignacia Rodríguez. Without being considered a political prisoner, there is a common prisoner who is connected to the movement: the mother of a young woman who dis-appeared on October 2 in Tlatelolco and who, after a number of protests demanding her daughter at the police station, was incarcerated alongside "the disturbed." The memories of the women of the movement who were in Santa Martha are almost nonexistent, in spite of the fact that many such women passed through that prison. If we go by the memoirs or interviews in circulation, it would seem that only La Tita and Ignacia "La Nacha" Rodríguez were political prisoners at Santa Martha, thereby erasing a number of other women.

17 Avendaño, *De la libertad y el encierro*, 29.

18 It was decades later that domestic work became part of a more systematic agenda of struggles. According to Lisette González Juárez, domestic work was not a priority in the feminist agenda of the 1970s, and it has yet to become a struggle for which a social consciousness has to arise. Lisette González Juárez, "Trabajo invisible: Trabajo doméstico; Revindicación en el movimiento feminista mexicano," in García, Millán,

and Pech, *Cartografías del feminismo mexicano,* 118–19. For a view on the different tones and registers in which the issue is received in some feminist circles, see Hortensia Morenos, "Trabajo doméstico," *Debate feminista* 11, no. 22 (2000): 26–51.

19 Avendaño, *De la libertad y el encierro,* 26.

20 I refer to Argüeyo Pazmiño's thorough study of the stereotypes that were dominant in the media at the time, particularly figures that stigmatized homosexuality. In "Identidades en disputa," she shows how the figures that stigmatized homosexuality in public media were then strategically used in the homosexual liberation movement's counterinformation campaigns.

21 Avendaño, *De la libertad y el encierro,* 1.

22 Avendaño, *De la libertad y el encierro,* 40.

23 Avendaño, *De la libertad y el encierro,* 41.

24 Poniatowska, *Massacre in Mexico,* 158.

25 Avendaño, *De la libertad y el encierro,* 83.

26 Avendaño, *De la libertad y el encierro,* 63.

27 Avendaño, *De la libertad y el encierro,* 133.

28 Avendaño, *De la libertad y el encierro,* 89.

29 Avendaño, *De la libertad y el encierro,* 144.

30 Avendaño, *De la libertad y el encierro,* 144.

31 Avendaño, *De la libertad y el encierro,* 119.

32 The abject, for Julia Kristeva, is linked to that which makes meaning collapse, disturbing order and the categories we use to maintain it. Julia Kristeva, *Powers of Horror: An Essay on Abjection,* trans. Leon S. Roudiez (New York: Columbia University Press, 1982), 2. In *De la libertad y el encierro,* it would seem that the text itself was a way of traversing and reconstructing an experience that Avendaño went through in order to be able to make it legible.

33 Williams, *The Mexican Exception,* 167–68; Carlos Montemayor, *Guerra en el paraíso* (Mexico City: Del Bolsillo, 2009).

34 Avendaño, *De la libertad y el encierro,* 143.

35 Étienne Balibar, *Equaliberty: Political Essays,* trans. James Ingram (Durham, NC: Duke University Press, 2014), 114.

36 López Hernández, interview with Draper and Rubio-Pueyo.

37 López Hernández, *Ovarimonio,* 13–16.

38 López Hernández, *Ovarimonio,* 18.

39 López Hernández, *Ovarimonio,* 38.

40 Although '68 was the great moment for questioning knowledge and reconfiguring the university, this problem has been put forth in different ways in Latin America throughout the decades. The student mobilizations that took place in high schools in Chile in 2011 introduced a problem similar to that set forth in Mexico in '68: the problem of social class and access to education. The struggle against privatization and for the right to schooling as a right to a time (the future) was carried out through the occupation of education centers and made use of self-management. Reviewing memories of the intense months of political activity of young people between fifteen and eighteen years of age, many discourses recall the key points that initiated the

popular high schools in Mexico. For a closer look at the event, see *Tres instantes, un grito* (*Three Moments, a Shout*), a 2013 documentary by Cecilia Barriga.

41 Del Valle, "La visión actual del 68 es totalmente machista," 2, emphasis mine.

42 Híjar, "Autonomía, autogestión, autogobierno."

43 Híjar, "Autonomía, autogestión, autogobierno."

44 Esperanza Lili Aparicio Hoyo, *Voces de la Preparatoria Popular* (Mexico City: Plaza y Valdés, 2007); Carlos Muñoz López, "La preparatoria popular 'Mártires de Tlatelolco': A. C. orígenes y desarrollo y desincorporación de la UNAM" (bachelor's thesis, Universidad Pedagógica Nacional, 2012), http://200.23.113.51/pdf/28805.pdf. "La escuela imposible," written by Fernando Castillo Bolaños and Jorge Maza, circulates outside the bookstore circuit among a group of alumni.

45 Aparicio Hoyo et al., *Voces de la Preparatoria Popular*, 265.

46 In his conversations with Gastón García Cantú, Javier Barrios Sierra sets the scene that gave rise to the struggle of the Popular Preparatory from elsewhere, explaining the problem that the university faced with regard to the extremely high number of students. See Gastón García Cantú, *Javier Barrios Sierra, 1968: Conversaciones con Gastón García Cantú* (Mexico City: Siglo XXI, 1972).

47 Alberto Híjar, "La hora de la autogestión," *Izquierda Revolucionaria Internacionalista Buenaventura Durruti* (blog), October 2008, http://colectivobuenaventuradurruti .weebly.com/hora-de-la-autogestion.html.

48 "Declaración de principios de la Preparatoria Popular." *Noticias de la Rebelión* (blog), July 18, 2005. Because of the provisional and sometimes clandestine nature of this activity, it is difficult to cite reliably; this particular document, written by a coalition of groups, was available online until 2016 online, but has since been removed. See an archived version at https://web.archive.org/web/20140331114704/http://www .noticiasdelarebelion.info/?p=14.

49 López Hernández, interview with Draper and Rubio-Pucyo.

50 López Hernández, *Ovarimonio*, 41.

51 López Hernández, *Ovarimonio*, 38.

52 López Hernández, *Ovarimonio*, 39.

53 López Hernández, *Ovarimonio*, 149.

54 In *Voces de la Preparatoria Popular* (68–74) there are some memories of these trips to the United States from one of the participants in the Emiliano Zapata group. See also Julio César López Cabrera, "El teatro campesino y Mascarones: La búsqueda de una identidad," *Casa del tiempo*, no. 86 (2006): 36–39. A more detailed history of these cultural and political exchanges is yet to be written.

55 Aparicio Hoyo et al., *Voces de la Preparatoria Popular*, 107.

56 López Hernández, *Ovarimonio*, 41.

57 Híjar, "La hora de la autogestión."

58 Aparicio Hoyo et al., *Voces de la Preparatoria Popular*, 44.

59 Aparicio Hoyo et al., *Voces de la Preparatoria Popular*, 111.

60 López Hernández remembers that she gained several Chicano friends who participated in the pedagogical laboratory, as some were interested in replicating the model in some parts of the United States. López Hernández, *Ovarimonio*, 57.

61 López Hernández, *Ovarimonio*, 89.

62 López Hernández, *Ovarimonio*, 95.

63 López Hernández, *Ovarimonio*, 111.

64 Reynoso, interview with Draper and Rubio-Pueyo.

65 López Hernández, *Ovarimonio*, 112.

66 Castillo Nájera, "Ovarimonio."

67 López Hernández, *Ovarimonio*, 150.

68 Benjamin, *The Arcades Project*, 458.

Conclusion

1 Iván Benumea Gómez, "Trascendiendo la coyuntura electoral: Consensos y tensiones al interior de #YoSoy132," in *Del internet a las calles: #YoSoy132, una opción alternativa de hacer política*, ed. Raúl Diego Rivera Hernández (Raleigh, NC: Editorial A Contracorriente, 2016), 217.

2 Sergio Aguayo, *De Tlatelolco a Ayotzinapa* (Mexico City: Ediciones Proceso, 2015).

3 In the context of the struggles of Guerrero, Carlos Ilíades frames events within a "mobilization—repression—self-defense continuum" and writes: "The mobilization—repression—self-defense continuum went through numerous cycles in Guerrero, from the Revolution until today, even though it currently has the particularity that social self-defense does not exclusively adopt the guerrilla form but rather as community policing (in the Mountains and the Costa Chica) and as citizen *autodefensas* in the rest of the state, with important differences between them that for now are not relevant to the discussion." Carlos Ilíades, "Guerrero: La violencia circular," *Nexos,* November 1, 2014, http://www.nexos.com.mx/?p=23092.

4 Elena Poniatowska, "Tlatelolco: 48 años después," *La Jornada,* October 1, 2016, http://www.jornada.unam.mx/2016/10/01/cultura/a04a1cul?partner=rss.

5 José Antonio Román and Emir Olivares, "Padres de Ayotzinapa encabezan la marcha del 2 de octubre," *La jornada*, October 3, 2016, http://www.jornada.unam.mx/2016/10/03/politica/010n1pol.

6 Ivonne del Valle and Estelle Tarica, "Radical Law and/or the Rule of Law in Mexico," *Política común* 7 (2015), https://quod.lib.umich.edu/p/pc/12322227.0007.001?view=text;rgn=main.

7 Yuri Herrera, "El sentido de la omisión: Sobre la impunidad en el México contemporáneo," *Politica común* 7 (2015), https://quod.lib.umich.edu/p/pc/12322227.0007.005/—el-sentido-de-la-omision-sobre-la-impunidad-en-el-mexico?rgn=main;view=fulltext.

8 Rossana Reguillo, "Rostros en escenas: Ayotzinapa y la imposibilidad del desentendimiento," *Magis*, December 1, 2014, https://magis.iteso.mx/content/rostros-en-escenas-ayotzinapa-y-la-imposibilidad-del-desentendimiento.

9 Rossana Reguillo, "Ayotzinapa: El nombre del horror," *Revista Anfibia*, 2014, http://www.revistaanfibia.com/ensayo/ayotzinapa-el-nombre-del-horror/.

10 Colectivo Situaciones, "Palabras previas," in *Los ritmos del Pachakuti (2000–2005)*, by Raquel Gutiérrez (Buenos Aires: Tinta Limón, 2008), 8.

11 Kristin Ross, *Communal Luxury: The Political Imaginary of the Paris Commune* (London: Verso, 2015), 29.

12 J. Revueltas, "Autogestión académica," *México 68*, 151.

13 Ross, *Communal Luxury*, 81.

14 Reynoso, interview with Draper and Rubio-Pueyo.

15 Ross, *Communal Luxury*, 5.

16 Bruno Bosteels, "The Mexican Commune," in *Communism in the 21st Century*, vol. 2, ed. Shannon Brincat (Santa Barbara, CA: Praeger, 2013), 161–89.

17 George Ciccariello-Maher, *Decolonizing Dialectics* (Durham, NC: Duke University Press, 2016), 6, emphasis mine.

18 The "discourse" of Occupy was not created around a political subject like the proletariat, nor was it developed around a specific form of cultural identification. Instead, Occupy assembled a group around the idea of the 99 percent ("We are the 99 percent") appealing directly to inequality in the distribution of wealth, which is highly concentrated in the hands of 1 percent of the population, and to the indebted subject. A month before the beginning of the encampment (that is, in August 2011), a Tumblr blog (see wearethe99percent.tumblr.com) was created with the power to produce a figure that linked different people through a common problem: *the indebted subject*. This opened a space capable of outlining a new subjectivity, stemming from a process of collective subjectification in which debt operates as a common, shared element. With the unfolding of tasks in September, commonalities began to surface through shared problems, and from these problems a subjectivity was generated. The blog compiled testimonies in which different people who felt like they were part of the movement narrated their situation. On the one hand, the figure of the 99 percent emerges as a heterogeneous space in which the disparity between "owners" of the financial apparatus and slaves of the system is outlined. On the other hand, the 99 percent is organized through debt linked to education, health, housing, and lack of employment: different people narrate the situation of the total precarity in which they live, unable to find exits from within the system. It is life transformed into a debt to pay off for the rest of one's life. All the stories end with the expression "We are the 99 percent," with which a subject of the movement is produced from feeling fed up and powerless toward the possibility of being able to act from this common place. Nonidentification with a race, an ethnic group, religion, or nationality was at first a great unifier, since in almost Rancierian terms, what was put into play was the distribution itself of the sensible and the two orders: the order of those who lay the foundation for the police (the places, the functions of each person) and the irruption of a protest that began to make another order visible.

19 Grace Lee Boggs and James Boggs, *Revolution and Evolution in the Twentieth Century* (New York: Monthly Review Press, 1974), 211–13, emphasis mine.

20 Ross, *Communal Luxury*.

21 The talk can be accessed online at http://www.makingworlds.org/documents/.

Bibliography

Aguayo, Sergio. *1968: Los archivos de la violencia*. Mexico City: Grijalbo, 1998.

———. *De Tlatelolco a Ayotzinapa*. Mexico City: Ediciones Proceso, 2015.

Aguilar Camín, Héctor, "Modelo para armar." In *Pensar el 68,* edited by Héctor Aguilar Camín and Hermann Bellinghausen, 13–14. Mexico City: Cal y Arena, 1988.

Aguilar Camín, Héctor, and Hermann Bellinghausen, eds. *Pensar el 68*. Mexico City: Cal y Arena, 1988.

Alexander, Sally. *Becoming a Woman: And Other Essays in 19th and 20th Century Feminist Theory*. London: Virago, 1994.

Allier Montaño, Eugenia. "Memory and History of Mexico '68." *European Review of Latin American and Caribbean Studies*, Revista Europea de Estudios Latinoamericanos y del Caribe 102 (2016): 7–25.

———. "Presentes-pasados del 68 mexicano." *Revista Mexicana de Sociología* 71, no. 2 (2009): 298–317.

Althusser, Louis. *Philosophy of the Encounter: Later Writings, 1978–87*. Edited by François Matheron and Oliver Corpet. Translated by G. M. Goshgarian. London: Verso, 2006.

Álvarez Garín, Raúl. *La estela de Tlatelolco: Una reconstrucción histórica del movimiento estudiantil del 68*. Mexico City: Grijalbo, 1998.

———. *Los procesos de México 1968: Acusaciones y defensa*. Mexico City: Editorial Estudiantes, 1970.

Ansa Goicoechea, Elixabete, and Óscar Ariel Cabezas, eds. *Efectos de imagen: ¿Qué fue y qué es el cine militante?* Santiago de Chile: LOM Ediciones, 2014.

Aparicio Hoyo, Esperanza Lili, José Manuel Galván Leguízamo, Rubén Dac Pérez, and Abraham Manuel Vidales Abrego. *Voces de la Preparatoria Popular*. Mexico City: Plaza y Valdés, 2007.

Argüeyo Pazmiño, Sofía. "Identidades en disputa: Discursos científicos, medios de comunicación y estrategias políticas del Movimiento de Liberación Homosexual mexicano, 1968–1984." In *La memoria y el deseo: Estudios gay y queer en México,* edited by Rodrigo Parrini and Alejandro Brito, 25–50. Mexico City: Universidad Nacional Autónoma de México, Programa Universitario de Estudios de Género, 2014.

Aricó, José. "Algunas consideraciones preliminares sobre la condición obrera." *Pasado y presente* 3, no. 9 (1965): 46–55.

Arrighi, Giovanni, Terence K. Hopkins, and Immanuel Wallerstein. *Antisystemic Movements*. London: Verso, 2012.

Ascencio, Esteban, ed. *1968: Más allá del mito*. Mexico City: Ediciones del Milenio, 1998.

Asociación de Documentalistas de México. *El cine independiente ¿hacia dónde?* Mexico City: Asociación de Documentalistas de México, 2007.

Avendaño, Roberta. *De la libertad y el encierro.* Mexico City: La idea dorada, 1998.

Ayala, Leopoldo. *Nuestra verdad: Memorial del movimiento estudiantil popular y el dos de octubre de 1968.* Mexico City: Porrúa, 1989.

Ayala Blanco, Jorge. *La búsqueda del cine mexicano (1968–1972).* Mexico City: Editorial Posada, 1986.

Badiou, Alain. "May 68 Revisited, 40 Years On." In *The Communist Hypothesis*, 43–67. London: Verso, 2010.

Balibar, Étienne. "El infinito adiós al marxismo." *Revista metapolítica*, September 9, 2015. http://www.revistametapolitica.com/#!El-infinto-adi%C3%B3s-al-marxismo/c2oh6 /55foa72bocf23dofefffc695.

———. *Equaliberty: Political Essays.* Translated by James Ingram. Durham, NC: Duke University Press, 2014.

———. *On the Dictatorship of the Proletariat.* London: NLB, 1977.

Barthes, Roland. *Camera Lucida: Reflections on Photography.* Translated by Richard Howard. New York: Farrar, Straus and Giroux, 1981.

Benjamin, Walter. *The Arcades Project.* Translated by Howard Eiland and Kevin McLaughlin. Cambridge, MA: Harvard University Press, 2002.

Bensaïd, Daniel. *Marx for Our Times: Adventures and Misadventures of a Critique.* London: Verso, 2002.

Bensaïd, Daniel, and Henri Weber. *Mai 1968: Une répétition générale.* Paris: F. Maspero, 1968.

Benumea Gómez, Iván. "Trascendiendo la coyuntura electoral: Consensos y tensiones al interior de #YoSoy132." In *Del internet a las calles: #YoSoy132, una opción alternativa de hacer política*, edited by Raúl Diego Rivera Hernández, 207–20. Raleigh, NC: Editorial A Contracorriente, 2016.

Bilbija, Ksenija, and Leigh A. Payne. *Accounting for Violence: Marketing Memory in Latin America.* Durham, NC: Duke University Press, 2011.

Bixler, Jacqueline. "Mexico 1968 and the Art(s) of Memory." In *The Long 1968: Revisions and New Perspectives*, edited by Daniel J. Sherman, Ruud van Dijk, Jasmine Alinder, and A. Aneesh, 169–215. Bloomington: Indiana University Press, 2013.

Blanco, José Joaquín. *José Revueltas.* Mexico City: Editorial Terra Nova, 1985.

Boggs, Grace Lee, and James Boggs. *Revolution and Evolution in the Twentieth Century.* New York: Monthly Review Press, 1974.

Bolado, Carlos, dir. *Tlatelolco: Verano del 68.* Mexico City: Eficine 226, Fidecine, Maíz Producciones, Producción corazones, Universidad Nacional Autónoma de México, 2013. DVD.

Bolaño, Roberto. *Amulet.* Translated by Chris Andrews. New York: New Directions, 2008.

———. *Amuleto.* Barcelona: Anagrama, 1999.

Boltanski, Luc, and Eve Chiapello. *The New Spirit of Capitalism.* Translated by Gregory Elliott. London: Verso, 2005.

Bosteels, Bruno. *Marx and Freud in Latin America: Politics, Psychoanalysis, and Religion in Times of Terror.* New York: Verso, 2012.

———. "The Mexican Commune." In *Communism in the 21st Century*, vol. 2, edited by Shannon Brincat, 161–89. Santa Barbara, CA: Praeger, 2013.

———. "Mexico 1968: The Revolution of Shame." *Radical Philosophy* 149 (May–June 2008): 5–11.

Brewster, Claire. "The Student Movement of 1968 and the Mexican Press: The Cases of *Excélsior* and *Siempre!*" *Bulletin of Latin American Research* 21, no. 2 (2002): 171–90.

Butler, Judith. *Giving an Account of Oneself.* New York: Fordham University Press, 2005.

———. *Notes toward a Performative Theory of Assembly.* Cambridge, MA: Harvard University Press, 2015.

Camín, Héctor Aguilar. "68, modelo para armar." In *Pensar el 68*, edited by Héctor Aguilar Camín and Hermann Bellinghausen, 13–14. Mexico City: Cal y Arena, 1988.

Camín, Héctor Aguilar, and Hermann Bellinghausen, eds. *Pensar el 68*. Mexico City: Cal y Arena, 1988.

Cárdenas Montaño, Macrina. "La participación de las mujeres en los movimientos armados." In *Movimientos armados en México, siglo XX*, vol. 2, edited by Verónika Oikión and Marta Eugenia García, 609–24. Mexico City: Centro de Investigación y Estudios Superiores en Antropología Social, 2006.

Carey, Elaine. "Los Dueños de México: Power and Masculinity in '68." In *Gender and Sexuality in 1968: Transformative Politics in the Cultural Imagination*, edited by Lessie Jo Frazier and Deborah Cohen, 59–83. New York: Palgrave Macmillan, 2009.

———. "Mexico's 1968 Olympic Dream." In *Protests in the Streets: 1968 across the Globe*, edited by Elaine Carey, 91–119. Indianapolis, IN: Hackett, 2016.

———. *Plaza of Sacrifices: Gender, Power, and Terror in 1968*. Albuquerque: University of New Mexico Press, 2005.

———. "The Streets Speak, 1968 and Today." In *Protests in the Streets: 1968 across the Globe*, edited by Elaine Carey, 120–32. Indianapolis, IN: Hackett, 2016.

Castañeda, Luis. *Spectacular Mexico: Design, Propaganda, and the 1968 Olympics*. Minneapolis: University of Minnesota Press, 2014.

Castillo, Heberto. *Si te agarran te van a matar*. Mexico City: Océano, 1983.

Castillo Nájera, Oralba. "Ovarimonio: Memorias de una presa política." *Siempre!*, September 24, 2013. http://www.siempre.mx/2013/09/ovarimonio-memorias-de-una-presa-politica/.

———. "Simone y yo." *Debate feminista* 38 (October 2008): 166–74.

Catela da Silva, L. "Poder local y violencia: Memorias de la represión en el noroeste argentino." In *Inseguridad y violencia en el Cono Sur*, edited by Alejandro Isla, 211–27. Buenos Aires: Paidós, 2007.

Cheah, Peng. "Non-Dialectical Materialism." In *New Materialisms: Ontology, Agency, and Politics*, edited by Diana Coole and Samantha Frost, 20–91. Durham, NC: Duke University Press, 2010.

Christiansen, Samantha, and Zachary A. Scarlett, eds. *The Third World in the Global Sixties*. New York: Berghahn Books, 2013.

Ciccariello-Maher, George. *Decolonizing Dialectics*. Durham, NC: Duke University Press, 2016.

Cohen, Deborah, and Lessie Jo Frazier. "'No sólo cocinábamos . . .': Historia inédita de la otra mitad del 68." In *La transición interrumpida: México 1968–1998*, edited by Ilán Semo, 75–105. Mexico City: Departamento de Historia, Universidad Iberoamericana, 1993.

Colectivo Situaciones. "Palabras previas." In *Los ritmos del Pachakuti (2000–2005)*, by Raquel Gutiérrez, 7–8. Buenos Aires: Tinta Limón, 2008.

———. "Talking Back to '68: Gendered Narratives, Participatory Spaces, and Political Cultures." In *Gender and Sexuality in 1968: Transformative Politics in the Cultural Imagination*, edited by Lessie Jo Frazier and Deborah Cohen, 145–72. New York: Palgrave Macmillan, 2009.

Cortázar, Julio. *62. Modelo para armar.* Buenos Aires: Editorial Sudamericana, 1968.

———. "Literatura en la revolución y revolución en la literatura. Algunos malentendidos a liquidar." In *Literatura en la revolución y revolución en la literatura*, edited by Óscar Collazos, Julio Cortázar and Mario Vargas Llosa, 38–77. Mexico City: Siglo XXI, 1970.

"Declaración de principios de la Preparatoria Popular." *Noticias de la Rebelión* (blog), July 18, 2005. Archived version available at https://web.archive.org/web/20140331114704/http://www.noticiasdelarebelion.info/?p=14.

de la Garza, Enrique, Tomás Ejea Mendoza, and Luis Fernando Macías García. *El otro movimiento estudiantil.* Mexico City: Universidad Autónoma Metropolitana–Azcapotzalco, 2014.

Del Campo, Jesús Martín. Interview with Susana Draper and Vicente Rubio-Pueyo. *México 68: Modelo para armar; Archivo de memorias desde los márgenes.* 2012. https://www.mexico68conversaciones.com/jesus-martin-del-campo

Delgado, Mónica V. "Las mujeres del 68: Mariposas en un mundo de palabras." *Vivir en Tlatelolco: Periodismo comunitario*, February 20, 2013. http://vivirtlatelolco.blogspot.com/2013/02/las-mujeres-del-68-mariposas-en-un.html.

Delphy, Christine. "For a Materialist Feminism." In *A Materialist Feminism: A Reader in Class, Difference, and Women's Lives,* edited by Rosemary Hennessy and Chrys Ingraham, 59–64. New York: Routledge, 1997.

del Valle, Ivonne, and Estelle Tarica. "Radical Politics and/or the Rule of Law in Mexico." *Política común* 7 (2015). https://quod.lib.umich.edu/p/pc/12322227.0007.001?view=text;rgn=main.

Del Valle, Sonia. "La visión actual del 68 es totalmente machista: Eugenia Espinosa Carbajal." September 30, 1998. http://generomexico.colmex.mx/textos/Lavisionactual68totalmentemachista-Carbajal.pdf.

Derrida, Jacques. *Rogues: Two Essays on Reason.* Translated by Pascale-Anne Brault and Michael Naas. Stanford, CA: Stanford University Press, 2005.

de Taboada, Javier. "Tercer cine: Tres manifiestos." *Revista de crítica literaria latinoamericana* 37, no. 73 (2011): 37–60.

Díaz, Guadalupe. "Roberta Avendaño: Entre Tlatelolco y Santa Martha Acatitla." *Fem: Publicación feminista mensual* 22, no. 187 (1998): 15–16.

Dindo, Richard, dir. *Ni olvido, ni perdón.* Zurich: Lea Produktion, Film Coopi, 2004. DVD.

Dozal, Martín. Interview with Susana Draper and Vicente Rubio-Pueyo. *México 68: Modelo para armar; Archivo de memorias desde los márgenes.* 2012. https://www.mexico68conversaciones.com/martin-dozal/.

Draper, Susana. "Fragmentos de futuro en los abismos del pasado: *Amuleto* (1968–1998)." In *Fuera de quicio: Sobre Roberto Bolaño en el tiempo de sus espectros*, edited by Raúl Rodríguez Freire, 53–76. Santiago de Chile: Editorial Ripio, 2012.

——. "Hegemonía, poder dual, post-hegemonía: Las derivas del concepto." In *Post-hegemonía: El final de un paradigma político de la filosofía en América Latina*, edited by Rodrigo Castro Orellana, 93–112. Madrid: Editorial Biblioteca Nueva, 2015.

Draper, Susana, and Vicente Rubio-Pueyo. *México 68: Modelo para armar; Archivo de memorias desde los márgenes.* 2012. https://www.mexico68conversaciones.com.

Dubinsky, Karen, Catherine Krull, Susan Lord, Sean Mills, and Scott Rutherford. "Introduction: The Global Sixties." In *New World Coming: The Sixties and the Shaping of Global Consciousness*, edited by Karen Dubinsky, Catherine Krull, Susan Lord, Sean Mills, and Scott Rutherford, 1–6. Toronto: Between the Lines, 2009.

Escudero, Roberto. "Prólogo." In José Revueltas, *México 68: Juventud y revolución*, 11–18. Mexico City: Era, 1978.

"Fernanda Sylvia Navarro y Solares (1941)," *Enciclopedia Electrónica de Filosofía Mexicana: Centro de Documentación en Filosofía Latinoamericana e Ibérica.* Mexico City: Universidad Autónoma Metropolitana—Unidad Iztapalapa, 2014. http://dcsh.izt.uam.mx/cen_doc/cefilibe/images/banners/enciclopedia/Diccionario/Autores/FilosofosMexicanos/Navarro_Fernanda.pdf.

Fernández-Savater, Amador. "How to Organize a Climate." In *Making Worlds: A Commons Coalition*, March 7, 2012. https://makingworlds.wikispaces.com/How+to+Organize+a+Climate?responseToken=c44721e2493b8c7b5730531d01b3a7bc.

Fernández-Savater, Amador, and David Cortés. *Con y contra el cine: En torno a mayo del 68.* Seville: Universidad Internacional de Andalucía, 1999.

Ferrer, Guadalupe. Interview with Susana Draper and Vicente Rubio-Pueyo. *México 68: Modelo para armar; Archivo de memorias desde los márgenes.* 2015. https://www.mexico68conversaciones.com/guadalupe-ferrer/.

Fons, Jorge, dir. *Rojo amanecer.* Mexico City: Quality Films, 1989. DVD.

Foucault, Michel. *Discipline and Punish: The Birth of the Prison.* Translated by Alan Sheridan. New York: Vintage Books, 1995.

Fraser, Nancy. *Fortunes of Feminism: From State-Managed Capitalism to Neoliberal Crisis.* New York: Verso, 2013.

Fraser, Nancy, and Axel Honnett. *Redistribution or Recognition? A Political Philosophical Exchange.* Translated by Joel Golb. London, New York: Verso: 2003.

Gandler, Stefan. *Marxismo crítico en México: Adolfo Sánchez Vázquez y Bolívar Echeverría.* Mexico City: Fondo de Cultura Económica, 2007.

García, Gustavo, and José Felipe Coria. *Nuevo cine mexicano.* Mexico City: Clío, 1997.

García, Nora Nínive, Márgara Millán, and Cynthia Pech, eds. *Cartografías del feminismo mexicano, 1970–2000.* Mexico City: Universidad Autónoma de la Ciudad de México, 2007.

García, Sergio. "Toward a Fourth Cinema." In "Superocheros," special issue, *Wide Angle: A Quarterly Journal of Film History, Theory, Criticism and Practice* 21, no. 3 (1999): 70–185.

García Cantú, Gastón. *Javier Barros Sierra, 1968: Conversaciones con Gastón García Cantú*. Mexico City: Siglo XXI, 1972.

Gargallo, Francesca. "1968: Una revolución en la que se manifestó un nuevo feminismo." *La calle es de quien la camina, las fronteras son asesinas*, 2008. https://francescagargallo .wordpress.com/ensayos/feminismo/feminismo-filosofia/1968-una-revolucion-en-la -que-se-manifesto-un-nuevo-feminismo/.

———. *Las ideas feministas lationamericanas*. Mexico City: Universidad de la Ciudad de México, 2004.

Gatens, Moira. *Feminism and Philosophy: Perspectives on Difference and Equality*. Cambridge, MA: Polity Press, 1991.

Georgi, Frank. "Construire l'autogestion." In *Autogestion: La dernière utopie?*, edited by Frank Georgi, 11–28. Paris: Publications de la Sorbonne, 2003.

Gilabert, César. *El hábito de la utopía: Análisis del imaginario sociopolítico en el movimiento estudiantil de México, 1968*. Mexico City: Porrúa, 1993.

Gilly, Adolfo. "1968: La ruptura en los bordes." *Nexos*, November 1, 1993. http://www .nexos.com.mx/?p=6916.

Gil Olivo, Ramón. *Cine y liberación: El nuevo cine latinoamericano (1954–1973); Fuentes para un lenguaje*. Guadalajara: Centro Universitario de Arte, Arquitectura y Diseño, Universidad de Guadalajara, 2009.

Giunta, Andrea. *Avant-Garde, Internationalism, and Politics: Argentine Art in the Sixties*. Translated by Peter Kahn. Durham, NC: Duke University Press, 2007.

Gómez Alvarez, Pablo. "Las enseñanzas: entrevista con Víctor Avilés." In *Pensar el 68*, edited by Héctor Aguilar Camín and Hermann Bellinghausen, 215–18. Mexico City: Cal y Arena, 1988.

Gómez Unamuno, Aurelia de. "Narrativas marginales y guerra sucia en México (1968– 1994)." PhD diss., University of Pittsburgh, 2008.

González, Alvarado. "El espíritu de una época." In *Cartografías del feminismo mexicano, 1970–2000*, edited by Nora Nínive García, Márgara Millán, and Cynthia Pech, 65–116. Mexico City: Universidad Autónoma de la Ciudad de México, 2007.

González de Alba, Luis. *Los días y los años*. Mexico City: Era, 1971.

González de Bustamante, Celeste. "Olympic Dreams and Tlatelolco Nightmares: Imagining and Imaging Modernity in Television." *Mexican Studies / Estudios Mexicanos* 26, no. 1 (2010): 1–30.

González Juárez, Lisette. "Trabajo invisible: Trabajo doméstico; Revindicación en el movimiento feminista mexicano." In *Cartografías del feminismo mexicano, 1970–2000*, edited by Nora Nínive García, Márgara Millán, and Cynthia Pech, 117–60. Mexico City: Universidad Autónoma de la Ciudad de México, 2007.

González Rojo, Enrique. "Las últimas concepciones teórico-políticas de J. Revueltas." In *Revueltas en la mira*, edited by Emmanuel Carballo et al., 101–27. Mexico City: Dirección de Difusión Cultural, 1984.

Gould-Wartofsky, Michael. *The Occupiers: The Making of the 99 Percent Movement*. New York: Oxford University Press, 2015.

Grindle, Merilee S., and Erin E. Goodman, eds. *Reflections on Memory and Democracy*. Cambridge, MA: David Rockefeller Center for Latin American Studies, Harvard University, 2016.

Grupo Mira. *The Graphics of 68: Honoring the Student Movement*. Mexico City: Ediciones Zurda, 1993.

Guevara Niebla, Gilberto. *1968: Largo camino a la democracia*. Mexico City: Cal y Arena, 2008.

———. *La democracia en la calle: Crónica del movimiento estudiantil mexicano*. Mexico City: Siglo XXI, 1988.

———. *La libertad nunca se olvida: Memoria del 68*. Mexico City: Cal y Arena, 2004.

Guillén, Abraham. *Democracia directa: Autogestión y socialismo*. Montevideo: Editorial Aconcagua, 1972.

Gurrola, Alfredo, dir. *Borrar de la memoria*. Mexico City: Magenta Films, 2014. DVD.

Gutiérrez, Marcia. "Éramos pocas las mujeres en el Consejo Nacional de Huelga." YouTube, September 29, 2011. https://www.youtube.com/watch?v=F6d1fL6lOUo.

Hancock, Ange-Marie. *Intersectionality: An Intellectual History*. Oxford: Oxford University Press, 2016.

Harari, José. *Contribución a la historia del ideario del M. L. N. Tupamaros: Análisis crítico*. Montevideo: Editorial MZ, 1986.

Hermosillo, Jaime Humberto. "Manifesto: 8 millimeters versus 8 millions / Manifiesto: 8 milímetros contra 8 millones." In "Superocheros," special issue, *Wide Angle: A Quarterly Journal of Film History, Theory, Criticism and Practice* 21, no. 3 (1999): 36–41.

Herrera, Yuri. "El sentido de la omisión: Sobre la impunidad en el México contemporáneo." *Política común* 7 (2015). https://quod.lib.umich.edu/p/pc/12322227.0007.005/—el-sentido-de-la-omision-sobre-la-impunidad-en-el-mexico?rgn=main;view=fulltext.

Híjar, Alberto. "Autonomía, autogestión, autogobierno." *Izquierda Revolucionaria Internacionalista Buenaventura Durruti*. http://colectivobuenaventuradurruti.weebly.com/autonomia-autogestion-autogobierno.html.

———. "Hora de la autogestión." *Izquierda Revolucionaria Internacionalista Buenaventura Durruti*, October 2008. http://colectivobuenaventuradurruti.weebly.com/hora-de-la-autogestion.html.

———. Interview with Susana Draper and Vicente Rubio-Pueyo. *México 68: Modelo para armar; Archivo de memorias desde los márgenes*. 2015. https://www.mexico68conversaciones.com/alberto-hijar/.

———. "Introducción." In *Hacia un tercer cine: Antología*, edited by Alberto Híjar, 7–27. Cuadernos de cine 20. Mexico City: Universidad Nacional Autónoma de México, 1972.

Hite, Katherine. *Politics and the Art of Commemoration: Memorials to Struggle in Latin America and Spain*. London: Routledge, 2013.

Hobsbawm, Eric. "1968: A Retrospective." *Marxism Today* 22, no. 5 (1978): 130–36.

Holloway, John. *Change the World without Taking Power*. London: Pluto, 2010.

Holmes, Brian. "1968 Olympic Dreams and Tlatelolco Nightmares: Imagining and Imaging Modernity on Television." November 18, 2015. https://prezi.com/47wxztjx0cr6/1968-olympic-dreams-and-tlatelolco-nightmares-imagining-and/.

Holzfeind, Heidrun. "Entrevista a Mercedes Perelló." *México 68: Entrevistas con activistas del movimiento estudiantil*. https://vimeo.com/77938520.

hooks, bell. *Feminism Is for Everybody*. Cambridge, MA: South End Press, 2000.

Huyssen, Andreas. *Present Pasts: Urban Palimpsests and the Politics of Memory*. Stanford, CA: Stanford University Press, 2003.

Ilíades, Carlos. "Guerrero: La violencia circular." *Nexos,* November 1, 2014, http://www
.nexos.com.mx/?p=23092.

Jaiven, Ana Lau. *La nueva ola del feminismo en México: Conciencia y acción de lucha de las mujeres.* Mexico City: Planeta, 1987.

Jameson, Fredric. "Periodizing the 60s." In *The 60s without Apology*, edited by Sohnya Sayres, Anders Stephanson, Stanley Aronomwitz, and Fredric Jameson, 178–209. Minneapolis: University of Minnesota Press, 1985.

———. *Valences of the Dialectic.* London: Verso, 2010.

Jardón, Raúl. *1968: El fuego de la esperanza.* Mexico City: Siglo XXI, 1998.

Jelin, Elizabeth. *State Repression and the Labors of Memory.* Translated by Judy Rein and Marcial Godoy-Anativia. Minneapolis: University of Minnesota Press, 2003.

Jenkins, Fiona, and Katrina Hutchison. "Introduction: Searching for Sofia; Gender and Philosophy in the 21st Century." In *Women in Philosophy: What Needs to Change?*, edited by Fiona Jenkins and Katrina Hutchison, 1–20. Oxford: Oxford University Press, 2014.

Joffroy, Michelle. "Ambiguous Subjects: The Autobiographical Situation and the Disembodiment of '68." In *Gender and Sexuality in 1968: Transformative Politics in the Cultural Imagination*, edited by Lessie Jo Frazier and Deborah Cohen, 219–34. New York: Palgrave Macmillan, 2009.

Katsiaficas, George. *The Imagination of the New Left: A Global Analysis of 1968.* Boston: South End Press, 1999.

Kornetis, Kostis. " 'Everything Links'? Temporality, Territoriality and Cultural Transfer in the '68 Protest Movements." *Historein* 9 (2009): 34–45.

———. "Introduction: 1968–2008: The Inheritance of Utopia." *Historein* 9 (2009): 7–20.

Kraniauskas, John. *Políticas literarias: Poder y acumulación en la literatura y el cine latinoamericanos.* Mexico City: Facultad Latinoamericana de Ciencias Sociales, 2012.

Kristeva, Julia. *Powers of Horror: An Essay on Abjection.* Translated by Leon S. Roudiez. New York: Columbia University Press, 1982.

Lacruz, Cecilia. "La comezón por el intercambio." In *Las rupturas del 68 en el cine de América Latina*, edited by Mariano Mestman, 311–51. Buenos Aires: Akal, 2016.

Lefebvre, Henri. *Critique of Everyday Life.* Translated by John Moore. London: Verso, 2014.

———. *Dialectical Materialism.* Translated by John Sturrock. Minneapolis: University of Minnesota Press, 2009.

———. "Theoretical Problems of Autogestion." In Henri Lefebvre, *State, Space, World: Selected Essays*, edited by Neil Brenner and Stuart Elden, 138–52. Translated by Gerald Moore, Neil Brenner, and Stuart Elden. Minneapolis: University of Minnesota Press, 2010.

Lemus, Rafael. "Ayotzinapa, la multitud y el antiguo régimen." *Política común* 7 (2015). http://quod.lib.umich.edu/p/pc/12322227.0007.010/—ayotzinapa-la-multitud-y-el-antiguo-regimen?rgn=main;view=fulltext.

Lerner, Jesse. "Superocheros." In "Superocheros," special issue, *Wide Angle: A Quarterly Journal of Film History, Theory, Criticism and Practice* 21, no. 3 (1999): 2–35.

Liscano, Carlos. "A Life Without Object(s)." In Carlos Liscano, *Truck of Fools*, translated by Elizabeth Hampsten, 1–14. Nashville, TN: Vanderbilt University Press, 2004.

Lonzi, Carla. *Escupamos sobre Hegel y otros escritos sobre liberación femenina.* Buenos Aires: Pléyade, 1975.

López Aretche, Leobardo, and Roberto Sánchez Martínez, dirs. *El grito.* México City: Centro Universitario de Estudios Cinematográficos, 1968. VHS.

López Cabrera, Julio César. "El teatro campesino y Mascarones: La búsqueda de una identidad." *Casa del tiempo*, no. 86 (March 2006): 36–39.

López Hernández, Gladys. Interview with Susana Draper and Vicente Rubio-Pueyo. *México 68: Modelo para armar; Archivo de memorias desde los márgenes.* 2015. https://www.mexico68conversaciones.com/gladys-lopez-hernandez/.

———. *Ovarimonio: ¿Yo guerrillera?* Mexico City: Itaca, 2013.

Ludec, Nathalie. "*La Boletina* de Morelia: Órgano informativo de la Red Nacional de Mujeres, 1982–1985." *Comunicación y sociedad*, no. 5 (January–June 2006): 89–113.

Markarian, Vania. "Debating Tlatelolco: Thirty Years of Public Debates about the Mexican Student Movement of 1968." In *Taking Back the Academy! History of Activism, History as Activism*, edited by Jim Downs and Jennifer Manion, 25–34. New York: Routledge, 2004.

———. *Uruguay 1968: Student Activism from Global Counterculture to Molotov Cocktails.* Berkeley: University of California Press, 2016.

Martínez, Gastón. "Todo el mundo era protagonista." In *1968: Más allá del mito*, edited by Esteban Ascencio, 99–103. Mexico City: Ediciones del Milenio, 1998.

Marx, Karl. *Historia crítica de la teoría de la plusvalía: Adam Smith y la idea del trabajo productivo.* Mexico City: Fondo de Cultura Económica, 1945.

———. *Theories of Surplus Value. Selections.* New York: International Publishers, 1952.

May, Todd. *The Political Thought of Jacques Rancière: Creating Equality.* Edinburgh: Edinburgh University Press, 2008.

Medina, Francisco. "El 68 un cambio social y no democrático: Esmeralda Reynoso." *almomento noticias*, October 10, 2013. http://www.almomento.mx/el-68-un-cambio-social-y-no-democratico-esmeralda-reynoso/.

Méndez, José Carlos. "Toward a Political Cinema: The Cooperative of Marginal Cinema / Hacia un cine político: La Cooperativa de Cine Marginal." In "Superocheros," special issue, *Wide Angle: A Quarterly Journal of Film History, Theory, Criticism and Practice* 21, no. 3 (1999): 42–65.

Mendoza, María Luisa. *Con él, conmigo, con nosotros tres: Cronovela.* Mexico City: Joaquín Mortiz, 1971.

Mendoza Rojas, Javier. *Los conflictos de la UNAM en el siglo XX.* Mexico City: Plaza y Valdés, 2001.

Menéndez, Óscar, dir., *Historia de un documento / Histoire d'un document.* Mexico City: Ediciones Pentagrama, 2004. DVD.

———. Interview with Susana Draper and Vicente Rubio-Pueyo. *México 68: Modelo para armar; Archivo de memorias desde los márgenes.* 2012. https://www.mexico68conversaciones.com/oscar-menendez/.

Mestman, Mariano. "Presentación: Las rupturas del 68 en el cine de América Latina; Contracultura, experimentación y política." In *Las rupturas del 68 en el cine de América Latina*, edited by Mariano Mestman, 7–60. Buenos Aires: Akal, 2016.

———. "Third Cinema/Militant Cinema: At the Origins of the Argentinian Experience (1968–1971)." *Third Text* 25, no. 1 (2011): 29–40.

Millán, Márgara. "Introducción: La construcción de la polivalencia del sujeto del feminismo." In *Cartografías del feminismo mexicano, 1970–2000*, edited by Nora Nínive García, Márgara Millán, and Cynthia Pech, 15–28. Mexico City: Universidad Autónoma de la Ciudad de México, 2007.

Mitchell, Juliet. *Woman's Estate*. Harmondsworth: Penguin, 1971.

Monsiváis, Carlos. "1968: Dramatis Personae." In *México: Una democracia utópica; El movimiento estudiantil del 68*, by Sergio Zermeño, xi–xxiv. Mexico City: Siglo XXI, 1978.

———. *El 68: La tradición de la resistencia*. Mexico City: Era, 2008.

Montemayor, Carlos. *Guerra en el paraíso*. Mexico City: Del Bolsillo, 2009.

Moreno, Hortensia. "Trabajo doméstico." *Debate feminista* 11, no. 22 (2000): 26–51.

Moreno-Caballud, Luis. *Cultures of Anyone: Studies on Cultural Democratization in the Spanish Neoliberal Crisis*. Liverpool: University of Liverpool Press, 2015.

Muñoz López, Carlos. "La preparatoria popular 'Mártires de Tlatelolco': A. C. orígenes y desarrollo y desincorporación de la UNAM." Bachelor's thesis, Universidad Pedagógica Nacional, 2012. http://200.23.113.51/pdf/28805.pdf.

Nancy, Jean-Luc. *Experience of Freedom*. Translated by Bridget McDonald. Stanford, CA: Stanford University Press, 1993.

Navarro, Fernanda. "Asfixiata (sketch teatral feminista en un acto)." *Lectura de la realidad en el aula. Textos de Fernanda Navarro*. 2010. http://www.lrealidad.filos.unam.mx /asfixiata.

———. "ETHOS versus EROS . . . y el silencio de la filosofía." *Lecturas Filosóficas* 1 (1978): 17–19.

———. *Existencia, encuentro y azar*. Mexico City: Universidad Michoacana, Secretaría de Difusión Cultural, Editorial Universitaria, 1995.

———. *Filosofía y marxismo: Entrevista a Louis Althusser*. Mexico City: Siglo XXI, 1988.

———. "La intersubjetividad en J. Sartre y Simone de Beauvoir." *Filósofos e ideas* (1990): 137–48.

———. "A New Way of Thinking in Action: The Zapatistas in Mexico—A Postmodern Guerrilla Movement?" *Rethinking Marxism: A Journal of Economics, Culture and Society* 10, no. 4 (2009): 155–65.

Negrín, Edith. *Entre la paradoja y la dialéctica: Una lectura de la narrativa de José Revueltas*. Mexico City: Universidad Nacional Autónoma de México, 1995.

Ochoa Sandy, Gerardo, and Pascal Beltrán del Río. "Louis Althusser en México: La generación del 68 lo hizo suyo por radical y antidogmático." *Proceso*, October 27, 1990. http://www.proceso.com.mx/155935/sanchez-vazquez-gonzalez-rojo-luis-zavala-hijar.

Osborne, Peter. *Politics of Time: Modernity and Avant-Garde*. London: Verso, 2007.

Passerini, Luisa. *Autobiography of a Generation: Italy, 1968*. Translated by Lisa Erdberg. Hanover, NH: University Press of New England, 1996.

———. "Foreword." In *Gender and Sexuality in 1968: Transformative Politics in the Cultural Imagination*, edited by Lessie Jo Frazier and Deborah Cohen, ix–xii. New York: Palgrave Macmillan, 2009.

———. *Memory and Utopia: The Primacy of Intersubjectivity*. London: Routledge, 2007.

———. "The Problematic Intellectual Repercussions of '68: Reflections in a Jump-Cut Style." *Historein* 9 (2009): 21–33.

Pech, Cynthia. "La presencia del cuerpo en el discurso feminista." In *Cartografías del feminismo mexicano, 1970–2000*, edited by Nora Nínive García, Márgara Millán, and Cynthia Pech, 327–343. Mexico City: Universidad Autónoma de la Ciudad de México, 2007.

Peña, Milagros. *Latina Activists across Borders: Women's Grassroots Organizing in Mexico and Texas*. Durham, NC: Duke University Press, 2007.

Petrich, Blanche. "Entrevista a Ana Ignacia Rodríguez, *La Nacha*." *La Jornada*, July 22, 2002. http://www.jornada.unam.mx/2002/07/22/009n1pol.php?origen=politica .html.

Poniatowska, Elena. *La noche de Tlatelolco: Testimonios de historia oral*. Mexico City: Era, 1971.

———. *Massacre in Mexico*. Translated by Helen R. Lane. New York: Viking, 1975.

———. "Tlatelolco: 48 años después." *La Jornada*, October 1, 2016. http://www.jornada .unam.mx/2016/10/01/cultura/a04a1cul?partner=rss.

Prieto, Emma. *Los testigos*. Mexico City: Porrúa, 2008.

Puga, María Luisa. *Pánico o peligro*. Mexico City: Siglo XXI Editores, 1983.

Ramírez Garrido, Jaime. *Dialéctica de lo terrenal: Ensayo sobre la obra de José Revueltas*. Mexico City: Consejo Nacional para la Cultura y las Artes, 1991.

Rancière, Jacques. "Democracy Means Equality: Jacques Rancière Interviewed by *Passages*." *Radical Philosophy: A Journal of Socialist and Feminist Philosophy* 82 (March/April 1997): 29–36.

———. "Desarrollar la temporalidad de los momentos de igualdad: Entrevista a Jacques Rancière por el Colectivo Situaciones." In *La noche de los proletarios*, 7–15. Translated by Emilio Bernini and Enrique Biondini. Buenos Aires: Tinta Limón, 2010.

———. *Disagreement: Politics and Philosophy*. Translated by Julie Rose. Minneapolis: University of Minnesota Press, 1999.

———. *Dissensus: On Politics and Aesthetics*. Translated by Steve Corcoran. New York: Continuum, 2010.

Reguillo, Rossana. "Ayotzinapa: El nombre del horror." *Revista Anfibia*, October 2014. http://www.revistaanfibia.com/ensayo/ayotzinapa-el-nombre-del-horror/.

———. "Rostros en escenas: Ayotzinapa y la imposibilidad del desentendimiento." *Magis*, December 1, 2014. https://magis.iteso.mx/content/rostros-en-escenas-ayotzinapa-y-la -imposibilidad-del-desentendimiento.

Revueltas, Andrea. "Aproximaciones a la obra teórico-política de J. Revueltas." In *Revueltas en la mira*, edited by Emmanuel Carballo et al., 83–100. Mexico City: Dirección de Difusión Cultural, 1984.

Revueltas, José. "A la generación 1965–1969 de sociología." In *México 68: Juventud y revolución*, edited by Andrea Revueltas and Philippe Cheron, 253. Mexico City: Era, 1978.

———. "Algunos puntos programáticos sobre la autogestión académica." In *México 68: Juventud y revolución*, edited by Andrea Revueltas and Philippe Cheron, 155–57. Mexico City: Era, 1978.

———. "Apuntes para un ensayo sobre la dialéctica de la conciencia." In *Dialéctica de la conciencia*, edited by Andrea Revueltas and Philippe Cheron, 19–82. Mexico City: Era, 1982.

———. "Autogestión académica y universidad crítica." In *México 68: Juventud y revolución*, edited by Andrea Revueltas and Philippe Cheron, 149–54. Mexico City: Era, 1978.

———. "Clase y partido: Los nuevos contenidos de la realidad en la segunda mitad del siglo XX." In *Dialéctica de la conciencia*, edited by Andrea Revueltas and Philippe Cheron, 230–35. Mexico City: Era, 1982.

———. "Consideraciones sobre la autogestión académica." In *México 68: Juventud y revolución*, edited by Andrea Revueltas and Philippe Cheron, 110–25. Mexico City: Era, 1978.

———. *Dialéctica de la conciencia,* edited by Andrea Revueltas and Philippe Cheron. Mexico City: Era, 1982.

———. "Diario de Lecumberri." In *México 68: Juventud y revolución*, edited by Andrea Revueltas and Philippe Cheron 248–49. Mexico City: Era, 1978.

———. *El apando.* Mexico City: Era, 1978.

———. *El tiempo y el número.* In *Las cenizas*, edited by Andrea Revueltas and Philippe Cheron, 127–54. Mexico City: Era, 1988.

———. *Ensayo sobre un proletariado sin cabeza.* Mexico City: Era, 1980.

———. "Esquema para conferencia sobre autogestión académica." In *México 68: Juventud y revolución*, edited by Andrea Revueltas and Philippe Cheron, 94–102. Mexico City: Era, 1978.

———. "Ezequiel, o la masacre de los inocentes." In *El material de los sueños*, edited by Andrea Revueltas and Philippe Cheron, 115–28. Mexico City: Era, 1974.

———. "Gris es toda teoría." In *México 68: Juventud y revolución*, edited by Andrea Revueltas and Philippe Cheron, 76–84. Mexico City: Era, 1978.

———. "Hegel y yo." In *El material de los sueños*, edited by Andrea Revueltas and Philippe Cheron, 9–24. Mexico City: Era, 1974.

———. "Intervención de José Revueltas en la audiencia de derecho de la vista de sentencia, Audiencia celebrada en la cárcel preventiva de la ciudad, del 17 al 18 de setiembre de 1970." In *México 68: Juventud y revolución*, edited by Andrea Revueltas and Philippe Cheron, 257–79. Mexico City: Era, 1978.

———. *Las cenizas.* Edited by Andrea Revueltas and Philippe Cheron. Mexico City: Era, 1988.

———. *Las evocaciones requeridas*, vol. 2. Edited by Andrea Revueltas and Philippe Cheron. Mexico City: Era, 1987.

———. "Las palabras prisioneras." In *México 68: Juventud y revolución,* edited by Andrea Revueltas and Philippe Cheron, 245–47. Mexico City: Era, 1978.

———. *Los muros del agua.* Mexico: Era, 1973.

———. *México, una democracia bárbara; y escritos acerca de Lombardo Toledano*. Mexico City: Era, 1983.

———. "Nuestra 'revolución de mayo' en México." In *México 68: Juventud y revolución*, edited by Andrea Revueltas and Philippe Cheron, 38–39. Mexico City: Era, 1978.

———. "Palabras finales." In *México 68: Juventud y revolución*, edited by Andrea Revueltas and Philippe Cheron, 282–83. Mexico City: Era, 1978.

———. "Prohibido prohibir la revolución." In *México 68: Juventud y revolución*, edited by Andrea Revueltas and Philippe Cheron, 25–37. Mexico City: Era, 1978.

———. "¿Qué es la autogestión académica?" In *México 68: Juventud y revolución*, edited by Andrea Revueltas and Philippe Cheron, 107–9. Mexico City: Era, 1978.

———. "Reforma educativa y universidad crítica." In *México 68: Juventud y revolución*, edited by Andrea Revueltas and Philippe Cheron, 165–73. Mexico City: Era, 1978.

———. "Un movimiento, una bandera, una revolución." In *México 68: Juventud y revolución*, edited by Andrea Revueltas and Philippe Cheron, 126–48. Mexico City: Era, 1978.

Reygadas, Rafael. *Universidad, autogestión y modernidad: Estudio comparado de la formación de arquitectos (1968–1996)*. Mexico City: Centro de Estudios Superiores Universitarios, Universidad Nacional Autónoma de México, 1998.

Reynoso, Esmeralda. Interview with Susana Draper and Vicente Rubio-Pueyo. *México 68: Modelo para armar; Archivo de memorias desde los márgenes*. 2015. https://www.mexico68conversaciones.com/esmeralda-reynoso/.

Rivera Cusicansqui, Silvia. *Ch'ixinacax utxiwa: Una reflexión sobre prácticas y discursos descolonizadores*. Buenos Aires: Tinta Limón, 2010.

Rivera Hernández, Raúl Diego. *Del Internet a las calles: #YoSoy132, una opción alternativa de hacer política*. Raleigh, NC: Editorial A Contracorriente, 2016.

Robles, Marta. *Los octubres del otoño*. Mexico City: Ediciones Océano, 1982.

Rojo, Juan. *Revisiting the Mexican Student Movement of 1968: Shifting Perspectives in Literature and Culture since Tlatelolco*. New York: Palgrave Macmillan, 2016.

Román, José Antonio, and Emir Olivares. "Padres de Ayotzinapa encabezan la marcha del 2 de octubre." *La jornada*, October 3, 2016. http://www.jornada.unam.mx/2016/10/03/politica/010n1pol.

Ross, Kristin. *Communal Luxury: The Political Imaginary of the Paris Commune*. London: Verso, 2015.

———. *May '68 and Its Afterlives*. Chicago: University of Chicago Press, 2002.

Roszak, Theodore. *The Making of a Counter Culture: Reflections on the Technocratic Society and Its Youthful Opposition*. Garden City, NJ: Doubleday, 1969.

Rowbotham, Sheila. *Promise of a Dream: Remembering the Sixties*. London: Verso, 2007.

Ruisánchez Serra, José Ramón. "Reading '68: The Tlatelolco Memorial and Gentrification in Mexico City." In *Accounting for Violence: Marketing Memory in Latin America*, edited by Leigh A. Payne and Ksenija Bilbija, 179–206. Durham, NC: Duke University Press, 2011.

Sáinz, Gustavo, ed. *Conversaciones con José Revueltas*. Mexico City: Centro de Investigaciones Lingüístico-Literarias, Universidad Veracruzana, 1977.

Sánchez Olvera, Alma Rosa. *El feminismo mexicano ante el movimiento urbano popular: Dos expresiones de lucha de género, 1970–1985*. Mexico City: Universidad Nacional Autónoma de México, 2002.

Sánchez Prado, Ignacio M. *Screening Neoliberalism: Transforming Mexican Cinema, 1988–2012*. Nashville, TN: Vanderbilt University Press, 2014.

Sánchez Vázquez, Adolfo. "La estética terrenal de José Revueltas." In *Revueltas en la mira*, edited by Emmanuel Carballo et al., 227–42. Mexico City: Dirección de Difusión Cultural, 1984.

Sartre, Jean-Paul. *No Exit, and Three Other Plays*. New York: Vintage International, 1989.

Scherer García, Julio, and Carlos Monsiváis. *Parte de guerra, Tlatelolco 1968: Documentos del general Marcelino García Barragán; Los hechos y la historia*. Mexico City: Nuevo Siglo/Aguilar, 1999.

Scott, Joan Wallach. *Gender and the Politics of History*. Revised edition. New York: Columbia University Press, 1999.

———. *Only Paradoxes to Offer: French Feminists and the Rights of Man*. Cambridge, MA: Harvard University Press, 1996.

Sherman, Daniel J., Ruud van Dijk, Jasmine Alinder, and A. Aneesh, eds. *The Long 1968: Revisions and New Perspectives*. Bloomington, IN: Indiana University Press, 2013.

Sitrin, Marina, and Dario Azzelini. *They Can't Represent Us! Reinventing Democracy from Greece to Occupy*. New York: Verso, 2014.

Solanas, Fernando, and Octavio Getino. "Hacia un tercer cine." *Testimonios* 1 (1969): 27–41.

———. "La hora de los hornos: Informe por el grupo Cine-Liberación." *Cine del tercer mundo*, no. 1 (1969): 19–23.

———. "Towards a Third Cinema: Notes and Experiences for the Development of a Cinema of Liberation in the Third World." In *Film Manifestos and Global Cinema Cultures: A Critical Anthology*, edited by Scott MacKenzie, 230–50. Berkeley: University of California Press, 2014.

Sorensen, Diana. *A Turbulent Decade Remembered: Scenes from the Latin American Sixties*. Stanford, CA: Stanford University Press, 2007.

Spivak, Gayatri Chakravorty. "Can the Subaltern Speak?" *Marxism and the Interpretation of Culture*, edited by Cary Nelson and Lawrence Grossberg, 271–313. Urbana: University of Illinois Press, 1988.

Steinberg, Samuel. *Photopoetics at Tlatelolco: Afterimages of Mexico, 1968*. Austin: University of Texas Press, 2016.

Taibo, Paco Ignacio, II. *'68*. Translated by Donald Nicholson Smith. New York: Seven Stories Press, 2004.

Tapia, Luis. *La condición multisocietal: Multiculturalidad, pluralismo, modernidad*. La Paz: Muela del Diablo, 2002.

Teshome, Gabriel. *Third Cinema in the Third World: The Aesthetics of Liberation*. Ann Arbor: University of Michigan Research Press, 1982.

Tirado Villegas, Gloria. *La otra historia: Voces de mujeres del 68, Puebla*. Puebla: Benemérita Universidad Autónoma de Puebla, 2004.

Toledo Garibaldi, Sandra Emma. "La sexualidad disidente: El movimiento lésbico en México." In *Cartografías del feminismo mexicano, 1970–2000*, edited by Nora Nínive García, Márgara Millán, and Cynthia Pech, 161–91. Mexico City: Universidad Autónoma de la Ciudad de México, 2007.

Tolosa, Carolina. "Las memorias públicas del movimiento estudiantil de 1968 a través de *El grito* and *Tlatelolco, las claves de la massacre.*" Presentation at the First University Colloquium of Film Analysis (Primer coloquio universitario de análisis cinematográfico), Mexico City, November 15–18, 2011.

Trejo Fuentes, Ignacio. "Las novelas de José Revueltas." In *Revueltas en la mira*, edited by Emmanuel Carballo et al., 15–24. Mexico City: Dirección de Difusión Cultural, 1984.

Trigo, Abril. "Una lectura materialista de la colonialidad (segunda parte)." *Alter/nativas* 3 (autumn 2014). https://alternativas.osu.edu/es/issues/autumn-2014/essays2/trigo2 .html.

Valle, Eduardo. *Escritos sobre el movimiento del 68*. Sinaloa: Universidad Autónoma de Sinaloa, 1984.

Vázquez Mantecón, Álvaro. *El cine súper 8 en México 1970–1989*. Mexico City: Universidad Nacional Autónoma de México, 2012.

———. "El 68 cinematográfico." In *Las rupturas del 68 en el cine de América Latina*, edited by Mariano Mestman, 285–310. Buenos Aires: Akal, 2016.

David Vega. "Una vida del Politécnico: Entrevista con Hermann Bellinghausen." In *Pensar el 68*, edited by Héctor Aguilar Camín and Hermann Bellinghausen, 43–48. Mexico City: Cal y Arena, 1988.

Velázquez, Carolina. "El 68, 'caldo de cultivo' para el movimiento de mujeres." *Cimac Noticias*, August 10, 2008. http://www.cimacnoticias.com.mx/node/46739.

Villoro, Luis. *Tres retos de la sociedad por venir: Justicia, democracia, pluralidad*. Mexico City: Siglo XXI, 2009.

Volpi, Jorge. *La imaginación y el poder: Una historia intelectual de 1968*. Mexico City: Era, 1998.

Williams, Gareth. *The Mexican Exception: Sovereignty, Police, and Democracy*. New York: Palgrave Macmillan, 2011.

Zancarini-Fournel, Michelle. *Le moment 68: Une histoire contestée*. Paris: Seuil, 2008.

Zavaleta Mercado, René. *El poder dual en América Latina: Estudios de los casos de Bolivia y Chile*. Mexico City: Siglo XXI, 1979.

Zermeño, Sergio. *México: Una democracia utópica; El movimiento estudiantil del 68*. Mexico City: Siglo XXI, 1978.

Zolov, Eric. *Refried Elvis: The Rise of the Mexican Counterculture*. Berkeley: University of California Press, 1999.

Index

8 mm film. *See* Super 8 film

16 mm film, 94, 99, 112

1968/'68; Christian narrative of, 14; cinema and, 94, 96–97, 119, 122, 124, 165, 188, 215n9; demobilization after, 31, 60, 93, 98–99, 186; democratic demands of, 168, 171–72; double temporality of, 7; experience of, 17, 36, 40, 85, 93, 99, 216n28; fiftieth anniversary of, 2; language and, 170; liberatory aspects of, 219n16; memory of, 5, 157, 161, 171; movements of, 42–43; myth of, 158; as national movement, 20, 50; as political movement, 10, 95, 127; prisoners of, 59, 75–75, 159; Revueltas and, 38–39; temporality of, 157, 173, 175; as theoretical act, 49; as Tlatelolco, 157, 203n37; as transition toward democracy, 5, 10–12, 18, 202n27; in Uruguay, 8, 215n17; as watershed moment, 7, 26. *See also* Mexico 1968/'68; women: of 1968/'68

activism, 11, 25

affirmation, 12, 29, 74; of militancy, 4

aleatory materialism. *See* materialism: aleatory

Algeria, 7, 10, 113, 201nn19–20

alienation, 37, 47, 51–58, 89; of architectural consciousness, 65; social, 52–53. *See also* disalienation

Allier Montaño, Eugenia, 12, 203n31

alterity, 17, 20, 138–40, 144–49, 152–55, 159, 164. *See also* otherness

Althusser, Louis, 36, 44, 88, 138, 141, 144–45, 147, 150–51, 164, 194, 196, 221n46, 223n51; Navarro and, 142–43. *See also* materialism: aleatory; encounter, the

Álvarez Garín, Raúl, 20, 23, 38

apando (punishment cell), 58, 61, 63, 69–70, 74, 82, 210n71; Revueltas on, 40, 57–58, 64, 67

The Apando (*El apando*) (Revueltas), 30, 57–73, 80–82

Aparicio Hoyo, Esperanza Lili, 178, 181–82

Argüeyo Pazmiño, Sofia, 137, 225n20

Aricó, José, 31, 88, 213n132

Arrighi, Giovanni, 1, 84

Ascencio, Esteban, 13, 157

authoritarianism, 10, 13, 22, 26–27, 30, 44, 50, 99, 114, 116

Avendaño, Roberta ("La Tita"), 17, 19–20, 32–33, 78, 138–39, 157–72, 174–75, 177, 182, 184, 186, 196, 223n15, 225n32; *Of Freedom and Imprisonment* (*De la libertad y el encierro*), 157–77, 183, 224n15; political life of, 223n11

Balibar, Étienne, 147, 172, 223n51

Barrios Sierra, Javier, 24, 54, 226n46

Benjamin, Walter, 42, 47, 88, 187

Bensaïd, Daniel, 1, 13

Boggs, Grace Lee, 21, 144, 197

Bolado, Carlos, 97, 188

Bolaño, Roberto, 157–58

Bosteels, Bruno, 4–5, 11, 14, 40, 42, 49, 86, 195

brigades, 9, 16, 25, 27, 41, 51–52, 96, 131–32, 137, 175, 195, 201n21, 214n4

Bussi de Allende, Hortensia, 141, 221n29

Butler, Judith, 19, 155

Castillo Nájera, Oralba, 143, 186, 221n37

censorship, 84, 86, 98, 112, 120–21, 200n14, 215n14. See also *History of a Document*: censorship of

cinema, 91–92, 97–98, 100–101, 105–108, 111, 151; of '68, 94, 96–97, 119, 122, 124, 165, 188, 215n9; commercial, 99, 120; cooperative, 98; history of, 103; independent, 92, 99, 215n14; Latin American, 91, 96–97, 119–20; liberation and, 31; mass, 188; militant, 31, 91, 94, 96, 98, 109–10, 121; new, 94, 98, 120 (*see also* third cinema); politics and, 93, 97. *See also* Cooperative of Marginal Cinema (Cooperativa de Cine Marginal); fourth cinema (*cuarto cine*); militant cinema; Super 8

cinema (continued)
filmmaking; *superocheros* (Super 8 filmmakers); third cinema
class difference, 17, 32, 134, 159, 162–63, 184, 189
clinamen, 45, 138, 145
cognitive democracy, 30, 36, 39–40, 44–45, 47–48, 70, 78, 137, 195; cinema and, 105; the encounter and, 197; equality of participation and, 42; self-management and, 39, 49, 52, 55, 57, 72, 92, 122, 179
cognitive democratization, 20, 32
Cohen, Deborah, 15, 64, 130–31, 134, 136
commemoration, 2; of the Tlatelolco massacre, 191–92, 218n9
committees of struggle (*comités de lucha*), 9
Communiqués of Labor Insurgency, 93, 102
Con la venda en los ojos (*With Blindfolded Eyes*), 107–108
Confederation of Mexican Workers (Confederación de Trabajadores de México, CTM), 93, 102, 104–106
Consejo Nacional de Huelga. *See* National Strike Council
Cooperative of Marginal Cinema (Cooperativa de Cine Marginal), 31, 92–93, 95, 98–100, 109, 111, 116, 159, 163, 216n27; communiqués of, 31, 95, 101–102, 105–107, 109, 112. *See also* *Communiqués of Labor Insurgency*; fourth cinema (*cuarto cine*); *History of a Document*; Menéndez, Óscar; *Otro país* (*Another Country*); *superocheros* (Super 8 filmmakers)
Corpus Christi massacre (*el Halconazo*), 100, 123, 176, 192
Cortázar, Julio, 207n12, 211n97
counterculture, 8, 91
criminality, 75–76, 163
Cuban Revolution, 24, 97

Davis, Angela, 21, 144
dehistoricization, 6, 207n19
democracy, 18, 25, 43, 51–52, 70, 90, 112, 127, 133, 137, 172, 208n38; absence of, 50; and arithmetic, 48, 51, 179; demand for, 20, 23, 26–27, 29, 85, 100, 125, 134; direct, 84; limited notion of, 162; meaning of, 23; as partyocracy, 23, 43, 194, 208n23; problematization of, 19; qualitative, 48, 51, 179; socialist, 43, 47, 195; of thought, 144; transition to, 10–11;

unfulfilled, 186; union, 100. *See also* cognitive democracy
democratization, 1, 8, 31–32, 39, 109, 140, 181, 202n27; demand for, 22, 26–27, 171–72; of knowledge, 9, 30, 57; of Mexico, 12; social, 22; of society, 134; unfulfilled, 161, 186; union, 93, 100, 103, 110
depoliticization, 6, 30–31, 42
de Taboada, Javier, 120, 217n36
developmentalism, 10, 41, 44, 63, 88–89, 154. *See also* nondevelopmentalism
dialectical materialism. *See* materialism: dialectical
dialectics, 30, 44, 55, 196, 208n20; local, 214n135; of nature, 89; Revueltas on, 35, 40, 42–43, 63, 66–67, 86. *See also* encounter: dialectic of
Díaz, Guadalupe, 164, 224n11
Díaz Ordaz, Gustavo, 76, 104, 111, 208n19; Fourth State of the Union Address, 28, 209n58
disagreement, 25, 27–30
disalienation, 47, 55, 57, 70, 90, 120, 123; social, 48
dissidence, 22, 29–30, 44, 66, 69, 109, 114, 117–18; political, 75–76, 116, 159
domestic work, 131, 162, 224n18
Dozal, Martín, 20, 38, 210n71, 211n97
dual power, 89, 208n37, 213n133

Echeverría, Luis, 113–14, 118
encounter, 15, 17, 20, 32–33, 100, 128, 137–40, 143–51, 153, 155, 159, 163, 173, 193–97; dialectic of, 43, 45; hypothetical, 158, 223n6; materialism of the, 32, 139; temporality of, 151. *See also* Althusser, Louis
equality, 4, 16–23, 25, 27, 29, 31–33, 42, 128–29, 134, 136–38, 145, 150, 169, 172, 174, 185, 204n53, 224n8; 1968 as a moment of, 17, 163; democratic, 127; forced, 129, 139–40; gender, 215n19; in participation, 16–19, 22, 25, 31, 33, 42–43, 50–51, 128, 131, 136, 173; practice of, 194, 204n52. *See also* inequality
Escuela Normal de Ayotzinapa students: disappearance of, 191–93, 202n27
Espinosa Carbajal, Eugenia, 127–28, 137, 178
everyday life, 26, 55, 59–60, 64, 86, 133, 154, 159, 193; of the movement, 52; of prison, 32, 166; reproduction of, 195, 198
everyday practices, 16, 22, 30, 36, 204n5

Existence, Encounter, and Chance (*Existencia, encuentro y azar*) (Navarro), 31, 141, 143–47, 151–52

Federici, Silvia, 144, 198
feminism, 16, 18, 132–35, 140–43, 200n14, 218n11, 219n16, 221n33, 221–22n40, 223n51, 224–25n18; lesbian, 129, 136, 220n28; materialist, 139; Mexican, 222n44; second-wave, 31–32, 133, 219n14
Fernández-Savater, Amador, 96, 205n59
Ferrer, Guadalupe, 20, 51, 101, 103, 106–107, 135, 204n52, 215n19, 216n26
Foucault, Michel, 117, 142, 155
fourth cinema (*cuarto cine*), 31, 94, 99–100, 119, 121–23. *See also* Cooperative of Marginal Cinema (Cooperativa de Cine Marginal); *superocheros* (Super 8 filmmakers)
France, 94, 101, 130, 201n19; *History of a Document* in, 113–14; May 1968 in, 1–4, 6–8, 10, 33, 36, 43, 96, 129, 144, 201n20, 208n19; Navarro in, 142; workers' cinema cooperatives in, 111, 124
Frazier, Lessie Jo, 15, 645, 130–31, 134, 136
freedom, 21, 27, 30, 36, 45, 49, 85, 90–92, 107–110, 140–41; autonomy and, 56; Avendaño and, 168–69, 171–72; cinema and, 122; collective, 22, 194; de-fetishization of, 67; democracy and, 44; encounter and, 138, 196, 198; López Hernández and, 183; meaning of, 22–23; Navarro on, 145–46, 148–49, 154, 163; philosophical history of, 37; for political prisoners, 24; Popular Preparatory and, 176; of the press, 29, 71–72; reconfiguring, 4, 17; redefining, 95, 139; re-signification of, 8, 20; rethinking, 174; Revueltas on, 39–40, 44, 48, 51, 57–70, 73–75, 77–84, 86–87, 110, 151–53, 193, 212n102; spatial and temporal meaning of, 169; Third-World struggles for, 201n19
future perfect, 158, 224n7

Galván Leguizamo, José Manuel, 178, 182
García, Sergio, 98–99, 119, 121, 123
gaze, 115, 124, 149, 151, 154, 180; dialectical materialist, 143; idealized, 140; feminist, 139, 200n14; patriarchal, 148; Revueltas's, 35; social, 111
gender inequality, 15, 27, 33, 175, 187
gender studies, 145, 222n40
Getino, Octavio, 120–22

Gilabert, César, 23, 25, 50
Global North, 2, 200n14
Global South, 5, 200n14, 203n37
González de Alba, Luis, 20, 146, 210n71
González Rojo, Enrique, 52, 144
Groupe de Recherches Technologiques—Atelier d'expérimentation Super 8, 31, 94, 113. *See also* Cooperative of Marginal Cinema (Cooperativa de Cine Marginal); *History of a Document*
Guevara Niebla, Gilberto, 20, 24, 26, 28

Heidegger, Martin, 73, 209n58
Híjar, Alberto, 20, 38, 54, 143–44, 178–79, 181, 209n58
historicization, 84–85, 133, 152, 215n12; self-, 129. *See also* dehistoricization
History of a Document, 31, 78, 93–95, 100, 102, 110–11, 113–18; censorship of, 31, 113–14, 117. *See also* Cooperative of Marginal Cinema (Cooperativa de Cine Marginal); Groupe de Recherches Technologiques—Atelier d'expérimentation Super 8; Super 8 filmmaking; *superocheros* (Super 8 filmmakers)
homosexuality, 140, 162, 220n28, 225n20
homosexual liberation, 129, 140, 163, 220n28
Hopkins, Terrence, 1, 84
horizontality, 9, 14, 21, 25, 43, 181; pedagogical, 173, 185
horizontal assemblies, 3, 13
horizontal organization, 30, 36
horizontal participation, 43, 131, 182

impunity, 117, 191–92
inappropriate, the, 114, 123
inequality, 18–19, 32, 127–28, 131, 134, 137, 160, 164, 171–74, 177, 181, 188; class, 20, 184, 187; gender, 15, 27, 33, 175, 187; relationships of, 176; system of, 105; of wealth distribution, 228n18. *See also* equality
internal colonialism, 6–7
intersubjectivity, 144–45, 147

Jameson, Fredric, 201n19, 214n135

knowledge, 39, 51–52, 55–58, 94, 106, 124, 182, 195; alienated, 65; Avendaño and, 169–71; categorical, 172; collective lack of, 130; communicability of, 53, 55, 71, 123, 179;

knowledge (continued)
  compartmentalization of, 110; counterfactual, 224n7; democratization of, 9, 30, 57, 70;
  deprivatization of, 125; ethics and, 155; forms
  of, 177, 185; questioning, 225n40; Revueltas's,
  38; right to, 180; subaltern, 181

language, 39–40, 59, 67–68, 70–75, 77–79, 86,
  120, 123, 152, 154, 166, 197, 211–12n97; '68 and,
  36, 84, 104, 135, 144, 147, 155, 170; alienation
  of, 56; alternative, 69; *apando* and, 60, 65;
  cinematic, 99–100, 102, 120; common, 21, 24,
  100, 103, 105–106, 108, 163; death and, 87;
  dissidence and, 30, 114; feminism and, 134,
  219n16, 222n40; freedom and, 57, 139, 141–42;
  official, 111, 116; political, 22; prisoners and, 58,
  212n102; as a site of struggle, 141
Lecumberri Prison, 64, 71, 93, 110, 123, 132, 159,
  171, 214n4; Avendaño and, 161; González de
  Alba and, 146; López Hernández and, 176,
  185; Revueltas and, 29–30, 37–38, 40, 44–45,
  49, 58, 60, 63, 65–66, 72, 74, 78, 80, 83,
  207n6, 210n71, 211n97; *superocheros* and, 31,
  79, 93, 99, 111, 116–17, 124
Lefebvre, Henri, 21, 42, 52, 55–56, 85, 88,
  208n20
Lerner, Jessee, 97, 122
lesbianism, 17, 159, 163
liberalism, 21, 89, 170
Liberation Cinema Group (Grupo Cine Liberación), 106, 120, 122
literature, 61, 68, 95, 158, 211n97, 220n26
López Aretche, Leobardo, 99, 102, 110, 214n4
López Hernández, Gladys, 19–20, 138–39, 160,
  173–77, 180–89, 205n90, 225n60; detention
  of, 132, 182; education and, 135, 171, 177, 183;
  encounter and, 17, 196; equality and, 204n52;
  Lecumberri prison and, 176, 185; memories
  of, 219n16; official memory of '68, 9; *Ovarimony: Me, a Guerrilla Fighter? (Ovarimonio:
  ¿Yo, guerrillera?)*, 32, 132, 173–77, 182–85;
  Popular Preparatory and, 177; release from
  prison, 185–86. *See also* ovarimony
love, 87, 135, 154, 165
Ludec, Nathalie, 141, 219n16

Marcuse, Herbert, 29, 208n20, 209n58
Markarian, Vania, 8, 203n31

Marx, Karl, 44, 56, 76, 194, 208n20, 209n45,
  209n58
Marxism, 36, 42–43, 46–50, 68, 76, 90, 143, 170,
  208n20; critical, 54–55, 57, 88, 138, 209n58;
  dogmatic, 8, 21, 50, 88–89; heterodox, 21;
  language of, 21–22; Leninist, 89; orthodox,
  89, 144. *See also* Stalinism
mass imprisonment, 29, 31, 59, 94
Massacre in Mexico (Poniatowska), 12, 130, 134,
  158, 165, 167
materialism, 30, 43–44, 49, 142, 144, 146,
  208n20; aleatory, 44, 138, 143–45, 147,
  150–51 (*see also* Althusser, Louis; Navarro,
  Fernanda); dialectical, 43, 45, 49, 68, 143;
  of the encounter, 32, 43, 139; feminist, 139;
  historical, 42; positivist notion of, 138
Memorial 68, 12–13, 132
memory, 3–5, 9–10, 13–17, 73, 87, 129, 132, 190,
  196, 216n33; of 1968/'68, 8–9, 12, 14–16,
  18, 30, 130–31, 157–59, 161, 171–72, 177–78,
  188, 220n26, 223n6, 224n15; act of, 189;
  democratization of, 9, 131; in Latin America,
  200n13; in *Ovarimony*, 186–88; places of, 19;
  political, 185, 201n20; singular plural, 1; social
  processes of, 12; of the university, 32
Méndez, José Carlos, 98–99, 101
Menéndez, Óscar, 31, 94, 98–99, 102, 111–13,
  216n28; *History of a Document*, 31, 78, 93–95,
  100, 102, 110–11, 113–18. *See also* Cooperative
  of Marginal Cinema (Cooperativa de Cine
  Marginal); *superocheros* (Super 8 filmmakers)
Mestman, Mariano, 91, 121–22
Mexican Communist Party (PCM, Partido
  Comunista Mexicano), 38, 41, 50
Mexico 1968/'68, 8–10, 23, 93, 97, 203n37; women
  of, 15, 27, 29, 131, 139, 196, 217n1, 218n9, 224n16
"Miguel Hernández" group, 32, 54, 174178–79,
  210n58
militancy, 4, 8, 81, 93, 108–109, 121–22, 135, 139,
  161; feminist, 143; political, 106, 171
Miller, Arthur, 71, 207n12
Monsiváis, Carlos, 20, 27
monumentalization, 2, 6
motley, the (*lo abigarrado*), 89, 153, 213–14n134
Muñoz López, Carlos, 178–79

National Strike Council (CNH, Consejo
  Nacional de Huelga), 9, 13, 15–16, 24–25, 35,

41, 51–52, 128, 160–61, 214n4; dominance of male leaders in, 13–14, 127, 131; list of demands (*pliego petitorio*) of, 22–26, 28–29, 162, 171, 201n21; women participants in, 32, 137, 218n8

Navarro, Fernanda, 17, 20–21, 31–32, 138–55, 159, 163–64, 194, 196, 221n33; "Asfixiata (A Feminist Theatrical Sketch)," 141–42; de Beauvoir's influence on, 221n37; *Existence, Encounter, and Chance* (*Existencia, encuentro y azar*), 31, 141, 143–47, 151–52; philosophical trajectory of, 221n29; on the Zapatistas, 221n36. *See also* VenSeremos

negation, 28, 43, 45, 53, 148; affirmative, 63; allotropic, 68–69, 72, 84

negativity, 12, 43, 46

Negrín, Edith, 80, 82

Noche de Tlatelolco: Masacre en México. See Massacre in Mexico (Poniatowska)

nondevelopmentalism, 30, 89, 124

Occupy Wall Street, 1, 41, 196, 205n59, 228n18

Olympic Games (1968), 9–10, 118, 189, 202n22, 208n19

Office de Radiodiffusion-Télévision Française (ORTF), 31, 113–14. *See also* Groupe de Recherches Technologiques—Atelier d'expérimentation Super 8; *History of a Document*

Of Freedom and Imprisonment (*De la libertad y el encierro*) (Avendaño), 157–77, 183, 224n15

Osborne, Peter, 87–88

otherness, 15, 32, 137, 148, 166, 170. *See also* alterity

Otro país (*Another Country*), 103–105

ovarimony, 138, 174–75, 189, 206n90. *See also* testimony

Ovarimony: Me, a Guerrilla Fighter? (*Ovarimonio: ¿Yo, guerrillera?*) (López Hernández), 32, 132, 173–77, 182–85

Panopticon, 118; Lecumberri as, 58, 114–15, 117, 119. *See also* surveillance

participation, 8, 10, 23, 122, 132, 134–35, 180, 182; collective, 42, 194; democratic, 29, 85, 101, 108; equality in/egalitarian, 16–19, 22, 25, 31, 33, 42–43, 50–51, 128, 131, 136, 173; grassroots, 64; political, 17, 21; of political prisoners in the movement, 75; of women in the movement, 15–16, 31, 127, 129–34, 138, 149–50, 175, 215n19, 218n8, 221n40

Partido de Acción Nacional (PAN, National Action Party), 12, 202n27

Partido Revolucionario Institucional (PRI, Institutional Revolutionary Party), 12, 18, 27, 41, 50, 67, 77, 98, 105, 202n27, 206n68; state monopoly of, 11, 27, 41, 67–68, 98, 117

Party of the Poor, 170, 191

Passerini, Luisa, 5, 15, 130, 202n29

Perelló, Mercedes, 21, 216n27

police repression, 24, 104

political, the, 17, 26–28, 47–49, 66, 77, 81, 95–97, 108–109, 123–24, 134, 145, 160, 165, 167, 172; equal participation in, 33; experience of, 27, 49, 90, 119; experimenting with, 3, 128; memory of, 187; reconceptualization of, 138; reconfiguration of, 23; redefining, 50; right to, 23, 30; transformation of, 11, 20–22; transformative potential of, 18

political imprisonment, 32–33, 75, 116

political prisoners, 24, 30, 32, 59–60, 65, 72–73, 75, 81, 112, 117–18, 130, 164, 166–67, 176; assault on, 78, 210n71; denial of existence of, 28, 31, 72–74, 76–77, 111, 114 (*see also* Díaz Ordaz, Gustavo); female, 159, 162, 224n16; hunger strike by, 70–71, 93–94, 111, 207n6

Polytechnic Institute (Instituto Politécnico), 14, 41, 99

Poniatowska, Elena, 20, 58, 135, 191; *Massacre in Mexico*, 12, 130, 134, 158, 165, 167

Popular Preparatory (Prepatoria Popular) schools, 9, 16, 19, 32, 53–54, 132, 160, 173–82, 184–85, 189, 226n46; Chicano movement and, 182, 226n60. *See also* rejected students (*rechazados*); self-management

prison, 91, 170, 211n79; Avendaño on, 17, 78–79, 160–169, 171–72, 177; double temporality of, 167; freedom and, 163, 165; language in, 212n102; lesbianism and, 17, 163; political, 95; politics and, 167; Revueltas on, 59–76, 78–82, 84, 87; as school, 169; self-management and, 94; social divisions and, 19; as system of signs, 164; women in, 18–19, 32, 165, 183–85, 224n16; women's 159–60, 165, 170, 175. *See also* Avendaño, Roberta ("La Tita"); *History of a Document*; Lecumberri prison; López Hernández, Gladys;

prison (continued)
  Panopticon; political prisoners; Revueltas, José; surveillance

racism, 7, 219n16
railroad workers movement, 23, 27, 46, 84, 206n68
Ramírez Garrido, Jaime, 60, 67
Rancière, Jacques, 29, 137, 193, 201n20, 217n48
rejected students (*rechazados*), 19, 54, 173, 176, 178–79, 184, 187, 196
re-signification, 8, 39, 87
revolutionary imaginary, 49–50, 63, 66
Revueltas, Andrea, 38, 40
Revueltas, José, 17, 20–21, 29–30, 32, 35–88, 92, 94, 105, 107, 110–11, 122–23, 137, 139, 141, 143, 146, 150–52, 154, 158, 164–65, 172, 179, 193–97, 207n6; *The Apando* (*El apando*), 30, 57–73, 80–82 (see also *apando*); on Communist Party in Mexico, 41, 50; 39–40, 53, 56–57; critical university, 39–40, 53, 56–57; on the Cuban Revolution, 211n97; *Dialectic of Consciousness*, 40, 63, 65, 68; fiction of, 65, 88; on freedom of consciousness, 57–58, 212n102; "Imprisoned Words," 72–75, 77, 123, 142, 185; incarceration of, 207n12; 212n97; language and, "Last Words," 75, 78; Lecumberri prison and, 29–30, 37–38, 40, 44–45, 49, 58, 60, 63, 65–66, 72, 74, 78, 80, 83, 207n6, 210n71, 211n97; literary workshop of, 39, 72, 74; on Marx, 208n20, 209n45, 212n112; Marxism of, 47; myth of, 38; on prisons, 65–66; "sea time" and, 80, 83; on self-management, 38–39, 42, 48, 51–59, 63, 68–69, 71–72, 92, 94, 105, 209n52; theoretical act, 17, 30, 39–45, 47, 49, 51, 54, 57, 59, 70, 80, 82, 84–86, 109–110, 137, 139, 143, 146, 150, 158; *Time and Number*, 30, 65, 79–84, 86–87, 151; visit to Cuba, 211n97; *Walls of Water*, 61, 65, 80–81. See also *apando*; cognitive democracy; democratization: of knowledge
Reynoso, Esmeralda, 11, 13, 16, 20, 25, 132, 186, 194, 204n52
riot police (*granaderos*), 24, 158
Rodríguez, Ana Ignacia ("La Nacha"), 15, 163, 175, 224n16
Ross, Kristin, 3, 5–8, 10, 129, 194–95, 198, 201n20

Sáiz, Paloma, 101, 215n19
Sánchez Vázquez, Adolfo, 47, 51, 209n45, 209n58
Sartre, Jean-Paul, 31, 60, 88, 112–13, 146, 148–49, 208n20
self-governance (*autogobierno*), 53–54, 68
self-management (*autogestión*), 30, 32, 35, 49, 54–55, 84–85, 89, 92–94, 110, 122–23, 169, 178, 185, 188–89, 194–95, 225n40; academic, 36, 51, 54, 57, 173; as daily practice, 182; of the Popular Preparatory, 16, 173–74, 176–77, 179–80, 182–84; Revueltas on, 38–39, 42, 48, 51–59, 63, 68–69, 71–72, 92, 94, 105, 209n52; social, 52, 92, 137
sexual difference, 128, 147, 162–63
sexuality, 133, 163
The Shout (*El grito*) (López Aretche and Sánchez Martínez), 93, 96, 100, 110, 214n4
singular-plural, the, 1, 7
small-gauge film, 95–97, 99–101, 104, 110. *See also* 16 mm film; Super 8 film (8mm); Super 8 filmmaking; *superocheros* (Super 8 filmmakers)
social class, 128, 139, 165, 170–71, 174, 184, 225n40; difference in, 159, 188; dislocation of, 8; erasure of, 129; freedom and, 147; historical formation of, 88; memory of '68 and, 9; women and, 19, 159–60, 164, 181
social connectivity, 20, 22, 140, 194
social movements, 1, 11–12, 30, 37, 40, 46, 82, 86, 89, 152
social transformation, 51–52, 55, 75, 89, 122, 138, 172, 193
Solanas, Fernando, 120–22
solidarity, 24–25, 27, 36, 52, 112, 114, 159, 165, 168, 182–83, 192, 201n21, 205n67
Soviet Union, 54–55
spatialization, 116–17
Spivak, Gayatri Chakravorty, 147, 224n7
Stalinism, 45, 47, 208n20
Steinberg, Samuel, 10, 14, 203n31
student (popular) movement, 10, 47–48, 50, 97, 161–62, 167, 173–76, 178–79, 186, 198, 205n67; beginning of, 23; cinema and, 105; demands of, 100, 171–72; demobilization of, 98; Díaz Ordaz's denial of, 28; filming of, 96, 216n28; image of, 13; memory of, 171; Olympic games and, 202n22; policing of, 14; railroad workers movement and, 46;

Revueltas and, 38, 41, 65, 72, 75, 79–80;
Topilejo and, 201n21
subjectivation, 27, 129, 137, 144, 146, 151
subjectivity, 58, 137, 144, 146–47, 150,
184, 228n18; revolutionary, 48. *See also*
intersubjectivity
Super 8 cameras, 31, 96, 98–99, 102, 111, 124
Super 8 film (8mm), 98–99, 113, 121
Super 8 filmmaking, 91, 95, 109; role of, 105;
as witness, 125
superocheros (Super 8 filmmakers), 20, 95,
97–99, 101, 121–22
surveillance, 60, 98, 114–17, 119

Taibo II, Paco Ignacio, 15, 101, 136, 149
temporality, 46, 70, 73, 82, 84, 109, 117, 151–53,
193, 202n29, 213n132; of change, 57; as
destiny, 174; double, 167; of the event, 31; of
movement, 90; multiple, 49; politics and,
11; in Revueltas, 20, 30, 74–75, 77, 80–81,
85, 87–88; of self-management, 42, 194
testimony, 85, 102, 115, 125, 135, 138, 163–64, 175.
See also ovarimony
third cinema ("new cinema"), 94, 99, 119–22,
217n36, 217n40. *See also* de Taboada, Javier
Third World, 1, 5–6, 120, 201n19
Tirado Villegas, Gloria, 15, 127, 130, 132, 218n1
Tlatelolco, 12, 66, 132
Tlatelolco massacre, 4, 9–10, 12–14, 29, 31, 59,
64, 75, 93–94, 97–100, 104, 111, 116–19, 124,
157, 166–67, 169, 175, 180, 187, 189, 191–92,
202n22, 203n37, 215n28, 218n9, 220n26
Tlatelolco: Summer of '68 (*Tlatelolco: Verano del
68*) (Bolado), 97, 188–89
Topilejo, 9, 16, 53, 106, 132, 163, 178, 182,
201–202n21
torture, 29, 83, 136, 182, 185, 188
trauma, 3, 11, 14, 186; Tlatelolco massacre and,
97, 11, 220n26
Topilejo, 16, 132, 163, 178, 182, 201–202n21; people
of, 9, 201n21; Popular Preparatory in, 53, 106

uncertainty, 21, 30, 37, 40, 55, 61, 82, 86, 90,
186
Universidad Nacional Autónoma de México
(UNAM, National Autonomous University of
Mexico), 22, 24, 32, 54, 99, 141, 143, 161, 173,
177–79, 188, 209n58
University Center for Film Studies (Centro
Universitario de Estudios Cinematográficos,
CUEC), 93, 99, 214n4
university strike, 35, 51, 93–94, 109, 167
utopia, 2, 23, 180

Valle, Eduardo ("El búho" ["The Owl"]), 15,
53, 136
Vázquez Mantecón, Álvaro, 91, 93, 97, 102–103,
106
VenSeremos, 141, 221n33
Vietnam, 36, 113
Villoro, Luis, 143, 208n23, 208n38
violence, 4, 13, 22, 148–50, 192–93; internal, 196;
micropolitical, 164; naturalized, 186; police,
216n33
Volpi, Jorge, 28, 36, 209n58

Wallerstein, Immanuel, 1, 84
Weber, Henri, 1
Williams, Gareth, 14, 28, 146, 170, 192
women: of 1968/'68, 15, 27, 29, 127–29, 131–32,
139, 196, 217–18n1, 218n9, 224n16; class
difference and, 159, 219n16; guerrillas and,
218n10; in philosophy, 143, 221n40; political
participation of, 132, 135–36, 175; political
prisoners, 224n16; roles of, 137; as a space
of open signification, 129; working-class,
219n16
women's liberation, 133, 139

#YoSoy132, 1, 41, 191, 193, 199n5

Zavaleta Mercado, René, 31, 88–89, 208n37
Zermeño, Sergio, 22, 25, 201n21